Cisco IOS Network Security

Cisco Systems, Inc.

Macmillan Technical Publishing
201 West 103rd Street
Indianapolis, IN 46290 USA

Published by:
Macmillan Technical Publishing
201 West 103rd Street
Indianapolis, IN 46290 USA

Printed in the United States of America 1 2 3 4 5 6 7 8 9 0

Library of Congress Cataloging-in-Publication Number 98-84219

ISBN: 1-57870-057-4

Warning and Disclaimer

This book is designed to provide information about **Cisco IOS Network Security**. Every effort has been made to make this book as complete and as accurate as possible, but no warranty or fitness is implied.

Associate Publisher	Jim LeValley
Executive Editor	Julie Fairweather
Cisco Systems Program Manager	H. Kim Lew
Managing Editor	Caroline Roop
Acquisitions Editor	Tracy Hughes
Development Editor	Stacia Mellinger
Project Editor	Sherri Fugit
Team Coordinator	Amy Lewis
Book Designer	Louisa Klucznik
Cover Designer	Karen Ruggles
Production Team	Argosy

Trademark
Acknowledgments

Acknowledgments

The Cisco IOS Reference Library is a result of collaborative efforts of many Cisco technical writers and editors over the years. This bookset represents the continuing development and integration of user documentation for the ever-increasing set of Cisco IOS networking features and functionality.

The current team of Cisco IOS writers and editors includes Katherine Anderson, Jennifer Bridges, Joelle Chapman, Christy Choate, Meredith Fisher, Tina Fox, Marie Godfrey, Dianna Johansen, Sheryl Kelly, Yvonne Ducher, Doug MacBeth, Lavanya Mandavilli, Mary Mangone, Spank McCoy, Greg McMillan, Madhu Mitra, Oralee Murillo, Vicki Payne, Jane Phillips, George Powers, Teresa Oliver Schuetz, Wink Schuetz, Karen Shell, Grace Tai, and Bethann Watson.

This writing team wants to acknowledge the many engineering, customer support, and marketing subject-matter experts for their participation in reviewing draft documents and, in many cases, providing source material from which this bookset is developed.

Table of Contents

v

CHAPTER 1

Security Overview

This chapter contains the following sections:

- **About this Network Security Book**

  Preview the topics in this book.

- **Creating Effective Security Policies**

  Learn tips and hints for creating a security policy for your organization. A security policy should be finalized and up-to-date *before* you configure any security features.

- **Identifying Security Risks and Cisco IOS Solutions**

  Identify common security risks that might be present in your network, and find the right Cisco IOS security feature to prevent security break-ins.

- **Creating a Firewall with Cisco IOS Software**

  Learn how to configure your Cisco networking device to be a firewall, using the features in this book.

ABOUT THIS NETWORK SECURITY BOOK

Cisco IOS Network Security describes how to configure Cisco IOS security features for your Cisco networking devices. It also outlines in great detail the many commands used for configuring security. The security features can protect your network against degradation or failure, and data loss or compromise, resulting from intentional attacks or from unintended but damaging mistakes by well-meaning network users.

This book is divided into five parts:

- Authentication, Authorization, and Accounting (AAA)
- Security Server Protocols

1

- Traffic Filtering
- Network Data Encryption
- Other Security Features

Each of these parts is briefly described next.

Authentication, Authorization, and Accounting (AAA)

This part describes how to configure Cisco's authentication, authorization, and accounting (AAA) paradigm, and offers corresponding chapters outlining in detail the related commands. AAA is an architectural framework for configuring a set of three independent security functions in a consistent, modular manner:

- Authentication—Provides the method of identifying users, including login and password dialog, challenge and response, messaging support, and, depending on the security protocol you select, encryption. Authentication is the way a user is identified prior to being allowed access to the network and network services. You configure AAA authentication by defining a named list of authentication methods, and then applying that list to various interfaces.

- Authorization—Provides the method for remote access control, including one-time authorization or authorization for each service, per-user account list and profile, user group support, and support of IP, IPX, ARA, and Telnet.

  Remote security servers, such as RADIUS and TACACS+, authorize users for specific rights by associating attribute-value (AV) pairs, which define those rights with the appropriate user. AAA authorization works by assembling a set of attributes that describe what the user is authorized to perform. These attributes are compared to the information contained in a database for a given user, and the result is returned to AAA to determine the user's actual capabilities and restrictions.

- Accounting—Provides the method for collecting and sending security server information used for billing, auditing, and reporting, such as user identities, start and stop times, executed commands (such as PPP), number of packets, and number of bytes. Accounting enables you to track the services users are accessing as well as the amount of network resources they are consuming.

NOTES

You can configure authentication outside of AAA. However, you must configure AAA if you want to use RADIUS, Kerberos, or TACACS+, or if you want to configure a backup authentication method.

Security Server Protocols

In many circumstances, AAA uses security protocols to administer its security functions. If your router or access server is acting as a network access server, AAA is the means through which you establish communication between your network access server and your RADIUS, TACACS+, or Kerberos security server.

The chapters in this part describe how to configure the following security server protocols:

- RADIUS—A distributed client/server system implemented through AAA that secures networks against unauthorized access. In the Cisco implementation, RADIUS clients run on Cisco routers and send authentication requests to a central RADIUS server that contains all user authentication and network service access information.

- TACACS+—A security application implemented through AAA that provides centralized validation of users attempting to gain access to a router or network access server. TACACS+ services are maintained in a database on a TACACS+ daemon that runs, typically, on a UNIX or Windows NT workstation. TACACS+ provides for separate and modular authentication, authorization, and accounting facilities.

- TACACS and Extended TACACS—TACACS is an older access protocol, which is incompatible with the newer TACACS+ protocol. TACACS provides password checking and authentication, and notification of user actions for security and accounting purposes. Extended TACACS is an extension to the older TACACS protocol, supplying additional functionality to TACACS.

- Kerberos—A secret-key network authentication protocol implemented through AAA that uses the Data Encryption Standard (DES) cryptographic algorithm for encryption and authentication. Kerberos was designed to authenticate requests for network resources. Kerberos is based on the concept of a trusted third party that performs secure verification of users and services. The primary use of Kerberos is to verify that users and the network services they use really are who and what they claim to be. To accomplish this, a trusted Kerberos server issues tickets to users. These tickets, which have a limited lifespan, are stored in a user's credential cache and can be used in place of the standard user-name-and-password authentication mechanism.

In addition to this configuration information, this part of the book also offers the standard corresponding chapters outlining in detail the commands related to these protocols.

Traffic Filtering

This part describes how to configure your networking devices to filter traffic (and again, includes extensive information on the related commands).

Cisco implements traffic filters with *access control lists* (also called *access lists*). Access lists determine what traffic is blocked and what traffic is forwarded at router interfaces. Cisco provides both basic and advanced access list capabilities:

- Basic access lists

  An overview of basic access lists is in Chapter 16, "Access Control Lists: Overview and Guidelines." This chapter describes tips, cautions, considerations, recommendations, and general guidelines for configuring access lists for the various network protocols.

You should configure basic access lists for all network protocols that will be routed through your networking device, such as IP, IPX, AppleTalk, and so forth.

- Advanced access lists

    The advanced access list capabilities and configuration are described in the remaining chapters in Part III, "Traffic Filtering." The advanced access lists provide sophisticated and dynamic traffic filtering capabilities for stronger, more flexible network security.

Network Data Encryption

This part describes how to configure network data encryption (with details on the related commands).

Network data encryption is used to prevent routed traffic from being examined or tampered with while it travels across a network. This feature allows IP packets to be encrypted at a Cisco router, routed across a network as encrypted information, and decrypted at the destination Cisco router.

Other Security Features

This part describes three important security features in the following main chapters:

- Chapter 25, "Configuring Passwords and Privileges"

    This chapter describes how to configure static passwords stored on your networking device. These passwords are used to control access to the device's command line prompt to view or change the device configuration.

    This chapter also describes how to assign privilege levels to the passwords. You can configure up to 16 different privilege levels, and assign each level to a password. For each privilege level, you define a subset of Cisco IOS commands that can be executed. You can use these different levels to allow some users the ability to execute all Cisco IOS commands and to restrict other users to a defined subset of commands.

    This chapter also describes how to recover lost passwords.

- Chapter 27, "Neighbor Router Authentication: Overview and Guidelines"

    This chapter describes the security benefits and operation of neighbor router authentication.

    When neighbor authentication is configured on a router, the router authenticates its neighbor router before accepting any route updates from that neighbor. This ensures that a router always receives reliable routing update information from a trusted source.

- Chapter 28, "Configuring IP Security Options"

    This chapter describes how to configure IP Security Options (IPSO) as described in RFC 1108. The IPSO is generally used to comply with the U.S. Government's Department of Defense security policy.

    Once again, each of these three main chapters is coupled with its own corresponding chapter outlining in detail the related commands.

CREATING EFFECTIVE SECURITY POLICIES

An effective security policy works to ensure that your organization's network assets are protected from sabotage and from inappropriate access—both intentional and accidental.

All network security features should be configured in compliance with your organization's security policy. If you don't have a security policy, or if your policy is out of date, you should ensure that the policy is created or updated before you decide how to configure security on your Cisco device.

The following sections provide guidelines to help you create an effective security policy:

- The Nature of Security Policies
- Two Levels of Security Policies
- Tips to Developing an Effective Security Policy

The Nature of Security Policies

You should recognize these aspects of security policies:

- Security policies represent trade-offs.

  With all security policies, there is some trade-off between user productivity and security measures that can be restrictive and time consuming. The goal of any security design is to provide maximum security with minimum impact on user access and productivity. Some security measures, such as network data encryption, do not restrict access and productivity. On the other hand, cumbersome or unnecessarily redundant verification and authorization systems can frustrate users and even prevent access to critical network resources.

- Security policies should be determined by business needs.

  Business needs should dictate the security policy; a security policy should not determine how a business operates.

- Security policies are living documents.

  Because organizations are constantly subject to change, security policies must be systematically updated to reflect new business directions, technological changes, and resource allocations.

Two Levels of Security Policies

You can think of a security policy as having two levels: a requirements level and an implementation level:

- At the requirements level, a policy defines the degree to which your network assets must be protected against intrusion or destruction and also estimates the cost (consequences) of a security breach. For example, the policy could state that only human resources personnel should be able to access personnel records, or that only IS personnel should be able to configure the backbone routers. The policy could also address the consequences of a network outage (due to sabotage), or the consequences of sensitive information inadvertently being made public.

- At the implementation level, a policy defines guidelines to implement the requirements-level policy, using specific technology in a predefined way. For example, the implementation-level policy could require access lists to be configured so that only traffic from human resources host computers can access the server containing personnel records.

When creating a policy, define security requirements before defining security implementations so that you don't end up merely justifying particular technical solutions that might not actually be required.

Tips to Developing an Effective Security Policy

To develop an effective security policy, consider the recommendations in the following sections:

- Identify Your Network Assets to Protect
- Determine Points of Risk
- Limit the Scope of Access
- Identify Assumptions
- Determine the Cost of Security Measures
- Consider Human Factors
- Keep a Limited Number of Secrets
- Implement Pervasive and Scalable Security
- Understand Typical Network Functions
- Remember Physical Security

Identify Your Network Assets to Protect

The first step to developing a security policy is to understand and identify your organization's network assets. Network assets include the following:

- Networked hosts (such as PCs; includes the hosts' operating systems, applications, and data)
- Networking devices (such as routers)
- Network data (data that travels across the network)

You must both identify your network's assets and determine the degree to which each of these assets must be protected. For example, one subnetwork of hosts might contain extremely sensitive data that should be protected at all costs, and a different subnetwork of hosts might require only modest protection against security risks, because there is less cost involved if the subnetwork is compromised.

Determine Points of Risk

You must understand how potential intruders can enter your organization's network or sabotage network operation. Special areas of consideration are network connections, dial-up access points, and misconfigured hosts. Misconfigured hosts, frequently overlooked as points of network entry, can be systems with unprotected login accounts (guest accounts), employ extensive trust in remote commands (such as rlogin and rsh), have illegal modems attached to them, and use easy-to-break passwords.

Limit the Scope of Access

Organizations can create multiple barriers within networks, so that unlawful entry to one part of the system does not automatically grant entry to the entire infrastructure. Although maintaining a high level of security for the entire network can be prohibitively expensive (in terms of systems and equipment as well as productivity), you can often provide higher levels of security to the more sensitive areas of your network.

Identify Assumptions

Every security system has underlying assumptions. For example, an organization might assume that its network is not tapped, that intruders are not very knowledgeable, that intruders are using standard software, or that a locked room is safe. It is important to identify, examine, and justify your assumptions: Any hidden assumption is a potential security hole.

Determine the Cost of Security Measures

In general, providing security comes at a cost. This cost can be measured in terms of increased connection times or inconveniences to legitimate users accessing the assets, or in terms of increased network management requirements, and sometimes in terms of actual dollars spent on equipment or software upgrades.

Some security measures inevitably inconvenience some sophisticated users. Security can delay work, create expensive administrative and educational overhead, use significant computing resources, and require dedicated hardware.

When you decide which security measures to implement, you must understand their costs and weigh these against potential benefits. If the security costs are out of proportion to the actual dangers, it is a disservice to the organization to implement them.

Consider Human Factors

If security measures interfere with essential uses of the system, users resist these measures and sometimes even circumvent them. Many security procedures fail because their designers do not take this fact into account. For example, because automatically generated "nonsense" passwords can be difficult to remember, users often write them on the undersides of keyboards. A "secure" door that leads to a system's only tape drive is sometimes propped open. For convenience, unauthorized modems are often connected to a network to avoid cumbersome dial-in security procedures. To ensure compliance with your security measures, users must be able to get their work done as well as understand and accept the need for security.

Any user can compromise system security to some degree. For example, an intruder can often learn passwords by simply calling legitimate users on the telephone claiming to be a system administrator and asking for them. If users understand security issues and understand the reasons for them, they are far less likely to compromise security in this way.

Defining such human factors and any corresponding policies needs to be included as a formal part of your complete security policy.

At a minimum, users must be taught never to release passwords or other secrets over unsecured telephone lines (especially through cordless or cellular telephones) or electronic mail. They should be wary of questions asked by people who call them on the telephone. Some companies have implemented formalized network security training for their employees in which employees are not allowed access to the network until they have completed a formal training program.

Keep a Limited Number of Secrets

Most security is based on secrets; for example, passwords and encryption keys are secrets. But the more secrets there are, the harder it is to keep all of them. It is prudent, therefore, to design a security policy that relies on a limited number of secrets. Ultimately, the most important secret an organization has is the information that can help someone circumvent its security.

Implement Pervasive and Scalable Security

Use a systematic approach to security that includes multiple, overlapping security methods.

Almost any change that is made to a system can affect security. This is especially true when new services are created. System administrators, programmers, and users need to consider the security implications of every change they make. Understanding the security implications of a change takes practice; it requires lateral thinking and a willingness to explore every way that a service could potentially be manipulated. The goal of any security policy is to create an environment that is not susceptible to every minor change.

Understand Typical Network Functions

Understand how your network system normally functions, know what is expected and unexpected behavior, and be familiar with how devices are usually used. This kind of awareness helps the organization detect security problems. Noticing unusual events can help catch intruders before they can damage the system. Software auditing tools can help detect, log, and track unusual events. In addition, an organization should know exactly what software it relies on to provide auditing trails, and a security system should not operate on the assumption that all software is bug-free.

Remember Physical Security

The physical security of your network devices and hosts cannot be neglected. For example, many facilities implement physical security by using security guards, closed circuit television, card-key entry systems, or other means to control physical access to network devices and hosts. Physical access to a computer or router usually gives a sophisticated user complete control over that device. Physical access to a network link usually allows a person to tap into that link, jam it, or inject traffic into it. Software security measures can often be circumvented when access to the hardware is not controlled.

IDENTIFYING SECURITY RISKS AND CISCO IOS SOLUTIONS

Cisco IOS software provides a comprehensive set of security features to guard against specific security risks.

This section describes a few common security risks that might be present in your network, and describes how to use Cisco IOS software to protect against each of these risks:

- Preventing Unauthorized Access into Networking Devices
- Preventing Unauthorized Access into Networks
- Preventing Network Data Interception
- Preventing Fraudulent Route Updates

Preventing Unauthorized Access into Networking Devices

If someone were to gain console or terminal access into a networking device, such as a router, switch, or network access server, that person could do significant damage to your network—perhaps by reconfiguring the device, or even by simply viewing the device's configuration information.

Typically, you want administrators to have access to your networking device; you do not want other users on your local-area network or those dialing in to the network to have access to the router.

Users can access Cisco networking devices by dialing in from outside the network through an asynchronous port, connecting from outside the network through a serial port, or connecting via a terminal or workstation from within the local network.

To prevent unauthorized access into a networking device, you should configure one or more of the following security features:

- At a minimum, you should configure passwords and privileges at each networking device for all device lines and ports, as described in Chapter 25, "Configuring Passwords and Privileges." These passwords are stored on the networking device. When users attempt to access the device through a particular line or port, they must enter the password applied to the line or port before they can access the device.

- For an additional layer of security, you can also configure username/password pairs, stored in a database on the networking device, as described in Chapter 25. These pairs are assigned to lines or interfaces and authenticate each user before that user can access the device. If you have defined privilege levels, you can also assign a specific privilege level (with associated rights and privileges) to each username/password pair.

- If you want to use username/password pairs, but you want to store them centrally instead of locally on each individual networking device, you can store them in a database on a security server. Multiple networking devices can then use the same database to obtain user authentication (and, if necessary, authorization) information. Cisco supports a variety of security server protocols, such as RADIUS, TACACS+, and Kerberos. If you decide to use the database on a security server to store login username/password pairs, you must configure your router or access server to support the applicable protocol; in addition, because most supported security protocols must be administered through the AAA security services, you will probably need to enable AAA. For more information about security protocols and AAA, refer to the chapters in Part I, "Authentication, Authorization, and Accounting (AAA)."

NOTES

Cisco recommends that whenever possible, use AAA to implement authentication.

- If you want to authorize individual users for specific rights and privileges, you can implement AAA's authorization feature, using a security protocol such as TACACS+ or RADIUS. For more information about security protocol features and AAA, refer to Part I.

- If you want to have a backup authentication method, you must configure AAA. AAA allows you to specify the primary method for authenticating users (for example, a username/password database stored on a TACACS+ server) and then specify backup methods (for example, a locally stored username/password database.) The backup method is used if the primary method's database cannot be accessed by the networking device. To configure AAA, refer to the chapters in Part I. You can configure up to four sequential backup methods.

NOTES

If you don't have backup methods configured, you will be denied access to the device if the username/password database cannot be accessed for any reason.

- If you want to keep an audit trail of user access, configure AAA accounting as described in Chapter 7, "Configuring Accounting."

Preventing Unauthorized Access into Networks

If someone were to gain unauthorized access to your organization's internal network, that person could cause damage in many ways, perhaps by accessing sensitive files from a host, by planting a virus, or by hindering network performance by flooding your network with illegitimate packets.

This risk can also apply to a person within your network attempting to access another internal network such as a Research and Development subnetwork with sensitive and critical data. That person could intentionally or inadvertently cause damage; for example, that person might access confidential files or tie up a time-critical printer.

To prevent unauthorized access through a networking device into a network, you should configure one or more of the following security features:

- Traffic Filtering

  Cisco uses access lists to filter traffic at networking devices. Basic access lists allow only specified traffic through the device; other traffic is simply dropped. You can specify individual hosts or subnets that should be allowed into the network, and you can specify what type of traffic should be allowed into the network. Basic access lists generally filter traffic based on source and destination addresses, and protocol type of each packet.

  Advanced traffic filtering is also available, providing additional filtering capabilities; for example, the Lock-and-Key Security feature requires each user to be authenticated via a username/password before that user's traffic is allowed onto the network.

  All the Cisco IOS traffic filtering capabilities are described in the chapters in Part III.

- Authentication

  You can require users to be authenticated before they gain access into a network. When users attempt to access a service or host (such as a Web site or file server) within the protected network, they must first enter certain data such as a username and password, and possibly additional information such as their date of birth or mother's maiden name. After successful authentication (depending on the method of authentication), users will be assigned specific privileges, allowing them to access specific network assets. In most cases, this type of authentication would be facilitated by using CHAP or PAP over a serial PPP connection in conjunction with a specific security protocol, such as TACACS+ or RADIUS.

  Just as in preventing unauthorized access to specific network devices, you need to decide whether or not you want the authentication database to reside locally or on a separate security server. In this case, a local security database is useful if you have very few routers providing network access. A local security database does not require a separate (and costly) security server. A remote, centralized security database is convenient when you have a large number of routers providing network access, because it prevents you from having to update each router with new or changed username authentication and authorization information for potentially hundreds of thousands of dial-in users. A centralized security database also helps establish consistent remote access policies throughout a corporation.

  Cisco IOS Release 11.3 supports a variety of authentication methods. Although AAA is the primary (and recommended) method for access control, Cisco IOS software provides additional features for simple access control that are outside the scope of AAA. For more information, see Chapter 3, "Configuring Authentication."

Preventing Network Data Interception

When packets travel across a network, they are susceptible to being read, altered, or *hijacked*. (Hijacking occurs when a hostile party intercepts a network traffic session and poses as one of the session endpoints.)

If the data is traveling across an unsecured network such as the Internet, the data is exposed to a fairly significant risk. Sensitive or confidential data could be exposed, critical data could be modified, and communications could be interrupted if data is altered.

To protect data as it travels across a network, configure network data encryption, as described in Chapter 23, "Configuring Network Data Encryption."

Network data encryption prevents routed traffic from being examined or tampered with while it travels across a network. This feature causes IP packets to be encrypted at a Cisco router, routed across a network as encrypted information, and decrypted at the destination Cisco router. In between the two routers, the packets are in encrypted form, and therefore the packets' contents cannot be read or altered. You define what traffic should be encrypted between the two routers, according to what data is more sensitive or critical.

If you want to protect traffic for protocols other than IP, you can encapsulate those other protocols into IP packets using GRE encapsulation, and then encrypt the IP packets.

Typically, you do not use network data encryption for traffic that is routed through networks that you consider secure. Consider using network data encryption for traffic that is routed across unsecured networks, such as the Internet, if your organization could be damaged if the traffic is examined or tampered with by unauthorized individuals.

Preventing Fraudulent Route Updates

All routing devices determine where to route individual packets by using information stored in route tables. This route table information is created using route updates obtained from neighboring routers.

If a router receives a fraudulent update, the router could be tricked into forwarding traffic to the wrong destination. This could cause sensitive data to be exposed, or could cause network communications to be interrupted.

To ensure that route updates are received only from known, trusted neighbor routers, configure neighbor router authentication as described in Chapter 27, "Neighbor Router Authentication: Overview and Guidelines."

CREATING A FIREWALL WITH CISCO IOS SOFTWARE

The following sections describe how you can configure your Cisco networking device to function as a firewall, using Cisco IOS security features:

- Overview of Firewalls
- Creating a Firewall
- Other Guidelines for Configuring a Firewall

Overview of Firewalls

Firewalls are networking devices that control access to your organization's network assets. Firewalls are positioned at the entrance points into your network. If your network has multiple entrance points, you must position a firewall at each point to provide effective network access control.

Firewalls are often placed in between the internal network and an external network such as the Internet. With a firewall between your network and the Internet, all traffic coming from the Internet must pass through the firewall before entering your network.

Firewalls can also be used to control access to a specific part of your network. For example, you can position firewalls at all the entry points into a research and development network to prevent unauthorized access to proprietary information.

The most basic function of a firewall is to monitor and filter traffic. Firewalls can be simple or elaborate, depending on your network requirements. Simple firewalls are usually easier to configure and manage. However, you might require the flexibility of a more elaborate firewall.

Creating a Firewall

Cisco IOS software provides an extensive feature set, allowing you to configure a simple or elaborate firewall, according to your particular requirements. You can configure a Cisco device as a firewall if the device is positioned appropriately at a network entry point.

To configure a basic firewall, you should at a minimum configure basic traffic filtering as described in Chapter 16. This chapter describes tips, cautions, considerations, recommendations, and general guidelines for configuring access lists for the various network protocols. You should configure basic access lists for all network protocols that will be routed through your firewall, such as IP, IPX, AppleTalk, and so forth.

To configure a more robust firewall, you should also configure one or more of the Cisco IOS features listed in Table 1-1.

Table 1-1 *Cisco IOS Features for a Robust Firewall*

Feature	Chapter	Comments
Lock-and-Key security	Chapter 17, "Configuring Lock-and-Key Security (Dynamic Access Lists)"	Lock-and-Key provides traffic filtering with the ability to allow temporary access through the firewall for certain individuals. These individuals must first be authenticated (by a username/password mechanism) before the firewall allows their traffic through the firewall, and afterwards, the firewall closes the temporary opening.
Reflexive access lists	Chapter 19, "Configuring IP Session Filtering (Reflexive Access Lists)"	Reflexive access lists filter IP traffic so that TCP or UDP "session" traffic is only permitted through the firewall if the session originated from within the internal network.

Table 1-1   *Cisco IOS Features for a Robust Firewall, Continued*

Feature	Chapter	Comments
TCP Intercept	Chapter 21, "Configuring TCP Intercept (Prevent Denial-of-Service Attacks)"	TCP Intercept protects TCP servers within your network from TCP SYN-flooding attacks, a type of denial-of-service attack.
Network Data Encryption	Chapter 23, "Configuring Network Data Encryption"	Network Data Encryption selectively encrypts IP packets that are transmitted across external networks.
User Authentication and Authorization	Chapter 3, "Configuring Authentication," and Chapter 5, "Configuring Authorization"	Authentication and authorization help protect your network from access by unauthorized users.
Network Address Translation (NAT)		NAT can be used to hide internal IP network addresses from the world outside the firewall. NAT was designed for internal IP networks that have unregistered (not globally unique) IP addresses: NAT translates these unregistered addresses into legal addresses at the firewall. NAT can also be configured to advertise only one address for the entire internal network to the outside world. This provides security by effectively hiding the entire internal network from the world.
Event Logging		Event Logging automatically logs output from system error messages and other events to the console terminal. You can also redirect these messages to other destinations such as virtual terminals, internal buffers, or syslog servers. You can also specify the severity of the event to be logged, and you can configure the logged output to be timestamped. The logged output can be used to assist real-time debugging and management and to track potential security breaches or other nonstandard activities throughout a network.

Other Guidelines for Configuring a Firewall

As with all networking devices, you should always protect access into the firewall by configuring passwords as described in Chapter 25. You should also consider configuring user authentication, authorization, and accounting as described in the chapters in Part I.

You should also consider the following recommendations:

- Configure neighbor router authentication (see Chapter 27).

- When setting passwords for accessing the firewall, use the **enable secret** command rather than the **enable password** command, which does not have as strong an encryption algorithm.

- Put a password on the console port. In authentication, authorization, and accounting (AAA) environments, use the same authentication for the console as for elsewhere. In a non-AAA environment, at a minimum configure the **login** and **password** *password* commands.

- Think about access control *before* you connect a console port to the network in any way, including attaching a modem to the port.

- Apply access lists and password protection to all virtual terminal ports.

- Use access lists to limit who can Telnet into your router.

- Don't enable any local service (such as SNMP or NTP) that you don't use. Cisco Discovery Protocol (CDP) and Network Time Protocol (NTP) are on by default, and you should turn these off if you don't absolutely need them.

  To turn off CDP, enter the **no cdp run** global configuration command. To turn off NTP, enter the **ntp disable** interface configuration command on each interface not using NTP.

  If you must run NTP, configure NTP only on required interfaces, and configure NTP to listen only to certain peers.

  Any enabled service could present a potential security risk. A determined, hostile party might be able to find creative ways to misuse the enabled services to access the firewall or the network.

  For local services that are enabled, protect against misuse by configuring the services to communicate only with specific peers and by configuring access lists to deny packets for the services at specific interfaces.

- Protect against spoofing: Protect the networks on both sides of the firewall from being spoofed from the other side. You could protect against spoofing by configuring access lists at all interfaces to pass only traffic from expected source addresses and to deny all other traffic.

  You can also disable source routing (for IP, enter the **no ip source-route** global configuration command). Disabling source routing at *all* routers can also help prevent spoofing.

  You can also disable minor services (for IP, enter the **no service tcp-small-servers** and **no service udp-small-servers** global configuration commands).

- Prevent the firewall from being used as relay by configuring access lists on any existing reverse Telnet ports.

- Disable directed broadcasts for all applicable protocols on your firewall and on all your other routers. (For IP, use the **no ip directed-broadcast** command.)

  Directed broadcasts can be misused to multiply the power of denial-of-service attacks, because every denial-of-service packet sent is broadcast to every host on a subnet. Furthermore, some hosts have other intrinsic security risks present when handling broadcasts.

- Configure the **no proxy-arp** command to prevent internal addresses from being revealed. (This is important to do if you don't have NAT configured to prevent internal addresses from being revealed.)

- Keep the firewall in a secured (locked) room.

PART I

Authentication, Authorization, and Accounting (AAA)

CHAPTER 2

AAA Overview

Access control is the way you control who is allowed access to the network server and what services they are allowed to use once they have access. Authentication, Authorization, and Accounting (AAA) network security services provide the primary framework through which you set up access control on your router or access server.

AAA SECURITY SERVICES

AAA is an architectural framework for configuring a set of three independent security functions in a consistent manner. AAA provides a modular way of performing the following services:

- Authentication—Provides the method of identifying users, including login and password dialog, challenge and response, messaging support, and, depending on the security protocol you select, encryption.

  Authentication is the way a user is identified prior to being allowed access to the network and network services. You configure AAA authentication by defining a named list of authentication methods and then applying that list to various interfaces. The method list defines the types of authentication to be performed and the sequence in which they will be performed; it must be applied to a specific interface before any of the defined authentication methods will be performed. The only exception is the default method list (which, by coincidence, is named "default"). The default method list is automatically applied to all interfaces if no other method list is defined. A defined method list overrides the default method list.

  All authentication methods, except for local, line password, and enable authentication, must be defined through AAA. For information about configuring all authentication methods, including those implemented outside of the AAA security services, see Chapter 3, "Configuring Authentication."

- Authorization—Provides the method for remote access control, including one-time authorization or authorization for each service, per-user account list and profile, user group support, and support of IP, IPX, ARA, and Telnet.

  AAA authorization works by assembling a set of attributes that describe what the user is authorized to perform. These attributes are compared to the information contained in a database for a given user, and the result is returned to AAA to determine the user's actual capabilities and restrictions. The database can be located locally on the access server or router or it can be hosted remotely on a RADIUS or TACACS+ security server. Remote security servers, such as RADIUS and TACACS+, authorize users for specific rights by associating attribute-value (AV) pairs, which define those rights, with the appropriate user. All authorization methods must be defined through AAA. When AAA authorization is activated, it is applied equally to all interfaces on the access server or router. For information about configuring authorization using AAA, see Chapter 5, "Configuring Authorization."

- Accounting—Provides the method for collecting and sending security server information used for billing, auditing, and reporting, such as user identities, start and stop times, executed commands (such as PPP), number of packets, and number of bytes.

  Accounting enables you to track the services users are accessing as well as the amount of network resources they are consuming. When AAA accounting is activated, the network access server reports user activity to the TACACS+ or RADIUS security server (depending on which security method you have implemented) in the form of accounting records. Each accounting record is comprised of accounting AV pairs and is stored on the access control server. This data can then be analyzed for network management, client billing, or auditing. All accounting methods must be defined through AAA. When AAA accounting is activated, it is applied equally to all interfaces on the access server or router. For information about configuring accounting using AAA, see Chapter 7, "Configuring Accounting."

In many circumstances, AAA uses protocols such as RADIUS, TACACS+, and Kerberos to administer its security functions. If your router or access server is acting as a network access server, AAA is the means through which you establish communication between your network access server and your RADIUS, TACACS+, or Kerberos security server.

Although AAA is the primary (and recommended) method for access control, Cisco IOS software provides additional features for simple access control that are outside the scope of AAA, such as local username authentication, line password authentication, and enable password authentication. However, these features do not provide the same degree of access control that is possible by using AAA.

Benefits of Using AAA

AAA provides the following benefits:

- Increased flexibility and control
- Scalability
- Standardized authentication methods, such as RADIUS, TACACS+, and Kerberos
- Multiple backup systems

NOTES

The deprecated protocols, TACACS and Extended TACACS, are not compatible with AAA; if you select these security protocols, you will not be able to take advantage of the AAA security services.

AAA Philosophy

AAA is designed to enable you to configure dynamically the type of authentication and authorization you want on a per-line (per-user) or per-service (for example, IP, IPX, or VPDN) basis. You define the type of authentication and authorization you want by creating method lists, then applying those method lists to specific services or interfaces.

Method Lists

A method list is simply a list defining the authentication methods to be used, in sequence, to authenticate a user. Method lists enable you to designate one or more security protocols to be used for authentication, thus ensuring a backup system for authentication in case the initial method fails. Cisco IOS software uses the first method listed to authenticate users; if that method fails to respond, the Cisco IOS software selects the next authentication method listed in the method list. This process continues until there is successful communication with a listed authentication method or the authentication method list is exhausted, in which case authentication fails.

NOTES

The Cisco IOS software attempts authentication with the next listed authentication method only when there is no response from the previous method. If authentication fails at any point in this cycle—meaning that the security server or local username database responds by denying the user access—the authentication process stops and no other authentication methods are attempted.

Figure 2–1 shows a typical AAA network configuration that includes four security servers: R1 and R2 are RADIUS servers, and T1 and T2 are TACACS+ servers.

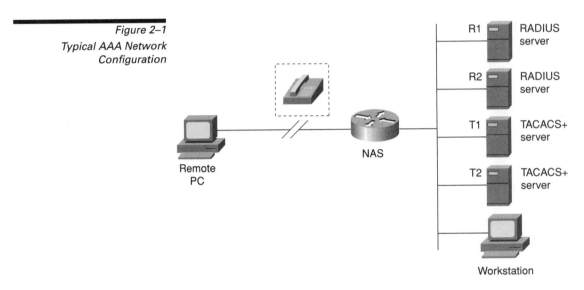

Figure 2–1
Typical AAA Network
Configuration

Suppose the system administrator has defined a method list where R1 will be contacted first for authentication information, then R2, T1, T2, and then finally the local username database on the access server itself. When a remote user attempts to dial in to the network, the network access server first queries R1 for authentication information. If R1 authenticates the user, it issues a PASS response to the network access server and the user is allowed to access the network. If R1 returns a FAIL response, the user is denied access and the session is terminated. If R1 fails to respond, then the network access server processes that as an ERROR and queries R2 for authentication information. This pattern would continue through the remaining designated methods until the user is either authenticated, rejected, or the session terminated. If all of the authentication methods fail, which the network access server would process as a failure, the session would be terminated.

NOTES

A FAIL response is significantly different from an ERROR. A FAIL means that the user has not met the criteria contained in the applicable authentication database to be authenticated successfully. Authentication ends with a FAIL response. An ERROR means that the security server has failed to respond to an authentication query. Because of this, no authentication has been attempted. Only when an ERROR is detected will AAA select the next authentication method defined in the authentication method list.

WHERE TO BEGIN

You must first decide what kind of security solution you want to implement. You need to assess the security risks in your particular network and decide on the appropriate means to prevent unauthorized entry and attack. For more information about accessing your security risks and possible security solutions, see Chapter 1, "Security Overview." We recommend that you use AAA, no matter how minor your security needs might be.

Overview of the AAA Configuration Process

Configuring AAA is relatively simple after you understand the basic process involved. To configure security on a Cisco router or access server using AAA, follow this process:

1. Enable AAA by using the **aaa new-model** global configuration command.
2. If you decide to use a separate security server, configure security protocol parameters, such as RADIUS, TACACS+, or Kerberos.
3. Define the method lists for authentication by using the **aaa authentication** command.
4. Apply the method lists to a particular interface or line, if required.
5. (Optional) Configure authorization using the **aaa authorization** command.
6. (Optional) Configure accounting using the **aaa accounting** command.

For a complete description of the commands used in this chapter, see Chapter 4, "Authentication Commands." To locate documentation of other commands that appear in this chapter, search online.

Enable AAA

Before you can use any of the services AAA network security services provide, you need to enable AAA.

To enable AAA, perform the following task in global configuration mode:

Task	Command
Enable AAA.	aaa new-model

NOTES

When you enable AAA, you can no longer access the commands to configure the older deprecated protocols, TACACS or Extended TACACS. If you decided to use TACACS or Extended TACACS in your security solution, do not enable AAA.

Disable AAA

You can disable AAA functionality with a single command if, for some reason, you decide that your security needs cannot be met by AAA but can be met by using TACACS, Extended TACACS, or a line security method that can be implemented without AAA.

To disable AAA, perform the following task in global configuration mode:

Task	Command
Disable AAA.	no aaa new-model

WHAT TO DO NEXT

Once you have enabled AAA, you are ready to configure the other elements relating to your selected security solution. Table 2–1 describes the configuration tasks you might want to complete and where to find that information.

Table 2–1   *AAA Access Control Security Solutions Methods*

Task	Chapter or Appendix in Book	Process Step
Configure local login authentication.	Chapter 3, "Configuring Authentication"	3
Control login using security server authentication.	Chapter 3, "Configuring Authentication"	3
Define method lists for authentication.	Chapter 3, "Configuring Authentication"	3
Apply method lists to a particular interface or line.	Chapter 3, "Configuring Authentication"	3
Configure RADIUS security protocol parameters.	Chapter 9, "Configuring RADIUS"	2
Configure TACACS+ security protocol parameters.	Chapter 11, "Configuring TACACS+"	2
Configure Kerberos security protocol parameters.	Chapter 14, "Configuring Kerberos"	2
Enable TACACS+ authorization.	Chapter 5, "Configuring Authorization"	5
Enable RADIUS authorization.	Chapter 5, "Configuring Authorization"	5
View supported IETF RADIUS attributes.	Appendix A, "RADIUS Attributes"	2

Table 2–1   *AAA Access Control Security Solutions Methods, Continued*

Task	Chapter or Appendix in Book	Process Step
View supported vendor-specific RADIUS attributes.	Appendix A, "RADIUS Attributes"	2
View supported TACACS+ AV pairs.	Appendix B, "TACACS+ Attribute-Value Pairs"	2
Enable accounting.	Chapter 7, "Configuring Accounting"	6

If you have elected not to use the AAA security services, Table 2–2 describes the configuration tasks you might want to complete and where to find that information.

Table 2–2   *Non-AAA Access Control Security Solutions Methods*

Tasks	Chapter in Book
Configure login authentication.	Chapter 3, "Configuring Authentication"
Configure TACACS.	Chapter 12, "Configuring TACACS and Extended TACACS"
Configure Extended TACACS.	Chapter 12, "Configuring TACACS and Extended TACACS"

CHAPTER 3

Configuring Authentication

Authentication identifies users before they are allowed access to the network and network services. Basically, the Cisco IOS software implementation of authentication is divided into two main categories:

- AAA Authentication Methods
- Non-AAA Authentication Methods

Authentication, for the most part, is implemented through the AAA security services. We recommend that, whenever possible, AAA be used to implement authentication.

This chapter describes both AAA and non-AAA authentication methods. For configuration examples, see section "Authentication Configuration Examples," found at the end of this chapter. For a complete description of the commands used in this chapter, see Chapter 4, "Authentication Commands." To locate documentation of other commands that appear in this chapter, search online.

AAA AUTHENTICATION METHOD LISTS

To configure AAA authentication, first define a named list of authentication methods, and then apply that list to various interfaces. The method list defines the types of authentication to be performed and the sequence in which they will be performed; it must be applied to a specific interface before any of the defined authentication methods will be performed. The only exception is the default method list (which, by coincidence, is named "default"). The default method list is automatically applied to all interfaces except those that have a named method list explicitly defined. A defined method list overrides the default method list.

A method list is simply a list describing the authentication methods to be queried, in sequence, to authenticate a user. Method lists enable you to designate one or more security protocols to be used for authentication, thus ensuring a backup system for authentication in case the initial method fails. Cisco IOS software uses the first method listed to authenticate users; if that method fails to respond, the Cisco IOS software selects the next authentication method listed in the method list. This process continues until there is successful communication with a listed authentication method, or all methods defined are exhausted.

It is important to note that the Cisco IOS software attempts authentication with the next listed authentication method only when there is no response from the previous method. If authentication fails at any point in this cycle—meaning that the security server or local username database responds by denying the user access—the authentication process stops and no other authentication methods are attempted.

Method List Examples

Figure 3–1 shows a typical AAA network configuration that includes four security servers: R1 and R2 are RADIUS servers, and T1 and T2 are TACACS+ servers. Suppose the system administrator has decided on a security solution where all interfaces will use the same authentication methods to authenticate PPP connections: R1 is contacted first for authentication information, then if there is no response, R2 is contacted. If R2 fails to respond, T1 is contacted; if T1 fails to respond, T2 is contacted. If all designated servers fail to respond, authentication falls over to the local username database on the access server itself. To implement this, the system administrator would create a default method list by entering the following command:

```
aaa authentication ppp default radius tacacs+ local
```

In this example, "default" is the name of the method list. The protocols included in this method list are listed after the name, in the order they are to be queried. The default list is automatically applied to all interfaces.

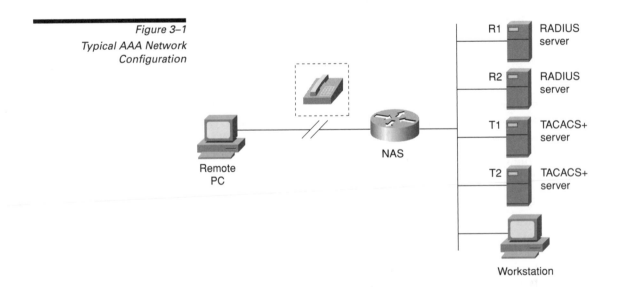

Figure 3–1
Typical AAA Network
Configuration

Suppose the system administrator wanted to apply this method list only to a particular interface or set of interfaces. In this case, the system administrator would create a named method list and then apply this named list to the applicable interfaces. The following example shows how the system administrator would implement the previous scenario if that authentication method were to be applied only to interface 3:

```
aaa authentication ppp apple radius tacacs+ local
  interface async 3
  ppp authentication chap apple
```

In this example, "apple" is the name of the method list, and the protocols included in this method list are listed after the name in the order in which they are to be performed. After the method list has been created, it is applied to the appropriate interface. Please note that the method list name in both the **aaa authentication** command and the **ppp authentication** commands must match.

When a remote user attempts to dial in to the network, the network access server first queries R1 for authentication information. If R1 authenticates the user, it issues a PASS response to the network access server and the user is allowed to access the network. If R1 returns a FAIL response, the user is denied access and the session is terminated. If R1 fails to respond, then the network access server processes that as an ERROR and queries R2 for authentication information. This pattern would continue through the remaining designated methods until the user is either authenticated, rejected, or the session terminated.

It is important to remember that a FAIL response is significantly different from an ERROR. A FAIL means that the user has not met the criteria contained in the applicable authentication database to be successfully authenticated. Authentication ends with a FAIL response. An ERROR means that the security server has failed to respond to an authentication query. Because of this, no authentication has been attempted. Only when an ERROR is detected will AAA select the next authentication method defined in the authentication method list.

AAA Authentication General Configuration Procedure

To configure AAA authentication, no matter what method of authentication you select, you need to perform the following tasks:

1. Enable AAA by using the **aaa new-model** global configuration command. For more information about configuring AAA, see Chapter 2, "AAA Overview."

2. Configure security protocol parameters, such as RADIUS, TACACS+, or Kerberos, if you are using a security server. For more information about RADIUS, see Chapter 9, "Configuring RADIUS." For more information about TACACS+, see Chapter 11, "Configuring TACACS+." For more information about Kerberos, see Chapter 14, "Configuring Kerberos."

3. Define the method lists for authentication by using the **aaa authentication** command.

4. Apply the method lists to a particular interface or line, if required.

AAA AUTHENTICATION METHODS

This section discusses the following AAA authentication methods:

- Configure Login Authentication Using AAA
- Configure PPP Authentication Using AAA
- Configure ARA Authentication Using AAA
- Configure NASI Authentication Using AAA
- Enable Password Protection at the Privileged Level
- Enable an Authentication Override
- Enable Double Authentication

NOTES

AAA features are not available for use until you enable AAA globally by issuing the **aaa new-model** command. For more information about enabling AAA, see Chapter 2, "AAA Overview."

Configure Login Authentication Using AAA

The AAA security services facilitate a variety of login authentication methods. Use the **aaa authentication login** command to enable AAA authentication no matter which of the supported login authentication methods you decide to use. With the **aaa authentication login** command, you create one or more lists of authentication methods that are tried at login. These lists are applied using the **login authentication** line configuration command.

To configure login authentication by using AAA, perform the following tasks, beginning in global configuration mode:

Task	Command
Enable AAA globally.	**aaa new-model**
Create a local authentication list.	**aaa authentication login** {**default** | *list-name*}*method1* [*method2...*]
Enter line configuration mode for the lines to which you want to apply the authentication list.	**line** [**aux** | **console** | **tty** | **vty**] *line-number* [*ending-line-number*]
Apply the authentication list to a line or set of lines.	**login authentication** {**default** | *list-name*}

The keyword *list-name* is any character string used to name the list you are creating. The keyword *method* refers to the actual method the authentication algorithm tries. The additional methods of authentication are used only if the previous method returns an error, not if it fails. To specify that the authentication should succeed even if all methods return an error, specify **none** as the final method in the command line.

For example, to specify that authentication should succeed even if (in this example) the TACACS+ server returns an error, enter the following:

```
aaa authentication login default tacacs+ none
```

NOTES

Because the **none** keyword enables *any* user logging in to authenticate successfully, it should be used only as a backup method of authentication.

To create a default list that is used if no list is specified in the **login authentication** command, use the **default** argument followed by the methods you want used in default situations. The default method list is automatically applied to all interfaces.

For example, to specify RADIUS as the default method for user authentication during login, enter the following:

```
aaa authentication login default radius
```

Table 3–1 lists the supported login authentication methods.

Table 3–1 *AAA Authentication Login Methods*

Keyword	Description
enable	Uses the enable password for authentication.
krb5	Uses Kerberos 5 for authentication.
line	Uses the line password for authentication.
local	Uses the local username database for authentication.
none	Uses no authentication.
radius	Uses RADIUS authentication.
tacacs+	Uses TACACS+ authentication.
krb5-telnet	Uses Kerberos 5 Telnet authentication protocol when using Telnet to connect to the router. If selected, this keyword must be listed as the first method in the method list.

Login Authentication Using Local Password

Use the **aaa authentication login** command with the **local** *method* keyword to specify that the Cisco router or access server will use the local username database for authentication. For example, to specify the local username database as the method of user authentication at login when no other method list has been defined, enter the following:

```
aaa authentication login default local
```

For information about adding users into the local username database, see section "Establish Username Authentication."

Login Authentication Using Line Password

Use the **aaa authentication login** command with the **line** *method* keyword to specify the line password as the login authentication method. For example, to specify the line password as the method of user authentication at login when no other method list has been defined, enter the following:

```
aaa authentication login default line
```

Before you can use a line password as the login authentication method, you need to define a line password. For more information about defining line passwords, see the section "Configure Line Password Protection."

Login Authentication Using Enable Password

Use the **aaa authentication login** command with the **enable** *method* keyword to specify the enable password as the login authentication method. For example, to specify the enable password as the method of user authentication at login when no other method list has been defined, enter:

```
aaa authentication login default enable
```

Before you can use the enable password as the login authentication method, you need to define the enable password. For more information about defining enable passwords, see Chapter 25, "Configuring Passwords and Privileges."

Login Authentication Using RADIUS

Use the **aaa authentication login** command with the **radius** *method* keyword to specify RADIUS as the login authentication method. For example, to specify RADIUS as the method of user authentication at login when no other method list has been defined, enter:

```
aaa authentication login default radius
```

Before you can use RADIUS as the login authentication method, you need to enable communication with the RADIUS security server. For more information about establishing communication with a RADIUS server, see Chapter 9, "Configuring Radius."

Login Authentication Using TACACS+

Use the **aaa authentication login** command with the **tacacs+** *method* keyword to specify TACACS+ as the login authentication method. For example, to specify TACACS+ as the method of user authentication at login when no other method list has been defined, enter:

```
aaa authentication login default tacacs+
```

Before you can use TACACS+ as the login authentication method, you need to enable communication with the TACACS+ security server. For more information about establishing communication with a TACACS+ server, see Chapter 11, "Configuring TACACS+."

Login Authentication Using Kerberos

Authentication via Kerberos is different from most other authentication methods: The user's password is never sent to the remote access server. Remote users logging in to the network are prompted for a username. If the key distribution center (KDC) has an entry for that user, it creates an encrypted ticket granting ticket (TGT) with the password for that user and sends it back to the router. The user is then prompted for a password, and the router attempts to decrypt the TGT with that password. If it succeeds, the user is authenticated and the TGT is stored in the user's credential cache on the router.

A user does not need to run the KINIT program to get a TGT to authenticate to the router. This is because KINIT has been integrated into the login procedure in the Cisco IOS implementation of Kerberos.

Use the **aaa authentication login** command with the **krb5** *method* keyword to specify Kerberos as the login authentication method. For example, to specify Kerberos as the method of user authentication at login when no other method list has been defined, enter:

```
aaa authentication login default krb5
```

Before you can use Kerberos as the login authentication method, you need to enable communication with the Kerberos security server. For more information about establishing communication with a Kerberos server, see Chapter 14, "Configuring Kerberos."

Configure PPP Authentication Using AAA

Many users access network access servers through dial-up via async or ISDN. Dial-up via async or ISDN bypasses the CLI completely; instead, a network protocol (such as PPP or ARAP) starts as soon as the connection is established.

The AAA security services facilitate a variety of authentication methods for use on serial interfaces running PPP. Use the **aaa authentication ppp** command to enable AAA authentication no matter which of the supported PPP authentication methods you decide to use.

To configure AAA authentication methods for serial lines using PPP, perform the following tasks in global configuration mode:

Task	Command
Enable AAA globally.	**aaa new-model**
Create a local authentication list.	**aaa authentication ppp** {**default** I *list-name*} *method1* [*method2...*]

Task	Command
Enter interface configuration mode for the interface to which you want to apply the authentication list.	**interface** *interface-type interface-number*
Apply the authentication list to a line or set of lines.	**ppp authentication** {**chap** I **pap** I **chap pap** I **pap chap**} [**if-needed**] {**default** I *list-name*} [**callin**]

With the **aaa authentication ppp** command, you create one or more lists of authentication methods that are tried when a user tries to authenticate via PPP. These lists are applied using the **ppp authentication** line configuration command.

To create a default list that is used if no list is specified in the **ppp authentication** command, use the **default** argument followed by the methods you want used in default situations.

For example, to specify the local username database as the default method for user authentication, enter the following:

```
aaa authentication ppp default local
```

The keyword *list-name* is any character string used to name the list you are creating. The keyword *method* refers to the actual method the authentication algorithm tries. The additional methods of authentication are used only if the previous method returns an error, not if it fails. To specify that the authentication should succeed even if all methods return an error, specify **none** as the final method in the command line.

For example, to specify that authentication should succeed even if (in this example) the TACACS+ server returns an error, enter the following:

```
aaa authentication ppp default tacacs+ none
```

NOTES

Because **none** allows all users logging in to authenticate successfully, it should be used as a backup method of authentication.

Table 3–2 lists the supported login authentication methods.

Table 3–2 *AAA Authentication PPP Methods*

Keyword	Description
if-needed	Does not authenticate if user has already been authenticated on a TTY line.
krb5	Uses Kerberos 5 for authentication (can only be used for PAP authentication).

Table 3–2 *AAA Authentication PPP Methods, Continued*

Keyword	Description
local	Uses the local username database for authentication.
none	Uses no authentication.
radius	Uses RADIUS authentication.
tacacs+	Uses TACACS+ authentication.

PPP Authentication Using Local Password

Use the **aaa authentication ppp** command with the *method* keyword **local** to specify that the Cisco router or access server will use the local username database for authentication. For example, to specify the local username database as the method of authentication for use on lines running PPP when no other method list has been defined, enter:

```
aaa authentication ppp default local
```

For information about adding users into the local username database, see section "Establish Username Authentication."

PPP Authentication Using RADIUS

Use the **aaa authentication ppp** command with the **radius** *method* keyword to specify RADIUS as the authentication method for use on interfaces running PPP. For example, to specify RADIUS as the method of user authentication when no other method list has been defined, enter:

```
aaa authentication ppp default radius
```

Before you can use RADIUS as the authentication method, you need to enable communication with the RADIUS security server. For more information about establishing communication with a RADIUS server, see Chapter 9.

PPP Authentication Using TACACS+

Use the **aaa authentication ppp** command with the **tacacs+** *method* keyword to specify TACACS+ as the authentication method for use on interfaces running PPP. For example, to specify TACACS+ as the method of user authentication when no other method list has been defined, enter:

```
aaa authentication ppp default tacacs+
```

Before you can use TACACS+ as the authentication method, you need to enable communication with the TACACS+ security server. For more information about establishing communication with a TACACS+ server, see Chapter 11.

PPP Authentication Using Kerberos

Use the **aaa authentication ppp** command with the **krb5** *method* keyword to specify Kerberos as the authentication method for use on interfaces running PPP. For example, to specify Kerberos as the method of user authentication when no other method list has been defined, enter:

```
aaa authentication ppp default krb5
```

Before you can use Kerberos as the login authentication method, you need to enable communication with the Kerberos security server. For more information about establishing communication with a Kerberos server, see Chapter 14.

NOTES

Kerberos login authentication works only with PPP PAP authentication.

Configure ARA Authentication Using AAA

With the **aaa authentication arap** command, you create one or more lists of authentication methods that are tried when AppleTalk Remote Access (ARA) users attempt to log in to the router. These lists are used with the **arap authentication** line configuration command.

Perform at least the first of the following tasks starting in global configuration mode:

Task	Command
Enable AAA globally.	**aaa new-model**
Enable authentication for ARA users.	**aaa authentication arap** {**default** I *list-name*} *method1* [*method2*...]
(Optional) Change to line configuration mode.	**line** *number*
(Optional) Enable autoselection of ARA.	**autoselect arap**
(Optional) Start the ARA session automatically at user login.	**autoselect during-login**
(Optional—not needed if **default** is used in the **aaa authentication arap** command) Enable TACACS+ authentication for ARA on a line.	**arap authentication** *list-name*

The *list-name* is any character string used to name the list you are creating. The *method* refers to the actual list of methods the authentication algorithm tries, in the sequence entered.

To create a default list that is used if no list is specified in the **arap authentication** command, use the **default** argument followed by the methods you want to be used in default situations.

The additional methods of authentication are used only if the previous method returns an error, not if it fails. To specify that the authentication should succeed even if all methods return an error, specify **none** as the final method in the command line.

Table 3–3 lists the supported login authentication methods.

Table 3–3 *AAA Authentication ARAP Methods*

Keyword	Description
guest	Allows guest logins.
auth-guest	Allows guest logins only if the user has already logged into EXEC.
line	Uses the line password for authentication.
local	Uses the local username database for authentication.
tacacs+	Uses TACACS+ authentication.
radius	Uses RADIUS authentication.

For example, to create a default AAA authentication method list used with the ARA protocol, enter:

```
aaa authentication arap default if-needed none
```

To create the same authentication method list for the ARA protocol but name the list *MIS-access*, enter:

```
aaa authentication arap MIS-access if-needed none
```

ARA Authentication Allowing Guest Logins

Use the **aaa authentication arap** command with the **guest** keyword to allow guest logins. This method must be the first listed in the ARA authentication method list, but it can be followed by other methods if it does not succeed. For example, to allow all guest logins as the default method of authentication, using RADIUS only if that method fails, enter:

```
aaa authentication arap default guest radius
```

ARA Authentication Allowing Authorized Guest Logins

Use the **aaa authentication arap** command with the **auth-guest** keyword to allow guest logins only if the user has already successfully logged in to the EXEC. This method must be first in the ARA authentication method list, but it can be followed by other methods if it does not succeed. For example, to allow all authorized guest logins—meaning logins by users who have already successfully logged in to the EXEC—as the default method of authentication, using RADIUS only if that method fails, enter:

```
aaa authentication arap default auth-guest radius
```

NOTES

By default, guest logins through ARAP are disabled when you initialize AAA. To allow guest logins, you must use the **aaa authentication arap** command with either the **guest** or **auth-guest** keyword.

ARA Authentication Using Local Password

Use the **aaa authentication arap** command with the *method* keyword **local** to specify that the Cisco router or access server will use the local username database for authentication. For example, to specify the local username database as the method of ARA user authentication when no other method list has been defined, enter:

```
aaa authentication arap default local
```

For information about adding users to the local username database, see section "Establish Username Authentication."

ARA Authentication Using Line Password

Use the **aaa authentication arap** command with the *method* keyword **line** to specify the line password as the authentication method. For example, to specify the line password as the method of ARA user authentication when no other method list has been defined, enter:

```
aaa authentication arap default line
```

Before you can use a line password as the ARA authentication method, you need to define a line password. For more information about defining line passwords, see section "Configure Line Password Protection."

ARA Authentication Using RADIUS

Use the **aaa authentication arap** command with the **radius** *method* keyword to specify RADIUS as the ARA authentication method. For example, to specify RADIUS as the method of ARA user authentication when no other method list has been defined, enter:

```
aaa authentication arap default radius
```

Before you can use RADIUS as the ARA authentication method, you need to enable communication with the RADIUS security server. For more information about establishing communication with a RADIUS server, see Chapter 9.

ARA Authentication Using TACACS+

Use the **aaa authentication arap** command with the **tacacs+** *method* keyword to specify TACACS+ as the ARA authentication method. For example, to specify TACACS+ as the method of ARA user authentication when no other method list has been defined, enter:

```
aaa authentication arap default tacacs+
```

Before you can use TACACS+ as the ARA authentication method, you need to enable communication with the TACACS+ security server. For more information about establishing communication with a TACACS+ server, see Chapter 11.

Configure NASI Authentication Using AAA

With the **aaa authentication nasi** command, you create one or more lists of authentication methods that are tried when Netware Asynchronous Services Interface (NASI) users attempt to log in to the router. These lists are used with the **nasi authentication** line configuration command.

Perform at least the first two of the following tasks starting in global configuration mode:

Task	Command
Enable AAA globally.	**aaa new-model**
Enable authentication for NASI users.	**aaa authentication nasi** {**default**	*list-name*} *method1* [*method2...*]
(Optional—not needed if **default** is used in the **aaa authentication nasi** command.) Change to line configuration mode.	**line** *number*
(Optional—not needed if **default** is used in the **aaa authentication nasi** command) Enable authentication for NASI on a line.	**nasi authentication** *list-name*

The *list-name* is any character string used to name the list you are creating. The *method* refers to the actual list of methods the authentication algorithm tries, in the sequence entered.

To create a default list that is used if no list is specified in the **aaa authentication nasi** command, use the **default** argument followed by the methods you want to be used in default situations.

The additional methods of authentication are used only if the previous method returns an error, not if it fails. To specify that the authentication should succeed even if all methods return an error, specify **none** as the final method in the command line.

NOTES

Because **none** allows all users logging in to authenticate successfully, it should be used as a backup method of authentication.

Table 3–4 lists the supported login authentication methods.

Table 3–4   *AAA Authentication NASI Methods*

Keyword	Description
enable	Uses the enable password for authentication.
line	Uses the line password for authentication.
local	Uses the local username database for authentication.
none	Uses no authentication.
tacacs+	Uses TACACS+ authentication.

NASI Authentication Using Enable Password

Use the **aaa authentication nasi** command with the argument **enable** to specify the enable password as the authentication method. For example, to specify the enable password as the method of NASI user authentication when no other method list has been defined, enter:

```
aaa authentication nasi default enable
```

Before you can use the enable password as the authentication method, you need to define the enable password. For more information about defining enable passwords, see Chapter 25, "Configuring Passwords and Privileges."

NASI Authentication Using Local Password

Use the **aaa authentication nasi** command with the *method* keyword **local** to specify that the Cisco router or access server will use the local username database for authentication information. For example, to specify the local username database as the method of NASI user authentication when no other method list has been defined, enter:

```
aaa authentication nasi default local
```

For information about adding users to the local username database, see section "Establish Username Authentication."

NASI Authentication Using Line Password

Use the **aaa authentication nasi** command with the *method* keyword **line** to specify the line password as the authentication method. For example, to specify the line password as the method of NASI user authentication when no other method list has been defined, enter:

```
aaa authentication nasi default line
```

Before you can use a line password as the NASI authentication method, you need to define a line password. For more information about defining line passwords, see section "Configure Line Password Protection."

NASI Authentication Using TACACS+

Use the **aaa authentication nasi** command with the **tacacs+** *method* keyword to specify TACACS+ as the NASI authentication method. For example, to specify TACACS+ as the method of NASI user authentication when no other method list has been defined, enter:

```
aaa authentication nasi default tacacs+
```

Before you can use TACACS+ as the authentication method, you need to enable communication with the TACACS+ security server. For more information about establishing communication with a TACACS+ server, see Chapter 11.

Enable Password Protection at the Privileged Level

Use the **aaa authentication enable default** command to create a series of authentication methods that are used to determine whether a user can access the privileged EXEC command level. You can specify up to four authentication methods. The additional methods of authentication are used only if the previous method returns an error, not if it fails. To specify that the authentication succeed even if all methods return an error, specify **none** as the final method in the command line.

Perform the following task in global configuration mode:

Task	Command
Enable user ID and password checking for users requesting privileged EXEC level.	**aaa authentication enable default** *method1* [*method2...*]

The *method* refers to the actual list of methods the authentication algorithm tries, in the sequence entered. Table 3–5 lists the supported login authentication methods.

Table 3–5 *AAA Authentication Enable Default Methods*

Keyword	Description
enable	Uses the enable password for authentication.
line	Uses the line password for authentication.
none	Uses no authentication.
tacacs+	Uses TACACS+ authentication.
radius	Uses RADIUS authentication.

Enable an Authentication Override

To configure the Cisco IOS software to check the local user database for authentication before attempting another form of authentication, use the **aaa authentication local-override** command.

This command is useful when you want to configure an override to the normal authentication process for certain personnel (such as system administrators).

Perform the following task in global configuration mode:

Task	Command
Create an override for authentication.	**aaa authentication local-override**

Enable Double Authentication

Double Authentication provides additional authentication for Point-to-Point Protocol (PPP) sessions. Previously, PPP sessions could only be authenticated by using a single authentication method: either PAP or CHAP. Double Authentication requires remote users to pass a second stage of authentication—after CHAP or PAP authentication—before gaining network access.

This second ("double") authentication requires a password that is known to the user but *not* stored on the user's remote host. Therefore, the second authentication is specific to a user, not to a host. This provides an additional level of security that will be effective even if information from the remote host is stolen. In addition, this also provides greater flexibility by allowing customized network privileges for each user.

The second stage authentication can use one-time passwords such as token card passwords, which are not supported by CHAP. If one-time passwords are used, a stolen user password is of no use to the perpetrator.

How Double Authentication Works

With Double Authentication, there are two authentication/authorization stages. These two stages occur after a remote user dials in and a PPP session is initiated.

In the first stage, the user logs in using the remote host name; CHAP (or PAP) authenticates the remote host, and then PPP negotiates with AAA to authorize the remote host. In this process, the network access privileges associated with the remote host are assigned to the user.

NOTES

We suggest that the network administrator restrict authorization at this first stage to allow only Telnet connections to the local host.

In the second stage, the remote user must Telnet to the network access server to be authenticated. When the remote user logs in, the user must be authenticated with AAA login authentication. The user then must enter the **access-profile** command to be reauthorized using AAA. When this authorization is complete, the user has been double authenticated, and can access the network according to per-user network privileges.

The system administrator determines what network privileges remote users will have after each stage of authentication by configuring appropriate parameters on a security server. To use Double Authentication, the user must activate it by issuing the **access-profile** command.

CAUTION

Double Authentication can cause certain undesirable events if multiple hosts share a PPP connection to a network access server, as shown in Figure 3–2.

First, if a user, Bob, initiates a PPP session and activates Double Authentication at the NAS (per Figure 3–2), any other user will automatically have the same network privileges as Bob until Bob's PPP session expires. This happens because Bob's authorization profile is applied to the NAS's interface during the PPP session and any PPP traffic from other users will use the PPP session Bob established.

Second, if Bob initiates a PPP session and activates Double Authentication, and then—before Bob's PPP session has expired—another user, Jane, executes the **access-profile** command (or, if she Telnets to the NAS and **autocommand access-profile** is executed), a reauthorization will occur and Jane's authorization profile will be applied to the interface—replacing Bob's profile. This can disrupt or halt Bob's PPP traffic, or grant Bob additional authorization privileges he should not have.

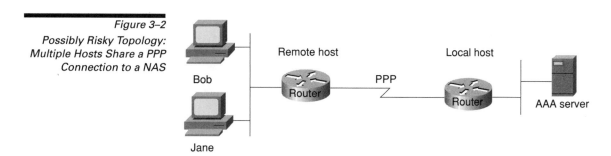

Figure 3–2
Possibly Risky Topology:
Multiple Hosts Share a PPP
Connection to a NAS

Configure Double Authentication

To configure Double Authentication, you must complete the following steps:

1. Enable AAA by using the **aaa-new model** global configuration command. For more information about enabling AAA, see Chapter 2.

2. Use the **aaa authentication** command to configure your network access server to use login and PPP authentication method lists, then apply those method lists to the appropriate lines or interfaces.

3. Use the **aaa authorization** command to configure AAA network authorization at login. For more information about configuring network authorization, see Chapter 5, "Configuring Authorization."

4. Configure security protocol parameters (for example, RADIUS or TACACS+). For more information about RADIUS, see Chapter 9. For more information about TACACS+, see Chapter 11.

5. Use access control list AV pairs on the security server that the user can connect to the local host only by establishing a Telnet connection.

6. (Optional) Configure the **access-profile** command as an autocommand. If you configure the autocommand, remote users will not have to manually enter the **access-profile** command to access authorized rights associated with their personal user profile.

NOTES ——

If the **access-profile** command is configured as an autocommand, users will still have to Telnet to the local host and log in to complete Double Authentication.

Follow these rules when creating the user-specific authorization statements (these rules relate to the default behavior of the **access-profile** command):

- Use valid AV pairs when configuring access control list AV pairs on the security server. For a list of valid AV pairs, see Chapter 4.

- If you want remote users to use the interface's existing authorization (that which existed prior to the second stage authentication/authorization), but you want them to have different access control lists (ACLs), you should specify *only* ACL AV pairs in the user-specific authorization definition. This might be desirable if you set up a default authorization profile to apply to the remote host, but want to apply specific ACLs to specific users.

- When these user-specific authorization statements are later applied to the interface, they can either be *added to* the existing interface configuration, or *replace* the existing interface configuration—depending on which form of the **access-profile** command is used to authorize the user. You should understand how the **access-profile** command works before configuring the authorization statements.

- If you will be using ISDN or Multilink PPP, you must also configure virtual templates at the local host.

To troubleshoot Double Authentication, use the **debug aaa per-user** debug command.

Access User Profile after Double Authentication

In Double Authentication, when a remote user establishes a PPP link to the local host using the local host name, the remote host is CHAP (or PAP) authenticated. After CHAP (or PAP) authentication, PPP negotiates with AAA to assign network access privileges associated with the remote host to the user. (We suggest that privileges at this stage be restricted to allow the user to connect to the local host only by establishing a Telnet connection.)

When the user needs to initiate the second phase of Double Authentication, establishing a Telnet connection to the local host, the user enters a personal username and password (different from the CHAP or PAP username and password). This action causes AAA reauthentication to occur according to the personal username/password. The initial rights associated with the local host, though, are still in place. By using the **access-profile** command, the rights associated with the local host are replaced by or merged with those defined for the user in the user's profile.

To access the rights associated with the user after Double Authentication, perform the following tasks in EXEC configuration mode:

Task	Command
Access the rights associated for the user after Double Authentication.	**access profile** [merge ׀ replace ׀ ignore-sanity-checks]

If you configured the **access-profile** command to be executed as an autocommand, it will be executed automatically after the remote user logs in.

Non-AAA Authentication Methods

This section discusses the following non-AAA authentication tasks:

- Configure Line Password Protection
- Establish Username Authentication
- Enable CHAP or PAP Authentication
- Configure TACACS and Extended TACACS Password Protection

Configure Line Password Protection

You can provide access control on a terminal line by entering the password and establishing password checking. To do so, perform the following tasks in line configuration mode:

Task	Command
Assign a password to a terminal or other device on a line.	**password** *password*
Enable password checking at login.	**login**

The password checker is case-sensitive and can include spaces; for example, the password "Secret" is different from the password "secret," and "two words" is an acceptable password.

You can disable line password verification by disabling password checking. To do so, perform the following task in line configuration mode:

Task	Command
Disable password checking or allow access to a line without password verification.	**no login**

If you configure line password protection and then configure TACACS or Extended TACACS, the TACACS username and password take precedence over line passwords. If you have not yet implemented a security policy, we recommend that you use AAA.

Establish Username Authentication

You can create a username-based authentication system, which is useful in the following situations:

- To provide a TACACS-like username and encrypted password-authentication system for networks that cannot support TACACS
- To provide special-case logins; for example, access list verification, no password verification, autocommand execution at login, and "no escape" situation

To establish username authentication, perform the following tasks in global configuration mode as needed for your system configuration:

Task	Command
Establish username authentication with encrypted passwords. or (Optional) Establish username authentication by access list.	**username** *name* [**nopassword** | **password** *encryption-type* **password**] **username** *name* [**access-class** *number*]
(Optional) Set the privilege level for the user.	**username** *name* **privilege** *level*
(Optional) Specify a command to automatically execute.	**username** *name* [**autocommand** *command*]
(Optional) Set a "no escape" login environment.	**username** *name* [**noescape**] [**nohangup**]

The keyword **noescape** prevents users from using escape characters on the hosts to which they are connected. The **nohangup** feature does not disconnect after using the autocommand.

CAUTION

Passwords will be displayed in cleartext in your configuration unless you enable the **service password-encryption** command. For more information about the **service password-encryption** command, see Chapter 26, "Passwords and Privileges Commands."

Enable CHAP or PAP Authentication

One of the most common transport protocols used in Internet Service Providers' (ISPs') dial solutions is the Point-to-Point Protocol (PPP). Traditionally, remote users dial in to an access server to initiate a PPP session. After PPP has been negotiated, remote users are connected to the ISP network and to the Internet.

Because ISPs want only customers to connect to their access servers, remote users are required to authenticate to the access server before they can start up a PPP session. Normally, a remote user authenticates by typing in a username and password when prompted by the access server. Although this is a workable solution, it is difficult to administer and awkward for the remote user.

A better solution is to use the authentication protocols built into PPP. In this case, the remote user dials in to the access server and starts up a minimal subset of PPP with the access server. This does not give the remote user access to the ISP's network—it merely allows the access server to talk to the remote device.

PPP currently supports two authentication protocols: Password Authentication Protocol (PAP) and Challenge Handshake Authentication Protocol (CHAP). Both are specified in RFC 1334 and are supported on synchronous and asynchronous interfaces. Authentication via PAP or CHAP is equivalent to typing in a username and password when prompted by the server. CHAP is considered to be more secure because the remote user's password is never sent across the connection.

PPP (with or without PAP or CHAP authentication) is also supported in dial-out solutions. An access server utilizes a dial-out feature when it initiates a call to a remote device and attempts to start up a transport protocol such as PPP.

NOTES

To use CHAP or PAP, you must be running PPP encapsulation.

When CHAP is enabled on an interface and a remote device attempts to connect to it, the access server sends a CHAP packet to the remote device. The CHAP packet requests or "challenges" the remote device to respond. The challenge packet consists of an ID, a random number, and the host name of the local router.

When the remote device receives the challenge packet, it concatenates the ID, the remote device's password, and the random number, and then encrypts all of it using the remote device's password. The remote device sends the results back to the access server, along with the name associated with the password used in the encryption process.

When the access server receives the response, it uses the name it received to retrieve a password stored in its user database. The retrieved password should be the same password the remote device used in its encryption process. The access server then encrypts the concatenated information with the newly retrieved password—if the result matches the result sent in the response packet, authentication succeeds.

The benefit of using CHAP authentication is that the remote device's password is never transmitted in cleartext. This prevents other devices from stealing it and gaining illegal access to the ISP's network.

CHAP transactions occur only at the time a link is established. The access server does not request a password during the rest of the call. (The local device can, however, respond to such requests from other devices during a call.)

When PAP is enabled, the remote router attempting to connect to the access server is required to send an authentication request. If the username and password specified in the authentication request are accepted, the Cisco IOS software sends an authentication acknowledgment.

After you have enabled CHAP or PAP, the access server will require authentication from remote devices dialing in to the access server. If the remote device does not support the enabled protocol, the call will be dropped.

To use CHAP or PAP, you must perform the following tasks:

1. Enable PPP encapsulation.
2. Enable CHAP or PAP on the interface.
3. For CHAP, configure host name authentication and the secret or password for each remote system with which authentication is required.

Enable PPP Encapsulation

To enable PPP encapsulation, perform the following task in interface configuration mode:

Task	Command
Enable PPP on an interface.	encapsulation ppp

Enable PAP or CHAP

To enable CHAP or PAP authentication on an interface configured for PPP encapsulation, perform the following task in interface configuration mode:

Task	Command
Define the authentication methods supported and the order in which they are used.	ppp authentication {chap	chap pap	pap chap	pap} [if-needed] [*list-name*	default] [callin] [one-time]

If you configure **ppp authentication chap** on an interface, all incoming calls on that interface that initiate a PPP connection will have to be authenticated using CHAP; likewise, if you configure **ppp authentication pap,** all incoming calls that start a PPP connection will have to be authenticated via PAP. If you configure **ppp authentication chap pap,** the access server will attempt to authenticate all incoming calls that start a PPP session with CHAP. If the remote device does not support CHAP, the access server will try to authenticate the call using PAP. If the remote device doesn't support either CHAP or PAP, authentication will fail and the call will be dropped. If you configure **ppp authentication pap chap,** the access server will attempt to authenticate all incoming calls that start a PPP session with PAP. If the remote device does not support PAP, the access server will try to authenticate the call using CHAP. If the remote device doesn't support either protocols, authentication will fail and the call will be dropped. If you configure the **ppp authentication** command with the **callin** keyword, the access server will only authenticate the remote device if the remote device initiated the call.

Authentication method lists and the **one-time** keyword are only available if you have enabled AAA—they will not be available if you are using TACACS or Extended TACACS. If you specify the name of an authentication method list with the **ppp authentication** command, PPP will attempt to authenticate the connection using the methods defined in the specified method list. If AAA is enabled and no method list is defined by name, PPP will attempt to authenticate the connection using the methods defined as the default. The **ppp authentication** command with the **one-time** keyword enables support for one-time passwords during authentication.

The **if-needed** keyword is only available if you are using TACACS or Extended TACACS. The **ppp authentication** command with the **if-needed** keyword means that PPP will only authenticate the remote device via PAP or CHAP if they have not yet authenticated during the life of the current call. If the remote device authenticated via a standard login procedure and initiated PPP from the EXEC prompt, PPP will not authenticate via CHAP, if **ppp authentication chap if-needed** is configured on the interface.

CAUTION

If you use a *list-name* that has not been configured with the **aaa authentication ppp** command, you disable PPP on the line.

For information about adding a **username** entry for each remote system from which the local router or access server requires authentication, see section "Establish Username Authentication."

Inbound and Outbound Authentication

PPP supports two-way authentication. Normally, when a remote device dials in to an access server, the access server requests that the remote device prove that it is allowed access. This is known as inbound authentication. At the same time, the remote device can also request that the access server prove that it is who it says it is. This is known as outbound authentication. An access server also does outbound authentication when it initiates a call to a remote device.

Enabling Outbound PAP Authentication

To enable outbound PAP authentication, perform the following task in interface configuration mode:

Task	Command
Enable outbound PAP authentication.	**ppp pap sent-username** *username* **password** *password*

The access server uses the username and password specified by the **ppp pap sent-username** command to authenticate itself whenever it initiates a call to a remote device or when it has to respond to a remote device's request for outbound authentication.

Create a Common CHAP Password

For remote CHAP authentication only, you can configure your router to create a common CHAP secret password to use in response to challenges from an unknown peer; for example, if your router calls a rotary of routers (either from another vendor, or running an older version of the Cisco IOS software) to which a new (that is, unknown) router has been added. The **ppp chap password** command allows you to replace several username and password configuration commands with a single copy of this command on any dialer interface or asynchronous group interface.

To enable a router calling a collection of routers to configure a common CHAP secret password, perform the following task in interface configuration mode:

Task	Command
Enable a router calling a collection of routers to configure a common CHAP secret password.	**ppp chap password** *secret*

Refuse CHAP Authentication Requests

To refuse CHAP authentication from peers requesting it (meaning that CHAP authentication is disabled for all calls) perform the following task in interface configuration mode:

Task	Command
Refuse CHAP authentication from peers requesting CHAP authentication.	**ppp chap refuse** [**callin**]

If the **callin** keyword is used, the router will refuse to answer CHAP authentication challenges received from the peer but will still require the peer to answer any CHAP challenges the router sends.

If outbound PAP has been enabled (using the **ppp pap sent-username** command), PAP will be suggested as the authentication method in the refusal packet.

Delay CHAP Authentication Until Peer Authenticates

To specify that the router will not authenticate to a peer requesting CHAP authentication until after the peer has authenticated itself to the router, perform the following task in interface configuration mode:

Task	Command
Configure the router to delay CHAP authentication until after the peer has authenticated itself to the router.	**ppp chap wait** *secret*

This command (which is the default) specifies that the router will not authenticate to a peer requesting CHAP authentication until the peer has authenticated itself to the router. The **no ppp chap wait** command specifies that the router will respond immediately to an authentication challenge.

Configure TACACS and Extended TACACS Password Protection

You can use TACACS or Extended TACACS to control login access to the router. Perform the tasks in the following sections:

- Set TACACS Password Protection at the User Level
- Disable Password Checking at the User Level

Before performing these tasks, you must have enabled communication with a TACACS host on the network. For more information, see Chapter 12, "Configuring TACACS and Extended TACACS."

Set TACACS Password Protection at the User Level

You can enable TACACS password checking at login by performing the following task in line configuration mode:

Task	Command
Set the TACACS-style user ID and password-checking mechanism.	**login tacacs**

Disable Password Checking at the User Level

If a TACACS server does not respond to a login request, the Cisco IOS software denies the request by default. However, you can prevent login failure in one of two ways:

- Allow a user to access privileged EXEC mode if that user enters the password set by the **enable** command.
- Ensure a successful login by allowing the user to access the privileged EXEC mode without further question.

To specify one of these features, perform either of the following tasks in global configuration mode:

Task	Command
Allow a user to access privileged EXEC mode, or set last resort options for logins.	**tacacs-server last-resort password** or **tacacs-server last-resort succeed**

AUTHENTICATION EXAMPLES

This section contains the following authentication configuration examples:

- RADIUS Authentication Examples
- TACACS+ Authentication Examples
- TACACS and Extended TACACS Authentication Examples
- Kerberos Authentication Examples
- Double Authentication Configuration Exampless

RADIUS Authentication Examples

This section provides two sample configurations using RADIUS.

The following example shows how to configure the router to authenticate and authorize using RADIUS:

```
aaa authentication login radius-login RADIUS local
aaa authentication ppp radius-ppp if-needed radius
aaa authorization exec radius if-authenticated
aaa authorization network radius
line 3
login authentication radius-login
interface serial 0
ppp authentication radius-ppp
```

The lines in this sample RADIUS authentication and authorization configuration are defined as follows:

- The **aaa authentication login radius-login RADIUS local** command configures the router to use RADIUS for authentication at the login prompt. If RADIUS returns an error, the user is authenticated using the local database.
- The **aaa authentication ppp radius-ppp if-needed radius** command configures the Cisco IOS software to use PPP authentication using CHAP or PAP if the user has not already logged in. If the EXEC facility has authenticated the user, PPP authentication is not performed.

- The **aaa authorization exec radius if-authenticated** command queries the RADIUS database for information that is used during EXEC authorization, such as autocommands and privilege levels, but only provides authorization if the user has successfully authenticated.

- The **aaa authorization network radius** command queries RADIUS for network authorization, address assignment, and other access lists.

- The **login authentication radius-login** command enables the user-radius method list for line 3.

- The **ppp authentication radius-ppp** command enables the user-radius method list for serial interface 0.

The following example shows how to configure the router to prompt for and verify a username and password, authorize the user's EXEC level, and specify it as the method of authorization for privilege level 2. In this example, if a local username is entered at the username prompt, that username is used for authentication.

If the user is authenticated using the local database, EXEC authorization using RADIUS will fail because no data is saved from the RADIUS authentication. The method list also uses the local database to find an autocommand. If there is no autocommand, the user becomes the EXEC user. If the user then attempts to issue commands that are set at privilege level 2, TACACS+ is used to attempt to authorize the command.

```
aaa authentication local-override
aaa authentication login default radius local
aaa authorization exec radius local
aaa authorization command 2 tacacs+ if-authenticated
```

The lines in this sample RADIUS authentication and authorization configuration are defined as follows:

- The **aaa authentication local-override** command specifies that the username prompt appear before authentication starts, and that the authentication always use the local database if the user has a local account.

- The **aaa authentication login default radius local** command specifies that the username and password are verified by RADIUS or, if RADIUS is not responding, by the router's local user database.

- The **aaa authorization exec radius local** command specifies that RADIUS authentication information be used to set the user's EXEC level if the user authenticates with RADIUS. If no RADIUS information is used, this command specifies that the local user database be used for EXEC authorization.

- The **aaa authorization command 2 tacacs+ if-authenticated** command specifies TACACS+ authorization for commands set at privilege level 2, if the user has already successfully authenticated.

TACACS+ Authentication Examples

The following example configures TACACS+ as the security protocol to be used for PPP authentication:

```
aaa new-model
aaa authentication ppp test tacacs+ local
interface serial 0
ppp authentication chap pap test
tacacs-server host 10.1.2.3
tacacs-server key goaway
```

The lines in this sample TACACS+ authentication configuration are defined as follows:

- The **aaa new-model** command enables the AAA security services.

- The **aaa authentication** command defines a method list, "test," to be used on serial interfaces running PPP. The keyword **tacacs+** means that authentication will be done through TACACS+. If TACACS+ returns an ERROR of some sort during authentication, the keyword **local** indicates that authentication will be attempted using the local database on the network access server.

- The **interface** command selects the line.

- The **ppp authentication** command applies the test method list to this line.

- The **tacacs-server host** command identifies the TACACS+ daemon as having an IP address of 10.1.2.3.

- The **tacacs-server key** command defines the shared encryption key to be "goaway."

The following example configures AAA authentication for PPP:

```
aaa authentication ppp default if-needed tacacs+ local
```

In this example, the keyword **default** means that PPP authentication is applied by default to all interfaces. The **if-needed** keyword means that if the user has already authenticated by going through the ASCII login procedure, then PPP is not necessary and can be skipped. If authentication is needed, the keyword **tacacs+** means that authentication will be done through TACACS+. If TACACS+ returns an ERROR of some sort during authentication, the keyword **local** indicates that authentication will be attempted using the local database on the network access server.

The following example creates the same authentication algorithm for PAP but calls the method list "MIS-access" instead of "default":

```
aaa authentication pap MIS-access if-needed tacacs+ local
interface serial 0
ppp authentication MIS-access
```

In this example, since the list does not apply to any interfaces (unlike the default list, which applies automatically to all interfaces), the administrator must select interfaces to which this authentication scheme should apply by using the **interface** command. The administrator must then apply this method list to those interfaces by using the **ppp authentication** command.

TACACS and Extended TACACS Authentication Examples

The following example shows TACACS enabled for PPP authentication:

```
int async 1
  ppp authentication chap
  ppp use-tacacs
```

The following example shows TACACS enabled for ARAP authentication:

```
line 3
  arap use-tacacs
```

Kerberos Authentication Examples

To specify Kerberos as the authentication method, use the following command:

```
aaa authentication login default krb5
```

Use the following command to specify Kerberos authentication for PPP:

```
aaa authentication ppp default krb5
```

Double Authentication Configuration Examples

The examples in this section illustrate possible configurations to be used with Double Authentication. Your configurations could differ significantly, depending on your network and security requirements.

These examples are included:

- Configuring the Local Host for AAA with Double Authentication Examples
- Configuring the AAA Server for First-Stage (PPP) Authentication/Authorization Example
- Configuring the AAA Server for Second-Stage (Per-User) Authentication/Authorization Examples
- Complete Sample Configuration with TACACS+

NOTES

These configuration examples include specific IP addresses and other specific information. This information is for illustration purposes only: your configuration will use different IP addresses, different usernames and passwords, and different authorization statements.

Configuring the Local Host for AAA with Double Authentication Examples

These two examples configure a local host to use AAA for PPP and login authentication, and for network and EXEC authorization. One example is shown for RADIUS and one example for TACACS+.

In both examples, the first three lines configure AAA, with a specific server as the AAA server. The next two lines configure AAA for PPP and login authentication, and the last two lines configure network and EXEC authorization. The last line is necessary only if the **access-profile** command will be executed as an autocommand.

Example Router Configuration with a RADIUS AAA

```
aaa new-model
radius-server host secureserver
radius-server key myradiuskey
aaa authentication ppp default radius
aaa authentication login default radius
aaa authorization network radius
aaa authorization exec radius
```

Example Router Configuration with a TACACS+ Server

```
aaa new-model
tacacs-server host security
tacacs-server key mytacacskey
aaa authentication ppp default tacacs+
aaa authentication login default tacacs+
aaa authorization network tacacs+
aaa authorization exec tacacs+
```

Configuring the AAA Server for First-Stage (PPP) Authentication/Authorization Example

This example shows a configuration on the AAA server. A partial sample AAA configuration is shown for RADIUS.

TACACS+ servers can be configured similarly. (See section "Complete Sample Configuration with TACACS+," found later in this chapter),

This example defines authentication/authorization for a remote host named "hostx" that will be authenticated by CHAP in the first stage of Double Authentication. Note that the ACL AV pair limits the remote host to Telnet connections to the local host. The local host has the IP address 10.0.0.2.

Example RADIUS AAA Server Configuration

```
hostx   Password = "welcome"
        User-Service-Type = Framed-User,
        Framed-Protocol = PPP,
        cisco-avpair = "lcp:interface-config=ip unnumbered ethernet 0",
        cisco-avpair = "ip:inacl#3=permit tcp any 172.21.114.0 0.0.0.255 eq telnet",
        cisco-avpair = "ip:inacl#4=deny icmp any any",
        cisco-avpair = "ip:route#5=55.0.0.0 255.0.0.0",
        cisco-avpair = "ip:route#6=66.0.0.0 255.0.0.0",
        cisco-avpair = "ipx:inacl#3=deny any"
```

Configuring the AAA Server for Second-Stage (Per-User) Authentication/Authorization Examples

This section contains partial sample AAA configurations on a RADIUS server. These configurations define authentication/authorization for a user (Bob) with the username "bobuser," who will be user-authenticated in the second stage of Double Authentication.

TACACS+ servers can be configured similarly. (See section "Complete Sample Configuration with TACACS+," found later in this chapter.)

Example RADIUS AAA Server Configurations

Three examples show sample RADIUS AAA configurations that could be used with each of the three forms of the **access-profile** command.

The first example shows a partial sample AAA configuration that works with the default form (no keywords) of the **access-profile** command. Note that only ACL AV pairs are defined. This example also sets up the **access-profile** command as an autocommand.

```
bobuser         Password = "welcome"
        User-Service-Type = Shell-User,
        cisco-avpair = "shell:autocmd=access-profile"
        User-Service-Type = Framed-User,
        Framed-Protocol = PPP,
        cisco-avpair = "ip:inacl#3=permit tcp any host 10.0.0.2 eq telnet",
        cisco-avpair = "ip:inacl#4=deny icmp any any"
```

The second example shows a partial sample AAA configuration that works with the **access-profile merge** form of the **access-profile** command. This example also sets up the **access-profile merge** command as an autocommand.

```
bobuser         Password = "welcome"
        User-Service-Type = Shell-User,
        cisco-avpair = "shell:autocmd=access-profile merge"
        User-Service-Type = Framed-User,
        Framed-Protocol = PPP,
        cisco-avpair = "ip:inacl#3=permit tcp any any"
        cisco-avpair = "ip:route=10.0.0.0 255.255.0.0",
        cisco-avpair = "ip:route=10.1.0.0 255.255.0.0",
        cisco-avpair = "ip:route=10.2.0.0 255.255.0.0"
```

The third example shows a partial sample AAA configuration that works with the **access-profile replace** form of the **access-profile** command. This example also sets up the **access-profile replace** command as an autocommand.

```
bobuser         Password = "welcome"
        User-Service-Type = Shell-User,
        cisco-avpair = "shell:autocmd=access-profile replace"
        User-Service-Type = Framed-User,
        Framed-Protocol = PPP,
        cisco-avpair = "ip:inacl#3=permit tcp any any",
```

```
cisco-avpair = "ip:inacl#4=permit icmp any any",
cisco-avpair = "ip:route=10.10.0.0 255.255.0.0",
cisco-avpair = "ip:route=10.11.0.0 255.255.0.0",
cisco-avpair = "ip:route=10.12.0.0 255.255.0.0"
```

Complete Sample Configuration with TACACS+

This example shows TACACS+ authorization profile configurations both for the remote host (used in the first stage of Double Authentication) and for specific users (used in the second stage of Double Authentication). This TACACS+ example contains approximately the same configuration information as shown in the previous RADIUS examples.

This sample configuration shows authentication/authorization profiles on the TACACS+ server for the remote host "hostx" and for three users, with the usernames "bob_default," "bob_merge," and "bob_replace." The configurations for these three usernames illustrate different configurations that correspond to the three different forms of the **access-profile** command. The three user configurations also illustrate setting up the autocommand for each form of the **access-profile** command.

Figure 3–3 shows the topology. The example following the figure shows a TACACS+ configuration file.

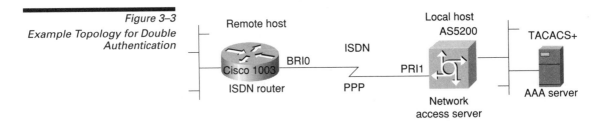

Figure 3–3
Example Topology for Double
Authentication

TACACS+ Configuration File

This sample configuration shows authentication/authorization profiles on the TACACS+ server for the remote host "hostx" and for three users, with the usernames "bob_default," "bob_merge," and "bob_replace."

```
key = "mytacacskey"

default authorization = permit


#--------------------------Remote Host (BRI)------------------------
#
# This allows the remote host to be authenticated by the local host
# during fist-stage authentication, and provides the remote host
# authorization profile.
#
#------------------------------------------------------------------
```

```
user = hostx
{
    login = cleartext "welcome"
    chap = cleartext "welcome"


    service = ppp protocol = lcp {
                interface-config="ip unnumbered ethernet 0"
    }

    service = ppp protocol = ip {
            # It is important to have the hash sign and some string after
            # it. This indicates to the NAS that you have a per-user
            # config.

            inacl#3="permit tcp any 172.21.114.0 0.0.0.255 eq telnet"
            inacl#4="deny icmp any any"

            route#5="55.0.0.0 255.0.0.0"
            route#6="66.0.0.0 255.0.0.0"
    }

    service = ppp protocol = ipx {
            # see previous comment about the hash sign and string, in protocol = ip
            inacl#3="deny any"
    }


}


#------------------ "access-profile" default user "only acls" ---------------
#
# - Without arguments, access-profile removes any access-lists it can find
#   in the old configuration (both per-user and per-interface), and makes sure
#   that the new profile contains ONLY access-list definitions.
#
#-------------------------------------------------------------------------------

user = bob_default
{
        login = cleartext "welcome"
        chap = cleartext "welcome"

        service = exec
        {
                # this is the autocommand that executes when bob_default logs in
                autocmd = "access-profile"
        }
```

```
        service = ppp protocol = ip {
                # Put whatever access-lists, static routes, whatever
                # here.
                # If you leave this blank, the user will have NO IP
                # access-lists (not even the ones installed prior to
                # this)!

                inacl#3="permit tcp any host 10.0.0.2 eq telnet"
                inacl#4="deny icmp any any"
        }


        service = ppp protocol = ipx {
                # Put whatever access-lists, static routes, whatever
                # here.
                # If you leave this blank, the user will have NO IPX
                # access-lists (not even the ones installed prior to
                # this)!
        }


}


#-------------------- "access-profile merge" user  ---------------------
#
# With the 'merge' option, first all old access-lists are removed (as before),
#  but then (almost) all AV pairs are uploaded and installed. This
#  will allow for uploading any custom static routes, sap-filters, and so on,
#  that the user may need in his or her profile. This needs to be used with
#  care, as it leaves open the possibility of conflicting configurations.
#
#-----------------------------------------------------------------------

user = bob_merge
{
        login = cleartext "welcome"
        chap = cleartext "welcome"


        service = exec
        {
                # this is the autocommand that executes when bob_merge logs in
                autocmd = "access-profile merge"
        }

        service = ppp protocol = ip
        {
                # Put whatever access-lists, static routes, whatever
                # here.
                # If you leave this blank, the user will have NO IP
```

```
                # access-lists (not even the ones installed prior to
                # this)!

                inacl#3="permit tcp any any"
                route#2="10.0.0.0 255.255.0.0"
                route#3="10.1.0.0 255.255.0.0"
                route#4="10.2.0.0 255.255.0.0"


        }

        service = ppp protocol = ipx
        {
                # Put whatever access-lists, static routes, whatever
                # here.
                # If you leave this blank, the user will have NO IPX
                # access-lists (not even the ones installed prior to
                # this)!


        }

}


#-------------------- "access-profile replace" user  ----------------------
#
#- With the 'replace' option,
#   ALL old configuration is removed and ALL new configuration is installed.
#
# One caveat: access-profile checks the new configuration for address-pool and
# address AV pairs. As addresses cannot be renegotiated at this point, the
# command will fail (and complain) when it encounters such an AV pair.
# Such AV pairs are considered to be "invalid" for this context.
#--------------------------------------------------------------------------


user = bob_replace
{
        login = cleartext "welcome"
        chap = cleartext "welcome"


        service = exec
        {
                # this is the autocommand that executes when bob_replace logs in
                autocmd = "access-profile replace"
        }

        service = ppp protocol = ip
        {
                # Put whatever access-lists, static routes, whatever
                # here.
```

```
        # If you leave this blank, the user will have NO IP
        # access-lists (not even the ones installed prior to
        # this)!

        inacl#3="permit tcp any any"
        inacl#4="permit icmp any any"


        route#2="10.10.0.0 255.255.0.0"
        route#3="10.11.0.0 255.255.0.0"
        route#4="10.12.0.0 255.255.0.0"
    }

service = ppp protocol = ipx
    {
        # put whatever access-lists, static routes, whatever
        # here.
        # If you leave this blank, the user will have NO IPX
        # access-lists (not even the ones installed prior to
        # this)!
    }

}
#-------------------------------------------------------------------------
```

CHAPTER 4

Authentication Commands

This chapter describes the commands used to configure both AAA and non-AAA authentication methods. Authentication identifies users before they are allowed access to the network and network services. Basically, the Cisco IOS software implementation of authentication is divided into two main categories:

- AAA Authentication Methods
- Non-AAA Authentication Methods

Authentication, for the most part, is implemented through the AAA security services. We recommend that, whenever possible, AAA be used to implement authentication.

For information on how to configure authentication using either AAA or non-AAA methods, see Chapter 3, "Configuring Authentication." For configuration examples using the commands in this chapter, see section "Authentication Configuration Examples" in Chapter 3.

AAA AUTHENTICATION ARAP

To enable an AAA authentication method for AppleTalk Remote Access (ARA) users using RADIUS or TACACS+, use the **aaa authentication arap** global configuration command. Use the **no** form of this command to disable this authentication.

> **aaa authentication arap** {**default** | *list-name*} *method1* [*method2...*]
> **no aaa authentication arap** {**default** | *list-name*} *method1* [*method2...*]

Syntax Description

default   Uses the listed methods that follow this argument as the default list of methods when a user logs in.

list-name   Character string used to name the following list of authentication methods tried when a user logs in.

method   One of the keywords described in Table 4–1.

Default

If the **default** list is not set, only the local user database is checked. This has the same effect as the following command:

```
aaa authentication arap default local
```

Command Mode

Global configuration

Usage Guidelines

This command first appeared in Cisco IOS Release 10.3.

The list names and default that you set with the **aaa authentication arap** command are used with the **arap authentication** command. Note that ARAP guest logins are disabled by default when you enable AAA. To allow guest logins, you must use either the **guest** or **auth-guest** method listed in Table 4–1. You can only use one of these methods; they are mutually exclusive.

Create a list by entering the **aaa authentication arap** *list-name method* command, where *list-name* is any character string used to name this list (such as *MIS-access.*) The *method* argument identifies the list of methods the authentication algorithm tries in the given sequence. See Table 4–1 for descriptions of method keywords.

To create a default list that is used if no list is specified in the **arap authentication** command, use the **default** keyword followed by the methods you want to be used in default situations.

The additional methods of authentication are used only if the previous method returns an error, not if it fails.

Use the **show running-config** command to view lists of authentication methods.

Table 4–1 *AAA Authentication ARAP Methods*

Keyword	Description
guest	Allows guest logins. This method must be the first method listed, but it can be followed by other methods if it does not succeed.

Table 4–1   *AAA Authentication ARAP Methods, Continued*

Keyword	Description
auth-guest	Allows guest logins only if the user has already logged in to EXEC. This method must be the first method listed, but can be followed by other methods if it does not succeed.
line	Uses the line password for authentication.
local	Uses the local username database for authentication.
tacacs+	Uses TACACS+ authentication.
radius	Uses RADIUS authentication.

NOTES

This command cannot be used with TACACS or extended TACACS.

Examples

The following example creates a list called *MIS-access*, which first tries TACACS+ authentication and then none:

```
aaa authentication arap MIS-access tacacs+ none
```

The following example creates the same list, but sets it as the default list that is used for all ARA protocol authentications if no other list is specified:

```
aaa authentication arap default tacacs+ none
```

Related Commands

Search online to find documentation for related commands.

aaa authentication local-override
aaa new-model

AAA AUTHENTICATION ENABLE DEFAULT

To enable AAA authentication to determine if a user can access the privileged command level, use the **aaa authentication enable default** global configuration command. Use the **no** form of this command to disable this authorization method.

> **aaa authentication enable default** *method1* [*method2...*]
> **no aaa authentication enable default** *method1* [*method2...*]

Syntax Description

method   At least one of the keywords described in Table 4–2.

Default

If the **default** list is not set, only the enable password is checked. This has the same effect as the following command:

```
aaa authentication enable default enable
```

On the console, the enable password is used if it exists. If no password is set, the process will succeed anyway.

Command Mode

Global configuration

Usage Guidelines

This command first appeared in Cisco IOS Release 10.3.

Use the **aaa authentication enable default** command to create a series of authentication methods that are used to determine whether a user can access the privileged command level. Method keywords are described in Table 4–2. The additional methods of authentication are used only if the previous method returns an error, not if it fails. To specify that the authentication should succeed even if all methods return an error, specify **none** as the final method in the command line.

If a default authentication routine is not set for a function, the default is **none** and no authentication is performed. Use the **show running-config** command to view currently configured lists of authentication methods.

Table 4–2 *AAA Authentication Enable Default Methods*

Keyword	Description
enable	Uses the enable password for authentication.
line	Uses the line password for authentication.
none	Uses no authentication.
tacacs+	Uses TACACS+ authentication.
radius	Uses RADIUS authentication.

NOTES

This command cannot be used with TACACS or extended TACACS.

Example

The following example creates an authentication list that first tries to contact a TACACS+ server. If no server can be found, AAA tries to use the enable password. If this attempt also returns an error (because no enable password is configured on the server), the user is allowed access with no authentication.

```
aaa authentication enable default tacacs+ enable none
```

Related Commands

Search online to find documentation for related commands.

aaa authentication local-override
aaa authorization
aaa new-model
enable password

AAA AUTHENTICATION LOCAL-OVERRIDE

To configure the Cisco IOS software to check the local user database for authentication before attempting another form of authentication, use the **aaa authentication local-override** global configuration command. Use the **no** form of this command to disable the override.

aaa authentication local-override
no aaa authentication local-override

Syntax Description

This command has no arguments or keywords.

Default

Override is disabled.

Command Mode

Global configuration

Usage Guidelines

This command first appeared in Cisco IOS Release 10.3.

This command is useful when you want to configure an override to the normal authentication process for certain personnel, such as system administrators.

When this override is set, the user is always prompted for the username. The system then checks to see if the entered username corresponds to a local account. If the username does not correspond to one in the local database, login proceeds with the methods configured with other **aaa** commands (such as **aaa authentication login**). Note that when using this command, the Username: prompt is fixed as the first prompt.

Example

The following example enables AAA authentication override:

```
aaa authentication local-override
```

Related Commands

Search online to find documentation for related commands.

aaa authentication arap
aaa authentication enable default
aaa authentication login
aaa authentication ppp
aaa new-model

AAA AUTHENTICATION LOGIN

To set AAA authentication at login, use the **aaa authentication login** global configuration command. Use the **no** form of this command to disable AAA authentication.

> **aaa authentication login** {**default** | *list-name*} *method1* [*method2...*]
> **no aaa authentication login** {**default** | *list-name*} *method1* [*method2...*]

Syntax Description

default   Uses the listed authentication methods that follow this argument as the default list of methods when a user logs in.

list-name   Character string used to name the following list of authentication methods activated when a user logs in.

method   At least one of the keywords described in Table 4–3.

Default

If the **default** list is not set, only the local user database is checked. This has the same effect as the following command:

```
aaa authentication login default local
```

NOTES

On the console, login will succeed without any authentication checks if **default** is not set.

Command Mode

Global configuration

Usage Guidelines

This command first appeared in Cisco IOS Release 10.3.

The default and optional list names that you create with the **aaa authentication login** command are used with the **login authentication** command.

Create a list by entering the **aaa authentication** *list-name method* command for a particular protocol, where *list-name* is any character string used to name this list (such as *MIS-access*). The *method* argument identifies the list of methods that the authentication algorithm tries, in the given sequence. Method keywords are described in Table 4–3.

To create a default list that is used if no list is assigned to a line, use the **login authentication** command with the default argument followed by the methods you want to use in default situations.

The additional methods of authentication are used only if the previous method returns an error, not if it fails. To ensure that the authentication succeeds even if all methods return an error, specify **none** as the final method in the command line.

If authentication is not specifically set for a line, the default is to deny access and no authentication is performed. Use the **show running-config** command to display currently configured lists of authentication methods.

Table 4–3 *AAA Authentication Login Methods*

Keyword	Description
enable	Uses the enable password for authentication.
krb5	Uses Kerberos 5 for authentication.
line	Uses the line password for authentication.
local	Uses the local username database for authentication.
none	Uses no authentication.
radius	Uses RADIUS authentication.
tacacs+	Uses TACACS+ authentication.
krb5-telnet	Uses Kerberos 5 Telnet authentication protocol when using Telnet to connect to the router.

NOTES

This command cannot be used with TACACS or extended TACACS.

Examples

The following example creates an AAA authentication list called *MIS-access*. This authentication first tries to contact a TACACS+ server. If no server is found, TACACS+ returns an error and AAA tries to use the enable password. If this attempt also returns an error (because no enable password is configured on the server), the user is allowed access with no authentication.

```
aaa authentication login MIS-access tacacs+ enable none
```

The following example creates the same list, but it sets it as the default list that is used for all login authentications if no other list is specified:

```
aaa authentication login default tacacs+ enable none
```

The following example sets authentication at login to use the Kerberos 5 Telnet authentication protocol when using Telnet to connect to the router:

```
aaa authentication login default KRB5-TELNET krb5
```

Related Commands

Search online to find documentation for related commands.

aaa authentication local-override
aaa new-model
login authentication

AAA AUTHENTICATION NASI

To specify AAA authentication for Netware Asynchronous Services Interface (NASI) clients connecting through the access server, use the **aaa authentication nasi** global configuration command. Use the **no** form of this command to disable authentication for NASI clients.

aaa authentication nasi {default | *list-name*} *method1* [*method2...*]
no aaa authentication nasi {default | *list-name*} *method1* [*method2...*]

Syntax Description

default	Makes the listed authentication methods that follow this argument the default list of methods used when a user logs in.
list-name	Character string used to name the following list of authentication methods activated when a user logs in.
methods	At least one of the methods described in Table 4–4

Default

If the **default** list is not set, only the local user database is selected. This has the same effect as the following command:

```
aaa authentication nasi default local
```

Command Mode

Global configuration

Usage Guidelines

This command first appeared in Cisco IOS Release 11.1.

The default and optional list names that you create with the **aaa authentication nasi** command are used with the **nasi authentication** command.

Create a list by entering the **aaa authentication nasi** command, where *list-name* is any character string that names this list (such as *MIS-access*). The *method* argument identifies the list of methods the authentication algorithm tries in the given sequence. Method keywords are described in Table 4–4.

To create a default list that is used if no list is assigned to a line with the **nasi authentication** command, use the default argument followed by the methods that you want to use in default situations.

The remaining methods of authentication are used only if the previous method returns an error, not if it fails. To ensure that the authentication succeeds even if all methods return an error, specify **none** as the final method in the command line.

If authentication is not specifically set for a line, the default is to deny access and no authentication is performed. Use the **show running-config** command to display currently configured lists of authentication methods.

Table 4–4 *AAA Authentication NASI Methods*

Keyword	Description
enable	Uses the enable password for authentication.
line	Uses the line password for authentication.
local	Uses the local username database for authentication.
none	Uses no authentication.
tacacs+	Uses TACACS+ authentication.

NOTES

This command cannot be used with TACACS or Extended TACACS.

Examples

The following example creates an AAA authentication list called *list1*. This authentication first tries to contact a TACACS+ server. If no server is found, TACACS+ returns an error, and AAA tries to use the enable password. If this attempt also returns an error (because no enable password is configured on the server), the user is allowed access with no authentication.

```
aaa authentication nasi list1 tacacs+ enable none
```

The following example creates the same list, but sets it as the default list that is used for all login authentications if no other list is specified:

```
aaa authentication nasi default tacacs+ enable none
```

Related Commands

Search online to find documentation for related commands.

ipx nasi-server enable
login authentication
show ipx nasi connections
show ipx spx-protocol

AAA AUTHENTICATION PASSWORD-PROMPT

To change the text displayed when users are prompted for a password, use the **aaa authentication password-prompt** global configuration command. Use the **no** form of this command to return to the default password prompt text.

> **aaa authentication password-prompt** *text-string*
> **no aaa authentication password-prompt** *text-string*

Syntax Description

text-string String of text that will be displayed when the user is prompted to enter a password. If this text-string contains spaces or unusual characters, it must be enclosed in double-quotes (for example, "Enter your password:").

Default

This command is disabled by default.

Command Mode

Global configuration

Usage Guidelines

This command first appeared in Cisco IOS Release 11.0.

Use the **aaa authentication password-prompt** command to change the default text that the Cisco IOS software displays when prompting a user to enter a password. This command changes the password prompt for the enable password as well as for login passwords that are not supplied by remote security servers. The **no** form of this command returns the password prompt to the default value:

```
Password:
```

The **aaa authentication password-prompt** command does not change any dialog that is supplied by a remote TACACS+ or RADIUS server.

Example

The following example changes the text for the password prompt:

```
aaa authentication password-prompt "Enter your password now:"
```

Related Commands

Search online to find documentation for related commands.

aaa authentication username-prompt
aaa new-model
enable password

AAA AUTHENTICATION PPP

To specify one or more AAA authentication methods for use on serial interfaces running Point-to-Point Protocol (PPP), use the **aaa authentication ppp** global configuration command. Use the **no** form of this command to disable authentication.

> **aaa authentication ppp** {default | *list-name*} *method1* [*method2...*]
> **no aaa authentication ppp** {default | *list-name*} *method1* [*method2...*]

Syntax Description

default   Uses the listed authentication methods that follow this argument as the default list of methods when a user logs in.

list-name   Character string used to name the following list of authentication methods tried when a user logs in.

method   At least one of the keywords described in Table 4–5.

Default

If the **default** list is not set, only the local user database is checked. This has the same effect as the following command:

```
aaa authentication ppp default local
```

Command Mode

Global configuration

Usage Guidelines

This command first appeared in Cisco IOS Release 10.3.

The lists that you create with the **aaa authentication ppp** command are used with the **ppp authentication** command. These lists contain up to four authentication methods that are used when a user tries to log in to the serial interface.

Create a list by entering the **aaa authentication ppp** *list-name method* command, where *list-name* is any character string used to name this list (such as *MIS-access*). The *method* argument identifies the list of methods that the authentication algorithm tries in the given sequence. You can enter up to four methods. Method keywords are described in Table 4–5.

The additional methods of authentication are only used if the previous method returns an error, not if it fails. Specify **none** as the final method in the command line to have authentication succeed even if all methods return an error.

If authentication is not specifically set for a function, the default is **none** and no authentication is performed. Use the **show running-config** command to display lists of authentication methods.

Table 4–5   *AAA Authentication PPP Methods*

Keyword	Description
if-needed	Does not authenticate if user has already been authenticated on a TTY line.
krb5	Uses Kerberos 5 for authentication (can only be used for PAP authentication).
local	Uses the local username database for authentication.
none	Uses no authentication.
radius	Uses RADIUS authentication.
tacacs+	Uses TACACS+ authentication.

NOTES

This command cannot be used with TACACS or Extended TACACS.

Example

The following example creates an AAA authentication list called *MIS-access* for serial lines that use PPP. This authentication first tries to contact a TACACS+ server. If this action returns an error, the user is allowed access with no authentication.

```
aaa authentication ppp MIS-access tacacs+ none
```

Related Commands

Search online to find documentation for related commands.

aaa authentication local-override
aaa new-model
ppp authentication

AAA AUTHENTICATION USERNAME-PROMPT

To change the text displayed when users are prompted to enter a username, use the **aaa authentication username-prompt** global configuration command. Use the **no** form of this command to return to the default username prompt text.

> **aaa authentication username-prompt** *text-string*
> **no aaa authentication username-prompt** *text-string*

Syntax Description

text-string   String of text that will be displayed when the user is prompted to enter a username. If this text-string contains spaces or unusual characters, it must be enclosed in double-quotes (for example, "Enter your name:").

Default

There is no user-defined *text-string*, and the username prompt appears as "Username."

Command Mode

Global configuration

Usage Guidelines

This command first appeared in Cisco IOS Release 11.0.

Use the **aaa authentication username-prompt** command to change the default text that the Cisco IOS software displays when prompting a user to enter a username. The **no** form of this command returns the username prompt to the default value:

    Username:

Some protocols (for example, TACACS+) have the ability to override the use of local username prompt information. Using the **aaa authentication username-prompt** command will not change the username prompt text in these instances.

─── **NOTES** ──

The **aaa authentication username-prompt** command does not change any dialog that is supplied by a remote TACACS+ server.

Example

The following example changes the text for the username prompt:

```
aaa authentication username-prompt "Enter your name here:"
```

Related Commands

Search online to find documentation for related commands.

aaa authentication password-prompt
aaa new-model
enable password

AAA NEW-MODEL

To enable the AAA access control model, issue the **aaa new-model** global configuration command. Use the **no** form of this command to disable this functionality.

> **aaa new-model**
> **no aaa new-model**

Syntax Description

This command has no arguments or keywords.

Default

AAA is not enabled.

Command Mode

Global configuration

Usage Guidelines

This command first appeared in Cisco IOS Release 10.0.

This command enables the AAA access control system. After you have enabled AAA, TACACS and Extended TACACS commands are no longer available. If you initialize AAA functionality and later decide to use TACACS or Extended TACACS, issue the **no** version of this command, and then enable the version of TACACS that you want to use.

Example

The following example initializes AAA:

```
aaa new-model
```

Related Commands

Search online to find documentation for related commands.

aaa accounting
aaa authentication arap
aaa authentication enable default
aaa authentication local-override
aaa authentication login
aaa authentication ppp
aaa authorization
tacacs-server key

ACCESS-PROFILE

To apply your per-user authorization attributes to an interface during a PPP session, use the **access-profile** EXEC command. Use the default form of the command (no keywords) to cause existing access control lists (ACLs) to be removed, and ACLs defined in your per-user configuration to be installed. See section "Usage Guidelines" that follows to learn what each form of the command specifically accomplishes.

access-profile [merge | replace] [ignore-sanity-checks]

Syntax Description

merge	(Optional) Like the default form of the command, this option removes existing ACLs while retaining other existing authorization attributes for the interface.
	However, using this option also installs per-user authorization attributes in addition to the existing attributes. (The default form of the command installs only new ACLs.) The per-user authorization attributes come from all AV pairs defined in the AAA per-user configuration (the user's authorization profile).
	The interface's resulting authorization attributes are a combination of the previous and new configurations.
replace	(Optional) This option removes existing ACLs *and* all other existing authorization attributes for the interface.
	A complete new authorization configuration is then installed, using all AV pairs defined in the AAA per-user configuration.
	This option is not normally recommended because it initially deletes *all* existing configuration, including static routes. This could be detrimental if the new user profile does not reinstall appropriate static routes and other critical information.
ignore-sanity-checks	(Optional) Enables you to use any AV pairs, whether or not they are valid.

Command Mode
User EXEC

Usage Guidelines
This command first appeared in Cisco IOS Release 11.2 F.

Remote users can use this command to activate Double Authentication for a PPP session. Double Authentication must be correctly configured for this command to have the desired effect.

You should use this command when you are a remote user and are establishing a PPP link to gain local network access.

After you have been authenticated with CHAP (or PAP), you will have limited authorization. To activate Double Authentication and gain your appropriate user network authorization, you must Telnet to the NAS and execute the **access-profile** command. (This command could also be set up as an autocommand, which would eliminate the need to manually enter the command.)

This command causes all subsequent network authorizations to be made in *your* username, instead of in the remote *host's* username.

Any changes to the interface caused by this command will stay in effect for as long as the interface stays up. These changes will be removed when the interface goes down. This command does not affect the normal operation of the router or the interface.

The default form of the command, **access-profile**, causes existing ACLs to be unconfigured (removed), and new ACLs to be installed. The new ACLs come from your per-user configuration on an AAA server (such as a TACACS+ server). The ACL replacement constitutes a reauthorization of your network privileges.

The default form of the command can fail if your per-user configuration contains statements other than ACL AV pairs. Any protocols with non-ACL statements will be deconfigured, and no traffic for that protocol can pass over the PPP link.

The **access-profile merge** form of the command causes existing ACLs to be unconfigured (removed) and new authorization information (including new ACLs) to be added to the interface. This new authorization information consists of your complete per-user configuration on an AAA server. If any of the new authorization statements conflict with existing statements, the new statements could "override" the old statements or be ignored, depending on the statement and applicable parser rules. The resulting interface configuration is a combination of the original configuration and the newly installed per-user configuration.

CAUTION

The new user authorization profile (per-user configuration) must *not* contain any invalid mandatory AV pairs; otherwise, the command will fail and the PPP protocol (containing the invalid pair) will be dropped. If invalid AV pairs are included as *optional* in the user profile, the command will succeed, but the invalid AV pair will be ignored. Invalid AV pair types are listed later in this section.

The **access-profile replace** form of the command causes the entire existing authorization configuration to be removed from the interface, and the complete per-user authorization configuration to be added. This per-user authorization consists of your complete per-user configuration on an AAA server. The caution of the previous paragraph applies.

CAUTION

Use extreme caution when using the **access-profile replace** form of the command. It might have detrimental and unexpected results, because this option deletes *all* authorization configuration information (including static routes) before reinstalling the new authorization configuration.

Invalid AV pair types:

- addr
- addr-pool
- zonelist
- tunnel-id
- ip-addresses
- x25-addresses
- frame-relay
- source-ip

NOTES

These AV pair types are only "invalid" when used with Double Authentication, in the user-specific authorization profile—they cause the **access-profile** command to fail. However, these AV pair types can be appropriate when used in other contexts.

Example

This example activates Double Authentication for a remote user. This example assumes that the **access-profile** command was *not* configured as an autocommand.

The remote user connects to the corporate headquarters network per Figure 4–1.

Figure 4–1
Network Topology for Activating Double Authentication (Example)

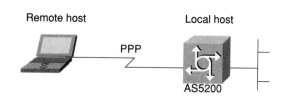

The remote user runs a terminal emulation application to Telnet to the corporate NAS, an AS5200 local host named "hqnas." The remote user, named Bob, has the username "BobUser."

This example replaces ACLs on the local host PPP interface. The ACLs previously applied to the interface during PPP authorization are replaced with ACLs defined in the per-user configuration AV pairs.

The remote user Telnets to the local host and logs in:

```
login: BobUser
Password: <welcome>
hqnas> access-profile
```

Bob is reauthenticated when he logs in to hqnas, because hqnas is configured for login AAA authentication using the corporate RADIUS server. When Bob enters the **access-profile** command, he is reauthorized with his per-user configuration privileges. This causes the access lists and filters in his per-user configuration to be applied to the NAS interface.

After the reauthorization is complete, Bob is automatically logged out of the AS5200 local host.

Related Commands

Search online to find documentation for related commands.

connect
telnet

ARAP AUTHENTICATION

To enable AAA authentication for ARA on a line, use the **arap authentication** line configuration command. Use the **no** form of the command to disable authentication for an ARA line.

>   arap authentication {default | *list-name*} [one-time]
>   no arap authentication {default | *list-name*}

──(CAUTION)──

If you use a *list-name* value that was not configured with the **aaa authentication arap** command, ARA protocol will be disabled on this line.

Syntax Description

default	Default list created with the **aaa authentication arap** command.
list-name	Indicated list created with the **aaa authentication arap** command.
one-time	(Optional) Accepts the username and password in the username field.

Default

ARA protocol authentication uses the default set with **aaa authentication arap** command. If no default is set, the local user database is checked.

Command Mode

Line configuration

Usage Guidelines

This command first appeared in Cisco IOS Release 11.0.

This command is a per-line command that specifies the name of a list of AAA authentication methods to try at login. If no list is specified, the default list is used (whether or not it is specified in the command line). You create defaults and lists with the **aaa authentication arap** command. Entering the **no** version of **arap authentication** has the same effect as entering the command with the **default** argument.

Before issuing this command, create a list of authentication processes by using the **aaa authentication arap** global configuration command.

Example

The following example specifies that the TACACS+ authentication list called *MIS-access* is used on ARA line 7:

```
line 7
  arap authentication MIS-access
```

Related Commands

Search online to find documentation for related commands.

aaa authentication arap

LOGIN AUTHENTICATION

To enable AAA authentication for logins, use the **login authentication** line configuration command. Use the **no** form of this command to either disable TACACS+ authentication for logins or to return to the default.

> **login authentication** {default | *list-name*}
> **no login authentication** {default | *list-name*}

Syntax Description

default	Uses the default list created with the **aaa authentication login** command.
list-name	Uses the indicated list created with the **aaa authentication login** command.

Default

Uses the default set with **aaa authentication login**

Command Mode

Line configuration

Usage Guidelines

This command first appeared in Cisco IOS Release 10.3.

This command is a per-line command used with AAA that specifies the name of a list of AAA authentication methods to try at login. If no list is specified, the default list is used (whether or not it is specified in the command line).

CAUTION
_____

If you use a *list-name* value that was not configured with the **aaa authentication login** command, you will disable login on this line.

Entering the **no** version of **login authentication** has the same effect as entering the command with the **default** argument.

Before issuing this command, create a list of authentication processes by using the global configuration **aaa authentication login** command.

Examples

The following example specifies that the default AAA authentication is to be used on line 4:

```
line 4
 login authentication default
```

The following example specifies that the AAA authentication list called *list1* is to be used on line 7:

```
line 7
 login authentication list1
```

Related Commands

Search online to find documentation for related commands.

aaa authentication login

LOGIN TACACS

To configure your router to use TACACS user authentication, use the **login tacacs** line configuration command. Use the **no** form of this command to disable TACACS user authentication for a line.

    login tacacs
    no login tacacs

Syntax Description

This command has no arguments or keywords.

Default

Disabled

Command Mode

Line configuration

Usage Guidelines

This command first appeared in Cisco IOS Release 10.0.

You can use TACACS security if you have configured a TACACS server and you have a command control language (CCL) script that allows you to use TACACS security.

NOTES

This command cannot be used with AAA. Use the **login authentication** command instead.

Example

In the following example, lines 1 through 16 are configured for TACACS user authentication:

```
line 1 16
  login tacacs
```

NASI AUTHENTICATION

To enable AAA authentication for NetWare Asynchronous Services Interface (NASI) clients connecting to a router, use the **nasi authentication** line configuration command. Use the **no** form of the command to return to the default, as specified by the **aaa authentication nasi** command.

nasi authentication {default | *list-name*}
no login authentication {default | *list-name*}

Syntax Description

default   Uses the default list created with the **aaa authentication nasi** command.

list-name   Uses the list created with the **aaa authentication nasi** command.

Default

Uses the default set with the **aaa authentication nasi** command

Command Mode

Line configuration

Usage Guidelines

This command first appeared in Cisco IOS Release 11.1.

This command is a per-line command used with AAA authentication that specifies the name of a list of authentication methods to try at login. If no list is specified, the default list is used, even if it is specified in the command line. (You create defaults and lists with the **aaa authentication nasi** command.) Entering the **no** form of this command has the same effect as entering the command with the **default** argument.

CAUTION

If you use a *list-name* value that was not configured with the **aaa authentication nasi** command, you will disable login on this line.

Before issuing this command, create a list of authentication processes by using the **aaa authentication nasi** global configuration command.

Examples

The following example specifies that the default AAA authentication be used on line 4:

```
line 4
  nasi authentication default
```

The following example specifies that the AAA authentication list called *list1* be used on line 7:

```
line 7
  nasi authentication list1
```

Related Commands

Search online to find documentation for related commands.

aaa authentication nasi
ipx nasi-server enable
show ipx nasi connections
show ipx spx-protocol

PPP AUTHENTICATION

To enable CHAP or PAP or both and to specify the order in which CHAP and PAP authentication are selected on the interface, use the **ppp authentication** interface configuration command. Use the **no** form of this command to disable this authentication.

> **ppp authentication** {chap | chap pap | pap chap | pap} [if-needed] [*list-name* | default]
>   [callin] [one-time]
> **no ppp authentication**

Syntax Description

chap   Enables CHAP on a serial interface.

pap   Enables PAP on a serial interface.

chap pap   Enables both CHAP and PAP, and performs CHAP authentication before PAP.

pap chap   Enables both CHAP and PAP, and performs PAP authentication before CHAP.

if-needed   (Optional) Used with TACACS and extended TACACS. Does not perform CHAP or PAP authentication if the user has already provided authentication. This option is available only on asynchronous interfaces.

list-name   (Optional) Used with AAA. Specifies the name of a list of methods of authentication to use. If no list name is specified, the system uses the default. The list is created with the **aaa authentication ppp** command.

default   The name of the method list is created with the **aaa authentication ppp** command.

callin   Specifies authentication on incoming (received) calls only.

one-time   (Optional) Accepts the username and password in the username field.

CAUTION

If you use a *list-name* value that was not configured with the **aaa authentication ppp** command, you will disable PPP on this interface.

Default

PPP authentication is not enabled.

Command Mode

Interface configuration

Usage Guidelines

This command first appeared in Cisco IOS Release 10.0.

When you enable CHAP or PAP authentication (or both), the local router requires the remote device to prove its identity before allowing data traffic to flow. PAP authentication requires the remote device to send a name and a password, which is checked against a matching entry in the local username database or in the remote security server database. CHAP authentication sends a Challenge to the remote device. The remote device encrypts the challenge value with a shared secret and returns the encrypted value and its name to the local router in a Response message. The local router attempts to match the remote device's name with an associated secret stored in the local username or remote security server database; it uses the stored secret to encrypt the original challenge and verify that the encrypted values match.

You can enable PAP or CHAP (or both) in either order. If you enable both methods, the first method specified is requested during link negotiation. If the peer suggests using the second method, or refuses the first method, the second method is tried. Some remote devices support only CHAP, and some support only PAP. Base the order in which you specify methods on the remote device's ability to negotiate correctly the appropriate method, and on the level of data line security you require. PAP usernames and passwords are sent as cleartext strings, which can be intercepted and reused. CHAP has eliminated most of the known security holes.

Enabling or disabling PPP authentication does not affect the local router's willingness to authenticate itself to the remote device.

If you are using autoselect on a TTY line, you probably want to use the ppp authentication command to turn on PPP authentication for the corresponding interface.

Example

The following example enables CHAP on asynchronous interface 4 and uses the authentication list MIS-access:

```
interface async 4
 encapsulation ppp
 ppp authentication chap MIS-access
```

Related Commands

Search online to find documentation for related commands.

aaa authentication ppp
aaa new-model
autoselect
encapsulation ppp
ppp-use-tacacs
username

PPP CHAP HOSTNAME

To create a pool of dial-up routers that all appear to be the same host when authenticating with CHAP, use the **ppp chap hostname** interface configuration command. To disable this function, use the **no** form of the command.

> **ppp chap hostname** *hostname*
> **no ppp chap hostname** *hostname*

Syntax Description

hostname   The name sent in the CHAP challenge.

Default

Disabled. The router name is sent in any CHAP challenges.

Command Mode

Interface configuration

Usage Guidelines

This command first appeared in Cisco IOS Release 11.2.

Currently, a router dialing a pool of access routers requires a username entry for each possible router in the pool because each router challenges with its host name. If a router is added to the dial-up rotary pool, all connecting routers must be updated. The **ppp chap hostname** command allows you to specify a common alias for all routers in a rotary group to use so that only one username must be configured on the dialing routers.

This command is normally used with local CHAP authentication (when the router authenticates to the peer), but it can also be used for remote CHAP authentication.

Example

The commands in the following example identify dialer interface 0 as the dialer rotary group leader and specifies ppp as the encapsulation method used by all member interfaces. This example shows that CHAP authentication is used on received calls only and the username *ISPCorp* will be sent in all CHAP challenges and responses:

```
interface dialer 0
 encapsulation ppp
 ppp authentication chap callin
 ppp chap hostname ISPCorp
```

Related Commands

Search online to find documentation for related commands.

aaa authentication ppp
ppp authentication
ppp chap password
ppp chap refuse
ppp chap wait

PPP CHAP PASSWORD

To enable a router calling a collection of routers that do not support this command (such as routers running older Cisco IOS software images) to configure a common CHAP secret password to use in response to challenges from an unknown peer, use the **ppp chap password** interface configuration command. To disable this function, use the **no** form of this command.

> **ppp chap password** *secret*
> **no ppp chap password** *secret*

Syntax Description

secret   The secret used to compute the response value for any CHAP challenge from an unknown peer.

Default

Disabled

Command Mode

Interface configuration

Usage Guidelines

This command first appeared in Cisco IOS Release 11.2.

This command allows you to replace several username and password configuration commands with a single copy of this command on any dialer interface or asynchronous group interface.

This command is used for remote CHAP authentication only (when routers authenticate to the peer) and does not affect local CHAP authentication.

Example

The commands in the following example specify ISDN Basic Rate Interface (BRI) number 0. The method of encapsulation on the interface is PPP. If a CHAP challenge is received from a peer whose name is not found in the global list of usernames, the encrypted secret 7 1267234591 is decrypted and used to create a CHAP response value.

```
interface bri 0
  encapsulation ppp
  ppp chap password 7 1234567891
```

Related Commands

Search online to find documentation for related commands.

aaa authentication ppp
ppp authentication

ppp chap hostname
ppp chap refuse
ppp chap wait

PPP CHAP REFUSE

To refuse CHAP authentication from peers requesting it, use the **ppp chap refuse** interface configuration command. To disable this function, use the **no** form of this command.

ppp chap refuse [callin]
no ppp chap refuse [callin]

Syntax Description

callin   (Optional) This keyword specifies that the router will refuse to answer CHAP authentication challenges received from the peer but will still require the peer to answer any CHAP challenges the router sends.

Default

Disabled

Command Mode

Interface configuration

Usage Guidelines

This command first appeared in Cisco IOS Release 10.3.

This command specifies that CHAP authentication is disabled for all calls, meaning that all attempts by the peer to force the user to authenticate using CHAP will be refused. If the **callin** keyword is used, CHAP authentication is disabled for incoming calls from the peer but will still be performed on outgoing calls to the peer.

If outbound PAP has been enabled (using the **ppp pap sent-username** command), PAP will be suggested as the authentication method in the refusal packet.

Example

The commands in the following example specify ISDN Basic Rate Interface (BRI) number 0. The method of encapsulation on the interface is PPP. This example disables CHAP authentication from occurring if a peer calls in requesting CHAP authentication:

```
interface bri 0
  encapsulation ppp
  ppp chap refuse
```

Related Commands

Search online to find documentation for related commands.

aaa authentication ppp
ppp authentication
ppp chap hostname
ppp chap password
ppp chap wait

PPP CHAP WAIT

To specify that the router will not authenticate to a peer requesting CHAP authentication until after the peer has authenticated itself to the router, use the **ppp chap wait** interface configuration command. To disable this function, use the **no** form of this command.

> **ppp chap wait** *secret*
> **no ppp chap wait** *secret*

Syntax Description

secret   The secret used to compute the response value for any CHAP challenge from an unknown peer.

Default

Enabled

Command Mode

Interface configuration

Usage Guidelines

This command first appeared in Cisco IOS Release 10.3.

This command (which is the default) specifies that the router will not authenticate to a peer requesting CHAP authentication until the peer has authenticated itself to the router. The **no** form of this command specifies that the router will respond immediately to an authentication challenge.

Example

The commands in the following example specify ISDN Basic Rate Interface (BRI) number 0. The method of encapsulation on the interface is PPP. This example disables the default, meaning that users do not have to wait for peers to complete CHAP authentication before authenticating themselves:

```
interface bri 0
  encapsulation ppp
  no ppp chap wait
```

Related Commands

Search online to find documentation for related commands.

aaa authentication ppp
ppp authentication
ppp chap hostname
ppp chap password
ppp chap refuse

PPP PAP SENT-USERNAME

To re-enable remote PAP support for an interface and use the **sent-username** and **password** in the PAP authentication request packet to the peer, use the **ppp pap sent-username** interface configuration command. Use the **no** form of this command to disable remote PAP support.

> **ppp pap sent-username** *username* **password** *password*
> **no ppp pap sent-username**

Syntax Description

username	Username sent in the PAP authentication request.
password	Password sent in the PAP authentication request.
password	Must contain from 1 to 25 uppercase and lowercase alphanumeric characters.

Default

Remote PAP support disabled

Command Mode

Interface configuration

Usage Guidelines

This command first appeared in Cisco IOS Release 11.2.

Use this command to re-enable remote PAP support (for example, to respond to the peer's request to authenticate with PAP) and to specify the parameters to be used when sending the PAP Authentication Request.

This is a per-interface command. You must configure this command for each interface.

Example

The commands in the following example identify dialer interface 0 as the dialer rotary group leader and specify PPP as the method of encapsulation used by the interface. Authentication is by CHAP or PAP on received calls only. *ISPCorp* is the username sent to the peer if the peer requires the router to authenticate with PAP.

```
interface dialer0
 encapsulation ppp
 ppp authentication chap pap callin
 ppp chap hostname ISPCorp
 ppp pap sent username ISPCorp password 7 fjhfeu
 ppp pap sent-username ISPCorp password 7 1123659238
```

Related Commands

Search online to find documentation for related commands.

aaa authentication ppp
ppp authentication
ppp chap hostname
ppp chap password
ppp use-tacacs

PPP USE-TACACS

To enable TACACS for PPP authentication, use the **ppp use-tacacs** interface configuration command. Use the **no** form of the command to disable TACACS for PPP authentication.

> **ppp use-tacacs [single-line]**
> **no ppp use-tacacs**

NOTES

This command is not used in TACACS+. It has been replaced with the **aaa authentication ppp** command.

Syntax Description

single-line   (Optional) Accept the username and password in the username field.
                     This option applies only when using CHAP authentication.

Default

TACACS is not used for PPP authentication.

Command Mode

Interface configuration

Usage Guidelines

This command first appeared in Cisco IOS Release 10.3.

This is a per-interface command. Use this command only when you have set up an extended TACACS server.

When CHAP authentication is being used, the **ppp use-tacacs** command with the **single-line** option specifies that if a username and password are specified in the username, separated by an asterisk (*), a standard TACACS login query is performed using that username and password. If the username does not contain an asterisk, then normal CHAP authentication is performed.

This feature is useful when integrating TACACS with other authentication systems that require a cleartext version of the user's password. Such systems include one-time password systems, token card systems, and Kerberos.

CAUTION

Normal CHAP authentications prevent the cleartext password from being transmitted over the link. When you use the single-line option, passwords cross the link as cleartext.

If the username and password are contained in the CHAP password, the CHAP secret is not used by the Cisco IOS software. Because most PPP clients require that a secret be specified, you can use any arbitrary string, and the Cisco IOS software ignores it.

Examples

In the following example, asynchronous interface 1 is configured to use TACACS for CHAP authentication:

```
interface async 1
  ppp authentication chap
  ppp use-tacacs
```

In the following example, asynchronous interface 1 is configured to use TACACS for PAP authentication:

```
interface async 1
  ppp authentication pap
  ppp use-tacacs
```

Related Commands

Search online to find documentation for related commands.

ppp authentication
tacacs-server extended
tacacs-server host

CHAPTER 5

Configuring Authorization

AAA authorization enables you to limit the services available to a user. When AAA authorization is enabled, the network access server uses information retrieved from the user's profile, which is located either in the local user database or on the security server, to configure the user's session. Once this is done, the user will be granted access to a requested service only if the information in the user profile allows it.

This chapter describes the following topics and tasks:

- AAA Authorization Types
- AAA Authorization Methods
- AAA Authorization Prerequisites
- AAA Authorization Configuration Task List
- Configuring Authorization
- Disabling Authorization for Global Configuration Commands
- Authorization Attribute-Value Pairs
- Authorization Configuration Examples

For a complete description of the authorization commands used in this chapter, see Chapter 6, "Authorization Commands."

AAA AUTHORIZATION TYPES

Cisco IOS software supports three different types of authorization:

- **EXEC**—Applies to the attributes associated with a user EXEC terminal session.
- **Command**—Applies to the EXEC mode commands a user issues. Command authorization attempts authorization for all EXEC mode commands, including global configuration commands, associated with a specific privilege level.
- **Network**—Applies to network connection. This can include a PPP, SLIP, or ARAP connection.

AAA AUTHORIZATION METHODS

AAA supports five different methods of authorization:

- **TACACS+**—The network access server exchanges authorization information with the TACACS+ security daemon. TACACS+ authorization defines specific rights for users by associating attribute-value (AV) pairs, which are stored in a database on the TACACS+ security server, with the appropriate user.
- **If-Authenticated**—The user is allowed to access the requested function provided the user has been authenticated successfully.
- **Local**—The router or access server consults its local database, as defined by the **username** command, to authorize specific rights for users. Only a limited set of functions can be controlled via the local database.
- **RADIUS**—The network access server requests authorization information from the RADIUS security server. RADIUS authorization defines specific rights for users by associating attributes, which are stored in a database on the RADIUS server, with the appropriate user.
- **Kerberos Instance Map**—The network access server uses the instance defined by the **kerberos instance map** command for authorization.

NOTES

Authorization, unlike authentication, cannot be applied selectively per interface.

AAA AUTHORIZATION PREREQUISITES

Before configuring authorization, you must first perform the following tasks:

- Enable AAA on your network access server. For more information about enabling AAA on your Cisco router or access server, see Chapter 2, "AAA Overview."
- Configure AAA authentication. Authorization generally takes place after authentication and relies on authentication to work properly. For more information about AAA authentication, refer to Chaper 3, "Configuring Authentication."

- Define the characteristics of your RADIUS or TACACS+ security server, if you are using RADIUS or TACACS+ authorization. For more information about configuring your Cisco network access server to communicate with your RADIUS security server, see Chapter 9, "Configuring RADIUS." For more information about configuring your Cisco network access server to communicate with your TACACS+ security server, see Chapter 11, "Configuring TACACS+."

- Define the rights associated with specific users by using the **username** command, if you are using local authorization.

- Create the administrative instances of users in the Kerberos key distribution center by using the kerberos instance map command, if you are using Kerberos. For more information about Kerberos, see Chapter 14, "Configuring Kerberos."

AAA AUTHORIZATION CONFIGURATION TASK LIST

This chapter describes the following tasks:

- Configuring Authorization
- Disabling Authorization for Global Configuration Commands

For authorization configuration examples using the commands in this chapter, see the section "Authorization Configuration Examples," located at the end of the this chapter.

CONFIGURING AUTHORIZATION

The **aaa authorization** command allows you to set parameters that restrict a user's network access. To enable AAA authorization, perform the following task in global configuration mode:

Task	Command
Set parameters that restrict a user's network access.	**aaa authorization** {**network** I **exec** I **command** *level*} {**tacacs+** I **if-authenticated** I **none** I **local** I **radius** I **krb5-instance**}

To enable authorization for all network-related service requests (including SLIP, PPP, PPP NCPs, and ARA protocols), use the **network** keyword. To enable authorization to determine if a user is allowed to run an EXEC shell, use the **exec** keyword.

To enable authorization for specific, individual EXEC commands associated with a specific privilege level, use the **command** keyword. This allows you to authorize all commands associated with a specified command level from 0 to 15.

TACACS+ Authorization

To have the network access server request authorization information via a TACACS+ security server, use the **aaa authorization** command with the **tacacs+** *method* keyword. For more specific information about configuring authorization using a TACACS+ security server, see Chapter 11. For an example of how to enable a TACACS+ server to authorize the use of network services, including PPP and ARA, see section "TACACS+ Authorization Examples," located at the end of this chapter.

If-Authenticated Authorization

To allow users to have access to the functions they request as long as they have been authenticated, use the **aaa authorization** command with the **if-authenticated** *method* keyword. If you select this method, all requested functions are automatically granted to authenticated users.

None Authorization

To perform no authorization for the actions associated with a particular type of authentication, use the **aaa authorization** command with the **none** *method* keyword. If you select this method, authorization is disabled for all actions.

Local Authorization

To select local authorization, which means that the router or access server consult its local user database to determine the functions a user is permitted, use the **aaa authorization** command with the **local** *method* keyword. The functions associated with local authorization are defined by using the **username** global configuration command. For a list of permitted functions, see Chapter 3, "Configuring Authentication."

RADIUS Authorization

To have the network access server request authorization via a RADIUS security server, use the **aaa authorization** command with the **radius** *method* keyword. For more specific information about configuring authorization using a RADIUS security server, see Chapter 9. For an example of how to enable a RADIUS server to authorize services, see section "RADIUS Authorization Example," located at the end of this chapter.

Kerberos Authorization

To run authorization to determine if a user is allowed to run an EXEC shell at a specific privilege level based on a mapped Kerberos instance, use the **krb5-instance** *method* keyword. For more information, see section "Enable Kerberos Instance Mapping" in Chapter 14. For an example of how to enable Kerberos instance mapping, see section "Kerberos Instance Mapping Examples," located at the end of this chapter.

DISABLING AUTHORIZATION FOR GLOBAL CONFIGURATION COMMANDS

The **aaa authorization** command with the keyword **command** attempts authorization for all EXEC mode commands, including global configuration commands, associated with a specific privilege level. Because there are configuration commands that are identical to some EXEC-level commands, there can be some confusion in the authorization process. Using **no aaa authorization config-commands** stops the network access server not from attempting configuration command authorization. To disable AAA authorization for all global configuration commands, perform the following task in global configuration mode:

Task	Command
Disable authorization for all global configuration commands.	**no aaa authorization config-command**

AUTHORIZATION ATTRIBUTE-VALUE PAIRS

RADIUS and TACACS+ authorization both define specific rights for users by processing attributes, which are stored in a database on the security server. For both RADIUS and TACACS+, attributes are defined on the security server, associated with the user, and sent to the network access server where they are applied to the user's connection.

For a list of supported RADIUS attributes, see Appendix A, "RADIUS Attributes." For a list of supported TACACS+ AV pairs, see Appendix B, "TACACS+ Attribute-Value Pairs."

AUTHORIZATION CONFIGURATION EXAMPLES

This section contains the following configuration examples:

- TACACS+ Authorization Exampless
- RADIUS Authorization Example
- Kerberos Instance Mapping Examples

TACACS+ Authorization Examples

The following example uses a TACACS+ server to authorize the use of network services, including PPP and ARA. If the TACACS+ server is not available or an error occurs during the authorization process, the fallback method (none) is to grant all authorization requests:

```
aaa authorization network tacacs+ none
```

The following example allows network authorization using TACACS+:

```
aaa authorization network tacacs+
```

The following example provides the same authorization, but also creates address pools called *mci* and *att*:

```
aaa authorization network tacacs+
ip address-pool local
ip local-pool mci 172.16.0.1 172.16.0.255
ip local-pool att 172.17.0.1 172.17.0.255
```

These address pools can then be selected by the TACACS daemon. A sample configuration of the daemon follows:

```
user = mci_customer1 {
    login = cleartext "some password"
    service = ppp protocol = ip {
        addr-pool=mci
    }
}

user = att_customer1 {
    login = cleartext "some other password"
    service = ppp protocol = ip {
        addr-pool=att
    }
}
```

RADIUS Authorization Example

The following example shows how to configure the router to authorize using RADIUS:

```
aaa authorization exec radius if-authenticated
aaa authorization network radius
```

The lines in this sample RADIUS authorization configuration are defined as follows:

- The **aaa authorization exec radius if-authenticated** command configures the network access server to contact the RADIUS server to determine if users are permitted to start an EXEC shell when they log in. If an error occurs when the network access server contacts the RADIUS server, the fallback method is to permit the CLI to start, provided the user has been properly authenticated.

  The RADIUS information returned may be used to specify an autocommand or a connection access list be applied to this connection.

- The **aaa authorization network radius** command configures network authorization via RADIUS. This can be used to govern address assignment, the application of access lists, and various other per-user quantities.

NOTES
Because no fallback method is specified in this example, authorization will fail if, for any reason, there is no response from the RADIUS server.

Kerberos Instance Mapping Examples

The following global configuration example maps the Kerberos instance, *admin*, to enable mode:

```
kerberos instance map admin 15
```

The following example configures the router to check users' Kerberos instances and set appropriate privilege levels:

```
aaa authorization exec krb5-instance
```

For more information about configuring Kerberos, see Chapter 14, "Configuring Kerberos."

## CHAPTER 6

Authorization Commands

This chapter describes the commands used to configure authentication, authorization, and accounting (AAA) authorization. AAA authorization enables you to limit the services available to a user. When AAA authorization is enabled, the network access server uses information retrieved from the user's profile, which is located either in the local user database or on the security server, to configure the user's session. Once this is done, the user will be granted access to a requested service only if the information in the user profile allows it.

For information on how to configure authorization using AAA, see Chapter 5, "Configuring Authorization." For configuration examples using the commands in this chapter, see section "Authorization Configuration Examples," located at the end of Chapter 5.

AAA AUTHORIZATION

Use the **aaa authorization** global configuration command to set parameters that restrict a user's network access. Use the **no** form of this command to disable authorization for a function.

> **aaa authorization** {network | exec | command *level*} *method*
> **no aaa authorization** {network | exec | command *level*}

Syntax Description

network	Runs authorization for all network-related service requests, including SLIP, PPP, PPP NCPs, and ARA protocol.
exec	Runs authorization to determine if the user is allowed to run an EXEC shell. This facility might return user profile information such as **autocommand** information.

command	Runs authorization for all commands at the specified privilege level.
level	Specific command level that should be authorized. Valid entries are 0 through 15.
method	One of the keywords in Table 6–1.

Default

Authorization is disabled for all actions (equivalent to the keyword **none**).

Command Mode

Global configuration

Usage Guidelines

This command first appeared in Cisco IOS Release 10.0.

NOTES

There are five commands associated with privilege level 0: **disable**, **enable**, **exit**, **help**, and **logout**. If you configure AAA authorization for a privilege level greater than 0, these five commands will not be included in the privilege level command set.

Use the **aaa authorization** command to create at least one, and up to four, authorization methods that can be used when a user accesses the specified function. Method keywords are described in Table 6–1.

NOTES

This command, along with **aaa accounting**, replaces the **tacacs-server** suite of commands in previous versions of TACACS.

The additional methods of authorization are used only if the previous method returns an error, not if it fails. Specify **none** as the final method in the command line to have authorization succeed even if all methods return an error.

If authorization is not specifically set for a function, the default is **none** and no authorization is performed.

Table 6-1 *AAA Authorization Methods*

Keyword	Description
tacacs+	Requests authorization information from the TACACS+ server.
if-authenticated	Allows the user to access the requested function if the user is authenticated.
none	No authorization is performed.
local	Uses the local database for authorization.
radius	Uses RADIUS to get authorization information.
krb5-instance	Uses the instance defined by the **Kerberos instance map** command.

The authorization command causes a request packet containing a series of attribute-value (AV) pairs to be sent to the RADIUS or TACACS daemon as part of the authorization process. The daemon can do one of the following:

- Accept the request as is
- Make changes to the request
- Refuse the request and refuse authorization

For a list of supported RADIUS attributes, see Appendix A, "RADIUS Attributes." For a list of supported TACACS+ AV pairs, see Appendix B, "TACACS+ Attribute-Value Pairs."

Examples

The following example specifies that TACACS+ authorization is used for all network-related requests. If this authorization method returns an error (if the TACACS+ server cannot be contacted), no authorization is performed and the request succeeds.

```
aaa authorization network tacacs+ none
```

The following example specifies that TACACS+ authorization is run for level 15 commands. If this authorization method returns an error (if the TACACS+ server cannot be contacted), no authorization is performed and the request succeeds.

```
aaa authorization command 15 tacacs+ none
```

Related Commands

Search online to find documentation for related commands.

aaa accounting
aaa new-model

AAA AUTHORIZATION CONFIG-COMMANDS

To disable AAA configuration command authorization in the EXEC mode, use the **no** form of the **aaa authorization config-commands** global configuration command. Use the standard form of this command to re-establish the default created when the **aaa authorization** *command level method* command was issued.

> **aaa authorization config-commands**
> **no aaa authorization config-commands**

Syntax Description

This command has no arguments or keywords.

Default

After the **aaa authorization** *command level method* has been issued, this command is enabled by default—meaning that all configuration commands in the EXEC mode will be authorized.

Command Mode

Global configuration

Usage Guidelines

This command first appeared in Cisco IOS Release 11.2.

If **aaa authorization** *command level method* is enabled, all commands, including configuration commands, are authorized by AAA using the method specified. Because there are configuration commands that are identical to some EXEC-level commands, there can be some confusion in the authorization process. Using **no aaa authorization config-commands** stops the network access server not from attempting configuration command authorization.

After the **no** form of this command has been entered, AAA authorization of configuration commands is completely disabled. Care should be taken before entering the **no** form of this command, because it potentially reduces the amount of administrative control on configuration commands.

Use the **aaa authorization config-commands command** if, after using the no form of this command, you need to re-establish the default set by the **aaa authorization** *command level method* command.

Example

The following example specifies that TACACS+ authorization is run for level 15 commands and that AAA authorization of configuration commands is disabled:

```
aaa new-model
aaa authorization command 15 tacacs+ none
no aaa authorization config-commands
```

Related Commands

Search online to find documentation for related commands.

aaa authorization

AAA NEW-MODEL

To enable the AAA access control model, use the **aaa new-model** global configuration command. Use the **no** form of this command to disable this functionality.

>aaa new-model
>no aaa new-model

Syntax Description

This command has no arguments or keywords.

Default

AAA is not enabled.

Command Mode

Global configuration

Usage Guidelines

This command first appeared in Cisco IOS Release 10.0.

This command enables the AAA access control system. After you have enabled AAA, TACACS and Extended TACACS commands are no longer available. If you initialize AAA functionality and later decide to use TACACS or extended TACACS, issue the **no** version of this command, then enable the version of TACACS that you want to use.

Example

The following example initializes AAA:

```
aaa new-model
```

Related Commands

Search online to find documentation for related commands.

aaa accounting
aaa authentication arap
aaa authentication enable default
aaa authentication local-override
aaa authentication login
aaa authentication ppp
aaa authorization
tacacs-server key

## CHAPTER 7

Configuring Accounting

The AAA accounting feature enables you to track the services users are accessing as well as the amount of network resources they are consuming. When **aaa accounting** is enabled, the network access server reports user activity to the TACACS+ or RADIUS security server (depending on which security method you have implemented) in the form of accounting records. Each accounting record contains accounting attribute-value (AV) pairs and is stored on the security server. This data can then be analyzed for network management, client billing, or auditing.

This chapter describes the following topics and tasks:

- AAA Accounting Types
- AAA Accounting Prerequisites
- AAA Accounting Configuration Task List
- Enabling Accounting
- Monitoring Accounting
- Accounting Attribute-Value Pairs
- Accounting Configuration Example

For a complete description of the accounting commands used in this chapter, see Chapter 8, "Accounting Commands."

AAA ACCOUNTING TYPES

Cisco IOS software supports five different kinds of accounting:

- Network Accounting
- Connection Accounting
- EXEC Accounting

- System Accounting
- Command Accounting

Network Accounting

Network accounting provides information for all PPP, SLIP, or ARAP sessions, including packet and byte counts.

The following example shows the information contained in a RADIUS network accounting record for a PPP user who comes in through an EXEC session:

```
Wed Jun 25 04:44:45 1997
        NAS-IP-Address = "172.16.25.15"
        NAS-Port = 5
        User-Name = "fgeorge"
        Client-Port-DNIS = "4327528"
        Caller-ID = "562"
        Acct-Status-Type = Start
        Acct-Authentic = RADIUS
        Service-Type = Exec-User
        Acct-Session-Id = "0000000D"
        Acct-Delay-Time = 0
        User-Id = "fgeorge"
        NAS-Identifier = "172.16.25.15"
Wed Jun 25 04:45:00 1997
        NAS-IP-Address = "172.16.25.15"
        NAS-Port = 5
        User-Name = "fgeorge"
        Client-Port-DNIS = "4327528"
        Caller-ID = "562"
        Acct-Status-Type = Start
        Acct-Authentic = RADIUS
        Service-Type = Framed
        Acct-Session-Id = "0000000E"
        Framed-IP-Address = "10.1.1.2"
        Framed-Protocol = PPP
        Acct-Delay-Time = 0
        User-Id = "fgeorge"
        NAS-Identifier = "172.16.25.15"
Wed Jun 25 04:47:46 1997
        NAS-IP-Address = "172.16.25.15"
        NAS-Port = 5
        User-Name = "fgeorge"
        Client-Port-DNIS = "4327528"
        Caller-ID = "562"
        Acct-Status-Type = Stop
        Acct-Authentic = RADIUS
        Service-Type = Framed
        Acct-Session-Id = "0000000E"
        Framed-IP-Address = "10.1.1.2"
        Framed-Protocol = PPP
```

```
                    Acct-Input-Octets = 3075
                    Acct-Output-Octets = 167
                    Acct-Input-Packets = 39
                    Acct-Output-Packets = 9
                    Acct-Session-Time = 171
                    Acct-Delay-Time = 0
                    User-Id = "fgeorge"
                    NAS-Identifier = "172.16.25.15"
        Wed Jun 25 04:48:45 1997
                    NAS-IP-Address = "172.16.25.15"
                    NAS-Port = 5
                    User-Name = "fgeorge"
                    Client-Port-DNIS = "4327528"
                    Caller-ID = "408"
                    Acct-Status-Type = Stop
                    Acct-Authentic = RADIUS
                    Service-Type = Exec-User
                    Acct-Session-Id = "0000000D"
                    Acct-Delay-Time = 0
                    User-Id = "fgeorge"
                    NAS-Identifier = "172.16.25.15"
```

The following example shows the information contained in a TACACS+ network accounting record for a PPP user who first started an EXEC session:

```
Wed Jun 25 04:00:35 1997          172.16.25.15    fgeorge   tty4    562/4327528
starttask_id=28       service=shell
Wed Jun 25 04:00:46 1997          172.16.25.15   fgeorge  tty4 562/4327528    starttask_id=30
addr=10.1.1.1    service=ppp
Wed Jun 25 04:00:49 1997          172.16.25.15    fgeorge   tty4    408/4327528      update
task_id=30        addr=10.1.1.1    service=ppp      protocol=ip      addr=10.1.1.1
Wed Jun 25 04:01:31 1997          172.16.25.15    fgeorge   tty4    562/4327528
stoptask_id=30        addr=10.1.1.1    service=ppp      protocol=ip      addr=10.1.1.1
bytes_in=2844         bytes_out=1682  paks_in=36       paks_out=24      elapsed_time=51
Wed Jun 25 04:01:32 1997          172.16.25.15    fgeorge   tty4    562/4327528
stoptask_id=28        service=shell   elapsed_time=57
```

NOTES

The precise format of accounting packets records may vary depending on your particular security server daemon.

The following example shows the information contained in a RADIUS network accounting record for a PPP user who comes in through autoselect:

```
Wed Jun 25 04:30:52 1997
            NAS-IP-Address = "172.16.25.15"
            NAS-Port = 3
            User-Name = "fgeorge"
            Client-Port-DNIS = "4327528"
            Caller-ID = "562"
```

```
            Acct-Status-Type = Start
            Acct-Authentic = RADIUS
            Service-Type = Framed
            Acct-Session-Id = "0000000B"
            Framed-Protocol = PPP
            Acct-Delay-Time = 0
            User-Id = "fgeorge"
            NAS-Identifier = "172.16.25.15"
Wed Jun 25 04:36:49 1997
            NAS-IP-Address = "172.16.25.15"
            NAS-Port = 3
            User-Name = "fgeorge"
            Client-Port-DNIS = "4327528"
            Caller-ID = "562"
            Acct-Status-Type = Stop
            Acct-Authentic = RADIUS
            Service-Type = Framed
            Acct-Session-Id = "0000000B"
            Framed-Protocol = PPP
            Framed-IP-Address = "10.1.1.1"
            Acct-Input-Octets = 8630
            Acct-Output-Octets = 5722
            Acct-Input-Packets = 94
            Acct-Output-Packets = 64
            Acct-Session-Time = 357
            Acct-Delay-Time = 0
            User-Id = "fgeorge"
            NAS-Identifier = "172.16.25.15"
```

The following example shows the information contained in a TACACS+ network accounting record for a PPP user who comes in through autoselect:

```
Wed Jun 25 04:02:19 1997          172.16.25.15      fgeorge    Async5   562/4327528
starttask_id=35        service=ppp
Wed Jun 25 04:02:25 1997          172.16.25.15    fgeorge   Async5  562/4327528      update
task_id=35        service=ppp        protocol=ip      addr=10.1.1.2
Wed Jun 25 04:05:03 1997          172.16.25.15    fgeorge   Async5  562/4327528
stoptask_id=35          service=ppp        protocol=ip      addr=10.1.1.2   bytes_in=3366
bytes_out=2149          paks_in=42        paks_out=28      elapsed_time=164
```

Connection Accounting

Connection accounting provides information about all outbound connections made from the network access server, such as Telnet, local-area transport (LAT), TN3270, packet assembly-disassembly (PAD), and rlogin.

The following example shows the information contained in a RADIUS connection accounting record for an outbound Telnet connection:

```
Wed Jun 25 04:28:00 1997
          NAS-IP-Address = "172.16.25.15"
          NAS-Port = 2
```

```
        User-Name = "fgeorge"
        Client-Port-DNIS = "4327528"
        Caller-ID = "5622329477"
        Acct-Status-Type = Start
        Acct-Authentic = RADIUS
        Service-Type = Login
        Acct-Session-Id = "00000008"
        Login-Service = Telnet
        Login-IP-Host = "171.68.202.158"
        Acct-Delay-Time = 0
        User-Id = "fgeorge"
        NAS-Identifier = "172.16.25.15"
Wed Jun 25 04:28:39 1997
        NAS-IP-Address = "172.16.25.15"
        NAS-Port = 2
        User-Name = "fgeorge"
        Client-Port-DNIS = "4327528"
        Caller-ID = "5622329477"
        Acct-Status-Type = Stop
        Acct-Authentic = RADIUS
        Service-Type = Login
        Acct-Session-Id = "00000008"
        Login-Service = Telnet
        Login-IP-Host = "171.68.202.158"
        Acct-Input-Octets = 10774
        Acct-Output-Octets = 112
        Acct-Input-Packets = 91
        Acct-Output-Packets = 99
        Acct-Session-Time = 39
        Acct-Delay-Time = 0
        User-Id = "fgeorge"
        NAS-Identifier = "172.16.25.15"
```

The following example shows the information contained in a TACACS+ connection accounting record for an outbound Telnet connection:

```
Wed Jun 25 03:47:43 1997        172.16.25.15   fgeorge   tty3   5622329430/4327528  start
task_id=10       service=connection       protocol=telnet addr=171.68.202.158 cmd=telnet
fgeorge-sun
Wed Jun 25 03:48:38 1997        172.16.25.15   fgeorge   tty3   5622329430/4327528  stop
task_id=10       service=connection       protocol=telnet addr=171.68.202.158 cmd=telnet
fgeorge-sun      bytes_in=4467   bytes_out=96      paks_in=61         paks_out=72 e
lapsed_time=55
```

The following example shows the information contained in a RADIUS connection accounting record for an outbound rlogin connection:

```
Wed Jun 25 04:29:48 1997
        NAS-IP-Address = "172.16.25.15"
        NAS-Port = 2
        User-Name = "fgeorge"
        Client-Port-DNIS = "4327528"
```

```
          Caller-ID = "5622329477"
          Acct-Status-Type = Start
          Acct-Authentic = RADIUS
          Service-Type = Login
          Acct-Session-Id = "0000000A"
          Login-Service = Rlogin
          Login-IP-Host = "171.68.202.158"
          Acct-Delay-Time = 0
          User-Id = "fgeorge"
          NAS-Identifier = "172.16.25.15"
Wed Jun 25 04:30:09 1997
          NAS-IP-Address = "172.16.25.15"
          NAS-Port = 2
          User-Name = "fgeorge"
          Client-Port-DNIS = "4327528"
          Caller-ID = "5622329477"
          Acct-Status-Type = Stop
          Acct-Authentic = RADIUS
          Service-Type = Login
          Acct-Session-Id = "0000000A"
          Login-Service = Rlogin
          Login-IP-Host = "171.68.202.158"
          Acct-Input-Octets = 18686
          Acct-Output-Octets = 86
          Acct-Input-Packets = 90
          Acct-Output-Packets = 68
          Acct-Session-Time = 22
          Acct-Delay-Time = 0
          User-Id = "fgeorge"
          NAS-Identifier = "172.16.25.15"
```

The following example shows the information contained in a TACACS+ connection accounting record for an outbound rlogin connection:

```
Wed Jun 25 03:48:46 1997      172.16.25.15    fgeorge   tty3    5622329430/4327528  start
task_id=12       service=connection        protocol=rlogin addr=171.68.202.158 cmd=rlogin
fgeorge-sun /user fgeorge
Wed Jun 25 03:51:37 1997      172.16.25.15    fgeorge   tty3    5622329430/4327528  stop
task_id=12       service=connection        protocol=rlogin addr=171.68.202.158 cmd=rlogin
fgeorge-sun /user fgeorge bytes_in=659926 bytes_out=138   paks_in=2378       paks_
out=1251         elapsed_time=171
```

The following example shows the information contained in a TACACS+ connection accounting record for an outbound LAT connection:

```
Wed Jun 25 03:53:06 1997      172.16.25.15    fgeorge   tty3    5622329430/4327528  start
task_id=18       service=connection      protocol=lat    addr=VAX        cmd=lat VAX
Wed Jun 25 03:54:15 1997      172.16.25.15    fgeorge   tty3    5622329430/4327528  stop
task_id=18       service=connection      protocol=lat    addr=VAX        cmd=lat VAX
bytes_in=0       bytes_out=0      paks_in=0       paks_out=0       elapsed_time=6
```

EXEC Accounting

EXEC accounting provides information about user EXEC terminal sessions (user shells) on the network access server, including username, date, start and stop times, the access server IP address, and (for dial-in users) the telephone number the call originated from.

The following example shows the information contained in a RADIUS EXEC accounting record for a dial-in user:

```
Wed Jun 25 04:26:23 1997
        NAS-IP-Address = "172.16.25.15"
        NAS-Port = 1
        User-Name = "fgeorge"
        Client-Port-DNIS = "4327528"
        Caller-ID = "5622329483"
        Acct-Status-Type = Start
        Acct-Authentic = RADIUS
        Service-Type = Exec-User
        Acct-Session-Id = "00000006"
        Acct-Delay-Time = 0
        User-Id = "fgeorge"
        NAS-Identifier = "172.16.25.15"
Wed Jun 25 04:27:25 1997
        NAS-IP-Address = "172.16.25.15"
        NAS-Port = 1
        User-Name = "fgeorge"
        Client-Port-DNIS = "4327528"
        Caller-ID = "5622329483"
        Acct-Status-Type = Stop
        Acct-Authentic = RADIUS
        Service-Type = Exec-User
        Acct-Session-Id = "00000006"
        Acct-Session-Time = 62
        Acct-Delay-Time = 0
        User-Id = "fgeorge"
        NAS-Identifier = "172.16.25.15"
```

The following example shows the information contained in a TACACS+ EXEC accounting record for a dial-in user:

```
Wed Jun 25 03:46:21 1997        172.16.25.15   fgeorge  tty3   5622329430/4327528 start
task_id=2        service=shell
Wed Jun 25 04:08:55 1997        172.16.25.15   fgeorge  tty3   5622329430/4327528 stop
task_id=2        service=shell   elapsed_time=1354
```

The following example shows the information contained in a RADIUS EXEC accounting record for a Telnet user:

```
Wed Jun 25 04:48:32 1997
        NAS-IP-Address = "172.16.25.15"
        NAS-Port = 26
```

```
            User-Name = "fgeorge"
            Caller-ID = "171.68.202.158"
            Acct-Status-Type = Start
            Acct-Authentic = RADIUS
            Service-Type = Exec-User
            Acct-Session-Id = "00000010"
            Acct-Delay-Time = 0
            User-Id = "fgeorge"
            NAS-Identifier = "172.16.25.15"
Wed Jun 25 04:48:46 1997
            NAS-IP-Address = "172.16.25.15"
            NAS-Port = 26
            User-Name = "fgeorge"
            Caller-ID = "171.68.202.158"
            Acct-Status-Type = Stop
            Acct-Authentic = RADIUS
            Service-Type = Exec-User
            Acct-Session-Id = "00000010"
            Acct-Session-Time = 14
            Acct-Delay-Time = 0
            User-Id = "fgeorge"
            NAS-Identifier = "172.16.25.15"
```

The following example shows the information contained in a TACACS+ EXEC accounting record for a Telnet user:

```
Wed Jun 25 04:06:53 1997        172.16.25.15     fgeorge   tty26    171.68.202.158
starttask_id=41        service=shell
Wed Jun 25 04:07:02 1997        172.16.25.15     fgeorge   tty26    171.68.202.158
stoptask_id=41         service=shell   elapsed_time=9
```

System Accounting

System accounting provides information about all system-level events (for example, when the system reboots or when accounting is turned on or off). The following accounting record is an example of a typical TACACS+ system accounting record server indicating that AAA accounting has been turned off:

```
Wed Jun 25 03:55:32 1997        172.16.25.15    unknown unknown unknown start   task_id=25
service=system  event=sys_acct  reason=reconfigure
```

NOTES

The precise format of accounting packets records may vary depending on your particular TACACS+ daemon.

The following accounting record is an example of a TACACS+ system accounting record indicating that AAA accounting has been turned on:

```
Wed Jun 25 03:55:22 1997        172.16.25.15    unknown unknown unknown stop    task_id=23
service=system  event=sys_acct  reason=reconfigure
```

━━━ NOTES ━━━

Cisco's implementation of RADIUS does not support system accounting.

Command Accounting

Command accounting provides information about the EXEC shell commands for a specified privilege level that are being executed on a network access server. Each command accounting record includes a list of the commands executed for that privilege level, as well as the date and time each command was executed, and the user who executed it.

The following example shows the information contained in a TACACS+ command accounting record for privilege level 1:

```
Wed Jun 25 03:46:47 1997        172.16.25.15    fgeorge  tty3    5622329430/4327528  stop
task_id=3         service=shell   priv-lvl=1      cmd=show version <cr>
Wed Jun 25 03:46:58 1997        172.16.25.15    fgeorge  tty3    5622329430/4327528  stop
task_id=4         service=shell   priv-lvl=1      cmd=show interfaces Ethernet 0 <cr>
Wed Jun 25 03:47:03 1997        172.16.25.15    fgeorge  tty3    5622329430/4327528  stop
task_id=5         service=shell   priv-lvl=1      cmd=show ip route <cr>
```

The following example shows the information contained in a TACACS+ command accounting record for privilege level 15:

```
Wed Jun 25 03:47:17 1997        172.16.25.15    fgeorge  tty3    5622329430/4327528  stop
task_id=6         service=shell   priv-lvl=15     cmd=configure terminal <cr>
Wed Jun 25 03:47:21 1997        172.16.25.15    fgeorge  tty3    5622329430/4327528  stop
task_id=7         service=shell   priv-lvl=15     cmd=interface Serial 0 <cr>
Wed Jun 25 03:47:29 1997        172.16.25.15    fgeorge  tty3    5622329430/4327528  stop
task_id=8         service=shell   priv-lvl=15     cmd=ip address 1.1.1.1 255.255.255.0 <cr>
```

━━━ NOTES ━━━

Cisco's implementation of RADIUS does not support command accounting.

AAA ACCOUNTING PREREQUISITES

Before configuring AAA accounting, you must first complete these tasks:

- Enable AAA on your network access server. For more information about the AAA security services and how to enable AAA, see Chapter 2, "AAA Overview."
- Define the characteristics of your RADIUS or TACACS+ security server. For more information about defining RADIUS security server attributes, see Chapter 9, "Configuring RADIUS." For more information about defining TACACS+ security server attributes, see Chapter 11, "Configuring TACACS+."

AAA ACCOUNTING CONFIGURATION TASK LIST

This section describes the following tasks:

- Enabling Accounting
- Monitoring Accounting

For an accounting configuration example using the commands in this chapter, see section "Accounting Configuration Example," located at the end of the this chapter.

ENABLING ACCOUNTING

The **aaa accounting** command enables you to create a record for any or all of the accounting functions monitored. To enable AAA accounting, perform the following task in global configuration mode:

Task	Command
Enable accounting.	**aaa accounting** {**system** I **network** I **connection** I **exec** I **command** *level*} {**start-stop** I **wait-start** I **stop-only**} {**tacacs+** I **radius**}

For minimal accounting, use the **stop-only** keyword, which instructs the specified authentication system (RADIUS or TACACS+) to send a stop record accounting notice at the end of the requested user process. For more accounting information, use the **start-stop** keyword to send a start accounting notice at the beginning of the requested event and a stop accounting notice at the end of the event. You can further control access and accounting by using the **wait-start** keyword, which ensures that the RADIUS or TACACS+ security server acknowledges the start notice before granting the user's process request.

Suppress Generation of Accounting Records for Null Username Sessions

When **aaa accounting** is activated, the Cisco IOS software issues accounting records for all users on the system, including users whose username string (because of protocol translation) is NULL.

An example of this is users who come in on lines where the **aaa authentication login** *method-list* **none** command is applied. To prevent accounting records from being generated for sessions that do not have usernames associated with them, perform the following task in global configuration mode:

Task	Command
Prevent accounting records from being generated for users whose username string is NULL.	**aaa accounting suppress null-username**

Generate Interim Accounting Records

To enable periodic interim accounting records to be sent to the accounting server, perform the following task in global configuration mode:

Task	Command
Enable periodic interim accounting records to be sent to the accounting server.	**aaa accounting update** {**newinfo** | **periodic** *number*}

When the **aaa accounting update** command is activated, the Cisco IOS software issues interim accounting records for all users on the system. If the keyword **newinfo** is used, interim accounting records will be sent to the accounting server every time there is new accounting information to report. An example of this would be when IPCP completes IP address negotiation with the remote peer. The interim accounting record will include the negotiated IP address used by the remote peer.

When used with the keyword **periodic**, interim accounting records are sent periodically as defined by the argument number. The interim accounting record contains all of the accounting information recorded for that user up to the time the interim accounting record is sent.

Both of these keywords are mutually exclusive, meaning that whichever keyword is configured last takes precedence over the previous configuration. For example, if you configure **aaa accounting update periodic**, and then configure **aaa accounting update newinfo**, all users currently logged in will continue to generate periodic interim accounting records. All new users will generate accounting records based on the **newinfo** algorithm.

CAUTION

Using the **aaa accounting update periodic** command can cause heavy congestion when many users are logged in to the network.

MONITORING ACCOUNTING

No specific **show** command exists for either RADIUS or TACACS+ accounting. To obtain accounting records displaying information about users currently logged in, perform the following task in Privileged EXEC mode:

Task	Command
Step through all active sessions and print all the accounting records for the actively accounted functions.	**show accounting**

ACCOUNTING ATTRIBUTE-VALUE PAIRS

The network access server monitors the accounting functions defined in either TACACS+ attribute-value (AV) pairs or RADIUS attributes, depending on which security method you have implemented. For a list of supported RADIUS accounting attributes, see Appendix A, "RADIUS Attributes." For a list of supported TACACS+ accounting AV pairs, see Appendix B, "TACACS+ Attribute-Value Pairs."

ACCOUNTING CONFIGURATION EXAMPLE

In the following sample configuration, RADIUS-style accounting is used to track all usage of EXEC commands and network services, such as SLIP, PPP, and ARAP:

```
aaa accounting exec start-stop radius
aaa accounting network start-stop radius
```

The **show accounting** command yields the following output for the above configuration:

```
Active Accounted actions on tty0, User georgef Priv 1
 Task ID 2, EXEC Accounting record, 00:02:13 Elapsed
 task_id=2 service=shell
 Task ID 3, Connection Accounting record, 00:02:07 Elapsed
 task_id=3 service=connection protocol=telnet address=172.21.14.90 cmd=synth
Active Accounted actions on tty1, User rubble Priv 1
 Task ID 5, Network Accounting record, 00:00:52 Elapsed
 task_id=5 service=ppp protocol=ip address=10.0.0.98
Active Accounted actions on tty10, User georgef Priv 1
 Task ID 4, EXEC Accounting record, 00:00:53 Elapsed
 task_id=4 service=shell
```

Table 7–1 describes the fields contained in this example.

Table 7-1 *Show Accounting Field Descriptions*

Field	Description
Active Accounted actions on	Terminal line or interface name user with which the user logged in.
User	User's ID
Priv	User's privilege level.
Task ID	Unique identifier for each accounting session.
Accounting Record	Type of accounting session.
Elapsed	Length of time (hh:mm:ss) for this session type.
attribute=value	AV pairs associated with this accounting session.

## CHAPTER 8

Accounting Commands

This chapter describes the commands used to manage accounting on the network. Accounting management allows you to track individual and group usage of network resources. The AAA accounting feature enables you to track the services users are accessing as well as the amount of network resources they are consuming. When **aaa accounting** is activated, the network access server reports user activity to the TACACS+ or RADIUS security server (depending on which security method you have implemented) in the form of accounting records. Each accounting record contains accounting attribute-value (AV) pairs and is stored on the security server. This data can then be analyzed for network management, client billing, or auditing.

For information on how to configure accounting using AAA, see Chapter 7, "Configuring Accounting." For a configuration example using the commands in this chapter, see section "Accounting Configuration Example," located at the end of Chapter 7.

AAA ACCOUNTING

To enable AAA accounting of requested services for billing or security purposes when you use RADIUS or TACACS+, use the **aaa accounting** global configuration command. Use the **no** form of this command to disable accounting.

> aaa accounting {system | network | exec | command *level*} {start-stop |
>   wait-start | stop-only} {tacacs+ | radius}
> no aaa accounting {system | network | exec | command *level*}

Syntax Description

system   Performs accounting for all system-level events not associated with users, such as reloads.

network   Runs accounting for all network-related service requests, including SLIP, PPP, PPP NCPs, and ARAP.

exec   Runs accounting for EXEC session (user shells). This keyword might return user profile information such as **autocommand** information.

command   Runs accounting for all commands at the specified privilege level.

level   Specifies the command level to track for accounting. Valid entries are 0 through 15.

start-stop   Sends a start accounting notice at the beginning of a process and a stop accounting notice at the end of a process. The start accounting record is sent in the background. The requested user process begins regardless of whether or not the start accounting notice was received by the accounting server.

wait-start   As in **start-stop**, sends both a start and a stop accounting notice to the accounting server. However, if you use the **wait-start** keyword, the requested user service does not begin until the start accounting notice is acknowledged. A stop accounting notice is also sent.

stop-only   Sends a stop accounting notice at the end of the requested user process.

tacacs+   Enables the TACACS-style accounting.

radius   Enables the RADIUS-style authorization.

Default

AAA accounting is not enabled.

Command Mode

Global configuration

Usage Guidelines

This command first appeared in Cisco IOS Release 10.3.

For minimal accounting, include the **stop-only** keyword to send a stop record accounting notice at the end of the requested user process. For more accounting, you can include the **start-stop** keyword, so that RADIUS or TACACS+ sends a start accounting notice at the beginning of the requested process and a stop accounting notice at the end of the process. For even more accounting control, you can include the **wait-start** keyword, which ensures that the start notice is received by the RADIUS or TACACS+ server before granting the user's process request. Accounting is done only to the RADIUS or TACACS+ server.

When **aaa accounting** is activated, the network access server monitors either RADIUS accounting attributes or TACACS+ AV pairs pertinent to the connection, depending on the security method you have implemented. The network access server reports these attributes as accounting records, which are then stored in an accounting log on the security server. For a list of supported RADIUS accounting attributes, see Appendix A, "RADIUS Attributes." For a list of supported TACACS+ accounting AV pairs, see Appendix B, "TACACS+ Attribute-Value Pairs."

Example

In the following example, accounting is configured for a TACACS+ security server, set for privilege level 15 commands with a wait-start restriction:

```
aaa accounting command 15 wait-start tacacs+
```

Related Commands

Search online to find documentation for related commands.

aaa authorization
aaa new-model

AAA ACCOUNTING SUPPRESS NULL-USERNAME

To prevent the Cisco IOS software from sending accounting records for users whose username string is NULL, use the **aaa accounting suppress null-username** global configuration command. Use the **no** form of this command to disable this feature.

aaa accounting suppress null-username
no aaa accounting suppress null-username

Syntax Description

This command has no arguments or keywords.

Default

Disabled

Command Mode

Global configuration

Usage Guidelines

This command first appeared in Cisco IOS Release 11.2.

When **aaa accounting** is activated, the Cisco IOS software issues accounting records for all users on the system, including users whose username string (because of protocol translation) is NULL. This command prevents accounting records from being generated for those users who do not have usernames associated with them.

Example

In the following example, accounting records for users who do not have usernames associated with them have been suppressed:

```
aaa accounting suppress null-username
```

Related Commands

Search online to find documentation for related commands.

aaa accounting

AAA ACCOUNTING UPDATE

To enable periodic interim accounting records to be sent to the accounting server, use the **aaa accounting update** global configuration command. Use the **no** form of this command to disable this feature.

> aaa accounting update {newinfo | periodic *number*}
> no aaa accounting update

Syntax Description

newinfo   Causes an interim accounting record to be sent to the accounting server whenever there is new accounting information to report relating to the user in question.

periodic   Causes an interim accounting record to be sent to the accounting server periodically, as defined by the argument *number*.

number   Integer specifying number of minutes.

Default

Disabled

Command Mode

Global configuration

Usage Guidelines

This command first appeared in Cisco IOS Release 11.3.

When **aaa accounting update** is activated, the Cisco IOS software issues interim accounting records for all users on the system. If the keyword **newinfo** is used, interim accounting records will be sent to the accounting server every time there is new accounting information to report. An example of this would be when IPCP completes IP address negotiation with the remote peer. The interim accounting record will include the negotiated IP address used by the remote peer.

When used with the keyword **periodic**, interim accounting records are sent periodically as defined by the argument number. The interim accounting record contains all of the accounting information recorded for that user up to the time the accounting record is sent.

Both of these keywords are mutually exclusive, meaning that whichever keyword is configured last takes precedence over the previous configuration. For example, if you configure **aaa accounting update periodic**, and then configure **aaa accounting update newinfo**, all users currently logged in will continue to generate periodic interim accounting records. All new users will generate accounting records based on the **newinfo** algorithm.

CAUTION

Using the **aaa accounting update periodic** command can cause heavy congestion when many users are logged in to the network.

Example

The following example sends PPP accounting records to a remote RADIUS server, and when IPCP completes negotiation, sends an interim accounting record to the RADIUS server that includes the negotiated IP address for this user:

```
aaa accounting network start-stop radius
aaa accounting update newinfo
```

Related Commands

Search online to find documentation for related commands.

aaa accounting exec
aaa accounting network

SHOW ACCOUNTING

Use the **show accounting** command to step through all active sessions and to print all the accounting records for actively accounted functions. Use the **no** form of this command to disable this function.

```
show accounting {system | network | exec | command level} {start-stop |
    wait-start | stop-only} tacacs+
no show accounting {system | network | exec | command level}
```

Syntax Description

system	Displays accounting for all system-level events not associated with users, such as reloads.
network	Displays accounting for all network-related service requests, including SLIP, PPP, PPP NCPs, and ARAP.
exec	Displays accounting for EXEC session (user shells). This keyword might return user profile information such as **autocommand** information.
command	Displays accounting for all commands at the specified privilege level.
level	Specifies the command level to display. Valid entries are 0 through 15.
start-stop	Displays a start record accounting notice at the beginning of a process and a stop record at the end of a process. The start accounting record is sent in the background. The requested user process begins regardless of whether or not the start accounting record was received by the accounting server.
wait-start	Displays both a start and a stop accounting notice to the accounting server.
stop-only	Displays a stop record accounting notice at the end of the requested user process.
tacacs+	Displays the TACACS-style accounting.

Default

Disabled

Command Mode

EXEC

Usage Guidelines

This command first appeared in Cisco IOS Release 11.1.

The **show accounting** command allows you to display the active accountable events on the network. It provides system administrators with a quick look at what is going on, and it also can help collect information in the event of a data loss on the accounting server.

The **show accounting** command displays additional data on the internal state of AAA if **debug aaa accounting** is activated.

Sample Displays

The following is sample output from the **show accounting** command, showing accounting records for an EXEC login and an outgoing Telnet session:

```
router# show accounting
Active Accounted actions on tty0, User (not logged in) Priv 1
  Task ID 1, EXEC Accounting record, 00:22:14 Elapsed
  task_id=1 service=shell
  Task ID 10, Connection Accounting record, 00:00:03 Elapsed
  task_id=10 service=connection protocol=telnet addr=172.16.57.11 cmd=connect tom-ss20
Active Accounted actions on tty66, User tom Priv 1
  Task ID 9, EXEC Accounting record, 00:02:14 Elapsed
  task_id=9 service=shell
```

The following is sample output from the **show accounting** command, showing accounting records for a network connection:

```
router# show accounting
Active Accounted actions on tty33, User tom Priv 1
  Task ID 13, Network Accounting record, 00:00:10 Elapsed
  task_id=13 service=ppp protocol=ip addr=10.0.0.1
```

The following is sample output from the **show accounting** command, showing accounting records for a PPP session started from an EXEC prompt:

```
router# show accounting
Active Accounted actions on tty0, User (not logged in) Priv 1
  Task ID 1, EXEC Accounting record, 00:35:16 Elapsed
  task_id=1 service=shell
Active Accounted actions on tty33, User ellie Priv 1
  Task ID 16, EXEC Accounting record, 00:00:17 Elapsed
  task_id=16 service=shell
Active Accounted actions on Interface Async33, User tom Priv 1
  Task ID 17, Network Accounting record, 00:00:13 Elapsed
  task_id=17 service=ppp protocol=ip addr=10.0.0.1
```

Table 8–1 describes the fields contained in this example.

Table 8–1 *Show Accounting Field Descriptions*

Field	Description
Active Accounted actions on	Terminal line or interface name user with which the user logged in.
User	User's ID
Priv	User's privilege level.

Table 8-1 *Show Accounting Field Descriptions, Continued*

Field	Description
Task ID	Unique identifier for each accounting session.
Accounting Record	Type of accounting session.
Elapsed	Length of time (hh:mm:ss) for this session type.
attribute=value	AV pairs associated with this accounting session.

Related Commands

Search online to find documentation for related commands.

debug aaa accounting
show line
show users

PART II

Security Server Protocols

## CHAPTER 9

Configuring RADIUS

This chapter describes the Remote Authentication Dial-In User Service (RADIUS) security system, defines its operation, and identifies appropriate and inappropriate network environments for using RADIUS technology. Section "RADIUS Configuration Task List" describes how to configure RADIUS with the authentication, authorization, and accounting (AAA) command set. Section "RADIUS Authentication and Authorization Examples," located at the end of this chapter, offers two possible implementation scenarios.

This chapter begins with the following main topics:

- RADIUS Overview
- RADIUS Operation
- RADIUS Configuration Task List

For a complete description of the commands used in this chapter, see Chapter 10, "RADIUS Commands."

RADIUS OVERVIEW

RADIUS is a distributed client/server system that secures networks against unauthorized access. In the Cisco implementation, RADIUS clients run on Cisco routers and send authentication requests to a central RADIUS server that contains all user authentication and network service access information.

RADIUS is a fully open protocol, distributed in source code format, that can be modified to work with any security system currently available on the market.

Cisco supports RADIUS under its AAA security paradigm. RADIUS can be used with other AAA security protocols, such as TACACS+, Kerberos, or local username lookup. RADIUS is supported on all Cisco platforms.

RADIUS has been implemented in a variety of network environments that require high levels of security while maintaining network access for remote users.

Use RADIUS in the following network environments that require access security:

- Networks with multiple-vendor access servers, each supporting RADIUS. For example, access servers from several vendors use a single RADIUS server-based security database. In an IP-based network with multiple vendors' access servers, dial-in users are authenticated through a RADIUS server that has been customized to work with the Kerberos security system.

- Turnkey network security environments in which applications support the RADIUS protocol, such as in an access environment that uses a "smart card" access control system. In one case, RADIUS has been used with Enigma's security cards to validate users and grant access to network resources.

- Networks already using RADIUS. You can add a Cisco router with RADIUS to the network. This might be the first step when you make a transition to a Terminal Access Controller Access Control System (TACACS+) server.

- Networks in which a user must only access a single service. Using RADIUS, you can control user access to a single host, to a single utility such as Telnet, or to a single protocol such as Point-to-Point Protocol (PPP). For example, when a user logs in, RADIUS identifies this user as having authorization to run PPP using IP address 10.2.3.4 and the defined access list is started.

- Networks that require resource accounting. You can use RADIUS accounting independent of RADIUS authentication or authorization. The RADIUS accounting functions allow data to be sent at the start and end of services, indicating the amount of resources (such as time, packets, bytes, and so on) used during the session. An Internet Service Provider (ISP) might use a freeware-based version of RADIUS access control and accounting software to meet special security and billing needs.

RADIUS is not suitable in the following network security situations:

- Multiprotocol access environments. RADIUS does not support the following protocols:
  - AppleTalk Remote Access Protocol (ARAP)
  - NetBIOS Frame Protocol Control Protocol (NBFCP)
  - NetWare Asynchronous Services Interface (NASI)
  - X.25 PAD connections

- Router-to-router situations. RADIUS does not provide two-way authentication. RADIUS can be used to authenticate from one router to a non-Cisco router if the non-Cisco router requires RADIUS authentication.

- Networks using a variety of services. RADIUS generally binds a user to one service model.

RADIUS OPERATION

When a user attempts to log in and authenticate to an access server using RADIUS, the following steps occur:

1. The user is prompted for and enters a username and password.

2. The username and encrypted password are sent over the network to the RADIUS server.

3. The user receives one of the following responses from the RADIUS server:

   ○ ACCEPT—The user is authenticated.

   ○ REJECT—The user is not authenticated and is prompted to re-enter the username and password, or access is denied.

   ○ CHALLENGE—A challenge is issued by the RADIUS server. The challenge collects additional data from the user.

   ○ CHANGE PASSWORD—A request is issued by the RADIUS server, asking the user to select a new password.

The ACCEPT or REJECT response is bundled with additional data that is used for EXEC or network authorization. You must first complete RADIUS authentication before using RADIUS authorization. The additional data included with the ACCEPT or REJECT packets consists of the following:

- Services that the user can access, including Telnet, rlogin, or local-area transport (LAT) connections, and PPP, Serial Line Internet Protocol (SLIP), or EXEC services.

- Connection parameters, including the host or client IP address, access list, and user timeouts.

RADIUS CONFIGURATION TASK LIST

To configure RADIUS on your Cisco router or access server, you must perform the following tasks:

- Use the **aaa new-model** global configuration command to enable AAA. AAA must be configured if you plan to use RADIUS. For more information about using the **aaa new-model** command, see Chapter 2, "AAA Overview."

- Use the **aaa authentication** global configuration command to define method lists for RADIUS authentication. For more information about using the **aaa authentication** command, see Chapter 3, "Configuring Authentication."

- Use **line** and **interface** commands to enable the defined method lists to be used. For more information, see Chapter 3.

The following configuration tasks are optional:

- If needed, use the **aaa authorization** global command to authorize specific user functions. For more information about using the **aaa authorization** command, see Chapter 5, "Configuring Authorization."

- If needed, use the **aaa accounting** command to enable accounting for RADIUS connections. For more information about using the **aaa accounting** command, see Chapter 7, "Configuring Accounting."

The upcoming sections describe how to set up RADIUS for authentication, authorization, and accounting on your network, as follows:

- Configuring Router to RADIUS Server Communication
- Configuring Router for Vendor-Proprietary RADIUS Server Communication
- Configuring Router to Query RADIUS Server for Static Routes and IP Addresses
- Specifying RADIUS Authentication
- Specifying RADIUS Authorization
- Specifying RADIUS Accounting

CONFIGURING ROUTER TO RADIUS SERVER COMMUNICATION

The RADIUS host is normally a multiuser system running RADIUS server software from Livingston, Merit, Microsoft, or another software provider. A RADIUS server and a Cisco router use a shared secret text-string to encrypt passwords and exchange responses.

To configure RADIUS to use the AAA security commands, you must specify the host running the RADIUS server daemon and a secret text-string that it shares with the router. Use the **radius-server** commands to specify the RADIUS server host and a secret text-string.

To specify a RADIUS server host and shared secret text-string, perform the following tasks in global configuration mode:

Task	Command
Specify the IP address or host name of the remote RADIUS server host and assign authentication and accounting destination port numbers.	**radius-server host** {*hostname* | *ip-address*} [**auth-port** *port-number*] [**acct-port** *port-number*]
Specify the shared secret text-string used between the router and the RADIUS server.	**radius-server key** *string*

To customize communication between the router and the RADIUS server, use the following optional **radius-server** global configuration commands:

Task	Command
Specify the number of times the router transmits each RADIUS request to the server before giving up (default is three).	**radius-server retransmit** *retries*
Specify the number of seconds a router waits for a reply to a RADIUS request before retransmitting the request.	**radius-server timeout** *seconds*
Specify the number of minutes a RADIUS server, which is not responding to authentication requests, is passed over by requests for RADIUS authentication.	**radius-server dead-time** *minutes*

CONFIGURING ROUTER FOR VENDOR-PROPRIETARY RADIUS SERVER COMMUNICATION

Although an Internet Engineering Task Force (IETF) draft standard for RADIUS specifies a method for communicating vendor-proprietary information between the network access server and the RADIUS server, some vendors have extended the RADIUS attribute set in a unique way. Cisco IOS software supports a subset of vendor-proprietary RADIUS attributes.

As mentioned earlier, to configure RADIUS (whether vendor-proprietary or IETF draft-compliant), you must specify the host running the RADIUS server daemon and the secret text-string it shares with the Cisco device. You specify the RADIUS host and secret text-string by using the **radius-server** commands. To identify that the RADIUS server is using a vendor-proprietary implementation of RADIUS, use the **radius-server host non-standard** command. Vendor-proprietary attributes will not be supported unless you use the **radius-server host non-standard** command.

To specify a vendor-proprietary RADIUS server host and a shared secret text-string, perform the following tasks in global configuration mode:

Task	Command
Specify the IP address or host name of the remote RADIUS server host and identify that it is using a vendor-proprietary implementation of RADIUS.	**radius-server host** {*hostname*	*ip-address*} **non-standard**

Task	Command
Specify the shared secret text-string used between the router and the vendor-proprietary RADIUS server. The router and the RADIUS server use this text-string to encrypt passwords and exchange responses.	**radius-server key** *string*

CONFIGURING ROUTER TO QUERY RADIUS SERVER FOR STATIC ROUTES AND IP ADDRESSES

Some vendor-proprietary implementations of RADIUS let the user define static routes and IP pool definitions on the RADIUS server instead of on each individual network access server in the network. Each network access server then queries the RADIUS server for static route and IP pool information.

To have the Cisco router or access server query the RADIUS server for static routes and IP pool definitions when the device first starts up, perform the following task in global configuration mode:

Task	Command
Tell the Cisco router or access server to query the RADIUS server for the static routes and IP pool definitions used throughout its domain.	**radius-server configure-nas**

NOTES

Because the **radius-server configure-nas** command is performed when the Cisco router starts up, it will not take effect until you issue a **copy running-config startup-config** command.

SPECIFYING RADIUS AUTHENTICATION

After you have identified the RADIUS server and defined the RADIUS authentication key, you need to define method lists for RADIUS authentication. Because RADIUS authentication is facilitated through AAA, you need to issue the **aaa authentication** command, specifying RADIUS as the authentication method. For more information, see Chapter 3.

SPECIFYING RADIUS AUTHORIZATION

AAA authorization lets you set parameters that restrict a user's network access. Authorization using RADIUS provides one method for remote access control, including one-time authorization or authorization for each service, per-user account list and profile, user group support, and support of IP, IPX, ARA, and Telnet. Because RADIUS authorization is facilitated through AAA, you need to issue the **aaa authorization** command, specifying RADIUS as the authorization method. For more information, see Chapter 5.

SPECIFYING RADIUS ACCOUNTING

The AAA accounting feature enables you to track the services users are accessing as well as the amount of network resources they are consuming. Because RADIUS accounting is facilitated through AAA, you need to issue the **aaa accounting** command, specifying RADIUS as the accounting method. For more information, see Chapter 7.

RADIUS ATTRIBUTES

The network access server monitors the RADIUS authorization and accounting functions defined by RADIUS attributes in each user profile. For a list of supported RADIUS attributes, see Appendix A, "RADIUS Attributes."

VENDOR-PROPRIETARY RADIUS ATTRIBUTES

An Internet Engineering Task Force (IETF) draft standard for RADIUS specifies a method for communicating vendor-proprietary information between the network access server and the RADIUS server. Some vendors, nevertheless, have extended the RADIUS attribute set in a unique way. Cisco IOS software supports a subset of vendor-proprietary RADIUS attributes. For a list of supported vendor-proprietary RADIUS attributes, see Appendix A.

RADIUS CONFIGURATION EXAMPLES

RADIUS configuration examples in this section include the following:

- RADIUS Authentication and Authorization Example
- RADIUS Authentication, Authorization, and Accounting Example
- Vendor-Proprietary RADIUS Configuration Example

RADIUS AUTHENTICATION AND AUTHORIZATION EXAMPLE

The following example shows how to configure the router to authenticate and authorize using RADIUS:

```
aaa authentication login use-radius radius local
aaa authentication ppp user-radius if-needed radius
aaa authorization exec radius
aaa authorization network radius
```

The lines in this sample RADIUS authentication and authorization configuration are defined as follows:

- The **aaa authentication login use-radius radius local** command configures the router to use RADIUS for authentication at the login prompt. If RADIUS returns an error, the user is authenticated using the local database. In this example, **use-radius** is the name of the method list, which specifies RADIUS and then local authentication.

- The **aaa authentication ppp user-radius if-needed radius** command configures the Cisco IOS software to use RADIUS authentication for lines using Point-to-Point Protocol (PPP) with CHAP or PAP if the user has not already been authorized. If the EXEC facility has authenticated the user, RADIUS authentication is not performed. In this example, **user-radius** is the name of the method list defining RADIUS as the if-needed authentication method.

- The **aaa authorization exec radius** command sets the RADIUS information that is used for EXEC authorization, autocommands, and access lists.

- The **aaa authorization network radius** command sets RADIUS for network authorization, address assignment, and access lists.

RADIUS Authentication, Authorization, and Accounting Example

The following sample is a general configuration using RADIUS with the AAA command set:

```
radius-server host 123.45.1.2
radius-server key myRaDiUSpassWoRd
username root password ALongPassword
aaa authentication ppp dialins radius local
aaa authorization network radius local
aaa accounting network start-stop radius
aaa authentication login admins local
aaa authorization exec local
line 1 16
 autoselect ppp
 autoselect during-login
 login authentication admins
 modem ri-is-cd
interface group-async 1
 encaps ppp
 ppp authentication pap dialins
```

The lines in this sample RADIUS authentication, authorization, and accounting configuration are defined as follows:

- The **radius-server host** command defines the IP address of the RADIUS server host.

- The **radius-server key** command defines the shared secret text-string between the network access server and the RADIUS server host.

- The **aaa authentication ppp dialins radius local** command defines the authentication method list "dialins," which specifies that RADIUS authentication, then (if the RADIUS server does not respond) local authentication will be used on serial lines using PPP.

- The **ppp authentication pap dialins** command applies the "dialins" method list to the lines specified.
- The **aaa authorization network radius local** command is used to assign an address and other network parameters to the RADIUS user.
- The **aaa accounting network start-stop radius** command tracks PPP usage.
- The **aaa authentication login admins local** command defines another method list, "admins," for login authentication.
- The **login authentication admins** command applies the "admins" method list for login authentication.

Vendor-Proprietary RADIUS Configuration Example

The following sample is a general configuration using vendor-proprietary RADIUS with the AAA command set:

```
radius-server host alcatraz non-standard
radius-server key myRaDiUSpassWoRd
radius-server configure-nas
username root password ALongPassword
aaa authentication ppp dialins radius local
aaa authorization network radius local
aaa accounting network start-stop radius
aaa authentication login admins local
aaa authorization exec local
line 1 16
autoselect ppp
autoselect during-login
login authentication admins
modem ri-is-cd
interface group-async 1
encaps ppp
ppp authentication pap dialins
```

The lines in this sample RADIUS authentication, authorization, and accounting configuration are defined as follows:

- The **radius-server host non-standard** command defines the name of the RADIUS server host and identifies that this RADIUS host uses a vendor-proprietary version of RADIUS.
- The **radius-server key** command defines the shared secret text-string between the network access server and the RADIUS server host.
- The **radius-server configure-nas** command defines that the Cisco router or access server will query the RADIUS server for static routes and IP pool definitions when the device first starts up.
- The **aaa authentication ppp dialins radius local** command defines the authentication method list "dialins," which specifies that RADIUS authentication, then (if the RADIUS server does not respond) local authentication will be used on serial lines using PPP.

- The **ppp authentication pap dialins** command applies the "dialins" method list to the lines specified.

- The **aaa authorization network radius local** command is used to assign an address and other network parameters to the RADIUS user.

- The **aaa accounting network start-stop radius** command tracks PPP usage.

- The **aaa authentication login admins local** command defines another method list, "admins," for login authentication.

- The **login authentication admins** command applies the "admins" method list for login authentication.

## CHAPTER 10

RADIUS Commands

This chapter describes the commands used to configure RADIUS.

RADIUS is a distributed client/server system that secures networks against unauthorized access. In the Cisco implementation, RADIUS clients run on Cisco routers and send authentication requests to a central RADIUS server that contains all user authentication and network service access information. Cisco supports RADIUS under its Authentication, Authorization, and Accounting (AAA) security paradigm.

For information on how to configure RADIUS, see Chapter 9, "Configuring RADIUS." For configuration examples using the commands in this chapter, see section "RADIUS Configuration Examples," located at the end of Chapter 9.

IP RADIUS SOURCE-INTERFACE

To force RADIUS to use the IP address of a specified interface for all outgoing RADIUS packets, use the **ip radius source-interface** global configuration command.

ip radius source-interface *subinterface-name*
no ip radius source-interface

Syntax Description

subinterface-name   Name of the interface that RADIUS uses for all of its outgoing packets.

Default

This command has no factory-assigned default.

Command Mode

Global configuration

Usage Guidelines

This command first appeared in Cisco IOS Release 11.3.

Use this command to set a subinterface's IP address to be used as the source address for all outgoing RADIUS packets. This address is used as long as the interface is in the *up* state. This way, the RADIUS server can use one IP address entry for every network access client instead of maintaining a list of IP addresses.

This command is especially useful in cases where the router has many interfaces and you want to ensure that all RADIUS packets from a particular router have the same IP address.

The specified interface must have an IP address associated with it. If the specified subinterface does not have a IP address or is in the *down* state, then RADIUS reverts to the default. To avoid this, add an IP address to the subinterface or bring the interface to the *up* state.

Example

The following example makes RADIUS use the IP address of subinterface s2 for all outgoing RADIUS packets:

```
ip radius source-interface s2
```

Related Commands

Search online to find documentation for related commands.

ip tacacs source-interface
ip telnet source-interface
ip tftp source-interface

RADIUS-SERVER CONFIGURE-NAS

To have the Cisco router or access server query the vendor-proprietary RADIUS server for the static routes and IP pool definitions used throughout its domain when the device starts up, use the **radius-server configure-nas** global configuration command.

radius-server configure-nas

Syntax Description

This command has no arguments or keywords.

Command Mode

Global configuration

Usage Guidelines

This command first appeared in Cisco IOS Release 11.3.

Use the **radius-server configure-nas** command to have the Cisco router query the vendor-proprietary RADIUS server for static routes and IP pool definitions when the router first starts up. Some vendor-proprietary implementations of RADIUS let the user define static routes and IP pool definitions on the RADIUS server instead of on each individual network access server in the network. As each network access server starts up, it queries the RADIUS server for static route and IP pool information. This command enables the Cisco router to obtain static routes and IP pool definition information from the RADIUS server.

NOTES

Because the **radius-server configure-nas** command is performed when the Cisco router starts up, it will not take effect until you issue a **copy running-config startup-config** command.

Example

The following example shows how to tell the Cisco router or access server to query the vendor-proprietary RADIUS server for already-defined static routes and IP pool definitions when the device first starts up:

```
radius-server configure-nas
```

Related Commands

Search online to find documentation for related commands.

radius-server host non-standard

RADIUS-SERVER DEAD-TIME

To improve RADIUS response times when some servers might be unavailable, use the **radius-server dead-time** global configuration command to cause the unavailable servers to be skipped immediately. Use the **no** form of this command to set **dead-time** to 0.

> **radius-server dead-time** *minutes*
> **no radius-server dead-time**

Syntax Description

minutes   Length of time a RADIUS server is skipped over by transaction requests, up to a maximum of 1440 minutes (24 hours).

Default

Dead time is set to 0.

Command Mode

Global configuration

Usage Guidelines

Use this command to cause the Cisco IOS software to mark as "dead" any RADIUS servers that fail to respond to authentication requests, thus avoiding the wait for the request to time out before trying the next configured server. A RADIUS server marked as "dead" is skipped by additional requests for the duration of *minutes,* or unless there are no servers not marked "dead."

Example

The following example specifies five minutes dead-time for RADIUS servers that fail to respond to authentication requests:

```
radius-server dead-time 5
```

Related Commands

Search online to find documentation for related commands.

radius-server host
radius-server retransmit
radius-server timeout

RADIUS-SERVER HOST

To specify a RADIUS server host, use the **radius-server host** global configuration command. Use the **no** form of this command to delete the specified RADIUS host.

> **radius-server host** {*hostname* | *ip-address*} [**auth-port** *port-number*] [**acct-port** *port-number*]
> **no radius-server host** {*hostname* | *ip-address*}

Syntax Description

hostname	DNS name of the RADIUS server host.
ip-address	IP address of the RADIUS server host.
auth-port	(Optional) Specifies the UDP destination port for authentication requests.
port-number	(Optional) Port number for authentication requests; the host is not used for authentication if set to 0.
acct-port	(Optional) Specifies the UDP destination port for accounting requests.
port-number	(Optional) Port number for accounting requests; the host is not used for accounting if set to 0.

Default

No RADIUS host is specified.

Command Mode

Global configuration

Usage Guidelines

You can use multiple **radius-server host** commands to specify multiple hosts. The software searches for hosts in the order you specify them.

Examples

The following example specifies *host1* as the RADIUS server and uses default ports for both accounting and authentication:

```
radius-server host host1.company.com
```

The following example specifies port 12 as the destination port for authentication requests and port 16 as the destination port for accounting requests on a RADIUS host named *host1*:

```
radius-server host host1.company.com auth-port 12 acct-port 16
```

Because entering a line resets all the port numbers, you must specify a host and configure accounting and authentication ports on a single line.

To use separate servers for accounting and authentication, use the zero port value as appropriate. The following example specifies that RADIUS server *host1* be used for accounting but not for authentication, and that RADIUS server *host2* be used for authentication but not for accounting:

```
radius-server host host1.company.com auth-port 0
radius-server host host2.company.com acct-port 0
```

Related Commands

Search online to find documentation for related commands.

aaa accounting
aaa authentication
aaa authorization
login authentication
login tacacs
ppp
ppp authentication
radius-server key
slip
tacacs-server
username

RADIUS-SERVER HOST NON-STANDARD

To identify that the security server is using a vendor-proprietary implementation of RADIUS, use the **radius-server host non-standard** global configuration command. This command tells the Cisco IOS software to support non-standard RADIUS attributes. Use the **no** form of this command to delete the specified vendor-proprietary RADIUS host.

> **radius-server host** {*hostname* | *ip-address*} **non-standard**
> **no radius-server host** {*hostname* | *ip-address*} **non-standard**

Syntax Description

hostname   DNS name of the RADIUS server host.

ip-address   IP address of the RADIUS server host.

Default

No RADIUS host is specified.

Command Mode

Global configuration

Usage Guidelines

This command first appeared in Cisco IOS Release 11.3.

The **radius-server host non-standard** command enables you to identify that the RADIUS server is using a vendor-proprietary implementation of RADIUS. Although an IETF draft standard for RADIUS specifies a method for communicating information between the network access server and the RADIUS server, some vendors have extended the RADIUS attribute set in a unique way. This command enables the Cisco IOS software to support the most common vendor-proprietary RADIUS attributes. Vendor-proprietary attributes will not be supported unless you use the **radius-server host non-standard** command.

For a list of supported vendor-specific RADIUS attributes, see Appendix A, "RADIUS Attributes."

Example

The following example specifies a vendor-proprietary RADIUS server host named *alcatraz*:

```
radius-server host alcatraz non-standard
```

Related Commands

Search online to find documentation for related commands.

radius-server host
radius-server configure-nas

RADIUS-SERVER KEY

To set the authentication and encryption key for all RADIUS communications between the router and the RADIUS daemon, use the **radius-server key** global configuration command. Use the **no** form of this command to disable the key.

> **radius-server key** {*string*}
> **no radius-server key**

Syntax Description

string   The key used to set authentication and encryption.
                  This key must match the encryption used on the RADIUS daemon.

Default

Disabled

Command Mode

Global configuration

Usage Guidelines

This command first appeared in Cisco IOS Release 11.1.

After enabling AAA authentication with the **aaa new-model** command, you must set the authentication and encryption key using the **radius-server key** command.

─── **NOTES** ──
Specify a RADIUS key after you issue the **aaa new-model** command.
───

The key entered must match the key used on the RADIUS daemon. All leading spaces are ignored, but spaces within and at the end of the key are used. If you use spaces in your key, do not enclose the key in quotation marks unless the quotation marks themselves are part of the key.

Example

The following example sets the authentication and encryption key to "dare to go":

```
radius-server key dare to go
```

Related Commands

Search online to find documentation for related commands.

login authentication
login tacacs

ppp
ppp authentication
radius-server host
slip
tacacs-server
username

RADIUS-SERVER RETRANSMIT

To specify the number of times the Cisco IOS software searches the list of RADIUS server hosts before giving up, use the **radius-server retransmit** global configuration command. Use the **no** form of this command to disable retransmission.

>   **radius-server retransmit** *retries*
>   **no radius-server retransmit**

Syntax Description

retries   Maximum number of retransmission attempts. The default is 3 attempts.

Default

Three retries

Command Mode

Global configuration

Usage Guidelines

This command first appeared in Cisco IOS Release 11.1.

The Cisco IOS software tries all servers, allowing each one to time out before increasing the retransmit count.

Example

The following example specifies a retransmit counter value of five times:

```
radius-server retransmit 5
```

RADIUS-SERVER TIMEOUT

To set the interval a router waits for a server host to reply, use the **radius-server timeout** global configuration command. Use the **no** form of this command to restore the default.

>   **radius-server timeout** *seconds*
>   **no radius-server timeout**

Syntax Description

seconds   Number that specifies the timeout interval in seconds. The default is 5 seconds.

Default

5 seconds

Command Mode

Global configuration

Usage Guidelines

This command first appeared in Cisco IOS Release 11.1.

Example

The following example changes the interval timer to 10 seconds:

```
radius-server timeout 10
```

Related Commands

Search online to find documentation for related commands.

login authentication
login tacacs
ppp
ppp authentication
slip
tacacs-server
username

## CHAPTER 11

Configuring TACACS+

Cisco IOS software currently supports three versions of the Terminal Access Controller Access Control System (TACACS) security protocol, each one of which is a separate and unique protocol:

- TACACS+—A recent protocol providing detailed accounting information and flexible administrative control over authentication and authorization processes. TACACS+ is facilitated through AAA and can be enabled only through AAA commands. A draft RFC details this protocol.

- TACACS—An older access protocol, incompatible with the newer TACACS+ protocol, that is now deprecated by Cisco. It provides password checking and authentication, and notification of user actions for security and accounting purposes.

- Extended TACACS—An extension to the older TACACS protocol, supplying additional functionality to TACACS. Extended TACACS provides information about protocol translator and router use. This information is used in UNIX auditing trails and accounting files. Extended TACACS is incompatible with TACACS+ and is also deprecated.

This chapter discusses how to enable and configure TACACS+. For information about the deprecated protocols TACACS or Extended TACACS, see Chapter 12, "Configuring TACACS and Extended TACACS."

For a complete description of the authorization commands used in this chapter, see Chapter 13, "TACACS, Extended TACACS, and TACACS+ Commands."

TACACS+ OVERVIEW

TACACS+ is a security application that provides centralized validation of users attempting to gain access to a router or network access server. TACACS+ services are maintained in a database on a TACACS+ daemon running, typically, on a UNIX or Windows NT workstation. You must have access to and must configure a TACACS+ server before the configured TACACS+ features on your network access server are available.

TACACS+ provides for separate and modular authentication, authorization, and accounting facilities. TACACS+ allows for a single access control server (the TACACS+ daemon) to provide each service—authentication, authorization, and accounting—independently. Each service can be tied into its own database to take advantage of other services available on that server or on the network, depending on the capabilities of the daemon.

The goal of TACACS+ is to provide a methodology for managing multiple network access points from a single management service. The Cisco family of access servers and routers and the Cisco IOS user interface (for both routers and access servers) can be network access servers.

Network access points enable traditional "dumb" terminals, terminal emulators, workstations, personal computers (PCs), and routers in conjunction with suitable adapters (for example, modems or ISDN adapters) to communicate using protocols such as Point-to-Point Protocol (PPP), Serial Line Internet Protocol (SLIP), Compressed SLIP (CSLIP), or AppleTalk Remote Access (ARA) Protocol. In other words, a network access server provides connections to a single user, to a network or subnetwork, and to interconnected networks. The entities connected to the network through a network access server are called *network access clients*; for example, a PC running PPP over a voice-grade circuit is a network access client. TACACS+, administered through the AAA security services, can provide the following services:

- Authentication—Provides complete control of authentication through login and password dialog, challenge and response, messaging support.

  The authentication facility provides the ability to conduct an arbitrary dialog with the user (for example, after a login and password are provided, to challenge a user with a number of questions, such as home address, mother's maiden name, service type, and social security number). In addition, the TACACS+ authentication service supports sending messages to user screens. For example, a message could notify users that their passwords must be changed because of the company's password aging policy.

- Authorization—Provides fine-grained control over user capabilities for the duration of the user's session, including but not limited to setting autocommands, access control, session duration, or protocol support. You can also enforce restrictions on what commands a user may execute with the TACACS+ authorization feature.

- Accounting—Collects and sends information used for billing, auditing, and reporting to the TACACS+ daemon. Network managers can use the accounting facility to track user activity for a security audit or to provide information for user billing. Accounting records include user identities, start and stop times, executed commands (such as PPP), number of packets, and number of bytes.

The TACACS+ protocol provides authentication between the network access server and the TACACS+ daemon, and it ensures confidentiality because all protocol exchanges between a network access server and a TACACS+ daemon are encrypted.

You need a system running TACACS+ daemon software to use the TACACS+ functionality on your network access server.

Cisco makes the TACACS+ protocol specification available as a draft RFC for those customers interested in developing their own TACACS+ software.

NOTES

TACACS+, in conjunction with AAA, is a separate and distinct protocol from the earlier TACACS or Extended TACACS, which are now deprecated. After AAA has been enabled, many of the original TACACS and extended TACACS commands can no longer be configured. For more information about TACACS or Extended TACACS, see Chapter 12.

TACACS+ OPERATION

When a user attempts a simple ASCII login by authenticating to a network access server using TACACS+, the following process typically occurs:

1. When the connection is established, the network access server will contact the TACACS+ daemon to obtain a username prompt, which is then displayed to the user. The user enters a username, and the network access server then contacts the TACACS+ daemon to obtain a password prompt. The network access server displays the password prompt to the user, the user enters a password, and the password is then sent to the TACACS+ daemon.

NOTES

TACACS+ allows an arbitrary conversation to be held between the daemon and the user until the daemon receives enough information to authenticate the user. This is usually done by prompting for a username and password combination but may include other items, such as mother's maiden name, all under the control of the TACACS+ daemon.

---

2. The network access server will eventually receive one of the following responses from the TACACS+ daemon:

    ○ ACCEPT—The user is authenticated, and service may begin. If the network access server is configured to requite authorization, authorization will begin at this time.

    ○ REJECT—The user has failed to authenticate. The user may be denied further access, or will be prompted to retry the login sequence depending on the TACACS+ daemon.

    ○ ERROR—An error occurred at some time during authentication. This can be either at the daemon or in the network connection between the daemon and the network access server. If an ERROR response is received, the network access server will typically try to use an alternative method for authenticating the user.

    ○ CONTINUE—The user is prompted for additional authentication information.

3. A PAP login is similar to an ASCII login, except that the username and password arrive at the network access server in a PAP protocol packet instead of being typed in by the user, so the user is not prompted. PPP CHAP logins are also similar in principle.

Following authentication, the user will also be required to undergo an additional authorization phase, if authorization has been enabled on the network access server. Users must first successfully complete TACACS+ authentication before proceeding to TACACS+ authorization.

4. If TACACS+ authorization is required, the TACACS+ daemon is again contacted and it returns an ACCEPT or REJECT authorization response. If an ACCEPT response is returned, the response will contain data in the form of attributes that are used to direct the EXEC or NETWORK session for that user, determining services that the user can access.

   Services include the following:

   ○ Telnet, rlogin, Point-to-Point Protocol (PPP), Serial Line Internet Protocol (SLIP), or EXEC services

   ○ Connection parameters, including the host or client IP address, access list, and user timeouts

TACACS+ CONFIGURATION TASK LIST

To configure your router to support TACACS+, you must perform the following tasks:

- Use the **aaa new-model** global configuration command to enable AAA. AAA must be configured if you plan to use TACACS+. For more information about using the **aaa new-model** command, see Chapter 2, "AAA Overview."

- Use the **tacacs-server host** command to specify the IP address of one or more TACACS+ daemons. Use the **tacacs-server key** command to specify an encryption key that will be used to encrypt all exchanges between the network access server and the TACACS+ daemon. This same key must also be configured on the TACACS+ daemon.

- Use the **aaa authentication** global configuration command to define method lists that use TACACS+ for authentication. For more information about using the **aaa authentication** command, see Chapter 3, "Configuring Authentication."

- Use **line** and **interface** commands to apply the defined method lists to various interfaces. For more information, see Chapter 3.

- If needed, use the **aaa authorization** global command to configure authorization for the network access server. Unlike authentication, which can be configured per line or per interface, authorization is configured globally for the entire network access server. For more information about using the **aaa authorization** command, see Chapter 5, "Configuring Authorization."

- If needed, use the **aaa accounting** command to enable accounting for TACACS+ connections. For more information about using the **aaa accounting** command, see Chapter 7, "Configuring Accounting."

To configure TACACS+, perform the tasks in the upcoming sections:

- Identifying the TACACS+ Server Host
- Setting the TACACS+ Authentication Key
- Specifying TACACS+ Authentication
- Specifying TACACS+ Authorization
- Specifying TACACS+ Accounting

For TACACS+ configuration examples using the commands in this chapter, see section "TACACS+ Configuration Examples," located at the end of the this chapter.

IDENTIFYING THE TACACS+ SERVER HOST

The **tacacs-server host** command enables you to specify the names of the IP host or hosts maintaining a TACACS+ server. Because the TACACS+ software searches for the hosts in the order specified, this feature can be useful for setting up a list of preferred daemons.

To specify a TACACS+ host, perform the following tasks in global configuration mode:

Task	Command
Specify a TACACS+ host.	**tacacs-server host** *name* [**single-connection**] [**port** *integer*] [**timeout** *integer*] [**key** *string*]

Using the **tacacs-server host** command, you can also configure the following options:

- Use the **single-connection** keyword to specify single-connection (only valid with CiscoSecure Release 1.0.1 or later). Rather than have the router open and close a TCP connection to the daemon each time it must communicate, the single-connection option maintains a single open connection between the router and the daemon. This is more efficient because it allows the daemon to handle a higher number of TACACS operations.

NOTES

The daemon must support single-connection mode for this to be effective; otherwise, the connection between the network access server and the daemon will lock up or you will receive spurious errors.

- Use the **port** *integer* argument to specify the TCP port number to be used when making connections to the TACACS+ daemon. The default port number is 49.
- Use the **timeout** *integer* argument to specify the period of time (in seconds) the router will wait for a response from the daemon before it times out and declares an error.

──● **NOTES** ●──

Specifying the timeout value with the **tacacs-server host** command overrides the default timeout value set with the **tacacs-server timeout** command for this server only.

───

- Use the **key** *string* argument to specify an encryption key for encrypting and decrypting all traffic between the network access server and the TACACS+ daemon.

──● **NOTES** ●──

Specifying the encryption key with the **tacacs-server host** command overrides the default key set by the global configuration **tacacs-server key** command for this server only.

───

Because some of the parameters of the **tacacs-server host** command override global settings made by the **tacacs-server timeout** and **tacacs-server key** commands, you can use this command to enhance security on your network by uniquely configuring individual TACACS+ connections.

SETTING THE TACACS+ AUTHENTICATION KEY

To set the TACACS+ authentication key and encryption key, perform the following task in global configuration mode:

Task	Command
Set the encryption key to match that used on the TACACS+ daemon.	**tacacs-server key** *key*

──● **NOTES** ●──

You must configure the same key on the TACACS+ daemon for encryption to be successful.

───

SPECIFYING TACACS+ AUTHENTICATION

After you have identified the TACACS+ daemon and defined an associated TACACS+ encryption key, you need to define method lists for TACACS+ authentication. Because TACACS+ authentication is operated via AAA, you need to issue the **aaa authentication** command, specifying TACACS+ as the authentication method. For more information, see Chapter 3.

SPECIFYING TACACS+ AUTHORIZATION

AAA authorization enables you to set parameters that restrict a user's network access. Authorization via TACACS+ may be applied to commands, network connections, and EXEC sessions.

Because TACACS+ authorization is facilitated through AAA, you need to issue the **aaa authorization** command, specifying TACACS+ as the authorization method. For more information, see Chapter 5.

SPECIFYING TACACS+ ACCOUNTING

AAA accounting enables you to track the services users are accessing as well as the amount of network resources they are consuming. Because TACACS+ accounting is facilitated through AAA, you need to issue the **aaa accounting** command, specifying TACACS+ as the accounting method. For more information, see Chapter 7.

TACACS+ AV PAIRS

The network access server implements TACACS+ authorization and accounting functions by transmitting and receiving TACACS+ attribute-value (AV) pairs for each user session. For a list of supported TACACS+ AV pairs, see Appendix B, "TACACS+ Attribute-Value Pairs."

TACACS+ CONFIGURATION EXAMPLES

TACACS+ configuration examples in this section include the following:

- TACACS+ Authentication Examples
- TACACS+ Authorization Example
- TACACS+ Accounting Example
- TACACS+ Daemon Configuration Example

TACACS+ Authentication Examples

The following example configures TACACS+ as the security protocol to be used for PPP authentication.

```
aaa new-model
aaa authentication ppp test tacacs+ local
tacacs-server host 10.1.2.3
tacacs-server key goaway
interface serial 0
 ppp authentication chap pap test
```

In this example:

- The **aaa new-model** command enables the AAA security services.
- The **aaa authentication** command defines a method list, "test," to be used on serial interfaces running PPP. The keyword **tacacs+** means that authentication will be done through TACACS+. If TACACS+ returns an ERROR of some sort during authentication, the keyword **local** indicates that authentication will be attempted using the local database on the network access server.

- The **tacacs-server host** command identifies the TACACS+ daemon as having an IP address of 10.1.2.3. The **tacacs-server key** command defines the shared encryption key to be "goaway."

- The **interface** command selects the line, and the **ppp authentication** command applies the test method list to this line.

The following example configures TACACS+ as the security protocol to be used for PPP authentication, but instead of the method list "test," the method list "default" is used.

```
aaa new-model
aaa authentication ppp default if-needed tacacs+ local
tacacs-server host 10.1.2.3
tacacs-server key goaway
interface serial 0
 ppp authentication default
```

In this example:

- The **aaa new-model** command enables the AAA security services.

- The **aaa authentication** command defines a method list, "default," to be used on serial interfaces running PPP. The keyword **default** means that PPP authentication is applied by default to all interfaces. The **if-needed** keyword means that if the user has already authenticated by going through the ASCII login procedure, then PPP authentication is not necessary and can be skipped. If authentication is needed, the keyword **tacacs+** means that authentication will be done through TACACS+. If TACACS+ returns an ERROR of some sort during authentication, the keyword **local** indicates that authentication will be attempted using the local database on the network access server.

- The **tacacs-server host** command identifies the TACACS+ daemon as having an IP address of 10.1.2.3. The **tacacs-server key** command defines the shared encryption key to be "goaway."

- The **interface** command selects the line, and the **ppp authentication** command applies the default method list to this line.

The following example creates the same authentication algorithm for PAP but calls the method list "MIS-access" instead of "default":

```
aaa new-model
aaa authentication pap MIS-access if-needed tacacs+ local
tacacs-server host 10.1.2.3
tacacs-server key goaway
interface serial 0
 ppp authentication pap MIS-access
```

In this example:

- The **aaa new-model** command enables the AAA security services.

- The **aaa authentication** command defines a method list, "MIS-access," to be used on serial interfaces running PPP. The method list "MIS-access" means that PPP authentication is applied to all interfaces. The **if-needed** keyword means that if the user has already authenticated by going through the ASCII login procedure, then PPP authentication is not necessary and can be skipped. If authentication is needed, the keyword **tacacs+** means that authentication will be done through TACACS+. If TACACS+ returns an ERROR of some sort during authentication, the keyword **local** indicates that authentication will be attempted using the local database on the network access server.

- The **tacacs-server host** command identifies the TACACS+ daemon as having an IP address of 10.1.2.3. The **tacacs-server key** command defines the shared encryption key to be "goaway."

- The **interface** command selects the line, and the **ppp authentication** command applies the default method list to this line.

The following example shows the configuration for a TACACS+ daemon with an IP address of 10.2.3.4 and an encryption key of "apple."

```
aaa new-model
aaa authentication login default tacacs+ local
tacacs-server host 10.2.3.4
tacacs-server key apple
```

In this example:

- The **aaa new-model** command enables the AAA security services.

- The **aaa authentication** command defines the default method method list. Incoming ASCII logins on all interfaces (by default) will use TACACS+ for authentication. If no TACACS+ server responds, then the network access server will use the information contained in the local username database for authentication.

- The **tacacs-server host** command identifies the TACACS+ daemon as having an IP address of 10.2.3.4. The **tacacs-server key** command defines the shared encryption key to be "apple."

TACACS+ Authorization Example

The following example configures TACACS+ as the security protocol to be used for PPP authentication using the default method list, and configures network authorization via TACACS+.

```
aaa new-model
aaa authentication ppp default if-needed tacacs+ local
aaa authorization network tacacs+
tacacs-server host 10.1.2.3
tacacs-server key goaway
interface serial 0
 ppp authentication default
```

In this example:

- The **aaa new-model** command enables the AAA security services.

- The **aaa authentication** command defines a method list, "default," to be used on serial interfaces running PPP. The keyword **default** means that PPP authentication is applied by default to all interfaces. The **if-needed** keyword means that if the user has already authenticated by going through the ASCII login procedure, then PPP authentication is not necessary and can be skipped. If authentication is needed, the keyword **tacacs+** means that authentication will be done through TACACS+. If TACACS+ returns an ERROR of some sort during authentication, the keyword **local** indicates that authentication will be attempted using the local database on the network access server.

- The **aaa authorization** command configures network authorization via TACACS+. Unlike authentication lists, this authorization list always applies to all incoming network connections made to the network access server.

- The **tacacs-server host** command identifies the TACACS+ daemon as having an IP address of 10.1.2.3. The **tacacs-server key** command defines the shared encryption key to be "goaway."

- The **interface** command selects the line, and the **ppp authentication** command applies the default method list to this line.

TACACS+ Accounting Example

The following example configures TACACS+ as the security protocol to be used for PPP authentication using the default method list, and configures accounting via TACACS+.

```
aaa new-model
aaa authentication ppp default if-needed tacacs+ local
aaa accounting network stop-only tacacs+
tacacs-server host 10.1.2.3
tacacs-server key goaway
interface serial 0
 ppp authentication default
```

In this example:

- The **aaa new-model** command enables the AAA security services.

- The **aaa authentication** command defines a method list, "default," to be used on serial interfaces running PPP. The keyword **default** means that PPP authentication is applied by default to all interfaces. The **if-needed** keyword means that if the user has already authenticated by going through the ASCII login procedure, then PPP authentication is not necessary and can be skipped. If authentication is needed, the keyword **tacacs+** means that authentication will be done through TACACS+. If TACACS+ returns an ERROR of some sort during authentication, the keyword **local** indicates that authentication will be attempted using the local database on the network access server.

- The **aaa accounting** command configures network accounting via TACACS+. In this example, accounting records describing the session that just terminated will be sent to the TACACS+ daemon whenever a network connection terminates.

- The **tacacs-server host** command identifies the TACACS+ daemon as having an IP address of 10.1.2.3. The **tacacs-server key** command defines the shared encryption key to be "goaway."

- The **interface** command selects the line, and the **ppp authentication** command applies the default method list to this line.

TACACS+ Daemon Configuration Example

The following example shows a sample configuration of the TACACS+ daemon. The precise syntax used by your TACACS+ daemon may be different than that included in this example.

```
user = mci_customer1 {
    chap = cleartext "some chap password"
    service = ppp protocol = ip {
  inacl#1="permit ip any any precedence immediate"
  inacl#2="deny igrp 0.0.1.2 255.255.0.0 any"
    }
}
```

## CHAPTER 12

Configuring TACACS and Extended TACACS

The Terminal Access Controller Access Control System (TACACS) provides a way to centrally validate users attempting to gain access to a router or access server. Basic Cisco TACACS support is modeled after the original Defense Data Network (DDN) application. TACACS services are maintained in a database on a TACACS server running, typically, on a UNIX workstation. You must have access to and must configure a TACACS server before configuring the TACACS features on your Cisco router.

Cisco implements TACACS in the Cisco IOS software to allow centralized control over access to routers and access servers. Authentication can also be provided for Cisco IOS administration tasks on the router and access server user interfaces. With TACACS enabled, the router or access server prompts for a username and password, then verifies the password with a TACACS server.

This chapter describes the TACACS and Extended TACACS protocols and the various ways you can use them to secure access to your network.

NOTES

Both TACACS and Extended TACACS are now deprecated by Cisco.

For a complete description of the authorization commands used in this chapter, see Chapter 13, "TACACS, Extended TACACS, and TACACS+ Commands."

TACACS PROTOCOL DESCRIPTION

Cisco IOS software currently supports three versions of the Terminal Access Controller Access Control System (TACACS) security protocol, each one of which is a separate and unique protocol:

- TACACS+—A recent protocol providing detailed accounting information and flexible administrative control over authentication and authorization processes. TACACS+ is facilitated through AAA and can be enabled only through AAA commands. A draft RFC details this protocol.

- TACACS—An older access protocol, incompatible with the newer TACACS+ protocol, that is now deprecated by Cisco. It provides password checking and authentication, and notification of user actions for security and accounting purposes.

- Extended TACACS—An extension to the older TACACS protocol, supplying additional functionality to TACACS. Extended TACACS provides information about protocol translator and router use. This information is used in UNIX auditing trails and accounting files. Extended TACACS is incompatible with TACACS+ and is also deprecated.

This chapter discusses how to enable and configure TACACS and Extended TACACS. For information about TACACS+, see Chapter 11, "Configuring TACACS+."

Table 12–1 identifies Cisco IOS commands available to the different versions of TACACS.

Table 12–1   *TACACS Command Comparison*

Cisco IOS Command	TACACS	Extended TACACS	TACACS+
aaa accounting	–	–	Yes
aaa authentication arap	–	–	Yes
aaa authentication enable default	–	–	Yes
aaa authentication login	–	–	Yes
aaa authentication local override	–	–	Yes
aaa authentication ppp	–	–	Yes
aaa authorization	–	–	Yes
aaa new-model	–	–	Yes
arap authentication	–	–	Yes
arap use-tacacs	Yes	Yes	–
enable last-resort	Yes	Yes	–
enable use-tacacs	Yes	Yes	–
ip tacacs source-interface	Yes	Yes	Yes
login authentication	–	–	Yes
login tacacs	Yes	Yes	–
ppp authentication	Yes	Yes	Yes
ppp use-tacacs	Yes	Yes	Yes
tacacs-server attempts	Yes	–	–
tacacs-server authenticate	Yes	Yes	–

Table 12–1 *TACACS Command Comparison, Continued*

Cisco IOS Command	TACACS	Extended TACACS	TACACS+
tacacs-server directed-request	Yes	Yes	Yes
tacacs-server extended	–	Yes	–
tacacs-server host	Yes	Yes	Yes
tacacs-server key	–	–	Yes
tacacs-server last-resort	Yes	Yes	–
tacacs-server notify	Yes	Yes	–
tacacs-server optional-passwords	Yes	Yes	–
tacacs-server retransmit	Yes	Yes	–
tacacs-server timeout	Yes	Yes	Yes

TACACS AND EXTENDED TACACS CONFIGURATION TASK LIST

You can establish TACACS-style password protection on both user and privileged levels of the system EXEC.

The following sections describe the features available with TACACS and extended TACACS. The extended TACACS software is available using the File Transfer Protocol (FTP).

NOTES

TACACS and Extended TACACS commands cannot be used after you have initialized AAA. To identify which commands can be used with the three versions, refer to Table 12–1 previously in this chapter.

- Setting TACACS Password Protection at the User Level
- Disabling Password Checking at the User Level
- Setting Optional Password Verification
- Setting TACACS Password Protection at the Privileged Level
- Disabling Password Checking at the Privileged Level
- Setting Notification of User Actions
- Setting Authentication of User Actions
- Establishing the TACACS Server Host
- Setting Limits on Login Attempts
- Specifying the Amount of Time for Login Input
- Enabling the Extended TACACS Mode

- Enabling TACACS for PPP Authentication
- Enabling Standard TACACS for ARA Authentication
- Enabling Extended TACACS for ARA Authentication
- Enabling TACACS to Use a Specific IP Address

For TACACS configuration examples, see section "TACACS Configuration Examples," located at the end of the this chapter.

SETTING TACACS PASSWORD PROTECTION AT THE USER LEVEL

To enable password checking at login, perform the following task in line configuration mode:

Task	Command
Set the TACACS-style user ID and password-checking mechanism.	login tacacs

DISABLING PASSWORD CHECKING AT THE USER LEVEL

If a TACACS server does not respond to a login request, the Cisco IOS software denies the request by default. However, you can prevent that login failure in one of the following two ways:

- Allow a user to access privileged EXEC mode if that user enters the password set by the **enable** command.
- Allow the user to access the privileged EXEC mode without further question.

To specify one of these features, perform either of the following tasks in global configuration mode:

Task	Command
Allow a user to access privileged EXEC mode.	tacacs-server last-resort password
Set last resort options for logins.	tacacs-server last-resort succeed

SETTING OPTIONAL PASSWORD VERIFICATION

You can specify that the first TACACS request to a TACACS server is made without password verification. To do so, perform the following task in global configuration mode:

Task	Command
Set TACACS password as optional.	tacacs-server optional-passwords

When the user enters the login name, the login request is transmitted with the name and a zero-length password. If accepted, the login procedure is completed. If the TACACS server refuses this request, the terminal server prompts for a password and tries again when the user supplies a password. The TACACS server must support authentication for users without passwords to make use of this feature. This feature supports all TACACS requests such as login, SLIP, and enable.

SETTING TACACS PASSWORD PROTECTION AT THE PRIVILEGED LEVEL

You can set the TACACS protocol to determine whether a user can access the privileged EXEC level. To do so, perform the following task in global configuration mode:

Task	Command
Set the TACACS-style user ID and password-checking mechanism at the privileged EXEC level.	enable use-tacacs

When you set TACACS password protection at the privileged EXEC level, the EXEC **enable** command will ask for both a new username and a password. This information is then passed to the TACACS server for authentication. If you are using the extended TACACS, it also passes any existing UNIX user identification code to the server.

CAUTION

If you use the **enable use-tacacs** command, you must also specify **tacacs-server authenticate enable**; otherwise, you will be locked out.

NOTES

When used without extended TACACS, this task allows anyone with a valid username and password to access the privileged command level, creating a potential security problem. This is because the TACACS query resulting from entering the **enable** command is indistinguishable from an attempt to log in without extended TACACS.

DISABLING PASSWORD CHECKING AT THE PRIVILEGED LEVEL

You can specify a last resort if the TACACS servers used by the **enable** command do not respond. To invoke this "last resort" login feature, perform either of the following tasks in global configuration mode:

Task	Command
Allow user to enable by asking for the privileged EXEC-level password.	**enable last-resort password**
Allow user to enable without further questions.	**enable last-resort succeed**

SETTING NOTIFICATION OF USER ACTIONS

The **tacacs-server notify** command allows you to configure the TACACS server to send a message when a user does the following:

- Makes a TCP connection
- Enters the **enable** command
- Logs out

To specify that the TACACS server send notification, perform the following task in global configuration mode:

Task	Command
Set server notification of user actions.	**tacacs-server notify {connection [always] | enable | logout [always] | slip [always]}**

The retransmission of the message is performed by a background process for up to five minutes. The terminal user, however, receives an immediate response, allowing access to the terminal.

The **tacacs-server notify** command is available only if you have set up an extended TACACS server using the latest Cisco extended TACACS server software, available via FTP.

SETTING AUTHENTICATION OF USER ACTIONS

For a SLIP or PPP session, you can specify that if a user tries to start a session, the TACACS software requires a response (either from the TACACS server host or the router) indicating whether the user can start the session. You can specify that the TACACS software perform authentication even when a user is not logged in; you can also request that the TACACS software install access lists.

If a user issues the **enable** command, the TACACS software must respond indicating whether the user can give the command. You can also specify authentication when a user enters the **enable** command.

To configure any of these scenarios, perform the following task in global configuration mode:

Task	Command
Set server authentication of user actions.	**tacacs-server authenticate** {**connection**[**always**] **enable**	**slip** [**always**] [**access-lists**]}

The **tacacs-server authenticate** command is available only when you have set up an extended TACACS server using the latest Cisco extended TACACS server software, which is available via FTP.

ESTABLISHING THE TACACS SERVER HOST

The **tacacs-server host** command allows you to specify the names of the IP host or hosts maintaining a TACACS server. Because the TACACS software searches for the hosts in the order specified, this feature can be useful for setting up a list of preferred servers.

With TACACS and extended TACACS, the **tacacs-server retransmit** command allows you to modify the number of times the system software searches the list of TACACS servers (from the default of two times) and the interval it waits for a reply (from the default of five seconds).

To define the number of times the Cisco IOS software searches the list of servers, and how long the server waits for a reply, perform the following tasks as needed for your system configuration in global configuration mode:

Task	Command
Specify a TACACS host.	**tacacs-server host** *name*
Specify the number of times the server will search the list of TACACS and extended TACACS server hosts before giving up.	**tacacs-server retransmit** *retries*
Set the interval the server waits for a TACACS and extended TACACS server host to reply.	**tacacs-server timeout** *seconds*

SETTING LIMITS ON LOGIN ATTEMPTS

The **tacacs-server attempts** command allows you to specify the number of login attempts that can be made on a line set up for TACACS. Perform the following task in global configuration mode to limit login attempts:

Task	Command
Control the number of login attempts that can be made on a line set for TACACS verification.	tacacs-server attempts *count*

SPECIFYING THE AMOUNT OF TIME FOR LOGIN INPUT

The **tacacs-server login-timeout** command allows you to specify how long the system will wait for login input (such as username and password) before timing out. The default login value is 30 seconds; with the **tacacs-server login-timeout** command, you can specify a timeout value from 1 to 300 seconds. Perform the following task in global configuration mode to change the login timeout value from the default of 30 seconds:

Task	Command
Specify how long the system will wait for login information before timing out.	tacacs-server login-timeout *seconds*

ENABLING THE EXTENDED TACACS MODE

While standard TACACS provides only username and password information, extended TACACS mode provides information about the terminal requests to help set up UNIX auditing trails and accounting files for tracking the use of protocol translators, access servers, and routers. The information includes responses from these network devices and validation of user requests.

An unsupported, extended TACACS server is available via FTP for UNIX users who want to create the auditing programs.

To enable extended TACACS mode, perform the following task in global configuration mode:

Task	Command
Enable an extended TACACS mode.	tacacs-server extended

ENABLING TACACS FOR PPP AUTHENTICATION

You can use extended TACACS for authentication within PPP sessions. To do so, perform the following steps in interface configuration mode:

Task	Command
Step 1 Enable CHAP or PAP.	ppp authentication {chap | chap pap | pap chap | pap} [if-needed] [*list-name* | default] [callin]

Task	Command
Step 2 Enable TACACS under PPP.	**ppp use-tacacs [single-line]**

For an example of enabling TACACS for PPP protocol authentication, see section "TACACS Configuration Examples," located at the end of this chapter.

ENABLING STANDARD TACACS FOR ARA AUTHENTICATION

You can use the Standard TACACS protocol for authentication within AppleTalk Remote Access (ARA) protocol sessions. To do so, perform the following tasks starting in line configuration mode:

Task	Command
Enable standard TACACS under the ARA protocol.	**arap use-tacacs single-line**
Enable autoselection of ARA.	**autoselect arap**
(Optional) Have the ARA session start automatically at user login.	**autoselect during-login**

The **arap use-tacacs single-line** command is useful when integrating TACACS with other authentication systems that require a cleartext version of the user's password. Such systems include one-time passwords, token card systems, and others.

By using the optional **during-login** argument with the **autoselect** command, you can display the username or password prompt without pressing the **Return** key. While the username or password name is displayed, you can choose to answer these prompts or to start sending packets from an autoselected protocol.

The remote user logs in through ARA as follows:

Step 1   When prompted for a username by the ARA application, the remote user enters *username*password* and presses **Return**.

Step 2   When prompted for password by the ARA application, the remote user enters **arap** and presses **Return**.

For examples of enabling TACACS for ARA protocol authentication, see section "TACACS Configuration Examples," located at the end of this chapter.

ENABLING EXTENDED TACACS FOR ARA AUTHENTICATION

You can use extended TACACS for authentication within AppleTalk Remote Access (ARA) protocol sessions. The extended TACACS server software is available via FTP.

NOTES

Before entering the commands listed in the following task table, you must edit the file called "Makefile" in the extended TACACS server software to use ARA. To do this, you must uncomment the lines that enable ARA support and recompile the file.

After installing an extended TACACS server with ARA support, perform the following tasks in line configuration mode on each line:

Task	Command
Enable extended TACACS under the ARA protocol on each line.	**arap use-tacacs**
(Optional) Enable autoselection of ARA.	**autoselect arap**
(Optional) Have the ARA session start automatically at user login.	**autoselect during-login**

By using the optional **during-login** argument with the **autoselect** command, you can display the username or password prompt without pressing the Return key. While the Username or Password name is being presented, you can choose to answer these prompts, or to start sending packets from an autoselected protocol.

ENABLING TACACS TO USE A SPECIFIC IP ADDRESS

You can designate a fixed source IP address for all outgoing TACACS packets. The feature enables TACACS to use the IP address of a specified interface for all outgoing TACACS packets. This is especially useful if the router has many interfaces, and you want to make sure that all TACACS packets from a particular router have the same IP address.

To enable TACACS to use the address of a specified interface for all outgoing TACACS packets, perform the following task in configuration mode:

Task	Command
Enable TACACS to use the IP address of a specified interface for all outgoing TACACS packets.	**ip tacacs source-interface** *subinterface-name*

TACACS CONFIGURATION EXAMPLES

The following example shows TACACS enabled for PPP authentication:

```
int async 1
  ppp authentication chap
  ppp use-tacacs
```

The following example shows TACACS enabled for ARAP authentication:

```
line 3
 arap use-tacacs
```

The following example shows a complete TACACS configuration for the Cisco AS5200 using Cisco IOS Release 11.1:

```
version 11.1
service udp-small-servers
service tcp-small-servers
!
hostname isdn-14
!
enable password ww
!
username cisco password lab
isdn switch-type primary-5ess
!
controller T1 1
 framing esf
 clock source line primary
 linecode b8zs
 pri-group timeslots 1-24
!
interface Loopback20
 no ip address
!
interface Ethernet0
 ip address 172.16.25.15 255.255.255.224
!
interface Serial0
 no ip address
 shutdown
!
interface Serial1
 no ip address
 shutdown
 no cdp enable
!
interface Serial1:23
 ip address 150.150.150.2 255.255.255.0
 no ip mroute-cache
 encapsulation ppp
 isdn incoming-voice modem
 no peer default ip address pool
 dialer idle-timeout 1
 dialer map ip 150.150.150.1 name isdn-5 broadcast 1234
 dialer-group 1
 no fair-queue
 ppp multilink
 ppp authentication pap
 ppp pap sent-username isdn-14 password 7 05080F1C2243
```

```
!
interface Group-Async1
 ip unnumbered Ethernet0
 encapsulation ppp
 async mode interactive
 peer default ip address pool default
 no cdp enable
 ppp authentication chap
 ppp use-tacacs
 group-range 1 24
!
ip local pool default 171.68.187.1 171.68.187.8
no ip classless
ip route 0.0.0.0 0.0.0.0 172.16.25.1
ip route 192.100.0.12 255.255.255.255 Serial1:23
tacacs-server host 171.68.186.35
tacacs-server last-resort succeed
tacacs-server extended
tacacs-server authenticate slip access-lists
tacacs-server notify connections always
tacacs-server notify logout always
tacacs-server notify slip always
!
dialer-list 1 protocol ip permit
!
line con 0
line 1 24
 session-timeout 30  output
 exec-timeout 1 0
 no activation-character
 autoselect during-login
 autoselect ppp
 no vacant-message
 modem InOut
 modem autoconfigure type microcom_hdms
 transport input all
 speed 115200
line aux 0
line vty 0 4
 password ww
 login
end
```

13

TACACS, Extended TACACS, and TACACS+ Commands

This chapter describes the commands used to configure TACACS, Extended TACACS, and TACACS+.

TACACS Command Comparison

There are currently three versions of the TACACS security protocol, each a separate entity. The Cisco IOS software supports the following versions of TACACS:

- TACACS+—Provides detailed accounting information and flexible administrative control over authentication and authorization processes. TACACS+ is facilitated through AAA and can be enabled only through AAA commands.

- Extended TACACS—Provides information about protocol translator and router use. This information is used in UNIX auditing trails and accounting files.

- TACACS—Provides password checking and authentication, and notification of user actions for security and accounting purposes.

Although TACACS+ is enabled through AAA and uses commands specific to AAA, there are some commands that are common to TACACS, Extended TACACS, and TACACS+. Table 13–1 identifies Cisco IOS commands available to the different versions of TACACS.

Table 13–1 *TACACS Command Comparison*

Cisco IOS Command	TACACS	Extended TACACS	TACACS+
aaa accounting	–	–	Yes
aaa authentication arap	–	–	Yes
aaa authentication enable default	–	–	Yes
aaa authentication login	–	–	Yes

Table 13–1   *TACACS Command Comparison, Continued*

Cisco IOS Command	TACACS	Extended TACACS	TACACS+
aaa authentication local override	–	–	Yes
aaa authentication ppp	–	–	Yes
aaa authorization	–	–	Yes
aaa new-model	–	–	Yes
arap authentication	–	–	Yes
arap use-tacacs	Yes	Yes	–
enable last-resort	Yes	Yes	–
enable use-tacacs	Yes	Yes	–
ip tacacs source-interface	Yes	Yes	Yes
login authentication	–	–	Yes
login tacacs	Yes	Yes	–
ppp authentication	Yes	Yes	Yes
ppp use-tacacs	Yes	Yes	Yes
tacacs-server attempts	Yes	–	–
tacacs-server authenticate	Yes	Yes	–
tacacs-server directed-request	Yes	Yes	Yes
tacacs-server extended	–	Yes	–
tacacs-server host	Yes	Yes	Yes
tacacs-server key	–	–	Yes
tacacs-server last-resort	Yes	Yes	–
tacacs-server notify	Yes	Yes	–
tacacs-server optional-passwords	Yes	Yes	–
tacacs-server retransmit	Yes	Yes	–
tacacs-server timeout	Yes	Yes	–

For information on how to configure TACACS or Extended TACACS, see Chapter 12, "Configuring TACACS and Extended TACACS." For configuration examples using the commands in this chapter, see section "TACACS Configuration Examples," located at the end of Chapter 12.

For information on how to configure TACACS+, see Chapter 11, "Configuring TACACS+." For configuration examples using the commands in this chapter, see section "TACACS+ Configuration Examples," located at the end of Chapter 11.

ARAP USE-TACACS

To enable TACACS for ARAP authentication, use the **arap use-tacacs** line configuration command. Use the **no** form of this command to disable TACACS for ARAP authentication.

> **arap use-tacacs** [single-line]
> **no arap use-tacacs**

Syntax Description

single-line   (Optional) Accepts the username and password in the username field. If you are using an older version of TACACS (before Extended TACACS), you must use this keyword.

Default

Disabled

Command Mode

Line configuration

Usage Guidelines

Use this command only when you have set up an extended TACACS server. This command requires the new Extended TACACS server.

NOTES

This command cannot be used with TACACS+. Use the **arap authentication** command instead.

The command specifies that if a username and password are specified in the username, separated by an asterisk (*), than a standard TACACS login query is performed using that username and password. If the username does not contain an asterisk, then normal ARAP authentication is performed using TACACS.

This feature is useful when integrating TACACS with other authentication systems that require a cleartext version of the user's password. Such systems include one-time passwords, token card systems, and others.

Normal ARAP authentications prevent the cleartext password from being transmitted over the link. When you use the single-line keyword, passwords cross the link in the clear, exposing them to anyone looking for such information.

Due to the two-way nature of the ARAP authentication, the ARA application requires that a password value be entered in the Password field in the ARA dialog box. This secondary password must be "arap." First enter the username and password in the form *username*password* in the Name field of the dialog box, then enter **arap** in the Password field.

Example

The following example enables TACACS for ARAP authentication:

```
line 3
  arap use-tacacs
```

Related Commands

Search online to find documentation for related commands.

arap enable
arap noguest
autoselect
tacacs-server extended
tacacs-server host

ENABLE LAST-RESORT

To specify what happens if the TACACS and Extended TACACS servers used by the enable command do not respond, use the **enable last-resort** global configuration command. Use the **no** form of this command to restore the default.

```
      enable last-resort {password | succeed}
      no enable last-resort {password | succeed}
```

Syntax Description

password   Allows you to enter enable mode by entering the privileged command level password. A password must contain from 1 to 25 uppercase and lowercase alphanumeric characters.

succeed   Allows you to enter enable mode without further question.

Default

Access to enable mode is denied.

Command Mode

Global configuration

Usage Guidelines

This secondary authentication is used only if the first attempt fails.

NOTES

This command is not used with TACACS+, which uses the **aaa authentication** suite of commands instead.

Example

In the following example, if the TACACS servers do not respond to the enable command, the user can enable by entering the privileged level password:

```
enable last-resort password
```

Related Commands

Search online to find documentation for related commands.

enable

ENABLE USE-TACACS

To enable the use of TACACS to determine whether a user can access the privileged command level, use the **enable use-tacacs** global configuration command. Use the **no** form of this command to disable TACACS verification.

enable use-tacacs
no enable use-tacacs

CAUTION

If you use the **enable use-tacacs** command, you must also use the **tacacs-server authenticate enable** command or you will be locked out of the privileged command level.

Syntax Description

This command has no arguments or keywords.

Default

Disabled

Command Mode

Global configuration

Part II

Command Reference

Usage Guidelines

When you add this command to the configuration file, the EXEC enable command prompts for a new username and password pair. This pair is then passed to the TACACS server for authentication. If you are using Extended TACACS, it also passes any existing UNIX user identification code to the server.

NOTES

This command initializes TACACS. Use the **tacacs server-extended** command to initialize Extended TACACS, or use the **aaa new-model** command to initialize AAA and TACACS+.

Example

The following example sets TACACS verification on the privileged EXEC-level login sequence:

```
enable use-tacacs
tacacs-server authenticate enable
```

Related Commands

Search online to find documentation for related commands.

tacacs-server authenticate enable

IP TACACS SOURCE-INTERFACE

To use the IP address of a specified interface for all outgoing TACACS packets, use the **ip tacacs source-interface** global configuration command. Use the **no** form of this command to disable use of the specified interface IP address.

> **ip tacacs source-interface** *subinterface-name*
> **no ip tacacs source-interface**

Syntax Description

subinterface-name   Name of the interface that TACACS uses for all of its outgoing packets.

Default

This command has no factory-assigned default.

Command Mode

Global configuration

Usage Guidelines

Use this command to set a subinterface's IP address for all outgoing TACACS packets. This address is used as long as the interface is in the *up* state. In this way, the TACACS server can use one IP address entry associated with the network access client instead of maintaining a list of all IP addresses.

This command is especially useful in cases where the router has many interfaces and you want to ensure that all TACACS packets from a particular router have the same IP address.

The specified interface must have an IP address associated with it. If the specified subinterface does not have an IP address or is in a *down* state, TACACS reverts to the default. To avoid this, add an IP address to the subinterface or bring the interface to the *up* state.

Example

The following example makes TACACS use the IP address of subinterface s2 for all outgoing TACACS (TACACS, Extended TACACS, or TACACS+) packets:

```
ip tacacs source-interface s2
```

Related Commands

Search online to find documentation for related commands.

ip radius source-interface
ip telnet source-interface
ip tftp source-interface

TACACS-SERVER ATTEMPTS

To control the number of login attempts that can be made on a line set up for TACACS verification, use the **tacacs-server attempts** global configuration command. Use the **no** form of this command to remove this feature and restore the default.

> **tacacs-server attempts** *count*
> **no tacacs-server attempts**

Syntax Description

count   Integer that sets the number of attempts. The default is 3 attempts.

Default

Three attempts

Command Mode

Global configuration

Example

The following example changes the login attempt to just one try:

```
tacacs-server attempts 1
```

Part
II

Command Reference

TACACS-SERVER AUTHENTICATE

To configure the Cisco IOS software to indicate whether a user can perform an attempted action under TACACS and Extended TACACS, use the **tacacs-server authenticate** global configuration command. Use the **no** form of this command to disable this feature.

> **tacacs-server authenticate** {connection [always] enable | slip [always] [access-lists]}
> **no tacacs-server authenticate**

Syntax Description

connection   Configures a required response when a user makes a TCP connection.

enable   Configures a required response when a user enters the **enable** command.

slip   Configures a required response when a user starts a SLIP or PPP session.

always   (Optional) Performs authentication even when a user is not logged in. This option only applies to the **slip** keyword.

access-lists   (Optional) Requests and installs access lists. This option only applies to the **slip** keyword.

Default

Disabled

Command Mode

Global configuration

Usage Guidelines

The **tacacs-server authenticate** [connection | enable] command first appeared in Cisco IOS Release 10.0. The **tacacs-server authenticate** {connection [always] enable | slip [always] [access-lists]} command first appeared in Cisco IOS Release 10.3.

Enter one of the keywords to specify the action (when a user enters enable mode, for example).

Before you use the **tacacs-server authenticate** command, you must enable the **tacacs-server extended** command.

NOTES

This command is not used in TACACS+. It has been replaced by the **aaa authorization** command.

Example

The following example configures TACACS logins that authenticate users to use Telnet or rlogin:

```
tacacs-server authenticate connect
```

Related Commands

Search online to find documentation for related commands.

enable secret
enable use-tacacs

TACACS-SERVER DIRECTED-REQUEST

To send only a username to a specified server when a direct request is issued, use the **tacacs-server directed-request** global configuration command. Use the **no** form of this command to disable the direct-request feature.

> **tacacs-server directed-request**
> **no tacacs-server directed-request**

Syntax Description

This command has no arguments or keywords.

Default

Enabled

Command Mode

Global configuration

Usage Guidelines

This command first appeared in Cisco IOS Release 11.1.

This command sends only the portion of the username before the "@" symbol to the host specified after the "@" symbol. In other words, with the directed-request feature enabled, you can direct a request to any of the configured servers, and only the username is sent to the specified server.

Disabling **tacacs-server directed-request** causes the whole string, both before and after the "@" symbol, to be sent to the default TACACS server. When the directed-request feature is disabled, the router queries the list of servers, starting with the first one in the list, sending the whole string, and accepting the first response that it gets from the server. The **tacacs-server directed-request** command is useful for sites that have developed their own TACACS server software that parses the whole string and makes decisions based on it.

Part II

Command Reference

With **tacacs-server directed-request** enabled, only configured TACACS servers can be specified by the user after the "@" symbol. If the host name specified by the user does not match the IP address of a TACACS server configured by the administrator, the user input is rejected.

Use **no tacacs-server directed-request** to disable the ability of the user to choose between configured TACACS servers and to cause the entire string to be passed to the default server.

Example

The following example enables **tacacs-server directed-request** so that the entire user input is passed to the default TACACS server:

```
no tacacs-server directed-request
```

TACACS-SERVER EXTENDED

To enable an Extended TACACS mode, use the **tacacs-server extended** global configuration command. Use the **no** form of this command to disable the mode.

> **tacacs-server extended**
> **no tacacs-server extended**

Syntax Description

This command has no arguments or keywords.

Default

Disabled

Command Mode

Global configuration

Usage Guidelines

This command first appeared in Cisco IOS Release 10.0.

This command initializes Extended TACACS.

Example

The following example enables Extended TACACS mode:

```
tacacs-server extended
```

Related Commands

Search online to find documentation for related commands.

aaa new-model

TACACS-SERVER HOST

To specify a TACACS host, use the **tacacs-server host** global configuration command. Use the **no** form of this command to delete the specified name or address.

> **tacacs-server host** *hostname* [**single-connection**] [**port** *integer*] [**timeout** *integer*] [**key** *string*]
> **no tacacs-server host** *hostname*

Syntax Description

hostname	Name or IP address of the host.
single-connection	(Optional) Specify that the router maintain a single open connection for confirmation from a AAA/TACACS+ server (CiscoSecure Release 1.0.1 or later). This command contains no autodetect and fails if the specified host is not running a CiscoSecure daemon.
port	(Optional) Specify a server port number. This option overrides the default, which is port 49.
integer	(Optional) Port number of the server. Valid port numbers range from 1 to 65535.
timeout	(Optional) Specify a timeout value. This overrides the global timeout value set with the **tacacs-server timeout** command for this server only.
integer	(Optional) Integer value, in seconds, of the timeout interval.
key	(Optional) Specify an authentication and encryption key. This must match the key used by the TACACS+ daemon. Specifying this key overrides the key set by the global command **tacacs-server key** for this server only.
string	(Optional) Character string specifying authentication and encryption key.

Default

No TACACS host is specified.

Command Mode

Global configuration

Usage Guidelines

This command first appeared in Cisco IOS Release 10.0.

You can use multiple **tacacs-server host** commands to specify additional hosts. The Cisco IOS software searches for hosts in the order in which you specify them. Use the **single-connection, port, timeout,** and **key** options only when running a AAA/TACACS+ server.

Because some of the parameters of the **tacacs-server host** command override global settings made by the **tacacs-server timeout** and **tacacs-server key** commands, you can use this command to enhance security on your network by uniquely configuring individual routers.

Examples

The following example specifies a TACACS host named Sea_Change:

```
tacacs-server host Sea_Change
```

The following example specifies that, for AAA confirmation, the router consult the CiscoSecure TACACS+ host named Sea_Cure on port number 51. The timeout value for requests on this connection is three seconds; the encryption key is a_secret.

```
tacacs-server host Sea_Cure single-connection port 51 timeout 3 key a_secret
```

Related Commands

Search online to find documentation for related commands.

login tacacs
PPP
slip
tacacs-server key
tacacs-server timeout

TACACS-SERVER KEY

To set the authentication encryption key used for all TACACS+ communications between the access server and the TACACS+ daemon, use the **tacacs-server key** global configuration command. Use the **no** form of this command to disable the key.

> **tacacs-server key** *key*
> **no tacacs-server key** [*key*]

Syntax Description

key   Key used to set authentication and encryption. This key must match the key used on the TACACS+ daemon.

Command Mode

Global configuration

Usage Guidelines

This command first appeared in Cisco IOS Release 11.1.

After enabling AAA with the **aaa new-model** command, you must set the authentication and encryption key using the **tacacs-server key** command.

The key entered must match the key used on the TACACS+ daemon. All leading spaces are ignored; spaces within and at the end of the key are not. If you use spaces in your key, do not enclose the key in quotation marks unless the quotation marks themselves are part of the key.

Example

The following example sets the authentication and encryption key to "dare to go":

```
tacacs-server key dare to go
```

Related Commands

Search online to find documentation for related commands.

aaa new-model
tacacs-server host

TACACS-SERVER LAST-RESORT

To cause the network access server to request the privileged password as verification, or to allow successful login without further input from the user, use the **tacacs-server last-resort** global configuration command. Use the **no** form of this command to restore the system to the default behavior.

```
tacacs-server last-resort {password | succeed}
no tacacs-server last-resort {password | succeed}
```

Syntax Description

password   Allows the user to access the EXEC command mode by entering the password set by the **enable** command.

succeed   Allows the user to access the EXEC command mode without further question.

Default

If, when running the TACACS server, the TACACS server does not respond, the default action is to deny the request.

Command Mode

Global configuration

Usage Guidelines

This command first appeared in Cisco IOS Release 10.0.

Use the **tacacs-server last-resort** command to be sure that login can occur; for example, when a systems administrator needs to log in to troubleshoot TACACS servers that might be down.

NOTES

This command is not used in TACACS+.

Example

The following example forces successful login:

```
tacacs-server last-resort succeed
```

Related Commands

Search online to find documentation for related commands.

enable password
login (EXEC)

TACACS-SERVER LOGIN-TIMEOUT

To specify how long the system will wait for login input (such as username and password) before timing out, use the **tacacs-server login-timeout** global configuration command. Use the **no** form of this command to restore the default value of 30 seconds.

> **tacacs-server login-timeout** *seconds*
> **no tacacs-server login-timeout** *seconds*

Syntax Description

seconds   Integer that determines the number of seconds the system will wait for login input before timing out. Available settings are from 1 to 300 seconds.

Default

The default login timeout value is 30 seconds.

Command Mode

Global configuration

Usage Guidelines

With **aaa new-model** enabled, the default login timeout value is 30 seconds. The **tacacs-server login-timeout** command lets you change this timeout value from 1 to 300 seconds. To restore the default login timeout value of 30 seconds, use the **no tacacs-server login-timeout** command.

Example

The following example changes the login timeout value to 60 seconds:

```
tacacs-server login-timeout 60
```

TACACS-SERVER NOTIFY

To cause a message to be transmitted to the TACACS server, with retransmission being performed by a background process for up to five minutes, use the **tacacs-server notify** global configuration command. Use the **no** form of this command to disable notification.

> **tacacs-server notify {connection [always] | enable | logout [always] | slip [always]}**
> **no tacacs-server notify**

Syntax Description

connection Specifies that a message be transmitted when a user makes a TCP connection.

always (Optional) Sends a message even when a user is not logged in. This option applies only to SLIP or PPP sessions and can be used with the **logout** or **slip** keywords.

enable Specifies that a message be transmitted when a user enters the **enable** command.

logout Specifies that a message be transmitted when a user logs out.

slip Specifies that a message be transmitted when a user starts a SLIP or PPP session.

Default

No message is transmitted to the TACACS server.

Command Mode

Global configuration

Usage Guidelines

This command first appeared in Cisco IOS Release 10.0. The **always** and **slip** commands first appeared in Cisco IOS Release 11.0.

Part
II

Command Reference

The terminal user receives an immediate response, allowing access to the feature specified. Enter one of the keywords to specify notification of the TACACS server upon receipt of the corresponding action (when user logs out, for example).

NOTES

This command is not used in TACACS+. It has been replaced by the **aaa accounting** suite of commands.

Example

The following example sets up notification of the TACACS server when a user logs out:

```
tacacs-server notify logout
```

TACACS-SERVER OPTIONAL-PASSWORDS

To specify that the first TACACS request to a TACACS server be made without password verification, use the **tacacs-server optional-passwords** global configuration command. Use the **no** form of this command to restore the default.

tacacs-server optional-passwords
no tacacs-server optional-passwords

Syntax Description

This command has no arguments or keywords.

Default

Disabled

Command Mode

Global configuration

Usage Guidelines

This command first appeared in Cisco IOS Release 10.0.

When the user enters the login name, the login request is transmitted with the name and a zero-length password. If accepted, the login procedure completes. If the TACACS server refuses this request, the server software prompts for a password and tries again when the user supplies a password. The TACACS server must support authentication for users without passwords to make use of this feature. This feature supports all TACACS requests, such as login, SLIP, and enable.

NOTES

This command is not used by TACACS+.

Example

The following example configures the first login to not require TACACS verification:

```
tacacs-server optional-passwords
```

TACACS-SERVER RETRANSMIT

To specify the number of times the Cisco IOS software searches the list of TACACS server hosts before giving up, use the **tacacs-server retransmit** global configuration command. Use the **no** form of this command to disable retransmission.

> **tacacs-server retransmit** *retries*
> **no tacacs-server retransmit**

Syntax Description

retries   Integer that specifies the retransmit count.

Default

Two retries

Command Mode

Global configuration

Usage Guidelines

This command first appeared in Cisco IOS Release 10.0.

The Cisco IOS software will try all servers, allowing each one to time out before increasing the retransmit count.

Example

The following example specifies a retransmit counter value of five times:

```
tacacs-server retransmit 5
```

TACACS-SERVER TIMEOUT

To set the interval that the server waits for a server host to reply, use the **tacacs-server timeout** global configuration command. Use the **no** form of this command to restore the default.

> **tacacs-server timeout** *seconds*
> **no tacacs-server timeout**

Syntax Description

seconds   Integer that specifies the timeout interval in seconds (between 1 and 300). The default is 5 seconds.

Default

5 seconds

Command Mode

Global configuration

Usage Guidelines

This command first appeared in Cisco IOS Release 10.0.

Example

The following example changes the interval timer to 10 seconds:

```
tacacs-server timeout 10
```

Related Commands

Search online to find documentation for related commands.

tacacs-server host

CHAPTER 14

Configuring Kerberos

This chapter describes the Kerberos security system and includes the following topics and tasks:

- Kerberos Overview
- Kerberos Client Support Operation
- Kerberos Configuration Task List

For a complete description of the commands used in this chapter, see Chapter 15, "Kerberos Commands."

KERBEROS OVERVIEW

Kerberos is a secret-key network authentication protocol, developed at Massachusetts Institute of Technology (MIT), that uses the Data Encryption Standard (DES) cryptographic algorithm for encryption and authentication. Kerberos was designed to authenticate requests for network resources. Kerberos, like other secret-key systems, is based on the concept of a trusted third party that performs secure verification of users and services. In the Kerberos protocol, this trusted third party is called the key distribution center (KDC).

The primary use of Kerberos is to verify that users and the network services they use are really who and what they claim to be. To accomplish this, a trusted Kerberos server issues tickets to users. These tickets, which have a limited lifespan, are stored in a user's credential cache and can be used in place of the standard username-and-password authentication mechanism.

The Kerberos credential scheme embodies a concept called "single logon." This process requires authenticating a user once, and then allows secure authentication (without encrypting another password) wherever that user's credential is accepted.

Starting with Cisco IOS Release 11.2, Cisco IOS software includes Kerberos 5 support, which allows organizations already deploying Kerberos 5 to use the same Kerberos authentication database on their routers that they are already using on their other network hosts (such as UNIX servers and PCs).

The following network services are supported by the Kerberos authentication capabilities in Cisco IOS software:

- Telnet
- rlogin
- rsh
- rcp

Table 14–1 lists common Kerberos-related terms and their definitions.

Table 14–1 *Kerberos Terminology*

Term	Definition
Authentication	A process by which a user or service identifies itself to another service. For example, a client can authenticate to a router or a router can authenticate to another router.
Authorization	A means by which the router determines what privileges you have in a network or on the router and what actions you can perform.
Credential	A general term that refers to authentication tickets, such as ticket granting tickets (TGTs) and service credentials. Kerberos credentials verify the identity of a user or service. If a network service decides to trust the Kerberos server that issued a ticket, it can be used in place of retyping in a username and password. Credentials have a default lifespan of eight hours.
Instance	An authorization level label for Kerberos principals. Most Kerberos principals are of the form user@REALM (for example, smith@BOO.COM). A Kerberos principal with a Kerberos instance has the form user/instance@REALM (for example, smith/admin@BOO.COM). The Kerberos instance can be used to specify the authorization level for the user if authentication is successful. It is up to the server of each network service to implement and enforce the authorization mappings of Kerberos instances. Note that the Kerberos realm name must be in uppercase characters.
Kerberized	Applications and services that have been modified to support the Kerberos credential infrastructure.

Table 14–1 *Kerberos Terminology, Continued*

Term	Definition
Kerberos realm	A domain consisting of users, hosts, and network services that are registered to a Kerberos server. The Kerberos server is trusted to verify the identity of a user or network service to another user or network service. Kerberos realms must always be in uppercase characters.
Kerberos server	A daemon running on a network host. Users and network services register their identity with the Kerberos server. Network services query the Kerberos server to authenticate to other network services.
Key distribution center (KDC)	A Kerberos server and database program running on a network host.
Principal	Also known as a Kerberos identity, this is who you are or what a service is according to the Kerberos server.
Service credential	A credential for a network service. When issued from the KDC, this credential is encrypted with the password shared by the network service and the KDC, and with the user's TGT.
SRVTAB	A password that a network service shares with the KDC. The network service authenticates an encrypted service credential by using the SRVTAB (also known as a KEYTAB) to decrypt it.
Ticket granting ticket (TGT)	A credential that the key distribution center (KDC) issues to authenticated users. When users receive a TGT, they can authenticate to network services within the Kerberos realm represented by the KDC.

KERBEROS CLIENT SUPPORT OPERATION

This section describes how the Kerberos security system works with a Cisco router functioning as the security server. Although (for convenience or technical reasons) you can customize Kerberos in a number of ways, remote users attempting to access network services must pass through the following three layers of security before they can access network services:

- Authenticate to the Boundary Router
- Obtain a TGT from a KDC
- Authenticate to Network Services

Authenticate to the Boundary Router

This section describes the first layer of security that remote users must pass through when they attempt to access a network. The first step in the Kerberos authentication process is for users to authenticate themselves to the boundary router. The following process describes how users authenticate to a boundary router:

1. The remote user opens a PPP connection to the corporate site router.

2. The router prompts the user for a username and password.

3. The router requests a TGT from the KDC for this particular user.

4. The KDC sends an encrypted TGT to the router that includes (among other things) the user's identity.

5. The router attempts to decrypt the TGT using the password the user entered. If the decryption is successful, the remote user is authenticated to the router.

A remote user who successfully initiates a PPP session and authenticates to the boundary router is inside the firewall but still must authenticate to the KDC directly before being allowed to access network services. This is because the TGT issued by the KDC is stored on the router and is not useful for additional authentication unless the user physically logs on to the router.

Obtain a TGT from a KDC

This section describes how remote users who are authenticated to the boundary router authenticate themselves to a KDC.

When a remote user authenticates to a boundary router, that user technically becomes part of the network; that is, the network is extended to include the remote user and the user's machine or network. To gain access to network services, however, the remote user must obtain a TGT from the KDC. The following process describes how remote users authenticate to the KDC:

1. The remote user, at a workstation on a remote site, launches the KINIT program (part of the client software provided with the Kerberos protocol).

2. The KINIT program finds the user's identity and requests a TGT from the KDC.

3. The KDC creates a TGT, which contains the identity of the user, the identity of the KDC, and the TGT's expiration time.

4. Using the user's password as a key, the KDC encrypts the TGT and sends the TGT to the workstation.

5. When the KINIT program receives the encrypted TGT, it prompts the user for a password (this is the password that is defined for the user in the KDC).

6. If the KINIT program can decrypt the TGT with the password the user enters, the user is authenticated to the KDC, and the KINIT program stores the TGT in the user's credential cache.

At this point, the user has a TGT and can communicate securely with the KDC. In turn, the TGT allows the user to authenticate to other network services.

Authenticate to Network Services

The following process describes how a remote user with a TGT authenticates to network services within a given Kerberos realm. Assume the user is on a remote workstation (Host A) and wants to log in to Host B.

1. The user on Host A initiates a Kerberized application (such as Telnet) to Host B.

2. The Kerberized application builds a service credential request and sends it to the KDC. The service credential request includes (among other things) the user's identity and the identity of the desired network service. The TGT is used to encrypt the service credential request.

3. The KDC tries to decrypt the service credential request with the TGT it issued to the user on Host A. If the KDC can decrypt the packet, it is assured that the authenticated user on Host A sent the request.

4. The KDC notes the network service identity in the service credential request.

5. The KDC builds a service credential for the appropriate network service on Host B on behalf of the user on Host A. The service credential contains the client's identity and the desired network service's identity.

6. The KDC then encrypts the service credential twice. It first encrypts the credential with the SRVTAB that it shares with the network service identified in the credential. It then encrypts the resulting packet with the TGT of the user (who, in this case, is on Host A).

7. The KDC sends the twice-encrypted credential to Host A.

8. Host A attempts to decrypt the service credential with the user's TGT. If Host A can decrypt the service credential, it is assured the credential came from the real KDC.

9. Host A sends the service credential to the desired network service. Note that the credential is still encrypted with the SRVTAB shared by the KDC and the network service.

10. The network service attempts to decrypt the service credential using its SRVTAB.

    If the network service can decrypt the credential, it is assured the credential was in fact issued from the KDC. Note that the network service trusts anything it can decrypt from the KDC, even if it receives it indirectly from a user. This is because the user first authenticated with the KDC.

At this point, the user is authenticated to the network service on Host B. This process is repeated each time a user wants to access a network service in the Kerberos realm.

KERBEROS CONFIGURATION TASK LIST

In order for hosts and the KDC in your Kerberos realm to communicate and mutually authenticate, you must identify them to each other. To do this, you add entries for the hosts to the Kerberos database on the KDC and add SRVTAB files generated by the KDC to all hosts in the Kerberos realm. You also make entries for users in the KDC database.

The upcoming sections describe how to set up a Kerberos-authenticated server-client system, as follows:

- Configuring the KDC Using Kerberos Commands
- Configuring the Router to Use the Kerberos Protocol

This section assumes that you have installed the Kerberos administrative programs on a UNIX host, known as the KDC, initialized the database, and selected a Kerberos realm name and password. For instructions about completing these tasks, refer to documentation that came with your Kerberos software.

NOTES

Write down the host name or IP address of the KDC, the port number you want the KDC to monitor for queries, and the name of the Kerberos realm it will serve. You need this information to configure the router.

CONFIGURING THE KDC USING KERBEROS COMMANDS

After you set up a host to function as the KDC in your Kerberos realm, you must make entries to the KDC database for all principals in the realm. Principals can be network services on Cisco routers and hosts or they can be users.

To use Kerberos commands to add services to the KDC database (and to modify existing database information), complete the tasks in the following sections:

- Add Users to the KDC Database
- Create SRVTABs on the KDC
- Extract SRVTABs

NOTES

All Kerberos command examples are based on Kerberos 5 Beta 5 of the original MIT implementation. Later versions use a slightly different interface.

Add Users to the KDC Database

To add users to the KDC and create privileged instances of those users, use the **su** command to become root on the host running the KDC and use the kdb5_edit program to perform the following tasks:

Task	Command
Use the **ank** (add new key) command to add a user to the KDC. This command prompts for a password, which the user must enter to authenticate to the router.	**ank** *username@REALM*
Use the **ank** command to add a privileged instance of a user.	**ank** *username/instance@REALM*

For example, to add user *loki* of Kerberos realm CISCO.COM, enter the following Kerberos command:

```
ank loki@CISCO.COM
```

NOTES

The Kerberos realm name must be in uppercase characters.

You might want to create privileged instances to allow network administrators to connect to the router at the enable level, for example, so that they need not enter a cleartext password (and compromise security) to enter enable mode.

To add an instance of *loki* with additional privileges (in this case, *enable*, although it could be anything) enter the following Kerberos command:

```
ank loki/enable@CISCO.COM
```

In each of these examples, you are prompted to enter a password, which you must give to user *loki* to use at login.

Section "Enable Kerberos Instance Mapping," found later in the chapter, describes how to map Kerberos instances to various Cisco IOS privilege levels.

Create SRVTABs on the KDC

All routers that you want to authenticate to use the Kerberos protocol must have a SRVTAB. This section and the following section, "Extract SRVTABs," describe how to create and extract SRVTABs for a router called *router1*. Section "Copy SRVTAB Files" describes how to copy SRVTAB files to the router.

To make SRVTAB entries on the KDC, use the **su** command to become root on the host running the KDC and use the kdb5_edit program to perform the following task:

Task	Command
Use the **ark** (add random key) command to add a network service supported by a host or router to the KDC.	**ark** *SERVICE/HOSTNAME@REALM*

For example, to add a Kerberized authentication service for a Cisco router called *router1* to the Kerberos realm CISCO.COM, enter the following Kerberos command:

```
ark host/router1.cisco.com@CISCO.COM
```

Make entries for all network services on all Kerberized hosts that use this KDC for authentication.

Extract SRVTABs

SRVTABs contain (among other things) the passwords or randomly generated keys for the service principals you entered into the KDC database. Service principal keys must be shared with the host running that service. To do this, you must save the SRVTAB entries to a file, then copy the file to the router and all hosts in the Kerberos realm. Saving SRVTAB entries to a file is called *extracting* SRVTABs. To extract SRVTABs, use the **su** command to become root on the host running the KDC and perform the following task:

Task	Command
Use the kdb5_edit command **xst** to write a SRVTAB entry to a file.	**xst** *router_name host*

For example, to write the host/router1.cisco.com@CISCO.COM SRVTAB to a file, enter the following Kerberos command:

```
xst router1.cisco.com@CISCO.COM host
```

Use the **quit** command to exit the kdb5_edit program.

CONFIGURING THE ROUTER TO USE THE KERBEROS PROTOCOL

To configure a Cisco router to function as a network security server and authenticate users using the Kerberos protocol, complete the tasks in the following sections:

- Define Kerberos Realm
- Copy SRVTAB Files

- Specify Kerberos Authentication
- Enable Credentials Forwarding
- Telnet to the Router
- Establish an Encrypted Kerberized Telnet Session
- Enable Mandatory Kerberos Authentication
- Enable Kerberos Instance Mapping
- Monitoring and Maintaining Kerberos

Define Kerberos Realm

For a router to authenticate a user defined in the Kerberos database, it must know the host name or IP address of the host running the KDC, the name of the Kerberos realm and, optionally, be able to map the host name or Domain Naming System (DNS) domain to the Kerberos realm.

To configure the router to authenticate to a specified KDC in a specified Kerberos realm, perform the following tasks in global configuration mode. Note that DNS domain names must begin with a leading dot (.):

Task	Command
Define the default realm for the router.	**kerberos local-realm** *kerberos-realm*
Specify to the router which KDC to use in a given Kerberos realm and, optionally, the port number the KDC is monitoring. (The default is 88.)	**kerberos server** *kerberos-realm* {*hostname* | *ip-address*} [*port-number*]
Optionally, map a host name or DNS domain to a Kerberos realm.	**kerberos realm** {*dns-domain* | *host*} *kerberos-realm*

NOTES

Because the machine running the KDC and all Kerberized hosts must interact within a 5-minute window or authentication fails, all Kerberized machines, and especially the KDC, should be running the Network Time Protocol (NTP).

The **Kerberos local realm**, **Kerberos realm**, and **Kerberos server** commands are equivalent to the UNIX *krb.conf* file. Table 14–2 identifies mappings from the Cisco IOS configuration commands to a Kerberos 5 configuration file (krb5.conf).

Table 14–2   *Kerberos 5 Configuration File and Commands*

krb5.conf file	Cisco IOS Configuration Command
[libdefaults]	(in config mode)
default_realm = *MURUGA.COM*	**kerberos local-realm** *MURUGA.COM*
[domain_realm]	(in config mode)
.muruga.com = *MURUGA.COM*	**kerberos realm** *.muruga.com MURUGA.COM*
muruga.com = *MURUGA.COM*	**kerberos realm** *muruga.com MURUGA.COM*
[realms]	(in config mode)
kdc = *MURUGA.PIL.COM:750*	**kerberos server** *MURUGA.COM 172.65.44.2*
admin_server = *MURUGA.PIL.COM*	(*172.65.44.2* is the example IP address for
default_domain = *MURUGA.COM*	*MURUGA.PIL.COM*)

For an example of defining a Kerberos realm, see section "Define Kerberos Realm Examples," found at the end of this chapter.

Copy SRVTAB Files

To make it possible for remote users to authenticate to the router using Kerberos credentials, the router must share a secret key with the KDC. To do this, you must give the router a copy of the SRVTAB you extracted on the KDC.

The most secure method to copy SRVTAB files to the hosts in your Kerberos realm is to copy them onto physical media and go to each host in turn and manually copy the files onto the system. To copy SRVTAB files to the router, which does not have a physical media drive, you must transfer them via the network using the Trivial File Transfer Protocol (TFTP).

To remotely copy SRVTAB files to the router from the KDC, perform the following task in global configuration mode:

Task	Command
Retrieve a SRVTAB file from the KDC.	**kerberos srvtab remote** {*hostname*	*ip-address*} {*file name*}

When you copy the SRVTAB file from the router to the KDC, the **kerberos srvtab remote** command parses the information in this file and stores it in the router's running configuration in the **kerberos srvtab entry** format. To ensure that the SRVTAB is available (does not need to be acquired from the KDC) when you reboot the router, use the **write memory** configuration command to write your running configuration (which contains the parsed SRVTAB file) to NVRAM.

For an example of copying SRVTAB files, see section "Copy SRVTAB Files Example," found at the end of this chapter.

Specify Kerberos Authentication

You have now configured Kerberos on your router. This makes it possible for the router to authenticate using Kerberos. The next step is to tell it to do so. Because Kerberos authentication is facilitated through AAA, you need to enter the **aaa authentication** command, specifying Kerberos as the authentication method. For more information, see Chapter 3, "Configuring Authentication."

Enable Credentials Forwarding

With Kerberos configured thus far, a user authenticated to a Kerberized router has a TGT and can use it to authenticate to a host on the network. However, if the user tries to list credentials after authenticating to a host, the output will show no Kerberos credentials present.

You can optionally configure the router to forward users' TGTs with them as they authenticate from the router to Kerberized remote hosts on the network when using Kerberized Telnet, rcp, rsh, and rlogin (with the appropriate flags).

To force all clients to forward users' credentials as they connect to other hosts in the Kerberos realm, perform the following task in global configuration mode:

Task	Command
Force all clients to forward user credential upon successful Kerberos authentication.	**kerberos credential forward**

With credentials forwarding enabled, users' TGTs are automatically forwarded to the next host they authenticate to. In this way, users can connect to multiple hosts in the Kerberos realm without running the KINIT program each time to get a new TGT.

Telnet to the Router

To use Kerberos to authenticate users opening a Telnet session to the router from within the network, perform the following task in global configuration mode:

Task	Command
Set login authentication to use the Kerberos 5 Telnet authentication protocol when using Telnet to connect to the router.	**aaa authentication login** {default | *list-name*} **krb5_telnet**

Although Telnet sessions to the router are authenticated, users must still enter a cleartext password if they want to enter enable mode. The **kerberos instance map** command, discussed in a later section, allows them to authenticate to the router at a predefined privilege level.

Establish an Encrypted Kerberized Telnet Session

Another way for users to open a secure Telnet session is to use Encrypted Kerberized Telnet. With Encrypted Kerberized Telnet, users are authenticated by their Kerberos credentials before a Telnet session is established. The Telnet session is encrypted using 56-bit Data Encryption Standard (DES) encryption with 64-bit Cipher Feedback (CFB). Because data sent or received is encrypted, not cleartext, the integrity of the dialed router or access server can be more easily controlled.

─ **NOTES** ───

This feature is available only if you have the 56-bit encryption image. 56-bit DES encryption is subject to U.S. government export control regulations.

───

To establish an encrypted Kerberized Telnet session from a router to a remote host, perform the following task in EXEC command mode:

Task	Command
Establish an encrypted Telnet session.	**connect** *host* [*port*] **/encrypt kerberos** or **telnet** *host* [*port*] **/encrypt kerberos**

When a user opens a Telnet session from a Cisco router to a remote host, the router and remote host negotiate to authenticate the user using Kerberos credentials. If this authentication is successful, the router and remote host then negotiate whether or not to use encryption. If this negotiation is successful, both inbound and outbound traffic is encrypted using 56-bit DES encryption with 64-bit CFB.

When a user dials in from a remote host to a Cisco router configured for Kerberos authentication, the host and router will attempt to negotiate whether or not to use encryption for the Telnet session. If this negotiation is successful, the router will encrypt all outbound data during the Telnet session.

If encryption is not successfully negotiated, the session will be terminated and the user will receive a message stating that the encrypted Telnet session was not successfully established.

For information about enabling bidirectional encryption from a remote host, refer to the documentation specific to the remote host device.

For an example of using encrypted Kerberized Telnet to open a secure Telnet session, see section "Specify an Encrypted Telnet Session Example," found at the end of this chapter.

Enable Mandatory Kerberos Authentication

As an added layer of security, you can optionally configure the router so that, after remote users authenticate to it, these users can authenticate to other services on the network only with Kerberized Telnet, rlogin, rsh, and rcp. If you do not make Kerberos authentication mandatory and Kerberos authentication fails, the application attempts to authenticate users using the default method of authentication for that network service; for example, Telnet and rlogin prompt for a password, rsh attempts to authenticate using the local rhost file.

To make Kerberos authentication mandatory, perform the following task in global configuration mode:

Task	Command
Set Telnet, rlogin, rsh, and rcp to fail if they cannot negotiate the Kerberos protocol with the remote server.	**kerberos clients mandatory**

Enable Kerberos Instance Mapping

As mentioned in section "Create SRVTABs on the KDC," you can create administrative instances of users in the KDC database. The **kerberos instance map** command allows you to map those instances to Cisco IOS privilege levels so that users can open secure Telnet sessions to the router at a predefined privilege level, obviating the need to enter a cleartext password to enter enable mode.

To map a Kerberos instance to a Cisco IOS privilege level, perform the following task in global configuration mode:

Task	Command
Map a Kerberos instance to a Cisco IOS privilege level.	**kerberos instance map** *instance privilege-level*

If there is a Kerberos instance for user *loki* in the KDC database (for example, *loki/admin*), user *loki* can now open a Telnet session to the router as loki/admin and authenticate automatically at privilege level 15, assuming instance "admin" is mapped to privilege level 15. (See section "Add Users to the KDC Database," found earlier in this chapter.)

Cisco IOS commands can be set to various privilege levels using the **privilege level** command.

After you map a Kerberos instance to a Cisco IOS privilege level, you must configure the router to check for Kerberos instances each time a user logs in. To run authorization to determine if a user is allowed to run an EXEC shell based on a mapped Kerberos instance, use the **aaa authorization** command with the **krb5-instance** keyword. For more information, see Chapter 5, "Configuring Authorization."

MONITORING AND MAINTAINING KERBEROS

To display or remove a current user's credentials, perform the following tasks in EXEC mode:

Task	Command
List the credentials in a current user's credentials cache.	show kerberos creds
Destroy all credentials in a current user's credentials cache.	clear kerberos creds

KERBEROS CONFIGURATION EXAMPLES

Configuration examples in this section include the following:

- Define Kerberos Realm Examples
- Copy SRVTAB Files Example
- Kerberos Configuration Exampless
- Specify an Encrypted Telnet Session Example

Define Kerberos Realm Examples

To define CISCO.COM as the default Kerberos realm, use the following command:

```
kerberos local-realm CISCO.COM
```

To tell the router that the CISCO.COM KDC is running on host 10.2.3.4 at port number 170, use the following Kerberos command:

```
kerberos server CISCO.COM 10.2.3.4 170
```

To map the DNS domain cisco.com to the Kerberos realm CISCO.COM, use the following command:

```
kerberos realm .cisco.com CISCO.COM
```

Copy SRVTAB Files Example

To copy over the SRVTAB file on a host named host123.cisco.com for a router named router1.cisco.com, the command would look like this:

```
kerberos srvtab remote host123.cisco.com router1.cisco.com-new-srvtab
```

Kerberos Configuration Examples

This section provides a typical non-Kerberos router configuration and shows output for this configuration from the **write term** command, then builds on this configuration by adding optional Kerberos functionality. Output for each configuration is presented for comparison against the previous configuration.

This example shows how to use the kdb5_edit program to perform the following configuration tasks:

- Add user chet to the Kerberos database
- Add a privileged Kerberos instance of user chet (chet/admin) to the Kerberos database
- Add a restricted instance of chet (chet/restricted) to the Kerberos database
- Add workstation chet-ss20.cisco.com
- Add router chet-2500.cisco.com to the Kerberos database
- Add workstation chet-ss20.cisco.com to the Kerberos database
- Extract SRVTABs for the router and workstations
- List the contents of the KDC database (with the **ldb** command)

Note that, in this sample configuration, host chet-ss20 is also the KDC:

```
chet-ss20# sbin/kdb5_edit
kdb5_edit:  ank chet
Enter password:
Re-enter password for verification:
kdb5_edit:  ank chet/admin
Enter password:
Re-enter password for verification:
kdb5_edit:  ank chet/restricted
Enter password:
Re-enter password for verification:
kdb5_edit:  ark host/chet-ss20.cisco.com
kdb5_edit:  ark host/chet-2500.cisco.com
kdb5_edit:  xst chet-ss20.cisco.com host
'host/chet-ss20.cisco.com@CISCO.COM' added to keytab
'WRFILE:chet-ss20.cisco.com-new-srvtab'
kdb5_edit:  xst chet-2500.cisco.com host
'host/chet-2500.cisco.com@CISCO.COM' added to keytab
'WRFILE:chet-2500.cisco.com-new-srvtab'
kdb5_edit:  ldb
entry: host/chet-2500.cisco.com@CISCO.COM
entry: chet/restricted@CISCO.COM
entry: chet@CISCO.COM
entry: K/M@CISCO.COM
entry: host/chet-ss20.cisco.com@CISCO.COM
entry: krbtgt/CISCO.COM@CISCO.COM
entry: chet/admin@CISCO.COM
kdb5_edit:  q
chet-ss20#
```

The following example shows output from a **write term** command, which displays the configuration of router chet-2500. This is a typical configuration with no Kerberos authentication.

```
chet-2500# write term
Building configuration...
```

```
Current configuration:
!
! Last configuration
change at 14:03:55 PDT Mon May 13 1996
!
version 11.2
service udp-small-servers
service tcp-small-servers
!
hostname chet-2500
!
clock timezone PST -8
clock summer-time PDT recurring
aaa new-model
aaa authentication login console none
aaa authentication ppp local local
enable password sMudgKin
!
username chet-2500 password 7 sMudgkin
username chet-3000 password 7 sMudgkin
username chetin password 7 sMudgkin
!
interface Ethernet0
 ip address 172.16.0.0 255.255.255.0
!
interface Serial0
 no ip address
 shutdown
 no fair-queue
!
interface Serial1
 no ip address
 shutdown
 no fair-queue
!
interface Async2
 ip unnumbered Ethernet0
 encapsulation ppp
 shutdown
 async dynamic routing
 async mode dedicated
 no cdp enable
 ppp authentication pap local
 no tarp propagate
!
interface Async3
 ip unnumbered Ethernet0
 encapsulation ppp
 shutdown
 async dynamic address
 async dynamic routing
```

```
 async mode dedicated
 no cdp enable
 ppp authentication pap local
 no tarp propagate
!
router eigrp 109
 network 172.17.0.0
 no auto-summary
!
ip default-gateway 172.30.55.64
ip domain-name cisco.com
ip name-server 192.168.0.0
ip classless
!
!
line con 0
 exec-timeout 0 0
 login authentication console
line 1 16
 transport input all
line aux 0
 transport input all
line vty 0 4
 password sMudgKin
!
ntp clock-period 17179703
ntp peer 172.19.10.0
ntp peer 172.19.0.0
end
```

The following example shows how to enable user authentication on the router via the Kerberos database. To enable user authentication via the Kerberos database, you would perform the following tasks:

- Enter configuration mode
- Define the Kerberos local realm
- Identify the machine hosting the KDC
- Enable credentials forwarding
- Specify Kerberos as the method of authentication for login
- Exit configuration mode (CTL-Z)
- Write the new configuration to the terminal

```
chet-2500# configure term
Enter configuration commands, one per line.  End with CNTL/Z.
chet-2500(config)# kerberos local-realm CISCO.COM
chet-2500(config)# kerberos server CISCO.COM chet-ss20
Translating "chet-ss20"...domain server (192.168.0.0) [OK]
```

```
chet-2500(config)# kerberos credentials forward
chet-2500(config)# aaa authentication login default krb5
chet-2500(config)#
chet-2500#
%SYS-5-CONFIG_I: Configured from console by console
chet-2500# write term
```

Compare the following configuration with the previous one. In particular, look at the lines beginning with the the words "aaa," "username," and "kerberos" (lines 10 through 20) in this new configuration.

```
Building configuration...

Current configuration:
!
! Last configuration change at 14:05:54 PDT Mon May 13 1996
!
version 11.2
service udp-small-servers
service tcp-small-servers
!
hostname chet-2500
!
clock timezone PST -8
clock summer-time PDT recurring
aaa new-model
aaa authentication login default krb5
aaa authentication login console none
aaa authentication ppp local local
enable password sMudgKin
!
username chet-2500 password 7 sMudgkin
username chet-3000 password 7 sMudgkin
username chetin password 7 sMudgkin
kerberos local-realm CISCO.COM
kerberos server CISCO.COM 172.71.54.14
kerberos credentials forward
!
interface Ethernet0
 ip address 172.16.0.0 255.255.255.0
!
interface Serial0
 no ip address
 shutdown
 no fair-queue
!
interface Serial1
 no ip address
 shutdown
 no fair-queue
!
interface Async2
```

```
 ip unnumbered Ethernet0
 encapsulation ppp
 shutdown
 async dynamic routing
 async mode dedicated
 no cdp enable
 ppp authentication pap local
 no tarp propagate
!
interface Async3
 ip unnumbered Ethernet0
 encapsulation ppp
 shutdown
 async dynamic address
 async dynamic routing
 async mode dedicated
 no cdp enable
 ppp authentication pap local
 no tarp propagate
!
router eigrp 109
 network 172.17.0.0
 no auto-summary
!
ip default-gateway 172.30.55.64
ip domain-name cisco.com
ip name-server 192.168.0.0
ip classless
!
!
line con 0
 exec-timeout 0 0
 login authentication console
line 1 16
 transport input all
line aux 0
 transport input all
line vty 0 4
 password sMudgKin
!
ntp clock-period 17179703
ntp peer 172.19.10.0
ntp peer 172.19.0.0
end
```

With the router configured thus far, user chet can log in to the router with a username and password and automatically obtain a TGT, as illustrated in the next example. With possession of a credential, user chet successfully authenticates to host chet-ss20 without entering a username/password.

```
chet-ss20% telnet chet-2500
Trying 172.16.0.0 ...
Connected to chet-2500.cisco.com.
```

```
Escape character is '^]'.


User Access Verification

Username: chet
Password:

chet-2500> show kerberos creds
Default Principal:  chet@CISCO.COM
Valid Starting           Expires                Service Principal
13-May-1996 14:05:39     13-May-1996 22:06:40   krbtgt/CISCO.COM@CISCO.COM

chet-2500> telnet chet-ss20
Trying chet-ss20.cisco.com (172.71.54.14)... Open
Kerberos:       Successfully forwarded credentials


SunOS UNIX (chet-ss20) (pts/7)

Last login: Mon May 13 13:47:35 from chet-ss20.cisco.c
Sun Microsystems Inc.   SunOS 5.4      Generic July 1994
unknown mode: new
chet-ss20%
```

The following example shows how to authenticate to the router using Kerberos credentials. To authenticate using Kerberos credentials, you would perform the following tasks:

- Enter configuration mode
- Remotely copy over the SRVTAB file from the KDC
- Set authentication at login to use the Kerberos 5 Telnet authentication protocol when using Telnet to connect to the router
- Write the configuration to the terminal

Note that the new configuration contains a **kerberos srvtab entry** line. This line is created by the **kerberos srvtab remote** command.

```
chet-2500# configure term
Enter configuration commands, one per line.  End with CNTL/Z.
chet-2500(config)#kerberos srvtab remote earth chet/chet-2500.cisco.com-new-srvtab
Translating "earth"...domain server (192.168.0.0) [OK]

Loading chet/chet-2500.cisco.com-new-srvtab from 172.68.1.123 (via Ethernet0): !
[OK - 66/1000 bytes]

chet-2500(config)# aaa authentication login default krb5-telnet krb5
chet-2500(config)#
chet-2500#
%SYS-5-CONFIG_I: Configured from console by console
chet-2500# write term
Building configuration...
```

```
Current configuration:
!
! Last configuration change at 14:08:32 PDT Mon May 13 1996
!
version 11.2
service udp-small-servers
service tcp-small-servers
!
hostname chet-2500
!
clock timezone PST -8
clock summer-time PDT recurring
aaa new-model
aaa authentication login default krb5-telnet krb5
aaa authentication login console none
aaa authentication ppp local local
enable password sMudgKin
!
username chet-2500 password 7 sMudgkin
username chet-3000 password 7 sMudgkin
username chetin password 7 sMudgkin
kerberos local-realm CISCO.COM
kerberos srvtab entry host/chet-2500.cisco.com@CISCO.COM 0 832015393 1 1 8 7 sMudgkin
kerberos server CISCO.COM 172.71.54.14
kerberos credentials forward
!
interface Ethernet0
 ip address 172.16.0.0 255.255.255.0
!
interface Serial0
 no ip address
 shutdown
 no fair-queue
!

interface Serial1
 no ip address
 shutdown
 no fair-queue
!
interface Async2
 ip unnumbered Ethernet0
 encapsulation ppp
 shutdown
 async dynamic routing
 async mode dedicated
 no cdp enable
 ppp authentication pap local
 no tarp propagate
!
interface Async3
```

```
  ip unnumbered Ethernet0
  encapsulation ppp
  shutdown
  async dynamic address
  async dynamic routing
  async mode dedicated
  no cdp enable
  ppp authentication pap local
  no tarp propagate
!
router eigrp 109
 network 172.17.0.0
 no auto-summary
!
ip default-gateway 172.30.55.64
ip domain-name cisco.com
ip name-server 192.168.0.0
ip classless
!
!
line con 0
 exec-timeout 0 0
 login authentication console
line 1 16
 transport input all
line aux 0
 transport input all
line vty 0 4
 password sMudgKin
!
ntp clock-period 17179703
ntp peer 172.19.10.0
ntp peer 172.19.0.0
end

  chet-2500#
```

With this configuration, the user can Telnet in to the router using Kerberos credentials, as illustrated in the next example.

```
chet-ss20% bin/telnet -a -F chet-2500
Trying 172.16.0.0...
Connected to chet-2500.cisco.com.
Escape character is '^]'.
[ Kerberos V5 accepts you as "chet@CISCO.COM" ]


User Access Verification

chet-2500>[ Kerberos V5 accepted forwarded credentials ]

chet-2500> show kerberos creds
Default Principal:  chet@CISCO.COM
```

```
Valid Starting          Expires              Service Principal
13-May-1996 15:06:25    14-May-1996 00:08:29 krbtgt/CISCO.COM@CISCO.COM

chet-2500>q
Connection closed by foreign host.
chet-ss20%
```

The following example shows how to map Kerberos instances to Cisco's privilege levels. To map Kerberos instances to privilege levels, you would perform the following tasks:

- Enter configuration mode
- Map the Kerberos instance, admin, to privilege level 15
- Map the Kerberos instance, restricted, to privilege level 3
- Specify that the instance defined by the **Kerberos instance map** command be used for AAA Authorization
- Write the configuration to the terminal

```
chet-2500# configure term
Enter configuration commands, one per line.  End with CNTL/Z.
chet-2500(config)# kerberos instance map admin 15
chet-2500(config)# kerberos instance map restricted 3
chet-2500(config)# aaa authorization exec krb5-instance
chet-2500(config)#
chet-2500#
%SYS-5-CONFIG_I: Configured from console by console
chet-2500# write term
Building configuration...

Current configuration:
!
! Last configuration change at 14:59:05 PDT Mon May 13 1996
!
version 11.2
service udp-small-servers
service tcp-small-servers
!
hostname chet-2500
!
aaa new-model
aaa authentication login default krb5-telnet krb5
aaa authentication login console none
aaa authentication ppp default krb5 local
aaa authorization exec krb5-instance
enable password sMudgKin
!
username chet-2500 password 7 sMudgKin
username chet-3000 password 7 sMudgKin
username chetin password 7 sMudgKin
ip domain-name cisco.com
ip name-server 192.168.0.0
kerberos local-realm CISCO.COM
```

```
kerberos srvtab entry host/chet-2500.cisco.com@CISCO.COM 0 832015393 1 1 8 7 sMudgkin
kerberos server CISCO.COM 172.71.54.14
kerberos instance map admin 15
kerberos instance map restricted 3
kerberos credentials forward
clock timezone PST -8
clock summer-time PDT recurring
!
interface Ethernet0
 ip address 172.16.0.0 255.255.255.0
!
interface Serial0
 no ip address
 shutdown
 no fair-queue
!
interface Serial1
 no ip address
 shutdown
 no fair-queue
!
interface Async2
 ip unnumbered Ethernet0
 encapsulation ppp
 shutdown
 async dynamic routing
 async mode dedicated
 no cdp enable
 ppp authentication pap local
 no tarp propagate
!
interface Async3
 ip unnumbered Ethernet0
 encapsulation ppp
 shutdown
 async dynamic address
 async dynamic routing
 async mode dedicated
 no cdp enable
 ppp authentication pap local
 no tarp propagate
!
router eigrp 109
 network 172.17.0.0
no auto-summary
!
ip default-gateway 172.30.55.64
ip classless
!
!
```

```
 line con 0
  exec-timeout 0 0
  login authentication console
 line 1 16
  transport input all
 line aux 0
  transport input all
 line vty 0 4
  password sMudgKin
 !
 ntp clock-period 17179703
 ntp peer 172.19.10.0
 ntp peer 172.19.0.0
 end

 chet-2500#
```

The following example shows output from the three types of sessions now possible for user chet with Kerberos instances turned on:

```
chet-ss20% telnet chet-2500
Trying 172.16.0.0 ...
Connected to chet-2500.cisco.com.
Escape character is '^]'.

User Access Verification

Username: chet
Password:

chet-2500> show kerberos creds
Default Principal:  chet@CISCO.COM
Valid Starting           Expires                  Service Principal
13-May-1996 14:58:28     13-May-1996 22:59:29     krbtgt/CISCO.COM@CISCO.COM

chet-2500> show privilege
Current privilege level is 1
chet-2500> q
Connection closed by foreign host.
chet-ss20% telnet chet-2500
Trying 172.16.0.0 ...
Connected to chet-2500.cisco.com.
Escape character is '^]'.

User Access Verification

Username: chet/admin
Password:

chet-2500# show kerberos creds
Default Principal:  chet/admin@CISCO.COM
Valid Starting           Expires                  Service Principal
13-May-1996 14:59:44     13-May-1996 23:00:45     krbtgt/CISCO.COM@CISCO.COM
```

```
chet-2500# show privilege
Current privilege level is 15
chet-2500# q
Connection closed by foreign host.
chet-ss20% telnet chet-2500
Trying 172.16.0.0 ...
Connected to chet-2500.cisco.com.
Escape character is '^]'.


User Access Verification

Username: chet/restricted
Password:

chet-2500# show kerberos creds
Default Principal:  chet/restricted@CISCO.COM
Valid Starting          Expires                 Service Principal
13-May-1996 15:00:32    13-May-1996 23:01:33    krbtgt/CISCO.COM@CISCO.COM

chet-2500# show privilege
Current privilege level is 3
chet-2500# q
Connection closed by foreign host.
chet-ss20%
```

Specify an Encrypted Telnet Session Example

The following example establishes an encrypted Telnet session from a router to a remote host named "host1":

```
Router> telnet host1 /encrypt kerberos
```

## CHAPTER 15

Kerberos Commands

This chapter describes the commands used to configure Kerberos. Kerberos is a secret-key network authentication protocol, developed at Massachusetts Institute of Technology (MIT), that uses the Data Encryption Standard (DES) cryptographic algorithm for encryption and authentication. Kerberos was designed to authenticate requests for network resources. Kerberos, like other secret-key systems, is based on the concept of a trusted third party that performs secure verification of users and services. In the Kerberos protocol, this trusted third party is called the *key distribution center* (KDC).

For information on how to configure Kerberos, see Chapter 14, "Configuring Kerberos." For configuration examples using the commands in this chapter, see section "Kerberos Configuration Examples," located at the end of Chapter 14.

CLEAR KERBEROS CREDS

To delete the contents of the credentials cache, use the **clear kerberos creds** EXEC command.

> **clear kerberos creds**

Syntax Description

This command has no keywords or arguments.

Command Mode

EXEC

Usage Guidelines

This command first appeared in Cisco IOS Release 11.1.

Credentials are cleared when the user logs out.

Cisco supports Kerberos 5.

Example

The following example illustrates the **clear kerberos creds** command:

```
cisco-2500> show kerberos creds
Default Principal: chet@cisco.com
Valid Starting           Expires               Service Principal
18-Dec-1995 16:21:07    19-Dec-1995 00:22:24   krbtgt/CISCO.COM@CISCO.COM

cisco-2500> clear kerberos creds
cisco-2500> show kerberos creds
No Kerberos credentials.

cisco-2500>
```

Related Commands

Search online to find documentation for related commands.

show kerberos creds

CONNECT

To log in to a host that supports Telnet, rlogin, or LAT, use the **connect** EXEC command.

> **connect** *host* [*port*] [*keyword*]

Syntax Description

host   A host name or an IP address.

port   (Optional) A decimal TCP port number; the default is the Telnet router port (decimal 23) on the host.

keyword   (Optional) One of the options listed in Table 15–1.

Table 15–1 describes the options that can be used for the argument *keyword*.

Table 15–1 *Connection Options*

Option	Description
/debug	Enables Telnet debugging mode.
/encrypt kerberos	Enables an encrypted Telnet session. This keyword is available only if you have the Kerberized Telnet subsystem. If you authenticate using Kerberos Credentials, the use of this keyword initiates an encryption negotiation with the remote server. If the encryption negotiation fails, the Telnet connection will be reset. If the encryption negotiation is successful, the Telnet connection will be established, and the Telnet session will continue in encrypted mode (all Telnet traffic for the session will be encrypted).

Table 15–1 *Connection Options, Continued*

Option	Description
/line	Enables Telnet line mode. In this mode, the Cisco IOS software sends no data to the host until you press **Return**. You can edit the line using the standard Cisco IOS software command editing characters. The **/line** keyword is a local switch; the remote router is not notified of the mode change.
/noecho	Disables local echo.
/route *path*	Specifies loose source routing. The *path* argument is a list of host names or IP addresses that specify network nodes and ends with the final destination.
/source-interface	Specifies source interface.
/stream	Turns on *stream* processing, which enables a raw TCP stream with no Telnet control sequences. A stream connection does not process Telnet options and can be appropriate for connections to ports running UUCP and other non-Telnet protocols.
port-number	Port number.
bgp	Border Gateway Protocol.
chargen	Character generator.
cmd *rcmd*	Remote commands.
daytime	Daytime.
discard	Discard.
domain	Domain Naming Service.
echo	Echo.
exec	EXEC.
finger	Finger.
ftp	File Transfer Protocol.
ftp-data	FTP data connections (used infrequently).
gopher	Gopher.
hostname	Network Information Center (NIC) host name server.
ident	Ident Protocol.
irc	Internet Relay Chat.
klogin	Kerberos login.

Part II

Command Reference

Table 15–1   *Connection Options, Continued*

Option	Description
kshell	Kerberos shell.
login	Login (rlogin).
lpd	Printer service.
nntp	Network News Transport Protocol.
node	Connect to a specific LAT node.
pop2	Post Office Protocol v2.
pop3	Post Office Protocol v3.
port	Destination LAT port name.
smtp	Simple Mail Transport Protocol.
sunrpc	Sun Remote Procedure Call.
syslog	Syslog.
tacacs	Specify TACACS security.
talk	Talk.
telnet	Telnet.
time	Time.
uucp	UNIX-to-UNIX Copy Program.
whois	Nickname.
www	World Wide Web (HTTP).

Command Mode

EXEC

Usage Guidelines

This command first appeared in a release prior to Cisco IOS Release 10.0.

With the Cisco IOS software implementation of TCP/IP, you are not required to enter the **connect**, **telnet**, **lat**, or **rlogin** commands to establish a terminal connection. You can just enter the learned host name—as long as the host name is different from a command word in the Cisco IOS software.

To display a list of the available hosts, enter the following command:

    show hosts

To display the status of all TCP connections, enter the following command:

show tcp

The Cisco IOS software assigns a logical name to each connection, and several commands use these names to identify connections. The logical name is the same as the host name, unless that name is already in use, or you change the connection name with the EXEC command **name-connection**. If the name is already in use, the Cisco IOS software assigns a null name to the connection.

Examples

The following example establishes an encrypted Telnet session from a router to a remote host named *host1*:

```
Router> connect host1 /encrypt kerberos
```

The following example routes packets from the source system host1 to kl.sri.com, then to 10.1.0.11, and finally back to host1:

```
Router> connect host1 /route:kl.sri.com 10.1.0.11 host1
```

The following example connects to a host with logical name *host1*:

```
Router> host1
```

Related Commands

Search online to find documentation for related commands.

kerberos clients mandatory
lat

KERBEROS CLIENTS MANDATORY

To cause the **rsh, rcp, rlogin,** and **telnet** commands to fail if they cannot negotiate the Kerberos protocol with the remote server, use the **kerberos clients mandatory** global configuration command. Use the **no** form of this command to disable this option.

kerberos clients mandatory
no kerberos clients mandatory

Syntax Description

This command has no arguments or keywords.

Default

Disabled

Command Mode

Global configuration

User Guidelines

This command first appeared in Cisco IOS Release 11.2.

If this command is not configured and the user has Kerberos credentials stored locally, the **rsh, rcp, rlogin,** and **telnet** commands attempt to negotiate the Kerberos protocol with the remote server and will use the non-Kerberized protocols if unsuccessful.

If this command is not configured and the user has no Kerberos credentials, the standard protocols for **rcp** and **rsh** are used to negotiate the Kerberos protocol.

Example

The following example causes the **rsh, rcp, rlogin,** and **telnet** commands to fail if they cannot negotiate the Kerberos protocol with the remote server:

```
kerberos clients mandatory
```

Related Commands

Search online to find documentation for related commands.

copy rcp
kerberos credentials forward
rlogin
rsh
telnet

KERBEROS CREDENTIALS FORWARD

To force all network application clients on the router to forward users' Kerberos credentials upon successful Kerberos authentication, use the **kerberos credentials forward** global configuration command. Use the **no** form of this command to turn off Kerberos credentials forwarding.

> **kerberos credentials forward**
> **no kerberos credentials forward**

Syntax Description

This command has no arguments or keywords.

Default

Disabled

Command Mode

Global configuration

Usage Guidelines

This command first appeared in Cisco IOS Release 11.2.

Enable credentials forwarding to have users' TGTs forwarded to the host on which they authenticate. In this way, users can connect to multiple hosts in the Kerberos realm without running the KINIT program each time they need to get a TGT.

Example

The following example forces all network application clients on the router to forward users' Kerberos credentials upon successful Kerberos authentication:

```
kerberos credentials forward
```

Related Commands

Search online to find documentation for related commands.

copy rcp
rlogin
rsh
telnet

KERBEROS INSTANCE MAP

To map Kerberos instances to Cisco IOS privilege levels, use the **kerberos instance map** global configuration command. Use the **no** form of this command to remove a Kerberos instance map.

> **kerberos instance map** *instance privilege-level*
> **no kerberos instance map** *instance*

Syntax Description

instance	Name of a Kerberos instance.
privilege-level	The privilege level at which a user is set if the user's Kerberos principal contains the matching Kerberos instance. You can specify up to 16 privilege levels, using numbers 0 through 15. Level 1 is normal EXEC-mode user privileges.

Default

Privilege level 1

Command Mode

Global configuration

Usage Guidelines

This command first appeared in Cisco IOS Release 11.2.

Use this command to create user instances with access to administrative commands.

Example

In the following example, the privilege level is set to 15 for authenticated Kerberos users with the *admin* instance in Kerberos realm:

```
kerberos instance map admin 15
```

Related Commands

Search online to find documentation for related commands.

aaa authorization

KERBEROS LOCAL-REALM

To specify the Kerberos realm in which the router is located, use the **kerberos local-realm** global configuration command. Use the **no** form of this command to remove the specified Kerberos realm from this router.

> **kerberos local-realm** *kerberos-realm*
> **no kerberos local-realm**

Syntax Description

kerberos-realm   The name of the default Kerberos realm. A Kerberos realm consists of users, hosts, and network services that are registered to a Kerberos server. The Kerberos realm must be in uppercase characters.

Default

Disabled

Command Mode

Global configuration

Usage Guidelines

This command first appeared in Cisco IOS Release 11.1.

The router can be located in more than one realm at a time. However, there can only be one instance of Kerberos local-realm. The realm specified with this command is the default realm.

Example

The following example specifies the Kerberos realm in which the router is located as MURUGA.COM:

```
kerberos local-realm MURUGA.COM
```

Related Commands

Search online to find documentation for related commands.

kerberos preauth
kerberos realm
kerberos server
kerberos srvtab entry
kerberos srvtab remote

KERBEROS PREAUTH

To specify a preauthentication method to use to communicate with the KDC, use the **kerberos preauth** global configuration command. Use the **no** form of this command to disable Kerberos preauthentication.

> **kerberos preauth [encrypted-unix-timestamp | none]**
> **no kerberos preauth**

Syntax Description

encrypted-unix-timestamp Use an encrypted UNIX timestamp as a quick authentication method when communicating with the KDC.

none   Do not use Kerberos preauthentication.

Default

Disabled

Command Mode

Global configuration

Usage Guidelines

This command first appeared in Cisco IOS Release 11.2.

It is more secure to use a preauthentication for communications with the KDC. However, communication with the KDC will fail if the KDC does not support this particular version of **kerberos preauth**. If that happens, turn off the preauthentication with the **none** option.

The **no** form of this command is equivalent to using the **none** keyword.

Examples

The following example enables Kerberos preauthentication:

```
kerberos preauth encrypted-unix-timestamp
```

The following example disables Kerberos preauthentication:

```
kerberos preauth none
```

Part II

Command Reference

Related Commands

Search online to find documentation for related commands.

kerberos local-realm
kerberos server
kerberos srvtab entry
kerberos srvtab remote

KERBEROS REALM

To map a host name or Domain Naming System (DNS) domain to a Kerberos realm, use the **kerberos realm** global configuration command. Use the **no** form of this command to remove a Kerberos realm map.

> **kerberos realm** {*dns-domain | host*} *kerberos-realm*
> **no kerberos realm** {*dns-domain | host*} *kerberos-realm*

Syntax Description

dns-domain	Name of a DNS domain or host.
host	Name of a DNS host.
kerberos-realm	Name of the Kerberos realm to which the specified domain or host belongs.

Default

Disabled

Command Mode

Global configuration

Usage Guidelines

This command first appeared in Cisco IOS Release 11.1.

DNS domains are specified with a leading dot (.) character; host names cannot begin with a dot (.) character. There can be multiple entries of this line.

A Kerberos realm consists of users, hosts, and network services that are registered to a Kerberos server. The Kerberos realm must be in uppercase characters. The router can be located in more than one realm at a time. Kerberos realm names must be in all uppercase characters.

Example

The following example maps the domain name, muraga.com, to the Kerberos realm, MURUGA.COM:

```
kerberos realm .muruga.com MURUGA.COM
kerberos realm muruga.com MURUGA.COM
```

Related Commands

Search online to find documentation for related commands.

kerberos local-realm
kerberos server
kerberos srvtab entry
kerberos srvtab remote

KERBEROS SERVER

To specify the location of the Kerberos server for a given Kerberos realm, use the **kerberos server** global configuration command. Use the **no** form of this command to remove a Kerberos server for a specified Kerberos realm.

> **kerberos server** *kerberos-realm* {*hostname* | *ip-address*} [*port-number*]
> **no kerberos server** *kerberos-realm* {*hostname* | *ip-address*}

Syntax Description

kerberos-realm	Name of the Kerberos realm. A Kerberos realm consists of users, hosts, and network services that are registered to a Kerberos server. The Kerberos realm must be in uppercase letters.
hostname	Name of the host functioning as a Kerberos server for the specified Kerberos realm (translated into an IP address at the time of entry).
ip-address	IP address of the host functioning as a Kerberos server for the specified Kerberos realm.
port-number	(Optional) Port that the KDC/TGS monitors (defaults to 88).

Default

Disabled

Command Mode

Global configuration

Usage Guidelines

This command first appeared in Cisco IOS Release 11.1.

Example

The following example specifies 192.168.47.66 as the Kerberos server for the Kerberos realm MURUGA.COM:

```
kerberos server MURUGA.COM 192.168.47.66
```

Part II

Command Reference

Related Commands

Search online to find documentation for related commands.

kerberos local-realm
kerberos realm
kerberos srvtab entry
kerberos srvtab remote

KERBEROS SRVTAB ENTRY

To retrieve a SRVTAB file from a remote host and automatically generate a Kerberos SRVTAB entry configuration, use the **kerberos srvtab remote** global configuration command (not **kerberos srvtab entry**). (The Kerberos SRVTAB entry is the router's locally stored SRVTAB.) Use the **no** form of this command to remove a SRVTAB entry from the router's configuration.

> **kerberos srvtab entry** *kerberos-principal principal-type timestamp key-version number key-type key-length encrypted-keytab*
> **no kerberos srvtab entry** *kerberos-principal principal-type*

Syntax Description

kerberos-principal   A service on the router.

principal-type   Version of the Kerberos SRVTAB.

timestamp   Number representing the date and time the SRVTAB entry was created.

key-version number   Version of the encryption key format.

key-type   Type of encryption used.

key-length   Length, in bytes, of the encryption key.

encrypted-keytab   Secret key the router shares with the KDC. It is encrypted with the private Data Encryption Standard (DES) key (if available) when you write out your configuration.

Command Mode

Global configuration

Usage Guidelines

This command first appeared in Cisco IOS Release 11.2.

When you use the **kerberos srvtab remote** command to copy the SRVTAB file from a remote host (generally the KDC), it parses the information in this file and stores it in the router's running configuration in the **kerberos srvtab entry** format. The key for each SRVTAB entry is encrypted with a private DES key if one is defined on the router. To ensure that the SRVTAB is available (that is, that it does not need to be acquired from the KDC) when you reboot the router, use the **write memory** router configuration command to write the router's running configuration to NVRAM.

If you reload a configuration, with a SRVTAB encrypted with a private DES key, on to a router that does not have a private DES key defined, the router displays a message informing you that the SRVTAB entry has been corrupted and discards the entry.

If you change the private DES key and reload an old version of the router's configuration that contains SRVTAB entries encrypted with the old private DES keys, the router will restore your Kerberos SRVTAB entries, but the SRVTAB keys will be corrupted. In this case, you must delete your old Kerberos SRVTAB entries and reload your Kerberos SRVTABs on to the router using the **kerberos srvtab remote** command.

Although you can configure **kerberos srvtab entry** on the router manually, generally you would not do this, because the keytab is encrypted automatically by the router when you copy the SRVTAB using the **kerberos srvtab remote** command.

Example

In the following example, host/new-router.loki.com@LOKI.COM is the host, 0 is the type, 817680774 is the timestamp, 1 is the version of the key, 1 indicates the DES is the encryption type, 8 is the number of bytes, and .cCN.YoU.okK is the encrypted key:

```
kerberos srvtab entry host/new-router.loki.com@LOKI.COM 0 817680774 1 1 8 .cCN.YoU.okK
```

Related Commands

Search online to find documentation for related commands.

kerberos srvtab remote
key config-key

KERBEROS SRVTAB REMOTE

To retrieve a krb5 SRVTAB file from the specified host, use the **kerberos srvtab remote** global configuration command.

> **kerberos srvtab remote** {*hostname* | *ip-address*} *filename*

Syntax Description

hostname	Machine with the Kerberos SRVTAB file.
ip-address	IP address of the machine with the Kerberos SRVTAB file.
filename	Name of the SRVTAB file.

Command Mode

Global configuration

Usage Guidelines

This command first appeared in Cisco IOS Release 11.2.

When you use the **kerberos srvtab remote** command to copy the SRVTAB file from the remote host (generally the KDC), it parses the information in this file and stores it in the router's running configuration in the **kerberos srvtab entry** format. The key for each SRVTAB entry is encrypted with the private Data Encryption Standard (DES) key if one is defined on the router. To ensure that the SRVTAB is available (that is, that it does not need to be acquired from the KDC) when you reboot the router, use the **write memory** configuration command to write the router's running configuration to NVRAM.

Example

The command in the following example copies the SRVTAB file residing on bucket.cisco.com to a router named scooter.cisco.com:

```
kerberos srvtab remote bucket.cisco.com scooter.cisco.com-new-srvtab
```

Related Commands

Search online to find documentation for related commands.

kerberos srvtab entry
key config-key

KEY CONFIG-KEY

To define a private DES key for the router, use the **key config-key** global configuration command. Use the **no** form of this command to delete a private DES key for the router.

```
key config-key 1 string
```

Syntax Description

string   Private DES key (can be up to eight alphanumeric characters).

Default

No DES-key defined

Command Mode

Global configuration

Usage Guidelines

This command first appeared in Cisco IOS Release 11.2.

This command defines a private DES key for the router that will not show up in the router configuration. This private DES key can be used to DES-encrypt certain parts of the router's configuration.

CAUTION

The private DES key is unrecoverable. If you encrypt part of your configuration with the private DES key and lose or forget the key, you will not be able to recover the encrypted data.

Example

The command in the following example sets *bubba* as the private DES key on the router:

```
key config-key 1 bubba
```

Related Commands

Search online to find documentation for related commands.

kerberos srvtab entry
kerberos srvtab remote

SHOW KERBEROS CREDS

To display the contents of your credentials cache, use the **show kerberos creds** EXEC command.

show kerberos creds

Syntax Description

This command has no keywords or arguments.

Command Mode

EXEC

Usage Guidelines

This command first appeared in Cisco IOS Release 11.1.

The **show kerberos creds** command is equivalent to the UNIX klist command.

When users authenticate themselves with Kerberos, they are issued an authentication ticket called a *credential*. The credential is stored in a credential cache.

Sample Displays

In the following example, the entries in the credentials cache are displayed:

```
Router> show kerberos creds

Default Principal: chet@cisco.com
Valid Starting         Expires                  Service Principal
18-Dec-1995 16:21:07   19-Dec-1995 00:22:24     krbtgt/CISCO.COM@CISCO.COM
```

Part II

Command Reference

In the following example, output is returned that acknowledges that credentials do *not* exist in the credentials cache:

```
Router> show kerberos creds

 No Kerberos credentials
```

Related Commands

Search online to find documentation for related commands.

clear kerberos creds

TELNET

To log in to a host that supports Telnet, use the **telnet** EXEC command.

> **telnet** *host* [*port*] [*keyword*]

Syntax Description

host   A host name or an IP address.

port   (Optional) A decimal TCP port number; the default is the Telnet router port (decimal 23) on the host.

keyword   (Optional) One of the options listed in Table 15–2.

Table 15–2 describes the options that can be used for the argument *keyword*.

Table 15–2   *Telnet Connection Options*

Option	Description
/debug	Enables Telnet debugging mode.
/encrypt kerberos	Enables an encrypted Telnet session. This keyword is available only if you have the Kerberized Telnet subsystem. If you authenticate using Kerberos Credentials, the use of this keyword initiates an encryption negotiation with the remote server. If the encryption negotiation fails, the Telnet connection will be reset. If the encryption negotiation is successful, the Telnet connection will be established, and the Telnet session will continue in encrypted mode (all Telnet traffic for the session will be encrypted).
/line	Enables Telnet line mode. In this mode, the Cisco IOS software sends no data to the host until you press **Return**. You can edit the line using the standard Cisco IOS software command-editing characters. The **/line** keyword is a local switch; the remote router is not notified of the mode change.

Table 15–2 *Telnet Connection Options, Continued*

Option	Description
/noecho	Disables local echo.
/route *path*	Specifies loose source routing. The *path* argument is a list of host names or IP addresses that specify network nodes and ends with the final destination.
/source-interface	Specifies source interface.
/stream	Turns on *stream* processing, which enables a raw TCP stream with no Telnet control sequences. A stream connection does not process Telnet options and can be appropriate for connections to ports running UUCP and other non-Telnet protocols.
port-number	Port number.
bgp	Border Gateway Protocol.
chargen	Character generator.
cmd *rcmd*	Remote commands.
daytime	Daytime.
discard	Discard.
domain	Domain Name System.
echo	Echo.
exec	EXEC.
finger	Finger.
ftp	File Transfer Protocol.
ftp-data	FTP data connections (used infrequently).
gopher	Gopher.
hostname	NIC hostname server.
ident	Ident Protocol.
irc	Internet Relay Chat.
klogin	Kerberos login.
kshell	Kerberos shell.
login	Login (rlogin).
lpd	Printer service.

Table 15–2   *Telnet Connection Options, Continued*

Option	Description
nntp	Network News Transport Protocol.
node	Connect to a specific LAT node.
pop2	Post Office Protocol v2.
pop3	Post Office Protocol v3.
port	Destination LAT port name.
smtp	Simple Mail Transport Protocol.
sunrpc	Sun Remote Procedure Call.
syslog	Syslog.
tacacs	Specify TACACS security.
talk	Talk.
telnet	Telnet.
time	Time.
uucp	UNIX-to-UNIX Copy Program.
whois	Nickname.
www	World Wide Web (HTTP).

Command Mode

EXEC

Usage Guidelines

This command first appeared in a release prior to Cisco IOS Release 10.0.

With the Cisco IOS implementation of TCP/IP, you are not required to enter the **connect** or **telnet** commands to establish a Telnet connection. You can just enter the learned host name—as long as the following conditions are met:

- The host name is different from a command word for the router
- The preferred transport protocol is set to Telnet

To display a list of the available hosts, use the **show hosts** command. To display the status of all TCP connections, use the **show tcp** command.

The Cisco IOS software assigns a logical name to each connection, and several commands use these names to identify connections. The logical name is the same as the host name, unless that name is already in use, or you change the connection name with the **name-connection** EXEC command. If the name is already in use, the Cisco IOS software assigns a null name to the connection.

The Telnet software supports special Telnet commands in the form of Telnet sequences that map generic terminal control functions to operating system-specific functions. To issue a special Telnet command, enter the escape sequence and then a command character. The default escape sequence is Ctrl-^ (press and hold the Control and Shift keys and the 6 key). You can enter the command character as you hold down Ctrl or with Ctrl released; you can use either uppercase or lowercase letters. Table 15–3 lists the special Telnet escape sequences.

Table 15–3 *Special Telnet Escape Sequences*

Task	Escape Sequence[1]
Break	Ctrl-^ b
Interrupt Process (IP)	Ctrl-^ c
Erase Character (EC)	Ctrl-^ h
Abort Output (AO)	Ctrl-^ o
Are You There? (AYT)	Ctrl-^ t
Erase Line (EL)	Ctrl-^ u

1. The caret (^) symbol refers to Shift-6 on your keyboard.

At any time during an active Telnet session, you can list the Telnet commands by pressing the escape sequence keys followed by a question mark at the system prompt:

    Ctrl-^ ?

A sample of this list follows. In this sample output, the first caret (^) symbol represents the Control key, while the second caret represents Shift-6 on your keyboard:

```
Router> ^^?
[Special telnet escape help]
^^B  sends telnet BREAK
^^C  sends telnet IP
^^H  sends telnet EC
^^O  sends telnet AO
^^T  sends telnet AYT
^^U  sends telnet EL
```

You can have several concurrent Telnet sessions open and switch back and forth between them. To open a subsequent session, first suspend the current connection by pressing the escape sequence (**Ctrl-Shift-6** then **x** [**Ctrl^x**] by default) to return to the system command prompt. Then open a new connection with the **telnet** command.

Part II

Command Reference

To terminate an active Telnet session, issue any of the following commands at the prompt of the device to which you are connecting:

close
disconnect
exit
logout
quit

Examples

The following example establishes an encrypted Telnet session from a router to a remote host named *host1*:

```
Router> telnet host1 /encrypt kerberos
```

The following example routes packets from the source system host1 to kl.sri.com, then to 10.1.0.11, and finally back to *host1*:

```
Router> telnet host1 /route:kl.sri.com 10.1.0.11 host1
```

The following example connects to a host with logical name *host1*:

```
Router> host1
```

Related Commands

Search online to find documentation for related commands.

connect
rlogin

PART III

Traffic Filtering

CHAPTER 16

Access Control Lists: Overview and Guidelines

Cisco provides basic traffic filtering capabilities with access control lists (also referred to as *access lists*). Access lists can be configured for all routed network protocols (IP, AppleTalk, and so on.) to filter those protocols' packets as the packets pass through a router.

You can configure access lists at your router to control access to a network: Access lists can prevent certain traffic from entering or exiting a network.

IN THIS CHAPTER

This chapter describes access lists as part of a security solution. This chapter includes tips, cautions, considerations, recommendations, and general guidelines for how to use access lists.

This chapter has these sections:

- About Access Control Lists
- Overview of Access List Configuration
  - Creating Access Lists
  - Applying Access Lists to Interfaces
- Find Complete Configuration and Command Information for Access Lists

ABOUT ACCESS CONTROL LISTS

This section briefly describes what access lists do; why and when you should configure access lists; and basic versus advanced access lists.

What Access Lists Do

Access lists filter network traffic by controlling whether routed packets are forwarded or blocked at the router's interfaces. Your router examines each packet to determine whether to forward or drop the packet, based on the criteria you specified within the access lists.

Access list criteria could be the source address of the traffic, the destination address of the traffic, the upper-layer protocol, or other information. Note that sophisticated users can sometimes successfully evade or fool basic access lists because no authentication is required.

Why You Should Configure Access Lists

There are many reasons to configure access lists—for example, you can use access lists to restrict contents of routing updates, or to provide traffic flow control. But one of the most important reasons to configure access lists is to provide security for your network; this is the reason focused on in this chapter.

You should use access lists to provide a basic level of security for accessing your network. If you do not configure access lists on your router, all packets passing through the router could be allowed onto all parts of your network.

For example, access lists can allow one host to access a part of your network, and prevent another host from accessing the same area. In Figure 16–1, Host A is allowed to access the Human Resources network and Host B is prevented from accessing the Human Resources network.

Figure 16–1

Using Traffic Filters to Prevent Traffic from being Routed to a Network

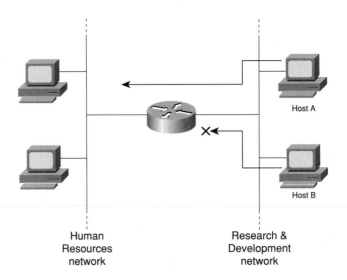

You can also use access lists to decide which types of traffic are forwarded or blocked at the router interfaces. For example, you can permit e-mail traffic to be routed but at the same time block all Telnet traffic.

When to Configure Access Lists

Access lists should be used in "firewall" routers, which are often positioned between your internal network and an external network such as the Internet. You can also use access lists on a router positioned between two parts of your network, to control traffic entering or exiting a specific part of your internal network.

To provide the security benefits of access lists, you should at a minimum configure access lists on border routers—routers situated at the edges of your networks. This provides a basic buffer from the outside network, or from a less controlled area of your own network into a more sensitive area of your network.

On these routers, you should configure access lists for each network protocol configured on the router interfaces. You can configure access lists so that inbound traffic or outbound traffic or both are filtered on an interface.

Access lists must be defined on a per-protocol basis. In other words, you should define access lists for every protocol enabled on an interface if you want to control traffic flow for that protocol. (Note that some protocols refer to access lists as *filters*.)

Basic versus Advanced Access Lists

This chapter describes how to use standard and static extended access lists, which are the basic types of access lists. Some type of basic access list should be used with each routed protocol that you have configured for router interfaces.

Besides the basic types of access lists described in this chapter, there are also more advanced access lists available, which provide additional security features and give you greater control over packet transmission. These advanced access lists and features are described in the other chapters within this part (Part III, "Traffic Filtering") of the book.

OVERVIEW OF ACCESS LIST CONFIGURATION

Although each protocol has its own set of specific tasks and rules required for you to provide traffic filtering, generally, most protocols require at least two basic steps to be accomplished. The first step is to create an access list definition, and the second step is to apply the access list to an interface.

The two steps are described next in the following sections:

- Creating Access Lists
- Applying Access Lists to Interfaces

Note that some protocols refer to access lists as *filters* and refer to the act of applying the access lists to interfaces as *filtering*.

Creating Access Lists

Create access lists for each protocol you want to filter, per router interface. For some protocols, you create one access list to filter inbound traffic and one access list to filter outbound traffic.

The protocols for which you can configure access lists are identified in Table 16–1 and Table 16–2 (following).

To create an access list, you specify the protocol to filter, you assign a unique name or number to the access list, and you define packet filtering criteria. A single access list can have multiple filtering criteria statements.

Cisco recommends that you create your access lists on a TFTP server, then download the access lists to your router. This can considerably simplify maintenance of your access lists. For details, see section "Creating and Editing Access List Statements on a TFTP Server," found later in this chapter.

Assigning a Unique Name or Number to Each Access List

When configuring access lists on a router, you must identify each access list uniquely within a protocol, by assigning either a name or a number to the protocol's access list.

NOTES
_____

Access lists of some protocols must be identified by a name, and access lists of other protocols must be identified by a number. Some protocols can be identified by either a name or a number. When a number is used to identify an access list, the number must be within the specific range of numbers that is valid for the protocol.

You can specify access lists by names for the protocols listed in Table 16–1.

Table 16–1   *Protocols with Access Lists Specified by Names*

Protocol
Apollo Domain
IP
IPX
ISO CLNS
NetBIOS IPX
Source-route bridging NetBIOS

You can specify access lists by numbers for the protocols listed in Table 16–2. Table 16–2 also lists the range of access list numbers that is valid for each protocol.

Table 16-2   *Protocols with Access Lists Specified by Numbers*

Protocol	Range
IP	1 to 99
Extended IP	100 to 199
Ethernet type code	200 to 299
Ethernet address	700 to 799
Transparent bridging (protocol type)	200 to 299
Transparent bridging (vendor code)	700 to 799
Extended transparent bridging	1100 to 1199
DECnet and extended DECnet	300 to 399
XNS	400 to 499
Extended XNS	500 to 599
AppleTalk	600 to 699
Source-route bridging (protocol type)	200 to 299
Source-route bridging (vendor code)	700 to 799
IPX	800 to 899
Extended IPX	900 to 999
IPX SAP	1000 to 1099
Standard VINES	1 to 100
Extended VINES	101 to 200
Simple VINES	201 to 300

Defining Criteria for Forwarding or Blocking Packets

When creating an access list, you define criteria which are applied to each packet that is processed by the router; the router decides whether to forward or block each packet based on whether or not the packet matches the criteria.

Typical criteria you define in access lists are packet source addresses, packet destination addresses, or upper-layer protocol of the packet. However, each protocol has its own specific set of criteria that can be defined.

For a single access list, you can define multiple criteria in multiple, separate access list statements. Each of these statements should reference the same identifying name or number to tie the statements to the same access list. You can have as many criteria statements as you want, limited only by the available memory. Of course, the more statements you have, the more difficult it will be to comprehend and manage your access lists.

The Implied "Deny All Traffic" Criteria Statement

At the end of every access list is an implied "deny all traffic" criteria statement. Therefore, if a packet does not match any of your criteria statements, the packet will be blocked.

NOTES

For most protocols, if you define an inbound access list for traffic filtering, you should include explicit access list criteria statements to permit routing updates. If you do not, you might effectively lose communication from the interface when routing updates are blocked by the implicit "deny all traffic" statement at the end of the access list.

The Order In Which You Enter Criteria Statements

Note that each additional criteria statement that you enter is appended to the *end* of the access list statements. Also note that you cannot delete individual statements after they have been created. You can only delete an entire access list.

The order of access list statements is important! When the router is deciding whether to forward or block a packet, the Cisco IOS software tests the packet against each criteria statement in the order the statements were created. After a match is found, no more criteria statements are checked.

If you create a criteria statement that explicitly permits all traffic, no statements added later will ever be checked. If you need additional statements, you must delete the access list and retype it with the new entries.

Creating and Editing Access List Statements on a TFTP Server

Because the order of access list criteria statements is important, and because you cannot reorder or delete criteria statements on your router, Cisco recommends that you create all access list statements on a TFTP server, and then download the entire access list to your router.

To use a TFTP server, create the access list statements using any text editor, and save the access list in ASCII format to a TFTP server that is accessible by your router. Then, from your router, use the **copy tftp running-config** *file_id* command to copy the access list to your router. Finally, perform the **copy running-config startup-config** command to save the access list to your router's NVRAM.

Then, if you ever want to make changes to an access list, you can make them to the text file on the TFTP server, and copy the edited file to your router as before.

NOTES

The first command of an edited access list file should delete the previous access list (for example, type a **no access-list** command at the beginning of the file). If you do not first delete the previous version of the access list, when you copy the edited file to your router you will merely be appending additional criteria statements to the end of the existing access list.

Applying Access Lists to Interfaces

For some protocols, you can apply up to two access lists to an interface: one inbound access list and one outbound access list. With other protocols, you apply only one access list which checks both inbound and outbound packets.

If the access list is inbound, when the router receives a packet, the Cisco IOS software checks the access list's criteria statements for a match. If the packet is permitted, the software continues to process the packet. If the packet is denied, the software discards the packet.

If the access list is outbound, after receiving and routing a packet to the outbound interface, the software checks the access list's criteria statements for a match. If the packet is permitted, the software transmits the packet. If the packet is denied, the software discards the packet.

FIND COMPLETE CONFIGURATION AND COMMAND INFORMATION FOR ACCESS LISTS

The guidelines discussed in this chapter apply in general to all protocols. The specific instructions for creating access lists and applying them to interfaces vary from protocol-to-protocol, and this specific information is not included in this chapter.

CHAPTER 17

Configuring Lock-and-Key Security (Dynamic Access Lists)

This chapter describes how to configure lock-and-key security at your router. Lock-and-key is a traffic filtering security feature available for the IP protocol.

For a complete description of lock-and-key commands, see Chapter 18, "Lock-and-Key Commands."

IN THIS CHAPTER

This chapter has the following sections:

- About Lock-and-Key
- Compatibility with Releases Prior to Cisco IOS Release 11.1
- Risk of Spoofing with Lock-and-Key
- Router Performance Impacts with Lock-and-Key
- Prerequisites to Configuring Lock-and-Key
- Configuring Lock-and-Key
- Verifying Lock-and-Key Configuration
- Lock-and-Key Maintenance
- Lock-and-Key Configuration Examples

ABOUT LOCK-AND-KEY

Lock-and-key is a traffic filtering security feature that dynamically filters IP protocol traffic. Lock-and-key is configured using IP dynamic extended access lists. Lock-and-key can be used in conjunction with other standard access lists and static extended access lists.

When lock-and-key is configured, designated users whose IP traffic is normally blocked at a router can gain temporary access through the router. When triggered, lock-and-key reconfigures the interface's existing IP access list to permit designated users to reach their designated host(s). Afterwards, lock-and-key reconfigures the interface back to its original state.

For a user to gain access to a host through a router with lock-and-key configured, the user must first Telnet to the router. When a user initiates a standard Telnet session to the router, lock-and-key automatically attempts to authenticate the user. If the user is authenticated, that user will then gain temporary access through the router and be able to reach the destination host.

Benefits of Lock-and-Key

Lock-and-key provides the same benefits as standard and static extended access lists (these benefits are discussed in Chapter 16, "Access Control Lists: Overview and Guidelines"). However, lock-and-key also has the following security benefits over standard and static extended access lists:

- Lock-and-key uses a challenge mechanism to authenticate individual users.
- Lock-and-key provides simpler management in large internetworks.
- In many cases, lock-and-key reduces the amount of router processing required for access lists.
- Lock-and-key reduces the opportunity for network break-ins by network hackers.

With lock-and-key, you can specify which users are permitted access to which source/destination hosts. These users must pass a user authentication process before they are permitted access to their designated host(s). Lock-and-key creates dynamic user access through a firewall, without compromising other configured security restrictions.

When to Use Lock-and-Key

Two examples of when you might use lock-and-key are as follows:

- When you want a specific remote user (or group of remote users) to be able to access a host within your network, connecting from their remote host(s) via the Internet. Lock-and-key authenticates the user, then permits limited access through your firewall router for the individual's host or subnet, for a finite period of time.
- When you want a subset of hosts on a local network to access a host on a remote network protected by a firewall. With lock-and-key, you can enable access to the remote host only for the desired set of local user's hosts. Lock-and-key requires the users to authenticate through a TACACS+ server, or other security server, before allowing their hosts to access the remote hosts.

How Lock-and-Key Works

The following process describes the lock-and-key access operation:

1. A user opens a Telnet session to a border (firewall) router configured for lock-and-key. The user connects via the virtual terminal port on the router.
2. The Cisco IOS software receives the Telnet packet, opens a Telnet session, prompts for a password, and performs a user authentication process. The user must pass authentication

before access through the router is allowed. The authentication process can be done by the router or by a central access security server such as a TACACS+ or RADIUS server.

3. When the user passes authentication, that user is logged out of the Telnet session, and the software creates a temporary entry in the dynamic access list. (Per your configuration, this temporary entry can limit the range of networks to which a user is given temporary access.)

4. The user exchanges data through the firewall.

5. The software deletes the temporary access list entry when a configured timeout is reached, or when the system administrator manually clears it. The configured timeout can either be an idle timeout or an absolute timeout.

NOTES

The temporary access list entry is not automatically deleted when the user terminates a session. The temporary access list entry remains until a configured timeout is reached or until it is cleared by the system administrator.

COMPATIBILITY WITH RELEASES PRIOR TO CISCO IOS RELEASE 11.1

Enhancements to the **access-list** command are used for lock-and-key. These enhancements are backward compatible—if you migrate from a release prior to Cisco IOS Release 11.1 to a newer release, your access lists will be automatically converted to reflect the enhancements. However, if you try to use lock-and-key with a release prior to Cisco IOS Release 11.1, you might encounter problems as described in the following caution paragraph.

CAUTION

Cisco IOS releases prior to Release 11.1 are not upwardly compatible with the lock-and-key access list enhancements. Therefore, if you save an access list with software older than Release 11.1, and then use this software, the resulting access list will not be interpreted correctly. *This could cause you severe security problems.* You must save your old configuration files with Cisco IOS Release 11.1 or later software before booting an image with these files.

RISK OF SPOOFING WITH LOCK-AND-KEY

CAUTION

Lock-and-key access allows an external event (a Telnet session) to place an opening in the firewall. While this opening exists, the router is susceptible to source address spoofing.

When lock-and-key is triggered, it creates a dynamic opening in the firewall by temporarily reconfiguring an interface to allow user access. While this opening exists, another host might spoof the authenticated user's address to gain access behind the firewall. Lock-and-key does not cause the address spoofing problem; the problem is only identified here as a concern to the user. Spoofing is a problem inherent to all access lists, and lock-and-key does not specifically address this problem.

To prevent spoofing, you could configure network data encryption as described in Chapter 23, "Configuring Network Data Encryption." Configure encryption so that traffic from the remote host is encrypted at a secured remote router and decrypted locally at the router interface providing lock-and-key. You want to ensure that all traffic using lock-and-key will be encrypted when entering the router; this way no hackers can spoof the source address, because they will be unable to duplicate the encryption or to be authenticated, as is a required part of the encryption setup process.

ROUTER PERFORMANCE IMPACTS WITH LOCK-AND-KEY

When lock-and-key is configured, router performance can be affected in the following ways:

- When lock-and-key is triggered, the dynamic access list forces an access list rebuild on the silicon switching engine (SSE). This causes the SSE switching path to slow down momentarily.

- Dynamic access lists require the idle timeout facility (even if the timeout is left to default) and therefore cannot be SSE switched. These entries must be handled in the protocol fast switching path.

- When remote users trigger lock-and-key at a border router, additional access list entries are created on the border router interface. The interface's access list will grow and shrink dynamically. Entries are dynamically removed from the list after either the idle timeout or max timeout period expires. Large access lists can degrade packet switching performance, so if you notice performance problems, you should look at the border router configuration to see if you should remove temporary access list entries generated by lock-and-key.

PREREQUISITES TO CONFIGURING LOCK-AND-KEY

Lock-and-key uses IP extended access lists. You must have a solid understanding of how access lists are used to filter traffic before you attempt to configure lock-and-key. Access lists are described in Chapter 16.

Lock-and-key employs user authentication and authorization as implemented in Cisco's Authentication, Authorization, and Accounting (AAA) paradigm. You must understand how to configure AAA user authentication and authorization before you configure lock-and-key. User authentication and authorization is explained in Part I, "Authentication, Authorization, and Accounting (AAA)."

Lock-and-key uses the **autocommand** command, which you should understand.

CONFIGURING LOCK-AND-KEY

To configure lock-and-key, perform the following tasks beginning in global configuration mode. While completing these steps, be sure to follow the guidelines listed afterward in the section "Lock-and-Key Configuration Tips":

Task	Command
Step 1 Configure a dynamic access list, which serves as a template and placeholder for temporary access list entries.	**access-list** *access-list-number* [**dynamic** *dynamic-name* [**timeout** *minutes*]] {**deny** | **permit**} **telnet** *source source-wildcard destination destination-wildcard* [**precedence** *precedence*] [**tos** *tos*] [**established**] [**log**]
Step 2 Configure an interface.	**interface** *type number*
Step 3 In interface configuration mode, apply the access list to the interface.	**ip access-group** *access-list-number*
Step 4 In global configuration mode, define one or more virtual terminal (VTY) ports. If you specify multiple VTY ports, they must all be configured identically, because the software hunts for available VTY ports on a round-robin basis. If you do not want to configure all your VTY ports for lock-and-key access, you can specify a group of VTY ports for lock-and-key support only.	**line VTY** *line-number* [*ending-line-number*]
Step 5 Configure user authentication.	**login tacacs** or **username** *name* **password** *secret* or **password** *password* **login local**
Step 6 Enable the creation of temporary access list entries. If the **host** argument is *not* specified, all hosts on the entire network are allowed to set up a temporary access list entry. The dynamic access list contains the network mask to enable the new network connection.	**autocommand access-enable** [**host**] [**timeout** *minutes*]

For an example of a lock-and-key configuration, see section "Lock-and-Key Configuration Examples," found later in this chapter.

Lock-and-Key Configuration Tips

You should understand the tips in this section before you configure lock-and-key.

Tips for Configuring Dynamic Access Lists

These tips correspond to Step 1 in the previous configuration task table.

- Do *not* create more than one dynamic access list for any one access list. The software only refers to the first dynamic access list defined.

- Do *not* assign the same *dynamic-name* to another access list. Doing so instructs the software to reuse the existing list. All named entries must be globally unique within the configuration.

- Assign attributes to the dynamic access list in the same way you assign attributes for a static access list. The temporary access list entries inherit the attributes assigned to this list.

- Configure Telnet as the protocol so that the user must Telnet into the router to be authenticated, before they can gain access through the router.

- Either define an idle timeout now with the **timeout** keyword in the **access-list** command, or define an absolute timeout value later with the **access-enable** command in the **autocommand** command. You must define either an idle timeout or an absolution timeout—otherwise, the temporary access list entry will remain configured indefinitely on the interface (even after the user has terminated the session) until the entry is removed manually by an administrator. (You could configure both idle and absolute timeouts if you wish.)

- If you configure an idle timeout, the idle timeout value should be equal to the WAN idle timeout value.

- If you configure both idle and absolute timeouts, the idle timeout value must be less than the absolute timeout value.

- The only values replaced in the temporary entry are the source or destination address, depending whether the access list was in the input access list or output access list. All other attributes such as port are inherited from the main dynamic access list.

- Each addition to the dynamic list is always put at the beginning of the dynamic list. You cannot specify the order of temporary access list entries.

- Temporary access list entries are never written to NVRAM.

- To manually clear or to display dynamic access lists, see section "Lock-and-Key Maintenance," found later in this chapter.

Tips for Configuring Lock-and-Key Authentication

These tips correspond to Step 5 in the previous configuration task table.

There are three possible methods to configure an authentication query process. These three methods are described in this section.

NOTES

Cisco recommends that you use the TACACS+ server for your authentication query process. TACACS+ provides authentication, authorization, and accounting services. It also provides protocol support, protocol specification, and a centralized security database. Using a TACACS+ server is described in the next section, "Method 1—Configure a Security Server."

Method 1—Configure a Security Server

Use a network access security server such as TACACS+ server. This method requires additional configuration steps on the TACACS+ server but allows for stricter authentication queries and more sophisticated tracking capabilities.

```
Router# login tacacs
```

Method 2—Configure the **username** Command

Use the **username** command. This method is more effective, because authentication is determined on a user basis.

```
Router# username name password password
```

Method 3—Configure the **password** and **login** Commands

Use the **password** and **login** commands. This method is less effective, because the password is configured for the port, not for the user. Therefore, any user who knows the password can authenticate successfully.

```
Router# password password
Router# login local
```

Tips for Configuring the autocommand Command

These tips correspond to Step 6 in the previous configuration task table.

- If you use a TACACS+ server to authenticate the user, you should configure the **autocommand** command on the TACACS+ server as a per-user autocommand. If you use local authentication, use the autocommand on the line.

- Configure all virtual terminal (VTY) ports with the same **autocommand** command. Omitting an **autocommand** command on a VTY port allows a random host to gain EXEC mode access to the router and does not create a temporary access list entry in the dynamic access list.

- If you did not previously define an idle timeout with the **access-list** command, you must define an absolute timeout now with the **autocommand access-enable** command. You must define either an idle timeout or an absolute timeout—otherwise, the temporary access list entry will remain configured indefinitely on the interface (even after the user has terminated the session) until the entry is removed manually by an administrator. (You could configure both idle and absolute timeouts if you want.)

- If you configure both idle and absolute timeouts, the absolute timeout value must be greater than the idle timeout value.

VERIFYING LOCK-AND-KEY CONFIGURATION

You can verify that lock-and-key is successfully configured on the router by asking a user to test the connection. The user should be at a host that is permitted in the dynamic access list, and the user should have AAA authentication and authorization configured for him or her.

To test the connection, the user should Telnet to the router, allow the Telnet session to close, and then attempt to access a host on the other side of the router. This host must be one that is permitted by the dynamic access list. The user should access the host with an application that uses the IP protocol.

The following sample display illustrates what end users might see if they are successfully authenticated. Notice that the Telnet connection is closed immediately after the password is entered and authenticated. The temporary access list entry is then created, and the host that initiated the Telnet session now has access inside the firewall.

```
Router% telnet corporate
Trying 172.21.52.1 ...
Connected to corporate.abc.com.
Escape character is '^]'.
User Access Verification
Password:Connection closed by foreign host.
```

You can then use the **show access-lists** command at the router to view the dynamic access lists, which should include an additional entry permitting the user access through the router.

LOCK-AND-KEY MAINTENANCE

When lock-and-key is in use, dynamic access lists will dynamically grow and shrink as entries are added and deleted. You need to make sure that entries are being deleted in a timely way, because while entries exist, the risk of a spoofing attack is present. Also, the more entries there are, the bigger the router performance impact will be.

If you don't have an idle or absolute timeout configured, entries will remain in the dynamic access list until you manually remove them. If this is the case for you, make sure that you are extremely vigilant about removing entries.

Display Dynamic Access List Entries

You can display temporary access list entries when they are in use. After a temporary access list entry is cleared by you or by the absolute or idle timeout parameter, it can no longer be displayed. The number of matches displayed indicates the number of times the access list entry was hit.

To view dynamic access lists and any temporary access list entries that are currently established, perform the following task in privileged EXEC mode:

Task	Command
Display dynamic access lists and temporary access list entries.	**show access-lists** [*access-list-number*]

Manually Delete Dynamic Access List Entries

To delete a temporary access list entry manually, perform the following task in privileged EXEC mode:

Task	Command
Delete a dynamic access list.	**clear access-template** [*access-list-number* | *name*] [*dynamic-name*] [*source*] [*destination*]

LOCK-AND-KEY CONFIGURATION EXAMPLES

There are two examples in this section:

- Example of Lock-and-Key with Local Authentication
- Example of Lock-and-Key with TACACS+ Authentication

Cisco recommends that you use a TACACS+ server for authentication, as shown in the second example.

Example of Lock-and-Key with Local Authentication

This example shows how to configure lock-and-key access, with authentication occurring locally at the router. Lock-and-key is configured on the Ethernet 0 interface.

```
interface ethernet0
 ip address 172.18.23.9 255.255.255.0
 ip access-group 101 in

access-list 101 permit tcp any host 172.18.21.2 eq telnet
access-list 101 dynamic mytestlist timeout 120 permit ip any any

line vty 0
login local
autocommand access-enable timeout 5
```

The first access list entry allows only Telnet into the router. The second access list entry is always ignored until lock-and-key is triggered.

After a user Telnets into the router, the router will attempt to authenticate the user. If authentication is successful, the **autocommand** executes and the Telnet session terminates. The autocommand creates a temporary inbound access list entry at the Ethernet 0 interface, based on the second access list entry (mytestlist). This temporary entry will expire after 5 minutes, as specified by the timeout.

Example of Lock-and-Key with TACACS+ Authentication

The following example shows how to configure lock-and-key access, with authentication on a TACACS+ server. Because login is on the TACACS+ server, no **autocommand** command appears in this configuration. Lock-and-key access is configured on the BRI0 interface. Four VTY ports are defined with the password "cisco."

```
aaa authentication login default tacacs+ enable
aaa accounting exec stop-only tacacs+
aaa accounting network stop-only tacacs+
enable password ciscotac
!
isdn switch-type basic-dms100
!
interface ethernet0
ip address 172.18.23.9 255.255.255.0
!!
interface BRI0
 ip address 172.18.21.1 255.255.255.0
 encapsulation ppp
 dialer idle-timeout 3600
 dialer wait-for-carrier-time 100
 dialer map ip 172.18.21.2 name diana
 dialer-group 1
 isdn spid1 2036333715291
 isdn spid2 2036339371566
 ppp authentication chap
 ip access-group 102 in
!
access-list 102 permit tcp any host 172.18.21.2 eq telnet
access-list 102 dynamic testlist timeout 5 permit ip any any
!
!
ip route 172.18.250.0 255.255.255.0 172.18.21.2
priority-list 1 interface BRI0 high
tacacs-server host 172.18.23.21
tacacs-server host 172.18.23.14
tacacs-server key test1
tftp-server rom alias all
!
dialer-list 1 protocol ip permit
!
line con 0
 password cisco
line aux 0
line VTY 0 4
password cisco
!
```

## CHAPTER 18

Lock-and-Key Commands

This chapter describes lock-and-key commands. Lock-and-key security is a traffic filtering security feature that uses dynamic access lists. Lock-and-key is available for IP traffic only.

For lock-and-key configuration information, see Chapter 17, "Configuring Lock-and-Key Security (Dynamic Access Lists)."

ACCESS-ENABLE

To enable the router to create a temporary access list entry in a dynamic access list, use the **access-enable** EXEC command.

```
access-enable [host] [timeout minutes]
```

Syntax Description

host
: (Optional) Tells the software to enable access only for the host from which the Telnet session originated. If not specified, the software allows all hosts on the defined network to gain access. The dynamic access list contains the network mask to use for enabling the new network.

timeout *minutes*
: (Optional) Specifies an idle timeout for the temporary access list entry. If the access list entry is not accessed within this period, it is automatically deleted and requires the user to authenticate again. The default is for the entries to remain permanently. We recommend that this value equal the idle timeout set for the WAN connection.

Command Mode

EXEC

Usage Guidelines

This command first appeared in Cisco IOS Release 11.1.

This command enables the lock-and-key access feature.

You should always define either an idle timeout (with the **timeout** keyword in this command) or an absolute timeout (with the **timeout** keyword in the **access-list** command). Otherwise, the temporary access list entry will remain, even after the user terminates the session.

Use the **autocommand** command with the **access-enable** command to cause the **access-enable** command to execute when a user Telnets into the router.

Example

The following example causes the software to create a temporary access list entry and tells the software to enable access only for the host from which the Telnet session originated. If the access list entry is not accessed within two minutes, it is deleted.

```
autocommand access-enable host timeout 2
```

Related Commands

Search online to find documentation for related commands.

access-list (extended)
autocommand

ACCESS-TEMPLATE

To manually place a temporary access list entry on a router to which you are connected, use the **access-template** EXEC command.

> **access-template** [*access-list-number* | *name*] [*dynamic-name*] [*source*] [*destination*] [*timeout minutes*]

Syntax Description

access-list-number   Number of the dynamic access list.

name   Name of an IP access list. The name cannot contain a space or quotation mark and must begin with an alphabetic character to avoid ambiguity with numbered access lists.

dynamic-name   (Optional) Name of a dynamic access list.

source   (Optional) Source address in a dynamic access list. The keywords **host** and **any** are allowed. All other attributes are inherited from the original access list entry.

destination   (Optional) Destination address in a dynamic access list. The keywords **host** and **any** are allowed. All other attributes are inherited from the original access list entry.

timeout *minutes*   (Optional) Specifies a maximum time limit for each entry within this dynamic list. This is an absolute time, from creation, that an entry can reside in the list. The default is an infinite time limit and allows an entry to remain permanently.

Command Mode

EXEC

Usage Guidelines

This command first appeared in Cisco IOS Release 11.1.

This command provides a way to enable the lock-and-key access feature.

You should always define either an idle timeout (with the **timeout** keyword in this command) or an absolute timeout (with the **timeout** keyword in the **access-list** command). Otherwise, the dynamic access list will remain, even after the user has terminated the session.

Example

In the following example, the software enables IP access on incoming packets in which the source address is 172.29.1.129 and the destination address is 192.168.52.12. All other source and destination pairs are discarded.

```
access-template 101 payroll host 172.29.1.129 host 192.168.52.12 timeout 2
```

Related Commands

Search online to find documentation for related commands.

access-list (extended)
autocommand
clear access-template

CLEAR ACCESS-TEMPLATE

To manually clear a temporary access list entry from a dynamic access list, use the **clear access-template** EXEC command.

clear access-template [*access-list-number* | *name*] [*dynamic-name*] [*source*] [*destination*]

Syntax Description

access-list-number	(Optional) Number of the dynamic access list from which the entry is to be deleted.
name	Name of an IP access list from which the entry is to be deleted. The name cannot contain a space or quotation mark, and must begin with an alphabetic character to avoid ambiguity with numbered access lists.
dynamic-name	(Optional) Name of the dynamic access list from which the entry is to be deleted.
source	(Optional) Source address in a temporary access list entry to be deleted.
destination	(Optional) Destination address in a temporary access list entry to be deleted.

Command Mode

EXEC

Usage Guidelines

This command first appeared in Cisco IOS Release 11.1.

This command is related to the lock-and-key access feature. It clears any temporary access list entries that match the parameters you define.

Example

The following example clears any temporary access list entries with a source of 172.20.1.12 from the dynamic access list named vendor:

```
clear access-template vendor 172.20.1.12
```

Related Commands

Search online to find documentation for related commands.

access-list (extended)
access-template

SHOW IP ACCOUNTING

To display the active accounting or checkpointed database or to display access list violations, use the **show ip accounting** privileged EXEC command.

> **show ip accounting [checkpoint] [output-packets | access-violations]**

Syntax Description

checkpoint   (Optional) Indicates that the checkpointed database should be displayed.

output-packets   (Optional) Indicates that information pertaining to packets that passed access control and were successfully routed should be displayed. This is the default value if neither **output-packet**s nor **access-violations** is specified.

access-violations   (Optional) Indicates that information pertaining to packets that failed access lists and were not routed should be displayed.

Defaults

If neither the **output-packet**s nor **access-violations** keyword is specified, **show ip accounting** displays information pertaining to packets that passed access control and were successfully routed.

Command Mode

EXEC

Usage Guidelines

This command first appeared in Cisco IOS Release 10.0.

To use this command, you must first enable IP accounting on a per-interface basis.

Sample Displays

Following is sample output from the **show ip accounting** command:

```
Router# show ip accounting

     Source          Destination          Packets          Bytes
  172.30.19.40      172.30.67.20              7              306
  172.30.13.55      172.30.67.20             67             2749
  172.30.2.50       172.30.33.51             17             1111
  172.30.2.50       172.30.2.1                5              319
  172.30.2.50       172.30.1.2              463            30991
  172.30.19.40      172.30.2.1                4              262
  172.30.19.40      172.30.1.2               28             2552
  172.30.20.2       172.30.6.100             39             2184
  172.30.13.55      172.30.1.2               35             3020
  172.30.19.40      172.30.33.51           1986            95091
  172.30.2.50       172.30.67.20            233            14908
  172.30.13.28      172.30.67.53            390            24817
  172.30.13.55      172.30.33.51         214669          9806659
  172.30.13.111     172.30.6.23           27739          1126607
```

```
172.30.13.44    172.30.33.51              35412            1523980
172.30.7.21     172.30.1.2                   11                824
172.30.13.28    172.30.33.2                  21               1762
172.30.2.166    172.30.7.130                797             141054
172.30.3.11     172.30.67.53                  4                246
172.30.7.21     172.30.33.51              15696             695635
172.30.7.24     172.30.67.20                 21                916
172.30.13.111   172.30.10.1                  16               1137
```

Table 18–1 describes fields shown in the display.

Table 18–1 *Show IP Accounting Field Descriptions*

Field	Description
Source	Source address of the packet.
Destination	Destination address of the packet.
Packets	Number of packets transmitted from the source address to the destination address.
Bytes	Number of bytes transmitted from the source address to the destination address.

Following is sample output from the **show ip accounting access-violations** command. (The following displays information pertaining to packets that failed access lists and were not routed.)

```
Router# show ip accounting access-violations

Source          Destination       Packets       Bytes      ACL
172.30.19.40    172.30.67.20      7             306        77
172.30.13.55    172.30.67.20      67            2749       185
172.30.2.50     172.30.33.51      17            1111       140
172.30.2.50     172.30.2.1        5             319        140
172.30.19.40    172.30.2.1        4             262        77
Accounting data age is 41
```

Table 18–2 describes fields shown in the display.

Table 18–2 *Show IP Accounting Access-Violation Field Descriptions*

Field	Description
Source	Source address of the packet.
Destination	Destination address of the packet.
Packets	For **accounting** keyword, number of packets transmitted from the source address to the destination address. For **access-violations** keyword, number of packets transmitted from the source address to the destination address that violated the access control list.

Table 18–2 *Show IP Accounting Access-Violation Field Descriptions, Continued*

Field	Description
Bytes	For **accounting** keyword, number of bytes transmitted from the source address to the destination address.
	For **access-violations** keyword, number of bytes transmitted from the source address to the destination address that violated the access control list.
ACL	Number of the access list of the last packet transmitted from the source to the destination that failed an access list.

Related Commands

Search online to find documentation for related commands.

clear ip accounting
ip accounting
ip accounting-list
ip accounting-threshold
ip accounting-transits

Part
III

Command Reference

## CHAPTER 19

Configuring IP Session Filtering (Reflexive Access Lists)

This chapter describes how to configure reflexive access lists on your router. Reflexive access lists provide the ability to filter network traffic at a router, based on IP upper-layer protocol "session" information.

For a complete description of reflexive access list commands, see Chapter 20, "Reflexive Access List Commands."

IN THIS CHAPTER

This chapter has the following sections:

- About Reflexive Access Lists
- Prework: Before You Configure Reflexive Access Lists
- Configuring Reflexive Access Lists
- Reflexive Access Lists Configuration Examples

ABOUT REFLEXIVE ACCESS LISTS

Reflexive access lists allow IP packets to be filtered based on upper-layer session information. You can use reflexive access lists to permit IP traffic for sessions originating from within your network, but deny IP traffic for sessions originating from outside your network. This is accomplished by *reflexive filtering,* a kind of session filtering.

Reflexive access lists can be defined with extended named IP access lists only. You cannot define reflexive access lists with numbered or standard named IP access lists or with other protocol access lists.

You can use reflexive access lists in conjunction with other standard access lists and static extended access lists.

Benefits of Reflexive Access Lists

Reflexive access lists are an important part of securing your network against network hackers, and can be included in a firewall defense. Reflexive access lists provide a level of security against spoofing and certain denial-of-service attacks. Reflexive access lists are simple to use, and, compared to basic access lists, provide greater control over which packets enter your network.

What Is a Reflexive Access List?

Reflexive access lists are similar in many ways to other access lists. Reflexive access lists contain condition statements (entries) that define criteria for permitting IP packets. These entries are evaluated in order; and when a match occurs, no more entries are evaluated.

However, reflexive access lists have significant differences from other types of access lists. Reflexive access lists contain only temporary entries; these entries are automatically created when a new IP session begins (for example, with an outbound packet), and the entries are removed when the session ends. Reflexive access lists are not themselves applied directly to an interface but are "nested" within an extended named IP access list that is applied to the interface. (For more information, see section "Configuring Reflexive Access Lists," found later in this chapter.) Also, reflexive access lists do not have the usual implicit "deny all traffic" statement at the end of the list, because of the nesting.

How Reflexive Access Lists Implement Session Filtering

This section compares session filtering with basic access lists to session filtering with reflexive access lists.

With Basic Access Lists

With basic standard and static extended access lists, you can approximate session filtering by using the **established** keyword with the **permit** command. The **established** keyword filters TCP packets based on whether the ACK or RST bits are set. (Set ACK or RST bits indicate that the packet is not the first in the session, and therefore, that the packet belongs to an established session.) This filter criterion would be part of an access list applied permanently to an interface.

With Reflexive Access Lists

Reflexive access lists, however, provide a truer form of session filtering, which is much harder to spoof, because more filter criteria must be matched before a packet is permitted through. (For example, source and destination addresses and port numbers are checked, not just ACK and RST bits.) Also, session filtering uses temporary filters, which are removed when a session is over. This limits the hacker's attack opportunity to a smaller time window.

Moreover, the previous method of using the **established** keyword was available only for the TCP upper-layer protocol. So, for the other upper-layer protocols (such as UDP, ICMP, and so forth), you would have to either permit all incoming traffic or define all possible permissible source/destination host/port address pairs for each protocol. (Besides being an unmanageable task, this could exhaust NVRAM space.)

Where to Configure Reflexive Access Lists

Configure reflexive access lists on border routers—routers that pass traffic between an internal and external network. Often, these are firewall routers.

NOTES

In this chapter, the words "within your network" and "internal network" refer to a network that is controlled (secured), such as your organization's intranet, or to a part of your organization's internal network that has higher security requirements than another part. "Outside your network" and "external network" refer to a network that is uncontrolled (unsecured), such as the Internet or to a part of your organization's network that is not as highly secured.

How Reflexive Access Lists Work

A reflexive access list is triggered when a new IP upper-layer session (such as TCP or UDP) is initiated from inside your network, with a packet traveling to the external network. When triggered, the reflexive access list generates a new, temporary entry. This entry will permit traffic to enter your network if the traffic is part of the session but will not permit traffic to enter your network if the traffic is not part of the session.

For example, if an outbound TCP packet is forwarded to outside of your network, and this packet is the first packet of a TCP session, then a new, temporary reflexive access list entry will be created. This entry is added to the reflexive access list, which applies to inbound traffic. The characteristics of the temporary entry are described in the following section.

Temporary Access List Entry Characteristics

- The entry is always a **permit** entry.
- The entry specifies the same protocol (TCP) as the original outbound TCP packet.
- The entry specifies the same source and destination addresses as the original outbound TCP packet, except the addresses are swapped.
- The entry specifies the same source and destination port numbers as the original outbound TCP packet, except the port numbers are swapped.

  (This entry characteristic applies only for TCP and UDP packets. Other protocols, such as ICMP and IGMP, do not have port numbers, and other criteria are specified. For example, for ICMP, type numbers are used instead.)

- Inbound TCP traffic will be evaluated against the entry, until the entry expires. If an inbound TCP packet matches the entry, the inbound packet will be forwarded into your network.

- The entry will expire (be removed) after the last packet of the session passes through the interface.
- If no packets belonging to the session are detected for a configurable length of time (the timeout period), the entry will expire.

When the Session Ends

Temporary reflexive access list entries are removed at the end of the session. For TCP sessions, the entry is removed 5 seconds after two set FIN bits are detected, or immediately after matching a TCP packet with the RST bit set. (Two set FIN bits in a session indicate that the session is about to end; the 5-second window allows the session to close gracefully. A set RST bit indicates an abrupt session close.) Or, the temporary entry is removed after no packets of the session have been detected for a configurable length of time (the timeout period).

For UDP and other protocols, the end of the session is determined differently than for TCP. Because other protocols are considered to be connectionless (sessionless) services, there is no session tracking information embedded in packets. Therefore, the end of a session is considered to be when no packets of the session have been detected for a configurable length of time (the timeout period).

Restrictions on Using Reflexive Access Lists

Reflexive access lists do not work with some applications that use port numbers that change during a session. For example, if the port numbers for a return packet are different from the originating packet, the return packet will be denied, even if the packet is actually part of the same session.

The TCP application of FTP is an example of an application with changing port numbers. With reflexive access lists, if you start an FTP request from within your network, the request will not complete. Instead, you must use Passive FTP when originating requests from within your network.

PREWORK: BEFORE YOU CONFIGURE REFLEXIVE ACCESS LISTS

Before you configure reflexive access lists, you must decide whether to configure reflexive access lists on an internal or external interface, as described in the next section, "Choose an Interface: Internal or External."

You should also be sure that you have a basic understanding of the IP protocol and of access lists; specifically, you should know how to configure extended named IP access lists.

Choose an Interface: Internal or External

Reflexive access lists are most commonly used with one of two basic network topologies. Determining which of these topologies is most like your own can help you decide whether to use reflexive access lists with an internal interface or with an external interface (the interface connecting to an internal network, or the interface connecting to an external network).

The first topology is shown in Figure 19–1. In this simple topology, reflexive access lists are configured for the *external* interface Serial 1. This prevents IP traffic from entering the router and the internal network, unless the traffic is part of a session already established from within the internal network.

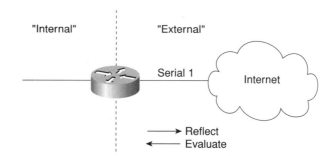

Figure 19–1

Simple Topology—Reflexive Access Lists Configured at the External Interface

The second topology is shown in Figure 19–2. In this topology, reflexive access lists are configured for the *internal* interface Ethernet 0. This allows external traffic to access the services in the Demilitarized Zone (DMZ), such as DNS services, but prevents IP traffic from entering your internal network—unless the traffic is part of a session already established from within the internal network.

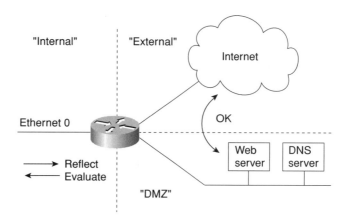

Figure 19–2

DMZ Topology—Reflexive Access Lists Configured at the Internal Interface

Use these two example topologies to help you decide whether to configure reflexive access lists for an internal or external interface.

CONFIGURING REFLEXIVE ACCESS LISTS

In the previous section, "Prework: Before You Configure Reflexive Access Lists," you decided whether to configure reflexive access lists for an internal or external interface.

Now, complete the tasks in one of the following configuration task lists.

External Interface Configuration Task List

To configure reflexive access lists for an external interface, perform these tasks:

1. Define the Reflexive Access List(s) in an *outbound* IP extended named access list.

2. Nest the Reflexive Access List(s) in an *inbound* IP extended named access list.

3. Set a Global Timeout Value (Optional).

These tasks are described in the sections following the internal interface configuration task list.

NOTES

The defined (outbound) reflexive access list evaluates traffic traveling out of your network: If the defined reflexive access list is matched, temporary entries are created in the nested (inbound) reflexive access list. These temporary entries will then be applied to traffic traveling into your network.

Internal Interface Configuration Task List

To configure reflexive access lists for an internal interface, perform these tasks:

1. Define the Reflexive Access List(s) in an *inbound* IP extended named access list.

2. Nest the Reflexive Access List(s) in an *outbound* IP extended named access list.

3. Set a Global Timeout Value (Optional).

These tasks are described in upcoming sections.

NOTES

The defined (inbound) reflexive access list is used to evaluate traffic traveling out of your network: If the defined reflexive access list is matched, temporary entries are created in the nested (outbound) reflexive access list. These temporary entries will then be applied to traffic traveling into your network.

Define the Reflexive Access List(s)

To define a reflexive access list, you use an entry in an extended named IP access list. This entry must use the **reflect** keyword.

- If you are configuring reflexive access lists for an external interface, the extended named IP access list should be one that is applied to outbound traffic.

- If you are configuring reflexive access lists for an internal interface, the extended named IP access list should be one that is applied to inbound traffic.

To define reflexive access lists, perform the following tasks, starting in global configuration mode:

Task	Command
External interface: Specify the outbound access list. or Internal interface: Specify the inbound access list. (Performing this task also causes you to enter the access-list configuration mode).	**ip access-list extended** *name*
Define the reflexive access list using the reflexive **permit** entry. Repeat this step for each IP upper-layer protocol; for example, you can define reflexive filtering for TCP sessions and also for UDP sessions. You can use the same *name* for multiple protocols. For additional guidelines for this task, see the following section, "Mixing Reflexive Access List Statements with Other Permit and Deny Entries."	**permit** *protocol* **any any reflect** *name* [**timeout** *seconds*]

If the extended named IP access list you just specified has never been applied to the interface, you must also complete this next task:

Apply the extended named IP access list to the interface, in interface configuration mode:

Task	Command
External interface: Apply the extended access list to the interface's outbound traffic. or Internal interface: Apply the extended access list to the interface's inbound traffic.	**ip access-group** *name* **out** or **ip access-group** *name* **in**

Mixing Reflexive Access List Statements with Other Permit and Deny Entries

The extended IP access list that contains the reflexive access list **permit** statement can also contain other normal **permit** and **deny** statements (entries). However, as with all access lists, the order of entries is important.

If you configure reflexive access lists for an external interface, when an outbound IP packet reaches the interface, the packet will be evaluated sequentially by each entry in the outbound access list until a match occurs.

If the packet matches an entry prior to the reflexive **permit** entry, the packet will not be evaluated by the reflexive **permit** entry, and no temporary entry will be created for the reflexive access list (reflexive filtering will not be triggered).

The outbound packet will be evaluated by the reflexive **permit** entry only if no other match occurs first. Then, if the packet matches the protocol specified in the reflexive **permit** entry, the packet is forwarded out of the interface and a corresponding temporary entry is created in the inbound reflexive access list (unless the corresponding entry already exists, indicating the outbound packet belongs to a session in progress). The temporary entry specifies criteria that permits inbound traffic only for the same session.

Nest the Reflexive Access List(s)

After you define a reflexive access list in one IP extended access list, you must "nest" the reflexive access list within a different extended named IP access list.

- If you are configuring reflexive access lists for an external interface, nest the reflexive access list within an extended named IP access list applied to inbound traffic.
- If you are configuring reflexive access lists for an internal interface, nest the reflexive access list within an extended named IP access list applied to outbound traffic.

After you nest a reflexive access list, packets heading into your internal network can be evaluated against any reflexive access list temporary entries, along with the other entries in the extended named IP access list.

To nest reflexive access lists, perform the following tasks, starting in global configuration mode:

Task	Command
External interface: Specify the inbound access list.	**ip access-list extended** *name*
or	
Internal interface: Specify the outbound access list.	
(Performing this task also causes you to enter the access-list configuration mode).	
Add an entry that "points" to the reflexive access list. Add an entry for each reflexive access list *name* previously defined.	**evaluate** *name*

Again, the order of entries is important. Normally, when a packet is evaluated against entries in an access list, the entries are evaluated in sequential order, and when a match occurs, no more entries are evaluated. With a reflexive access list nested in an extended access list, the extended access list entries are evaluated sequentially up to the nested entry, then the reflexive access list entries are evaluated sequentially, and then the remaining entries in the extended access list are evaluated sequentially. As usual, after a packet matches *any* of these entries, no more entries will be evaluated.

If the extended named IP access list you just specified has never been applied to the interface, you must also complete this next task:

Apply the extended named IP access list to the interface, in interface configuration mode:

Task	Command
External interface: apply the extended access list to the interface's inbound traffic. or Internal interface: apply the extended access list to the interface's outbound traffic.	**ip access-group** *name* **in** or **ip access-group** *name* **out**

Set a Global Timeout Value (Optional)

Reflexive access list entries expire after no packets in the session have been detected for a certain length of time (the "timeout" period). You can specify the timeout for a particular reflexive access list when you define the reflexive access list. But if you do not specify the timeout for a given reflexive access list, the list will use the global timeout value instead.

The global timeout value is 300 seconds by default. But, you can change the global timeout to a different value at any time.

To change the global timeout value, perform the following task in global configuration mode:

Task	Command
Change the global timeout value for temporary reflexive access list entries.	**ip reflexive-list timeout** *seconds*

REFLEXIVE ACCESS LISTS CONFIGURATION EXAMPLES

There are two examples in this section:

- External Interface Configuration Example
- Internal Interface Configuration Example

External Interface Configuration Example

This example has reflexive access lists configured for an external interface, for a topology similar to the one in Figure 19–1 (shown earlier in this chapter).

This configuration example permits both inbound and outbound TCP traffic at interface Serial 1, but only if the first packet (in a given session) originated from inside your network. The interface Serial 1 connects to the Internet.

Define the interface where the session filtering configuration is to be applied:

```
interface serial 1
 description Access to the Internet via this interface
```

Apply access lists to the interface, for inbound traffic and for outbound traffic:

```
ip access-group inboundfilters in
ip access-group outboundfilters out
```

Define the outbound access list. This is the access list that evaluates all outbound traffic on interface Serial 1.

```
ip access-list extended outboundfilters
```

Define the reflexive access list *tcptraffic*. This entry permits *all* outbound TCP traffic and creates a new access list named *tcptraffic*. Also, when an outbound TCP packet is the first in a new session, a corresponding temporary entry will be automatically created in the reflexive access list *tcptraffic*.

```
permit tcp any any reflect tcptraffic
```

Define the inbound access list. This is the access list that evaluates all inbound traffic on interface Serial 1.

```
ip access-list extended inboundfilters
```

Define the inbound access list entries. This example shows BGP and Enhanced IGRP running on the interface. Also, no ICMP traffic is permitted. The last entry points to the reflexive access list. If a packet does not match the first three entries, the packet will be evaluated against all the entries in the reflexive access list *tcptraffic*.

```
permit bgp any any
permit eigrp any any
deny icmp any any
evaluate tcptraffic
```

Define the global idle timeout value for all reflexive access lists. In this example, when the reflexive access list *tcptraffic* was defined, no timeout was specified, so *tcptraffic* uses the global timeout. Therefore, if for 120 seconds there is no TCP traffic that is part of an established session, the corresponding reflexive access list entry will be removed.

```
ip reflexive-list timeout 120
```

This is what the example configuration looks like:

```
interface Serial 1
 description Access to the Internet via this interface
 ip access-group inboundfilters in
 ip access-group outboundfilters out
!
ip reflexive-list timeout 120
!
ip access-list extended outboundfilters
 permit tcp any any reflect tcptraffic
!
ip access-list extended inboundfilters
 permit bgp any any
 permit eigrp any any
```

```
deny icmp any any
evaluate tcptraffic
!
```

With this configuration, before any TCP sessions have been initiated, the **show access-list** EXEC command displays the following:

```
Extended IP access list inboundfilters
 permit bgp any any
 permit eigrp any any
 deny icmp any any
 evaluate tcptraffic
Extended IP access list outboundfilters
 permit tcp any any reflect tcptraffic
```

Notice that the reflexive access list does not appear in this output. That is because before any TCP sessions have been initiated, no traffic has triggered the reflexive access list, and the list is empty (has no entries). When empty, reflexive access lists do not show up in **show access-list** output.

After a Telnet connection is initiated from within your network to a destination outside of your network, the **show access-list** EXEC command displays the following:

```
Extended IP access list inboundfilters
 permit bgp any any (2 matches)
 permit eigrp any any
 deny icmp any any
 evaluate tcptraffic
Extended IP access list outboundfilters
 permit tcp any any reflect tcptraffic
Reflexive IP access list tcptraffic
 permit tcp host 172.19.99.67 eq telnet host 192.168.60.185 eq 11005 (5 matches) (time
left 115 seconds)
```

Notice that the reflexive access list *tcptraffic* now appears, and displays the temporary entry generated when the Telnet session initiated with an outbound packet.

Internal Interface Configuration Example

This configuration example is for reflexive access lists configured for an internal interface. This example has a topology similar to the one in Figure 19–2 (shown earlier in this chapter).

This example is similar to the previous example; the only difference is that the entries for the outbound and inbound access lists are swapped. See the previous example for more details and descriptions.

```
interface Ethernet 0
 description Access from the I-net to our Internal Network via this interface
 ip access-group inboundfilters in
 ip access-group outboundfilters out
!
ip reflexive-list timeout 120
!
ip access-list extended outboundfilters
 permit bgp any any
```

```
  permit eigrp any any
  deny icmp any any
  evaluate tcptraffic
!
ip access-list extended inboundfilters
  permit tcp any any reflect tcptraffic
!
```

## CHAPTER 20

Reflexive Access List Commands

This chapter describes reflexive access list commands, which are used to configure IP session filtering. IP session filtering provides the capability to filter IP packets based on upper-layer protocol "session" information.

For reflexive access list configuration information, see Chapter 19, "Configuring IP Session Filtering (Reflexive Access Lists)."

EVALUATE

To nest a reflexive access list within an access list, use the **evaluate** access-list configuration command. Use the **no** form of this command to remove a nested reflexive access list from the access list.

> **evaluate** *name*
> **no evaluate** *name*

Syntax Description

name   The name of the reflexive access list that you want evaluated for IP traffic entering your internal network. This is the name defined in the **permit (reflexive)** command.

Default

Reflexive access lists are not evaluated.

Command Mode

Access-list configuration

Usage Guidelines

This command first appeared in Cisco IOS Release 11.3.

This command is used to achieve reflexive filtering, a form of session filtering.

Before this command will work, you must define the reflexive access list using the **permit (reflexive)** command.

This command nests a reflexive access list within an extended named IP access list.

If you are configuring reflexive access lists for an external interface, the extended named IP access list should be one that is applied to inbound traffic. If you are configuring reflexive access lists for an internal interface, the extended named IP access list should be one that is applied to outbound traffic. (In other words, use the access list opposite of the one used to define the reflexive access list.)

This command allows IP traffic entering your internal network to be evaluated against the reflexive access list. Use this command as an entry (condition statement) in the IP access list; the entry "points" to the reflexive access list to be evaluated.

As with all access list entries, the order of entries is important. Normally, when a packet is evaluated against entries in an access list, the entries are evaluated in sequential order, and when a match occurs, no more entries are evaluated. With a reflexive access list nested in an extended access list, the extended access list entries are evaluated sequentially up to the nested entry, then the reflexive access list entries are evaluated sequentially, and then the remaining entries in the extended access list are evaluated sequentially. As usual, after a packet matches *any* of these entries, no more entries are evaluated.

Example

This example is for reflexive filtering at an external interface. It defines an extended named IP access list *inboundfilters*, and applies it to inbound traffic at the interface. The access list definition permits all BGP and Enhanced IGRP traffic, denies all ICMP traffic, and causes all TCP traffic to be evaluated against the reflexive access list *tcptraffic*.

If the reflexive access list *tcptraffic* has an entry that matches an inbound packet, the packet will be permitted into the network. *tcptraffic* only has entries that permit inbound traffic for *existing* TCP sessions.

```
interface Serial 1
 description Access to the Internet via this interface
 ip access-group inboundfilters in
!
ip access-list extended inboundfilters
 permit bgp any any
 permit eigrp any any
 deny icmp any any
 evaluate tcptraffic
```

Related Commands

Search online to find documentation for related commands.

ip access-list (extended)
ip reflexive-list timeout
permit (reflexive)

IP REFLEXIVE-LIST TIMEOUT

To specify the length of time that reflexive access list entries will continue to exist when no packets in the session are detected, use the **ip reflexive-list timeout** global configuration command. Use the **no** form to reset the timeout period to the default timeout. This command applies only to reflexive access lists that do not already have a specified timeout.

> **ip reflexive-list timeout** *seconds*
> **no ip reflexive-list timeout**

Syntax Description

seconds   Specifies the number of seconds to wait (when no session traffic is being detected) before temporary access list entries expire. Use a positive integer from 0 to $2^{32}-1$.

Default

The reflexive access list entry is removed after no packets in the session are detected for 300 seconds.

Command Mode

Global configuration

Usage Guidelines

This command first appeared in Cisco IOS Release 11.3.

This command is used with reflexive filtering, a form of session filtering.

This command specifies when a reflexive access list entry will be removed after a period of no traffic for the session (the timeout period).

With reflexive filtering, when an IP upper-layer session begins from within your network, a temporary entry is created within the reflexive access list, and a timer is set. Whenever a packet belonging to this session is forwarded (inbound or outbound), the timer is reset. When this timer counts down to zero without being reset, the temporary reflexive access list entry is removed.

The timer is set to the *timeout period*. Individual timeout periods can be defined for specific reflexive access lists, but for reflexive access lists that do not have individually defined timeout periods, the global timeout period is used. The global timeout value is 300 seconds by default; however, you can change the global timeout to a different value at any time using this command.

This command does not take effect for reflexive access list entries that were already created when the command is entered; this command only changes the timeout period for entries created after the command is entered.

Examples

This example sets the global timeout period for reflexive access list entries to 120 seconds.

```
ip reflexive-list timeout 120
```

Part
III

Command Reference

This example returns the global timeout period to the default of 300 seconds.

```
no ip reflexive-list timeout
```

Related Commands

Search online to find documentation for related commands.

evaluate
ip access-list (extended)
permit (reflexive)

PERMIT (REFLEXIVE)

To create a reflexive access list and to enable its temporary entries to be generated automatically, use the **permit (reflexive)** access-list configuration command. Use the **no** form of this command to delete the reflexive access list (if only one protocol was defined) or to delete protocol entries from the reflexive access list (if multiple protocols defined).

> permit *protocol* **any any reflect** *name* [**timeout** *seconds*]
> **no permit** *protocol* **any any reflect** *name*

Syntax Description

protocol	Name or number of an IP protocol. It can be one of the keywords **gre, icmp, ip, ipinip, nos, tcp,** or **udp,** or an integer in the range 0 to 255 representing an IP protocol number. To match any Internet protocol (including ICMP, TCP, and UDP), use the keyword **ip.**
name	Specifies the name of the reflexive access list. Names cannot contain a space or quotation mark, and must begin with an alphabetic character to prevent ambiguity with numbered access lists. The name can be up to 64 characters long.
timeout *seconds*	(Optional) Specifies the number of seconds to wait (when no session traffic is being detected) before entries expire in this reflexive access list. Use a positive integer from 0 to $2^{32}-1$. If not specified, the number of seconds defaults to the global timeout value.

Default

If this command is not configured, no reflexive access lists will exist, and no session filtering will occur.

If this command is configured without specifying a **timeout** value, entries in this reflexive access list will expire after the global timeout period.

Command Mode

Access-list configuration

Usage Guidelines

This command first appeared in Cisco IOS Release 11.3.

This command is used to achieve reflexive filtering, a form of session filtering.

For this command to work, you must also nest the reflexive access list using the **evaluate** command.

This command creates a reflexive access list and triggers the creation of entries in the same reflexive access list. This command must be an entry (condition statement) in an extended named IP access list.

If you are configuring reflexive access lists for an external interface, the extended named IP access list should be one that is applied to outbound traffic.

If you are configuring reflexive access lists for an internal interface, the extended named IP access list should be one that is applied to inbound traffic.

IP sessions that originate from within your network are initiated with a packet exiting your network. When such packet is evaluated against the statements in the extended named IP access list, the packet is also evaluated against this reflexive **permit** entry.

As with all access list entries, the order of entries is important, because they are evaluated in sequential order. When an IP packet reaches the interface, it will be evaluated sequentially by each entry in the access list until a match occurs.

If the packet matches an entry prior to the reflexive **permit** entry, the packet will not be evaluated by the reflexive **permit** entry, and no temporary entry will be created for the reflexive access list (session filtering will not be triggered).

The packet will be evaluated by the reflexive **permit** entry if no other match occurs first. Then, if the packet matches the protocol specified in the reflexive **permit** entry, the packet is forwarded and a corresponding temporary entry is created in the reflexive access list (unless the corresponding entry already exists, indicating the packet belongs to a session in progress). The temporary entry specifies criteria that permits traffic into your network only for the same session.

Characteristics of Reflexive Access List Entries

This command enables the creation of temporary entries in the same reflexive access list that was defined by the command. The temporary entries are created when a packet exiting your network matches the protocol specified in this command. (The packet "triggers" the creation of a temporary entry.) These entries have the following characteristics:

- The entry is a **permit** entry.
- The entry specifies the same IP upper-layer protocol as the original triggering packet.
- The entry specifies the same source and destination addresses as the original triggering packet, except the addresses are swapped.
- If the original triggering packet is TCP or UDP, the entry specifies the same source and destination port numbers as the original packet, except the port numbers are swapped.

If the original triggering packet is a protocol other than TCP or UDP, port numbers do not apply, and other criteria are specified. For example, with ICMP, type numbers are used; the temporary entry specifies the same type number as the original packet (with only one exception: If the original ICMP packet is type 8, the returning ICMP packet must be type 0 to be matched).

- The entry inherits all the values of the original triggering packet, with exceptions only as noted in the previous four bullets.

- IP traffic entering your internal network will be evaluated against the entry, until the entry expires. If an IP packet matches the entry, the packet will be forwarded into your network.

- The entry will expire (be removed) after the last packet of the session is matched.

- If no packets belonging to the session are detected for a configurable length of time (the timeout period), the entry will expire.

Example

This example defines a reflexive access list *tcptraffic*, in an outbound access list that permits all BGP and Enhanced IGRP traffic and denies all ICMP traffic. This example is for an external interface (an interface connecting to an external network).

First, the interface is defined, and the access list is applied to the interface for outbound traffic.

```
interface Serial 1
  description Access to the Internet via this interface
  ip access-group outboundfilters out
```

Next, the outbound access list is defined, and the reflexive access list *tcptraffic* is created with a reflexive **permit** entry.

```
ip access-list extended outboundfilters
  permit tcp any any reflect tcptraffic
```

Related Commands

Search online to find documentation for related commands.

evaluate
ip access-list (extended)
ip reflexive-list timeout

## CHAPTER 21

Configuring TCP Intercept (Prevent Denial-of-Service Attacks)

This chapter describes how to configure your router to protect TCP servers from TCP SYN-flooding attacks, a type of denial-of-service attack. This is accomplished by configuring the Cisco IOS feature known as "TCP Intercept."

For a complete description of TCP Intercept commands, see Chapter 22, "TCP Intercept Commands."

IN THIS CHAPTER

This chapter has the following sections:

- About TCP Intercept
- TCP Intercept Configuration Task List
- Enabling TCP Intercept
- Setting the TCP Intercept Mode
- Setting the TCP Intercept Drop Mode
- Changing the TCP Intercept Timers
- Changing the TCP Intercept Aggressive Thresholds
- Monitoring and Maintaining TCP Intercept
- TCP Intercept Configuration Example

ABOUT TCP INTERCEPT

The TCP intercept feature implements software to protect TCP servers from TCP SYN-flooding attacks, which are a type of denial-of-service attack.

A SYN-flooding attack occurs when a hacker floods a server with a barrage of requests for connection. Because these messages have unreachable return addresses, the connections cannot be established. The resulting volume of unresolved open connections eventually overwhelms the server and can cause it to deny service to valid requests, thereby preventing legitimate users from connecting to a Web site, accessing e-mail, using FTP service, and so on.

The TCP intercept feature helps prevent SYN-flooding attacks by intercepting and validating TCP connection requests. In intercept mode, the TCP intercept software intercepts TCP synchronization (SYN) packets from clients to servers that match an extended access list. The software establishes a connection with the client on behalf of the destination server, and if successful, establishes the connection with the server on behalf of the client and knits the two half-connections together transparently. Thus, connection attempts from unreachable hosts will never reach the server. The software continues to intercept and forward packets throughout the duration of the connection.

In the case of illegitimate requests, the software's aggressive timeouts on half-open connections and its thresholds on TCP connection requests protect destination servers while still allowing valid requests.

When establishing your security policy using TCP intercept, you can choose to intercept all requests or only those coming from specific networks or destined for specific servers. You can also configure the connection rate and threshold of outstanding connections.

You can choose to operate TCP intercept in watch mode, as opposed to intercept mode. In watch mode, the software passively watches the connection requests flowing through the router. If a connection fails to get established in a configurable interval, the software intervenes and terminates the connection attempt.

TCP options that are negotiated on handshake (such as RFC 1323 on window scaling, for example) will not be negotiated, because the TCP intercept software does not know what the server can do or will negotiate.

TCP INTERCEPT CONFIGURATION TASK LIST

Perform the following tasks to configure TCP intercept. The first task is required; the rest are optional.

- Enabling TCP Intercept
- Setting the TCP Intercept Mode
- Setting the TCP Intercept Drop Mode
- Changing the TCP Intercept Timers
- Changing the TCP Intercept Aggressive Thresholds
- Monitoring and Maintaining TCP Intercept

ENABLING TCP INTERCEPT

To enable TCP intercept, perform the following tasks in global configuration mode:

Task	Command
Step 1 Define an IP extended access list.	**access-list** *access-list-number* {**deny** | **permit**} **tcp** **any** *destination destination-wildcard*
Step 2 Enable TCP intercept.	**ip tcp intercept list** *access-list-number*

You can define an access list to intercept all requests or only those coming from specific networks or destined for specific servers. Typically, the access list will define the source as **any** and define specific destination networks or servers. That is, you do not attempt to filter on the source addresses because you don't necessarily know who to intercept packets from. You identify the destination in order to protect destination servers.

If no access list match is found, the router allows the request to pass with no further action.

SETTING THE TCP INTERCEPT MODE

The TCP intercept can operate in either active intercept mode or passive watch mode. The default is intercept mode.

In intercept mode, the software actively intercepts each incoming connection request (SYN) and responds on behalf of the server with an ACK and SYN, then waits for an ACK of the SYN from the client. When that ACK is received, the original SYN is set to the server and the software performs a three-way handshake with the server. When this is complete, the two half-connections are joined.

In watch mode, connection requests are allowed to pass through the router to the server but are watched until they become established. If they fail to become established within 30 seconds (configurable with the **ip tcp intercept watch-timeout** command), the software sends a Reset to the server to clear up its state.

To set the TCP intercept mode, perform the following task in global configuration mode:

Task	Command
Set the TCP intercept mode.	**ip tcp intercept mode** {**intercept** | **watch**}

SETTING THE TCP INTERCEPT DROP-MODE

When under attack, the TCP intercept feature becomes more aggressive in its protective behavior. If the number of incomplete connections exceeds 1100, or the number of connections arriving in the last one minute exceeds 1100, each new arriving connection causes the oldest partial connection to be deleted. Also, the initial retransmission timeout is reduced by half to 0.5 seconds (so the total time trying to establish a connection is cut in half).

By default, the software drops the oldest partial connection. Alternatively, you can configure the software to drop a random connection. To set the drop mode, perform the following task in global configuration mode:

Task	Command
Set the drop mode.	ip tcp intercept drop-mode {oldest	random}

CHANGING THE TCP INTERCEPT TIMERS

By default, the software waits for 30 seconds for a watched connection to reach established state before sending a Reset to the server. To change this value, perform the following task in global configuration mode:

Task	Command
Change the time allowed to reach established state.	ip tcp intercept watch-timeout seconds

By default, the software waits for 5 seconds from receipt of a Reset or FIN-exchange before it ceases to manage the connection. To change this value, perform the following task in global configuration mode:

Task	Command
Change the time between receipt of a Reset or FIN-exchange and dropping the connection.	ip tcp intercept finrst-timeout seconds

By default, the software still manages a connection for 24 hours after no activity. To change this value, perform the following task in global configuration mode:

Task	Command
Change the time the software will manage a connection after no activity.	ip tcp intercept connection-timeout seconds

CHANGING THE TCP INTERCEPT AGGRESSIVE THRESHOLDS

Two factors determine when aggressive behavior begins and ends: total incomplete connections and connection requests during the last one-minute sample period. Both thresholds have default values that can be redefined.

When a threshold is exceeded, the TCP intercept assumes the server is under attack and goes into aggressive mode. When in aggressive mode, the following occurs:

- Each new arriving connection causes the oldest partial connection to be deleted. (You can change to a random drop mode.)

- The initial retransmission timeout is reduced by half to 0.5 seconds, and so the total time trying to establish the connection is cut in half. (When not in aggressive mode, the code does exponential back-off on its retransmissions of SYN segments. The initial retransmission timeout is 1 second. The subsequent timeouts are 2 seconds, 4 seconds, 8 seconds, and 16 seconds. The code retransmits 4 times before giving up, so it gives up after 31 seconds of no acknowledgment.)

- If in watch mode, the watch timeout is reduced by half. (If the default is in place, the watch timeout becomes 15 seconds).

The drop strategy can be changed from the oldest connection to a random connection with the **ip tcp intercept drop-mode** command.

NOTES

The two factors that determine aggressive behavior are related and work together. When *either* of the **high** values is exceeded, aggressive behavior begins. When *both* quantities fall below the **low** value, aggressive behavior ends.

You can change the threshold for triggering aggressive mode based on the total number of incomplete connections. The default values for **low** and **high** are 900 and 1100 incomplete connections, respectively. To change these values, perform the following tasks in global configuration mode:

Task	Command
Set the threshold for stopping aggressive mode.	**ip tcp intercept max-incomplete low** *number*
Set the threshold for triggering aggressive mode.	**ip tcp intercept max-incomplete high** *number*

You can also change the threshold for triggering aggressive mode based on the number of connection requests received in the last 1-minute sample period. The default values for **low** and **high** are 900 and 1100 connection requests, respectively. To change these values, perform the following tasks in global configuration mode:

Task	Command
Set the threshold for stopping aggressive mode.	**ip tcp intercept one-minute low** *number*
Set the threshold for triggering aggressive mode.	**ip tcp intercept one-minute high** *number*

MONITORING AND MAINTAINING TCP INTERCEPT

To display TCP intercept information, perform either of the following tasks in EXEC mode:

Task	Command
Display incomplete connections and established connections.	**show tcp intercept connections**
Display TCP intercept statistics.	**show tcp intercept statistics**

TCP INTERCEPT CONFIGURATION EXAMPLE

The following configuration defines extended IP access list 101, causing the software to intercept packets for all TCP servers on the 192.168.1.0/24 subnet:

```
ip tcp intercept list 101
!
access-list 101 permit tcp any 192.168.1.0 0.0.0.255
```

## CHAPTER 22

TCP Intercept Commands

This chapter describes TCP Intercept commands. TCP Intercept is a traffic filtering security feature that protects TCP servers from TCP SYN-flooding attacks, which are a type of denial-of-service attack. TCP Intercept is available for IP traffic only.

For TCP Intercept configuration information, see Chapter 21, "Configuring TCP Intercept (Prevent Denial-of-Service Attacks)."

IP TCP INTERCEPT CONNECTION-TIMEOUT

To change how long a TCP connection will still be managed by the TCP intercept after no activity, use the **ip tcp intercept connection-timeout** global configuration command. To restore the default value, use the **no** form of this command.

> **ip tcp intercept connection-timeout** *seconds*
> **no ip tcp intercept connection-timeout** [*seconds*]

Syntax Description

seconds	Time (in seconds) that the software will still manage the connection after no activity. The minimum value is 1 second. The default is 86400 seconds (24 hours).

Default

86400 seconds (24 hours)

Command Mode

Global configuration

Usage Guidelines

This command first appeared in Cisco IOS Release 11.2 F.

Example

The following example sets the software to manage the connection for 12 hours (43200 seconds) after no activity:

```
ip tcp intercept connection-timeout 43200
```

IP TCP INTERCEPT DROP-MODE

To set the TCP intercept drop mode, use the **ip tcp intercept drop-mode** global configuration command. To restore the default value, use the **no** form of this command.

> **ip tcp intercept drop-mode {oldest | random}**
> **no ip tcp intercept drop-mode [oldest | random]**

Syntax Description

oldest   Software drops the oldest partial connection. This is the default.

random   Software drops a randomly selected partial connection.

Default

oldest

Command Mode

Global configuration

Usage Guidelines

This command first appeared in Cisco IOS Release 11.2 F.

If the number of incomplete connections exceeds 1100, or the number of connections arriving in the last 1 minute exceeds 1100, the TCP intercept feature becomes more aggressive. When this happens, each new arriving connection causes the oldest partial connection to be deleted, and the initial retransmission timeout is reduced by half to 0.5 seconds (and so the total time trying to establish the connection will be cut in half).

Note that the 1100 thresholds can be configured with the **ip tcp intercept max-incomplete high** and **ip tcp intercept one-minute high** commands.

Use the **ip tcp intercept drop-mode** command to change the dropping strategy from oldest to a random drop.

Example

The following example sets the drop mode to random:

```
ip tcp intercept drop-mode random
```

Related Commands

Search online to find documentation for related commands.

ip tcp intercept max-incomplete high
ip tcp intercept max-incomplete low
ip tcp intercept one-minute high
ip tcp intercept one-minute low

IP TCP INTERCEPT FINRST-TIMEOUT

To change how long after receipt of a Reset or FIN-exchange the software ceases to manage the connection, use the **ip tcp intercept finrst-timeout** global configuration command. To restore the default value, use the **no** form of this command.

> **ip tcp intercept finrst-timeout** *seconds*
> **no ip tcp intercept finrst-timeout** [*seconds*]

Syntax Description

seconds   Time (in seconds) after receiving a Reset or FIN-exchange that the software ceases to manage the connection. The minimum value is 1 second. The default is 5 seconds.

Default

5 seconds

Command Mode

Global configuration

Usage Guidelines

This command first appeared in Cisco IOS Release 11.2 F.

Even after the two ends of the connection are joined, the software intercepts packets being sent back and forth. Use this command if you need to adjust how soon after receiving a Reset or FIN-exchange the software stops intercepting packets.

Example

The following example sets the software to wait for 10 seconds before forgetting about the connection:

```
ip tcp intercept finrst-timeout 10
```

IP TCP INTERCEPT LIST

To enable TCP intercept, use the **ip tcp intercept list** global configuration command. To disable TCP intercept, use the **no** form of this command.

>   **ip tcp intercept list** *access-list-number*
>   **no ip tcp intercept list** *access-list-number*

Syntax Description

access-list-number   Extended access list number in the range 100 to 199.

Default

Disabled

Command Mode

Global configuration

Usage Guidelines

This command first appeared in Cisco IOS Release 11.2 F.

The TCP intercept feature intercepts TCP connection attempts and shields servers from TCP SYN-flood attacks, also known as denial-of-service attacks.

TCP packets matching the access list are presented to the TCP intercept code for processing, as determined by the **ip tcp intercept mode** command. The TCP intercept code either intercepts or watches the connections.

To have all TCP connection attempts submitted to the TCP intercept code, have the access list match everything.

Example

The following configuration defines access list 101, causing the software to intercept packets for all TCP servers on the 192.168.1.0/24 subnet:

```
ip tcp intercept list 101
!
access-list 101 permit tcp any 192.168.1.0 0.0.0.255
```

Related Commands

Search online to find documentation for related commands.

access-list (extended)
ip tcp intercept mode
show tcp intercept connections
show tcp intercept statistics

IP TCP INTERCEPT MAX-INCOMPLETE HIGH

To define the maximum number of incomplete connections allowed before the software behaves aggressively, use the **ip tcp intercept max-incomplete high** global configuration command. To restore the default value, use the **no** form of this command.

> ip tcp intercept max-incomplete high *number*
> no ip tcp intercept max-incomplete high [*number*]

Syntax Description

number Defines the number of incomplete connections allowed, above which the software behaves aggressively. The range is 1 to 2147483647. The default is 1100.

Default

1100 incomplete connections

Command Mode

Global configuration

Usage Guidelines

This command first appeared in Cisco IOS Release 11.2 F.

If the number of incomplete connections exceeds the *number* configured, the TCP intercept feature becomes aggressive. These are the characteristics of aggressive mode:

- Each new arriving connection causes the oldest partial connection to be deleted.
- The initial retransmission timeout is reduced by half to 0.5 seconds (and so the total time trying to establish the connection is cut in half).
- The watch timeout is cut in half (from 30 seconds to 15 seconds).

You can change the drop strategy from the oldest connection to a random connection with the **ip tcp intercept drop-mode** command.

> **NOTES**

The two factors that determine aggressive behavior (connection requests and incomplete connections) are related and work together. When the value of *either* **ip tcp intercept one-minute high** or **ip tcp intercept max-incomplete high** is exceeded, aggressive behavior begins. When *both* connection requests and incomplete connections fall below the values of **ip tcp intercept one-minute low** and **ip tcp intercept max-incomplete low**, aggressive behavior ends.

The software will back off from its aggressive behavior when the number of incomplete connections falls below the number specified by the **ip tcp intercept max-incomplete low** command.

Example

The following example allows 1500 incomplete connections before the software takes its aggressive steps:

```
ip tcp intercept max-incomplete high 1500
```

Related Commands

Search online to find documentation for related commands.

ip tcp intercept drop-mode
ip tcp intercept max-incomplete low
ip tcp intercept one-minute high
ip tcp intercept one-minute low

IP TCP INTERCEPT MAX-INCOMPLETE LOW

To define the number of incomplete connections below which the software stops behaving aggressively, use the **ip tcp intercept max-incomplete low** global configuration command. To restore the default value, use the **no** form of this command.

> **ip tcp intercept max-incomplete low** *number*
> **no ip tcp intercept max-incomplete low** [*number*]

Syntax Description

number	Defines the number of incomplete connections below which the software stops behaving aggressively. The range is 1 to 2147483647. The default is 900.

Default

900 incomplete connections

Command Mode

Global configuration

Usage Guidelines

This command first appeared in Cisco IOS Release 11.2 F.

When *both* connection requests and incomplete connections fall below the values of **ip tcp intercept one-minute low** and **ip tcp intercept max-incomplete low,** the TCP intercept feature stops behaving aggressively.

NOTES

The two factors that determine aggressive behavior (connection requests and incomplete connections) are related and work together. When the value of *either* **ip tcp intercept one-minute high** or **ip tcp intercept max-incomplete high** is exceeded, aggressive behavior begins. When *both* connection requests and incomplete connections fall below the values of **ip tcp intercept one-minute low** and **ip tcp intercept max-incomplete low**, aggressive behavior ends.

See the **ip tcp intercept max-incomplete high** command for a description of aggressive behavior.

Example

The following example sets the software to stop behaving aggressively when the number of incomplete connections falls below 1000:

```
ip tcp intercept max-incomplete low 1000
```

Related Commands

Search online to find documentation for related commands.

ip tcp intercept drop-mode
ip tcp intercept max-incomplete high
ip tcp intercept one-minute high
ip tcp intercept one-minute low

IP TCP INTERCEPT MODE

To change the TCP intercept mode, use the **ip tcp intercept mode** global configuration command. To restore the default value, use the **no** form of this command.

ip tcp intercept mode {intercept | watch}
no ip tcp intercept mode [intercept | watch]

Syntax Description

intercept	Active mode in which the TCP intercept software intercepts TCP packets from clients to servers that match the configured access list and performs intercept duties. This is the default.
watch	Monitoring mode in which the software allows connection attempts to pass through the router and watches them until they are established.

Default

intercept

Command Mode

Global configuration

Usage Guidelines

This command first appeared in Cisco IOS Release 11.2 F.

When TCP intercept is enabled, it operates in intercept mode by default. In intercept mode, the software actively intercepts TCP SYN packets from clients to servers that match the specified access list. For each SYN, the software responds on behalf of the server with an ACK and SYN, and waits for an ACK of the SYN from the client. When that ACK is received, the original SYN is sent to the server, and the code then performs a three-way handshake with the server. Then the two half-connections are joined.

In watch mode, the software allows connection attempts to pass through the router, but watches them until they become established. If they fail to become established in 30 seconds (or the value set by the **ip tcp intercept watch-timeout** command), a Reset is sent to the server to clear up its state.

Example

The following example sets the mode to watch mode:

```
ip tcp intercept mode watch
```

Related Command

Search online to find documentation for related commands.

ip tcp intercept watch-timeout

IP TCP INTERCEPT ONE-MINUTE HIGH

To define the number of connection requests received in the last one-minute sample period before the software behaves aggressively, use the **ip tcp intercept one-minute high** global configuration command. To restore the default value, use the **no** form of this command.

> **ip tcp intercept one-minute high** *number*
> **no ip tcp intercept one-minute high** [*number*]

Syntax Description

number	Specifies the number of connection requests that can be received in the last one-minute sample period before the software behaves aggressively. The range is 1 to 2147483647. The default is 1100.

Default

1100 connection requests

Command Mode

Global configuration

Usage Guidelines

This command first appeared in Cisco IOS Release 11.2 F.

If the number of connection requests exceeds the *number* value configured, the TCP intercept feature becomes aggressive. These are the characteristics of aggressive mode:

- Each new arriving connection causes the oldest partial connection to be deleted.
- The initial retransmission timeout is reduced by half to 0.5 seconds (and so the total time trying to establish the connection is cut in half).
- The watch timeout is cut in half (from 30 seconds to 15 seconds).

You can change the drop strategy from the oldest connection to a random connection with the **ip tcp intercept drop-mode** command.

--- **NOTES** ---

The two factors that determine aggressive behavior (connection requests and incomplete connections) are related and work together. When the value of *either* **ip tcp intercept one-minute high** or **ip tcp intercept max-incomplete high** is exceeded, aggressive behavior begins. When *both* connection requests and incomplete connections fall below the values of **ip tcp intercept one-minute low** and **ip tcp intercept max-incomplete low**, aggressive behavior ends.

Example

The following example allows 1400 connection requests before the software behaves aggressively:

```
ip tcp intercept one-minute high 1400
```

Related Commands

Search online to find documentation for related commands.

ip tcp intercept drop-mode
ip tcp intercept max-incomplete high
ip tcp intercept max-incomplete low
ip tcp intercept one-minute low

IP TCP INTERCEPT ONE-MINUTE LOW

To define the number of connection requests below which the software stops behaving aggressively, use the **ip tcp intercept one-minute low** global configuration command. To restore the default value, use the **no** form of this command.

> **ip tcp intercept one-minute low** *number*
> **no ip tcp intercept one-minute low** [*number*]

Syntax Description

number   Defines the number of connection requests in the last one-minute sample
                            period below which the software stops behaving aggressively. The range is 1
                            to 2147483647. The default is 900.

Default

900 connection requests

Command Mode

Global configuration

Usage Guidelines

This command first appeared in Cisco IOS Release 11.2 F.

When *both* connection requests and incomplete connections fall below the values of **ip tcp intercept
one-minute low** and **ip tcp intercept max-incomplete low,** the TCP intercept feature stops behaving
aggressively.

NOTES
───

The two factors that determine aggressive behavior (connection requests and incomplete connections) are related and work together. When the value of *either* **ip tcp intercept one-minute high** or **ip
tcp intercept max-incomplete high** is exceeded, aggressive behavior begins. When *both* connection
requests and incomplete connections fall below the values of **ip tcp intercept one-minute low** and **ip
tcp intercept max-incomplete low,** aggressive behavior ends.

See the **ip tcp intercept one-minute high** command for a description of aggressive behavior.

Example

The following example sets the software to stop behaving aggressively when the number of connection requests falls below 1000:

```
ip tcp intercept one-minute low 1000
```

Related Commands

Search online to find documentation for related commands.

ip tcp intercept drop-mode
ip tcp intercept max-incomplete high
ip tcp intercept max-incomplete low
ip tcp intercept one-minute high

IP TCP INTERCEPT WATCH-TIMEOUT

To define how long the software will wait for a watched TCP intercept connection to reach established state before sending a Reset to the server, use the **ip tcp intercept watch-timeout** global configuration command. To restore the default value, use the **no** form of this command.

> **ip tcp intercept watch-timeout** *seconds*
> **no ip tcp intercept watch-timeout** [*seconds*]

Syntax Description

seconds   Time (in seconds) that the software waits for a watched connection to reach established state before sending a Reset to the server. The minimum value is 1 second. The default is 30 seconds.

Default

30 seconds

Command Mode

Global configuration

Usage Guidelines

This command first appeared in Cisco IOS Release 11.2 F.

Use this command if you have set the TCP intercept to passive watch mode and you want to change the default time the connection is watched. During aggressive behavior, the watch timeout time is cut in half.

Example

The following example sets the software to wait 60 seconds for a watched connection to reach established state before sending a Reset to the server:

```
ip tcp intercept watch-timeout 60
```

Related Commands

Search online to find documentation for related commands.

ip tcp intercept mode

SHOW TCP INTERCEPT CONNECTIONS

To display TCP incomplete connections or established connections, use the **show tcp intercept connections** EXEC command.

```
show tcp intercept connections
```

Syntax Description

This command has no arguments or keywords.

Command Mode

EXEC

Usage Guidelines

This command first appeared in Cisco IOS Release 11.2 F.

Sample Display

The following is sample output from the **show tcp intercept connections** command:

```
Router# show tcp intercept connections
Incomplete:
Client                    Server              State   Create    Timeout  Mode
172.19.160.17:58190       10.1.1.30:23        SYNRCVD 00:00:09  00:00:05 I
172.19.160.17:57934       10.1.1.30:23        SYNRCVD 00:00:09  00:00:05 I

Established:
Client                    Server              State   Create    Timeout  Mode
171.69.232.23:1045        10.1.1.30:23        ESTAB   00:00:08  23:59:54 I
```

Table 22–1 describes significant fields shown in the display.

Table 22–1   *Show TCP Intercept Connections Field Descriptions*

Field	Description
Incomplete:	Rows of information under "Incomplete" indicate connections that are not yet established.
Client	IP address and port of the client.
Server	IP address and port of the server being protected by TCP intercept.
State	SYNRCVD—establishing with client. SYNSENT—establishing with server. ESTAB—established with both, passing data.
Create	Hours:minutes:seconds since the connection was created.
Timeout	Hours:minutes:seconds until the retransmission timeout.
Mode	I—intercept mode. W—watch mode.

Table 22–1 *Show TCP Intercept Connections Field Descriptions, Continued*

Field	Description
Established:	Rows of information under "Established" indicate connections that are established. The fields are the same as those under "Incomplete" except for the Timeout field described below.
Timeout	Hours:minutes:seconds until the connection will timeout, unless the software sees a FIN exchange, in which case this indicates the hours:minutes:seconds until the FIN or Reset timeout.

Related Commands

Search online to find documentation for related commands.

ip tcp intercept connection-timeout
ip tcp intercept finrst-timeout
ip tcp intercept list
show tcp intercept statistics

SHOW TCP INTERCEPT STATISTICS

To display TCP intercept statistics, use the **show tcp intercept statistics** EXEC command.

```
show tcp intercept statistics
```

Syntax Description

This command has no arguments or keywords.

Command Mode

EXEC

Usage Guidelines

This command first appeared in Cisco IOS Release 11.2 F.

Sample Display

The following is sample output from the **show tcp intercept statistics** command:

```
Router# show tcp intercept statistics
intercepting new connections using access-list 101
2 incomplete, 1 established connections (total 3)
1 minute connection request rate 2 requests/sec
```

Related Commands

Search online to find documentation for related commands.

ip tcp intercept connection-timeout
ip tcp intercept finrst-timeout
ip tcp intercept list
show tcp intercept connections

PART IV

Network Data Encryption

## CHAPTER 23

Configuring Network Data Encryption

This chapter describes how to configure your router for network data encryption. This chapter includes the following sections:

- Why Encryption?
- Cisco's Implementation of Encryption
- Prework: Before You Configure Encryption
- Configuring Encryption
- Configuring Encryption with GRE Tunnels
- Configuring Encryption with an ESA in a VIP2
- Configuring Encryption with an ESA in a Cisco 7200 Series Router
- Customizing Encryption (Configure Options)
- Turning Off Encryption
- Testing and Troubleshooting Encryption
- Encryption Configuration Examples

NOTES

Whenever the term "encryption" is used in this chapter, it refers only to encryption of network data, not to other types of encryption.

For a complete description of the encryption commands in this chapter, see Chapter 24, "Network Data Encryption Commands."

WHY ENCRYPTION?

Data that traverses unsecured networks is open to many types of attacks. Data can be read, altered, or forged by anybody who has access to the route that your data takes. For example, a protocol analyzer can read packets and gain classified information. Or, a hostile party can tamper with packets and cause damage by hindering, reducing, or preventing network communications within your organization.

Encryption provides a means to safeguard network data that travels from one Cisco router to another across unsecured networks. Encryption is particularly important if classified, confidential, or critical data is being sent.

Figure 23–1 illustrates the encryption of an IP packet as it travels across an unsecured network.

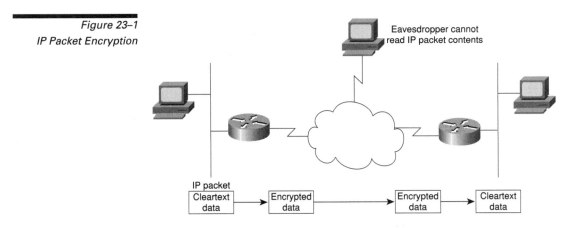

Figure 23–1
IP Packet Encryption

CISCO'S IMPLEMENTATION OF ENCRYPTION

The following sections answer these questions:

- What Gets Encrypted?
- Where Are Packets Encrypted and Decrypted in the Network?
- When Can Encrypted Packets Be Exchanged?
- How Does an Encrypting Router Identify Other Peer Encrypting Routers?
- What Standards Are Implemented in Cisco's Encryption?
- How Does Cisco's Encryption Work?

What Gets Encrypted?

Network data encryption is provided at the IP packet level—only IP packets can be encrypted. (If you want to encrypt a network protocol other than IP, you must encapsulate the protocol within an IP packet.)

An IP packet is encrypted/decrypted only if the packet meets criteria you establish when you configure a router for encryption.

When encrypted, individual IP packets can be detected during transmission, but the IP packet contents (payload) cannot be read. Specifically, the IP header and upper-layer protocol headers (for example, TCP or UDP) are not encrypted, but all payload data within the TCP or UDP packet will be encrypted, and therefore not readable during transmission.

Where Are Packets Encrypted and Decrypted in the Network?

The actual encryption and decryption of IP packets occur only at routers that you configure for network data encryption. Such routers are considered to be *peer encrypting routers* (or simply *peer routers*). Intermediate hops do not participate in encryption/decryption.

Often, peer routers are situated at the edges of unsecured networks (such as the Internet) in order to provide secure communications between two secured networks that are physically separated. Cleartext (not encrypted) traffic that enters a peer router from the secure network side is encrypted and forwarded across the unsecure network. When the encrypted traffic reaches the remote peer router, the router decrypts the traffic before forwarding it into the remote secure network.

Packets are encrypted at one peer router's outbound interface and decrypted at the other peer router's inbound interface.

When Can Encrypted Packets Be Exchanged?

Encrypted packets can be exchanged between peer routers only during encrypted sessions. When a peer router detects a packet that should be encrypted, an encrypted session must first be established. After an encrypted session is established, encrypted traffic can pass freely between peer routers. When the session expires, a new session must be established before encrypted traffic can continue to be sent.

How Does an Encrypting Router Identify Other Peer Encrypting Routers?

During the setup of every encrypted session, both participating peer routers attempt to authenticate each other. If either authentication fails, the encrypted session will not be established, and no encrypted traffic will pass. Peer authentication ensures that only known, trusted peer routers exchange encrypted traffic and prevents routers from being tricked into sending sensitive encrypted traffic to illegitimate or fraudulent destination routers.

What Standards Are Implemented in Cisco's Encryption?

To provide encryption services, Cisco implements the following standards: Digital Signature Standard (DSS), the Diffie-Hellman (DH) public key algorithm, and Data Encryption Standard (DES). DSS is used for peer router authentication. The DH algorithm and DES standard are used to initiate and conduct encrypted communication sessions between participating peer routers.

How Does Cisco's Encryption Work?

The following sections provide an overview of Cisco's encryption process:

- You Enable Peer Router Authentication with a DSS Key Exchange
- A Router Establishes an Encrypted Session with a Peer
- Peer Routers Encrypt and Decrypt Data During an Encrypted Session

You Enable Peer Router Authentication with a DSS Key Exchange

Peer router authentication occurs during the setup of each encrypted session. But before peer routers can authenticate each other, you must generate Digital Signature Standard (DSS) keys (both public and private DSS keys) for each peer, and you must exchange (and verify) the DSS public keys with each peer (see Figure 23–2). You generate and exchange DSS keys only once per peer, and afterwards these DSS keys will be used each time an encrypted session occurs. (Generating and exchanging DSS keys are described in section "Configuring Encryption," found later in the chapter.)

Each peer router's DSS keys are unique: a unique DSS public key, and a unique DSS private key. DSS public and private keys are stored in a private portion of the router's NVRAM, which cannot be viewed with commands such as **show configuration, show running-config,** or **write terminal.** If you have a router with an Encryption Service Adapter (ESA), DSS keys are stored in the tamper resistant memory of the ESA.

The DSS private key is not shared with any other device. However, the DSS public key is distributed to all other peer routers. You must cooperate with the peer router's administrator to exchange public keys between the two peer routers, and you and the other administrator must verbally verify to each other the public key of the other router. (The verbal verification is sometimes referred to as "voice authentication.")

When an encrypted session is being established, each router uses the peer's DSS public key to authenticate the peer. The process of authenticating peers and establishing encrypted sessions is described in the following section.

A Router Establishes an Encrypted Session with a Peer

An encrypted session must be established before a Cisco router can send encrypted data to a peer router. (See Figure 23–3.) An encrypted session is established whenever a router detects an IP packet that should be encrypted and no encrypted session already exists.

To establish a session, two peer routers exchange connection messages. These messages have two purposes. The first purpose is to authenticate each router to the other. Authentication is accomplished by attaching "signatures" to the connection messages: A signature is a character string that is created by each local router using its own DSS private key, and verified by the other (remote) router using the local router's DSS public key (previously exchanged). A signature is always unique

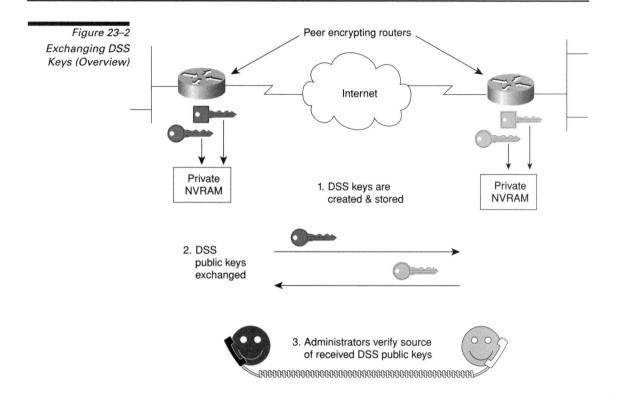

Figure 23–2
Exchanging DSS
Keys (Overview)

Peer encrypting routers

Internet

Private NVRAM

Private NVRAM

1. DSS keys are created & stored

2. DSS public keys exchanged

3. Administrators verify source of received DSS public keys

to the sending router and cannot be forged by any other device. When a signature is verified, the router that sent the signature is authenticated.

The second purpose of the connection messages is to generate a temporary DES key ("session key"), which is the key that will be used to actually encrypt data during the encrypted session. To generate the DES key, Diffie-Hellman (DH) numbers must be exchanged in the connection messages. Then, the DH numbers are used to compute a common DES session key that is shared by both routers.

Peer Routers Encrypt and Decrypt Data During an Encrypted Session

After both peer routers are authenticated and the session key (DES key) has been generated, data can be encrypted and transmitted. A DES encryption algorithm is used with the DES key to encrypt and decrypt IP packets during the encrypted session. (See Figure 23–4.)

An encrypted communication session will terminate when the session times out. When the session terminates, both the DH numbers and the DES key are discarded. When another encrypted session is required, new DH numbers and DES keys are generated.

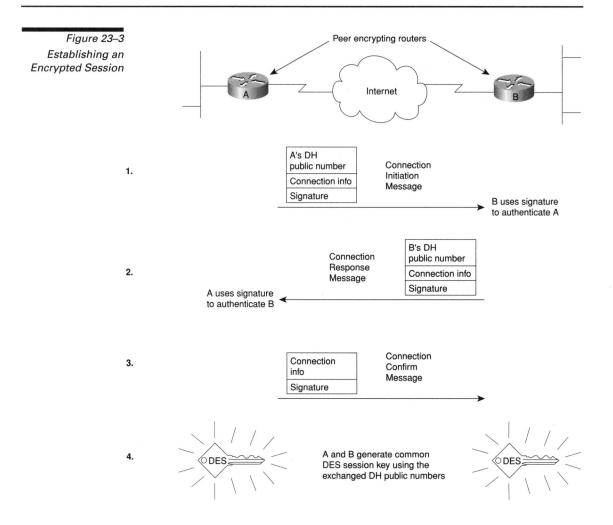

Figure 23–3
Establishing an
Encrypted Session

PREWORK: BEFORE YOU CONFIGURE ENCRYPTION

You should understand and follow the guidelines in this section *before* attempting to configure your system for network data encryption. This section describes the following guidelines:

- Identify Peer Routers
- Consider Your Network Topology
- Identify Crypto Engines within Each Peer Router
- Understand Implementation Issues and Limitations

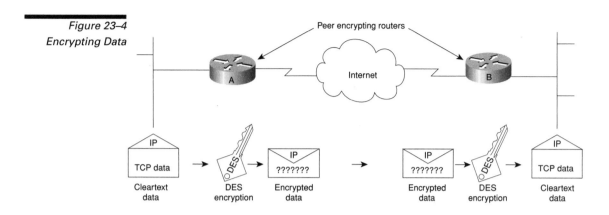

Figure 23–4
Encrypting Data

1. DES key is used by routers A and B to encrypt outbound IP traffic and to decrypt inbound IP traffic.

2.

When session terminates, DES keys and DH numbers are discarded.

Identify Peer Routers

You must identify all peer routers that will be participating in encryption. Peer routers are routers configured for encryption, between which all encrypted traffic is passed. These peers are usually routers within your administrative control that will be passing IP packets over an uncontrolled network (such as the Internet). Participating peer routers might also include routers not within your administrative control; however, this should only be the case if you share a trusted, cooperative relationship with the other router's administrator. This person should be known and trusted by both you and your organization.

Peer routers should be located within a network topology according to the guidelines listed in the following section.

Consider Your Network Topology

Take care in choosing a network topology between peer encrypting routers. Particularly, you should set up the network so that a stream of IP packets must use exactly one pair of encrypting routers at a time. Do not nest levels of encrypting routers. (That is, do not put encrypting routers in between two peer encrypting routers.)

Frequent route changes between pairs of peer encrypting routers, including for purposes of load balancing, will cause excessive numbers of connections to be set up and very few data packets to be delivered. Note that load balancing can still be used, but only if done transparently to the encrypting peer routers. That is, peer routers should not participate in the load balancing; only devices in between the peer routers should provide load balancing.

A common network topology used for encryption is a hub-and-spoke arrangement between an enterprise router and branch routers. Also, Internet firewall routers are often designated as peer encrypting routers.

Identify Crypto Engines within Each Peer Router

Encryption is provided by a software service called a *crypto engine*. To perform encryption at a router, you must first configure the router's crypto engine to be an encrypting peer; then you can configure any interface governed by that crypto engine to perform encryption. (To configure a crypto engine, you must at a minimum generate and exchange DSS keys for that engine, as described in section "Configuring Encryption," found later in the chapter.)

Depending on your hardware configuration, different crypto engines will govern different router interfaces. In some instances, you may even need to configure multiple crypto engines as peers within a single router, particularly if a router has multiple interfaces that you want to use for encryption, and those interfaces are governed by different crypto engines.

There are three types of crypto engines—the Cisco IOS crypto engine, the VIP2 crypto engine, and the ESA crypto engine.

If you have a Cisco 7200, RSP7000, or 7500 series router with one or more VIP2 boards (VIP2-40 or higher) or ESA cards, your router can have multiple crypto engines. All other routers have only one crypto engine, the Cisco IOS crypto engine.

When you configure a crypto engine on a Cisco 7200, RSP7000, or 7500 series router, you must identify which engine you are configuring by specifying the engine's chassis slot number when you enter the crypto commands.

The three different crypto engines are described in the upcoming three sections.

The Cisco IOS Crypto Engine

Every router with Cisco IOS encryption software has a Cisco IOS crypto engine. For many Cisco routers, the Cisco IOS crypto engine is the only crypto engine available. The only exceptions are the Cisco 7200, RSP7000, and 7500 series routers, which can also have additional crypto engines (as described in the next two sections).

If a router has no additional crypto engines, the Cisco IOS crypto engine governs all the router interfaces: You must configure the Cisco IOS crypto engine before you can configure any router interface for encryption.

The Cisco IOS crypto engine is identified by the chassis slot number of the Route Switch Processor (RSP). (For routers with no RSP, the Cisco IOS crypto engine is selected by default and does not need to be specifically identified during configuration.)

The VIP2 Crypto Engine (Cisco RSP7000 and 7500 Series Routers Only)

Cisco RSP7000 and 7500 series routers with a second-generation Versatile Interface Processor (VIP2) (version VIP2-40 or greater) have two crypto engines: the Cisco IOS crypto engine and the VIP2 crypto engine.

The VIP2 crypto engine governs all the VIP2 interfaces. The Cisco IOS crypto engine governs all remaining router interfaces. (These rules assume that there is no ESA installed in the VIP2. If the VIP2 has an installed ESA, the interfaces are governed differently, as explained in the next section.)

The VIP2 crypto engine is identified by the chassis slot number of the VIP2.

The Encryption Service Adapter Crypto Engine (Cisco 7200, RSP7000, and 7500 Series Routers Only)

Cisco 7200, RSP7000, and 7500 series routers with an Encryption Service Adapter (ESA) have an ESA crypto engine.

Cisco 7200 Series Routers with an ESA

When a Cisco 7200 router has an active ESA, the ESA crypto engine—not the Cisco IOS crypto engine—governs all the router interfaces. (With an inactive ESA, the Cisco IOS crypto engine governs all the router interfaces. On the Cisco 7200, you can select which engine is active; only one engine is active at a time.)

The ESA plugs into the Cisco 7200 chassis, and the ESA crypto engine is identified by the ESA's chassis slot number.

Cisco RSP7000 and 7500 Series Routers with an ESA

The ESA and an adjoining port adapter plug into a VIP2 board. The ESA crypto engine—not the VIP2 crypto engine—governs the adjoining VIP2 port interfaces. The Cisco IOS crypto engine governs all remaining interfaces.

In a Cisco RSP7000 or 7500 series router, the ESA crypto engine is identified by the chassis slot number of the VIP2.

Understand Implementation Issues and Limitations

Please note the following issues and limitations of encryption, described in this section:

- Encapsulation
- Multicast of Encrypted Traffic
- IP Fragmentation

- Restrictions for Switching Types with the VIP2
- Number of Simultaneous Encrypted Sessions
- Performance Impacts

Encapsulation

You can use any type of encapsulation with IP encryption, except as follows: If you have a second-generation Versatile Interface Processor (VIP2) with a serial interface, encryption will not work for traffic on the serial interface unless you use the Point-to-Point Protocol (PPP), High-Level Data Link Control (HDLC) protocol, or Frame Relay protocol. For example, you cannot use encryption if you have X.25 or SMDS configured for the serial interface of a VIP2.

Multicast of Encrypted Traffic

Encrypted multicast is not supported.

IP Fragmentation

IP fragmentation is supported with encryption for all platforms except the VIP2. If you configure encryption for VIP2 interfaces, all IP fragments will be dropped.

Restrictions for Switching Types with the VIP2

If you configure encryption for VIP2 interfaces on a Cisco RSP7000 or 7500 series router, you must use distributed switching (DSW) on the source and destination encrypting/decrypting interfaces.

This restriction means that any protocol that is not compatible with DSW, such as SMDS, cannot be used on VIP2 encrypting interfaces.

Number of Simultaneous Encrypted Sessions

Each encrypting router can set up encrypted sessions with many other routers—if these are peer encrypting routers. Encrypting routers can also set up multiple simultaneous encrypted sessions with multiple peer routers. Up to 299 concurrent encrypted sessions per router can be supported.

Performance Impacts

Because of the high amount of processing required for encryption, if you use encryption heavily, there will be performance impacts such as interface congestion or slowed CPU functioning. Using an ESA crypto engine rather than the Cisco IOS crypto engine can improve overall router performance, because the Cisco IOS software will not be impacted by encryption processing.

CONFIGURING ENCRYPTION

To pass encrypted traffic between two routers, you must configure encryption at both routers. This section describes the tasks required to configure encryption on one router: you must repeat these tasks for each peer encrypting router (routers that will participate in encryption).

To configure encryption on a router, complete the tasks described in the following sections:

1. Generate DSS Public/Private Keys (required to configure a crypto engine)
2. Exchange DSS Public Keys (required to configure a crypto engine)
3. Enable DES Encryption Algorithms (required to configure the router)
4. Define Crypto Maps and Assign Them to Interfaces (required to configure router interfaces)
5. Back Up Your Configuration

NOTES

There are additional steps required if you configure encryption with GRE tunnels or if you configure encryption with a Data Encryption Service Adaptor (ESA). These additional steps are described later in this chapter, in sections "Configuring Encryption with GRE Tunnels," "Configuring Encryption with an ESA in a VIP2," and "Configuring Encryption with an ESA in a Cisco 7200 Series Router." Before you configure encryption, refer to these other sections as appropriate.

For examples of the configuration in this section, see section "Encryption Configuration Examples," found at the end of this chapter.

Generate DSS Public/Private Keys

You must generate DSS keys for each crypto engine you will use. If you will use more than one crypto engine, you must generate DSS keys separately for each engine. (These are the crypto engines you previously identified according to the description in the earlier section "Identify Crypto Engines within Each Peer Router.")

The DSS key pair that you generate is used by peer routers to authenticate each other before each encrypted session. The same DSS key pair is used by a crypto engine with all its encrypted sessions (regardless of the peer encrypting router that it connects to).

To generate DSS keys for a crypto engine, perform at least the first of the following tasks, in global configuration mode:

Task	Command
Generate DSS public and private keys.	**crypto gen-signature-keys** *key-name* [*slot*]
View your DSS public key (private key not viewable).	**show crypto mypubkey** [*slot*]

Task	Command
Save DSS keys to private NVRAM. (Complete this task only for Cisco IOS crypto engines.)	copy running-config startup-config

If you are generating keys for an ESA crypto engine, the following occurs during DSS key generation:

- You are prompted to enter a password.
  - If you previously used the **crypto zeroize** command to reset the ESA, you should create a new password for the ESA at this time.
  - If you previously used the **crypto clear-latch** command to reset the ESA, you should now use the password you assigned when you reset the ESA. If you do not remember the password, you must clear the ESA with the **crypto zeroize** command; you can then generate keys and create a new password for the ESA.
- The DSS keys are automatically saved to the tamper-resistant memory of the ESA.

Configuring encryption with an ESA is described later in sections "Configuring Encryption with an ESA in a VIP2" and "Configuring Encryption with an ESA in a Cisco 7200 Series Router."

Exchange DSS Public Keys

You must exchange DSS public keys with all participating peer routers. This allows peer routers to authenticate each other at the start of encrypted communication sessions.

If your network contains several peer encrypting routers, you need to exchange DSS keys multiple times (once for each peer router). If you ever add an encrypting peer router to your network topology, you will then need to exchange DSS keys with the new router to enable encryption to occur with that new router.

You must exchange the DSS public keys of each crypto engine that you will use.

To exchange DSS public keys successfully, you must cooperate with a trusted administrator of the other peer router. You and the administrator of the peer router must complete the following steps in the order given (see Figure 23–5):

Step 1   Call the other administrator on the phone. Remain on the phone with this person until you complete all the steps in this list.

Step 2   You and the other administrator decide which of you will be called "PASSIVE" and which will be called "ACTIVE."

Step 3   PASSIVE enables a DSS exchange connection by performing the following task in global configuration mode:

Task	Command
Enable a DSS exchange connection.	**crypto key-exchange passive** [*tcp-port*]

Step 4   ACTIVE initiates a DSS exchange connection and sends a DSS public key by performing the following task in global configuration mode:

Task	Command
Initiate connection and send DSS public key.	**crypto key-exchange** *ip-address key-name* [*tcp-port*]

The serial number and Fingerprint of ACTIVE's DSS public key will display on both of your screens. The serial number and Fingerprint are numeric values generated from ACTIVE's DSS public key.

Step 5   You both verbally verify that the serial number is the same on both your screens, and that the Fingerprint is the same on both your screens.

Step 6   If the displayed serial numbers and Fingerprints match, PASSIVE should agree to accept ACTIVE's DSS key by typing **y** at the prompt.

Step 7   PASSIVE sends ACTIVE a DSS public key by pressing <Return> at the screen prompt and selecting a crypto engine at the next prompt.

Step 8   PASSIVE's DSS serial number and Fingerprint display on both of your screens.

Step 9   As before, you both verbally verify that the PASSIVE's DSS serial number and Fingerprint match on your two screens.

Step 10   ACTIVE agrees to accept PASSIVE's DSS public key.

Step 11   The exchange is complete, and you can end the phone call.

The previous steps (illustrated in Figure 23–5) must be accomplished between your router and a peer router for every peer router with which you will be conducting encrypted sessions.

Figure 23–5
Exchange DSS
Public Keys

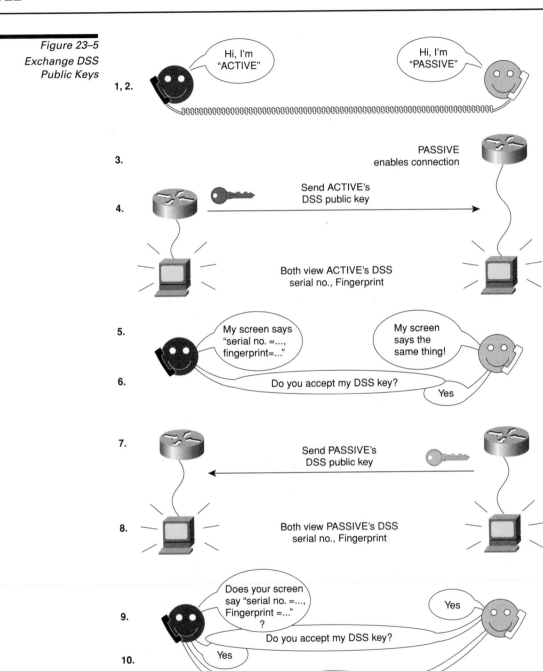

Figure 23–5
Exchange DSS
Public Keys

Enable DES Encryption Algorithms

Cisco routers use Data Encryption Standard (DES) encryption algorithms and DES keys to encrypt and decrypt data. You must globally enable (turn on) all the DES encryption algorithms that your router will use during encrypted sessions. If a DES algorithm is not enabled globally, you will not be able to use it. (Enabling a DES algorithm once allows it to be used by all crypto engines of a router.)

To conduct an encrypted session with a peer router, you must enable at least one DES algorithm that the peer router also has enabled. You must configure the same DES algorithm on both peer routers for encryption to work.

Cisco supports the following four types of DES encryption algorithms:

- DES with 8-bit Cipher FeedBack (CFB)
- DES with 64-bit CFB
- 40-bit variation of DES with 8-bit CFB
- 40-bit variation of DES with 64-bit CFB

The 40-bit variations use a 40-bit DES key, which is easier for attackers to "crack" than basic DES, which uses a 56-bit DES key. However, some international applications might require you to use 40-bit DES because of export laws. Also, 8-bit CFB is more commonly used than 64-bit CFB but requires more CPU time to process. Other conditions might also exist that require you to use one or another type of DES.

> **NOTES**
>
> If you are running an exportable image, you can only enable and use 40-bit variations of DES. You cannot enable or use the basic DES algorithms, which are not available with exportable images.

One DES algorithm is enabled for your router by default. If you do not plan to use the default DES algorithm, you may choose to disable it. If you are running a non-exportable image, the DES default algorithm will be basic DES with 64-bit CFB. If you are running an exportable image, the DES default algorithm will be the 40-bit variation of DES with 64-bit CFB.

If you do not know if your image is exportable or non-exportable, you can perform the **show crypto algorithms** command to determine which DES algorithms are currently enabled.

To globally enable one or more DES algorithms, perform one or more of the following tasks, in global configuration mode:

Task	Command
Enable DES with 8-bit or 64-bit CFB.	**crypto algorithm des [cfb-8	cfb-64]**
Enable 40-bit DES with 8-bit or 64-bit CFB.	**crypto algorithm 40-bit-des [cfb-8	cfb-64]**
View all enabled DES algorithms.	**show crypto algorithms**

Define Crypto Maps and Assign Them to Interfaces

The purpose of this task is to tell your router which interfaces should encrypt/decrypt traffic, which IP packets to encrypt or decrypt at those interfaces, and also which DES encryption algorithm to use when encrypting/decrypting the packets.

There are actually three steps required to complete this task:

Step 1	Set Up Encryption Access List (to be used in the crypto map definition)
Step 2	Define Crypto Maps
Step 3	Apply Crypto Maps to Interfaces

NOTES

You should select which interfaces to configure so that traffic is encrypted at the outbound interface of the local peer router, and traffic is decrypted at the input interface of the remote peer.

Set Up Encryption Access List

Encryption access lists are used in this step to define which IP packets will be encrypted and which IP packets will not be encrypted. Encryption access lists are defined using extended IP access lists. (Normally, IP access lists are used to filter traffic. Encryption access lists are *not* used to filter traffic but are used to specify which packets to encrypt or not encrypt.)

To set up encryption access lists for IP packet encryption, perform the following task in global configuration mode:

Task	Command
Specify conditions to determine which IP packets will be encrypted. (Enable or disable encryption for traffic that matches these conditions.)[1]	**access-list** *access-list-number* [**dynamic** *dynamic-name* [**timeout** *minutes*]] {**deny** | **permit**} *protocol source source-wildcard destination destination-wildcard* [**precedence** *precedence*] [**tos** *tos*] [**log**]
	or
	ip access-list extended *name* Follow with **permit** and **deny** statements as appropriate.

1. You specify conditions using an IP access list designated by either a number or a name. The **access-list** command designates a numbered access list; the **ip access-list extended** command designates a named access list.

Using the **permit** keyword will cause all traffic that is passed between the specified source and destination addresses to be encrypted/decrypted by peer routers. Using the **deny** keyword prevents that traffic from being encrypted/decrypted by peer routers.

The encryption access list you define at the local router must have a "mirror-image" encryption access list defined at the remote router, so that traffic that is encrypted locally is decrypted at the remote peer.

The encryption access list you define will be applied to an interface as an outbound encryption access list after you define a crypto map and apply the crypto map to the interface. (These two tasks are described in the following sections.)

CAUTION

When you create encryption access lists, Cisco recommends *against* using the **any** keyword to specify source or destination addresses. Using the **any** keyword could cause extreme problems if a packet enters your router and is destined for a router that is not configured for encryption. This would cause your router to attempt to set up an encryption session with a nonencrypting router.

NOTES

If your encryption access list defines more than 100 distinct source addresses or more than 10 destination addresses for a given source address, you need to change certain defaults as described in section "Change Encryption Access List Limits," found later in the chapter.

NOTES

If you view your router's access lists by using a command such as **show ip access-lists**, *all* extended IP access lists will be shown in the command output. This includes extended IP access lists that are used for traffic filtering purposes as well as those that are used for encryption. The **show** command output does not differentiate between the two uses of the extended access lists.

Define Crypto Maps

You must define exactly one crypto map for each physical interface that will send encrypted data to a peer encrypting router.

Crypto maps are used to specify which DES encryption algorithm(s) will be used in conjunction with each access list defined in the previous step. Crypto maps are also used to identify which peer routers will provide the remote end encryption services.

To define a crypto map, perform the following tasks. The first task is performed in global configuration mode; the other tasks are performed in crypto map configuration mode.

Task	Command
Name the crypto map. (Executing this command causes you to enter the crypto map configuration mode.)	**crypto map** *map-name seq-num*

Task	Command
Specify the remote peer router.	**set peer** *key-name*
Specify at least one encryption access list.	**match address** [*access-list-number* | *name*]
Specify at least one DES encryption algorithm. (This must be an algorithm you previously enabled.)	**set algorithm des** [**cfb-8** | **cfb-64**] or **set algorithm 40-bit-des** [**cfb-8** | **cfb-64**]

NOTES

If you are running an exportable image, you can only specify 40-bit variations of DES. You cannot enable or use the basic DES algorithms, which are not available with exportable images.

To define an additional, different set of parameters for the same interface, repeat the steps in the previous task list, using the same *map-name* but using a different *seq-num* for the crypto map command. For more information, refer to the **crypto map** command description in Chapter 24, "Network Data Encryption Commands."

Apply Crypto Maps to Interfaces

This step puts into effect the crypto maps just defined. You must apply exactly one crypto map to each physical interface that will encrypt outbound data and decrypt inbound data. This interface provides the encrypted connection to a peer encrypting router. An interface will not encrypt/decrypt data until you apply a crypto map to the interface.

To apply a crypto map to an interface, perform the following task in interface configuration mode:

Task	Command
Apply a crypto map to an interface.	**crypto map** *map-name*

Back Up Your Configuration

Cisco recommends that after you configure your router for encryption, you make a backup of your configuration. (Be careful to restrict unauthorized access of this backed-up configuration.)

CONFIGURING ENCRYPTION WITH GRE TUNNELS

When GRE tunnel endpoints are located at the peer encrypting routers, you can configure encryption so that all traffic through the GRE tunnel is encrypted.

Note that you cannot selectively encrypt GRE tunnel traffic: Either all the GRE tunnel traffic is encrypted, or no GRE tunnel traffic is encrypted.

To configure encryption with GRE tunnels, perform the same basic tasks described previously in section "Configuring Encryption." However, while you complete basic task 4—Define Crypto Maps and Assign Them to Interfaces—you also must follow the additional instructions described next (for two cases):

- Encrypt Only GRE Tunnel Traffic
- Encrypt GRE Tunnel Traffic and Other Traffic

For examples of configuring encryption with a GRE tunnel, see section "Examples of Configuring Encryption with GRE Tunnels," found later in this chapter.

Encrypt Only GRE Tunnel Traffic

To encrypt only traffic through the GRE tunnel, follow these two additional instructions:

- When you set up your encryption access list, the list should contain only one criteria statement. In this one statement, specify **gre** as the protocol, specify the tunnel source address as the source, and specify the tunnel destination address as the destination.
- Apply the crypto map to the physical interface and to the tunnel interface. (Without GRE tunnels, you only had to apply the crypto map to the physical interface.)

  Remember to apply a crypto map to the physical interface and tunnel interface at both ends of the GRE tunnel.

Encrypt GRE Tunnel Traffic and Other Traffic

To encrypt both GRE tunnel traffic and other specified non-GRE tunnel traffic, follow these three additional instructions:

- Create two separate encryption access lists as follows:
  - The first encryption access list should contain only one criteria statement. In this one statement, specify **gre** as the protocol, specify the tunnel source address as the source, and specify the tunnel destination address as the destination.
  - In the second encryption access list, specify which non-GRE traffic should be encrypted. (For example, you could specify **tcp** as a protocol, and specify a subnet source/wildcard and a subnet destination/wildcard.)
- Create two separate crypto maps as follows:
  - In the first crypto map, specify the first encryption access list, along with a DES algorithm and the remote peer.
  - In the second crypto map, create at least two separate subdefinitions. The first subdefinition should exactly match the statements in the first crypto map. The second subdefinition should specify the second encryption access list, a DES algorithm, and the remote peer.

- Apply the first crypto map to tunnel interface, and apply the second crypto map to the physical interface. (Without GRE tunnels, you only had to apply one crypto map to the physical interface.)

  Remember to apply a crypto map to the physical interface and tunnel interface at both ends of the GRE tunnel.

CONFIGURING ENCRYPTION WITH AN ESA IN A VIP2

To configure encryption with a Data Encryption Service Adaptor (ESA), there are additional instructions that you must follow, in addition to the basic encryption configuration tasks described previously in section "Configuring Encryption."

Before you start to accomplish the basic tasks, be sure to read the information in this section.

This section describes configuration for an ESA plugged into a VIP2 on a Cisco RSP7000 or 7500 series router.

To configure encryption with an ESA plugged into a VIP2, complete these tasks and in this order:

1. Reset the ESA
2. Perform Additional Encryption Configuration

NOTES

If you ever remove and reinstall the ESA or the VIP2, you must reset the ESA again.

For examples of ESA-specific configuration tasks, see section "Examples of ESA-Specific Encryption Configuration Tasks," found later in this chapter.

Reset the ESA

If you do not reset the ESA in a VIP2, the ESA crypto engine will not be used; instead, the VIP2 crypto engine will govern all the VIP2 interfaces (and the Cisco IOS crypto engine will govern the other router interfaces).

Before an ESA is reset, the ESA's "Tampered" LED is lit.

To reset an ESA, complete one of the following bulleted tasks:

- Reset an ESA that has never been used before. Complete the following task in global configuration mode:

Task	Command
Reset the ESA by clearing the ESA hardware latch.	**crypto clear-latch** *slot*
When prompted, create a new password for the ESA.	*password*

- Reset an ESA that was previously used, and you know the ESA password of. Complete the following task in global configuration mode:

Task	Command
Reset the ESA by clearing the ESA hardware latch.	**crypto clear-latch** *slot*
When prompted, type the ESA password previously assigned.	*password*

- Reset an ESA that was previously used, but you do not know the ESA password of. Complete this task in global configuration mode:

Task	Command
Clear the ESA. (This deletes all DSS keys for the ESA.)	**crypto zeroize** *slot*

Perform Additional Encryption Configuration

After you reset the ESA in a VIP2, continue configuring encryption by following the instructions in one of the following bullets.

- If the router, VIP2, and ESA were never previously configured for encryption, complete all the tasks described earlier in section "Configuring Encryption."
- If the ESA was never previously configured for encryption, but the router and VIP2 interfaces were configured for encryption, complete only the following two tasks, described earlier in section "Configuring Encryption":
  - Generate DSS Public/Private Keys (for the ESA crypto engine)
  - Exchange DSS Public Keys

NOTES

When you generate DSS keys for the ESA, you could give the keys the same *key-name* as you previously gave the VIP2 keys. If you do not give the keys the same *key-name*, you need to make sure that all remote peer routers update their crypto maps to include the new name of the ESA crypto engine as their peer.

As always, remember to back up your configuration when you are done.

- If the router, VIP2, and ESA were all previously configured for encryption, you might not need to complete any additional configuration. However, you will need additional configuration in at least the following cases (see section "Configuring Encryption" for descriptions of the tasks):
  - If you have any concern that the old ESA keys are compromised, you should regenerate and exchange new DSS keys for the ESA. (Use the same ESA *key-name* previously assigned.)

○ If the ESA was relocated and now governs different interfaces than before, either all peer routers must update their crypto maps to reflect the changed peers, or you must regenerate and exchange new DSS keys for the ESA, assigning the *key-name* that is currently in the peer routers' crypto maps.

○ If you previously reset the ESA with the **crypto zeroize** command because you did not know the ESA password, you must at a minimum generate and exchange DSS keys for the ESA crypto engine.

As always, remember to back up your configuration when you are done.

CONFIGURING ENCRYPTION WITH AN ESA IN A CISCO 7200 SERIES ROUTER

To configure encryption with a Data Encryption Service Adaptor (ESA), there are additional instructions that you must follow in addition to the basic encryption configuration tasks described previously in section "Configuring Encryption."

Before you start to accomplish the basic tasks, be sure to read the information in this section.

This section describes configuration for an ESA plugged into a Cisco 7200 series router.

For examples of ESA-specific configuration tasks, see section "Examples of ESA-Specific Encryption Configuration Tasks," found later in this chapter.

Required Tasks

Complete the following tasks and in this order (see following sections for descriptions):

1. Reset the ESA
2. Perform Additional Encryption Configuration
3. Enable the ESA

NOTES

If you ever remove and reinstall the ESA, you must reset the ESA again and re-enable the ESA.

Optional Tasks

You can optionally complete these additional tasks (see following sections for descriptions):

• Select a Crypto Engine (after encryption is configured, you might want to change which crypto engine to use—the Cisco IOS crypto engine or the ESA crypto engine.)

• Delete DSS Keys (if you ever remove or relocate the ESA or the Cisco 7200, you might want to delete DSS keys, to reduce any potential security risk.)

Reset the ESA

Before an ESA is reset, the ESA's "Tampered" LED is lit.

To reset an ESA in a Cisco 7200 series router, complete one of the following bulleted tasks:

- Reset an ESA that has never been used before. Complete the following tasks in global configuration mode:

Task	Command
Reset the ESA by clearing the ESA hardware latch.	**crypto clear-latch** *slot*
When prompted, create a new password for the ESA.	*password*

- Reset a previously used ESA when:

  ○ You know the ESA password.

  ○ You know or suspect that either the ESA, router, or router interfaces need additional configuration. (For example, the ESA's previous configuration was not complete or is uncertain; or you know you want to generate new DSS keys for the ESA; or the router is not configured for encryption.)

  If you meet all the criteria just described, reset the ESA, in global configuration mode:

Task	Command
Reset the ESA by clearing the ESA hardware latch.	**crypto clear-latch** *slot*
When prompted, type the ESA password previously assigned.	*password*
If prompted to enable the ESA, type **no**.	**no**

- Reset a previously used ESA when:

  ○ You know the ESA password.

  ○ The router has been configured for encryption (and may have already been encrypting traffic using the Cisco IOS crypto engine).

  ○ The ESA has already been configured for encryption with the same *key-name* as the Cisco IOS crypto engine and with DSS keys generated and exchanged, and you do not want to generate new keys.

  ○ All encryption configuration is already complete as described previously in section "Configuring Encryption," and you are ready to start encrypting traffic using the ESA crypto engine.

If you meet all the criteria just described, reset the ESA, in global configuration mode:

Task	Command
Reset the ESA by clearing the ESA hardware latch.	**crypto clear-latch** *slot*
When prompted, type the ESA password previously assigned.	*password*
When prompted to enable the ESA, type **yes**.	yes

NOTES

After you reset the ESA as just described, the ESA will automatically become active and begin encrypting traffic. For this case only, you do not need to complete any additional encryption configuration. (But as always, be sure to back up your configuration.)

- Reset a previously used ESA when you do not know the ESA password. Complete this task in global configuration mode:

Task	Command
Clear the ESA. (This deletes all DSS keys for the ESA.)	**crypto zeroize** *slot*

Perform Additional Encryption Configuration

After you reset the ESA in a Cisco 7200 series router, continue configuring encryption by following the instructions in one of the following bullets:

- If the router and ESA were never previously configured for encryption, complete all the tasks described earlier in section "Configuring Encryption," then enable the ESA as described in the next section, "Enable the ESA."
- If the ESA was never previously configured for encryption, but the router is configured for encryption, complete only the following two tasks described earlier in section "Configuring Encryption":
  - Generate DSS Public/Private Keys (for the ESA crypto engine)
  - Exchange DSS Public Keys (for the ESA crypto engine)

NOTES

When you generate DSS keys for the ESA, give the keys the same *key-name* previously assigned to the Cisco IOS crypto engine keys.

After you generate and exchange DSS keys for the ESA crypto engine, enable the ESA as described in the next section, "Enable the ESA."

- If the router and ESA are both already configured for encryption, you might only need to enable the ESA as described in the next section, "Enable the ESA."

However, in at least the following cases you will need additional configuration before you enable the ESA (see earlier section "Configuring Encryption" for descriptions of the tasks):

- If the ESA has DSS keys generated but not exchanged with the peer routers, you must exchange the keys.

- If you have any concern that the ESA's DSS keys are compromised, you should regenerate and exchange new DSS keys for the ESA, using the same *key-name* assigned to the router DSS keys.

- If the ESA was relocated from a different router, regenerate and exchange DSS keys, using the same *key-name* assigned to the router DSS keys.

- If you previously reset the ESA with the **crypto zeroize** command because you did not know the ESA password, you must at a minimum generate and exchange DSS keys for the ESA crypto engine.

Enable the ESA

To enable an ESA in a Cisco 7200 series router, complete the following task in global configuration mode:

Task	Command
Enable the ESA.	**crypto esa enable** *slot*

NOTES

If the Cisco IOS crypto engine is currently encrypting traffic when you enable the ESA, the session will be torn down, and a new session will be established using the ESA crypto engine. This could cause a momentary delay for encrypted traffic.

As always, remember to back up your configuration when you are done.

Select a Crypto Engine

This is an optional task.

After encryption is configured on a Cisco 7200 series router with an ESA, you might want to change which crypto engine to use—the Cisco IOS crypto engine or the ESA crypto engine. This section describes how to switch from one crypto engine to the other.

You should only select a crypto engine if the engine is fully configured for encryption.

If you boot the router with an operational ESA installed, the ESA will be the active crypto engine upon bootup, by default. Otherwise, the Cisco IOS crypto engine will be the default active crypto engine.

NOTES

If any encryption session is in progress when you switch from one crypto engine to the other, the session will be torn down, and a new session will be established using the newly selected crypto engine. This could cause a momentary delay for encrypted traffic.

Select the Cisco IOS Crypto Engine

If the ESA crypto engine is encrypting traffic, but you want to cause the Cisco IOS crypto engine to encrypt the traffic instead, you can switch to the Cisco IOS crypto engine without removing the ESA. (You might want to do this for testing purposes.)

CAUTION

Before you switch to the Cisco IOS crypto engine, be sure that the Cisco IOS crypto engine is configured with DSS keys generated and exchanged, and be sure that the DSS keys have the same *key-name* for both engines; otherwise, you will lose encryption capability when you switch engines.

To select the Cisco IOS crypto engine, perform the following task in global configuration mode:

Task	Command
Shut down the ESA.	**crypto esa shutdown** *slot*

After you select the Cisco IOS crypto engine, the Cisco IOS crypto engine will be the active engine, governing the router interfaces. The Cisco IOS crypto engine will perform the encryption services, and the ESA will be inactive.

Select the ESA Crypto Engine

If the Cisco IOS crypto engine is encrypting traffic, but you want to cause an installed ESA crypto engine to encrypt the traffic instead, you can switch to the ESA crypto engine.

NOTES

Before you switch to the ESA crypto engine, be sure that the ESA crypto engine is configured with DSS keys generated and exchanged, and be sure that the DSS keys have the same *key-name* for both engines; otherwise, you will lose encryption capability when you switch engines.

To select the ESA crypto engine, perform the following task in global configuration mode:

Task	Command
Enable the ESA.	**crypto esa enable** *slot*

After you select the ESA crypto engine, the ESA crypto engine will be the active engine, governing the router interfaces. The ESA crypto engine will perform encryption services for the router, and the Cisco IOS crypto engine will be inactive.

Delete DSS Keys

This is an optional task.

If you ever remove or relocate the ESA or the Cisco 7200, or if the DSS keys ever become compromised, or if you want to turn encryption off at the router, you might want to delete DSS keys to reduce any potential security risk. This section describes how to delete a DSS key pair for an ESA or for a Cisco 7200 series router.

To delete DSS keys, perform the following tasks beginning in EXEC mode:

Task	Command
View all existing sets of DSS keys (ESA and Cisco IOS keys).	**show crypto mypubkey**
Determine the current (active) crypto engine.	**show crypto engine configuration**
If the current engine is not the engine for which you want to delete keys, change engines. (When you delete keys, the software deletes keys for the current active engine.)	**crypto esa enable** *slot* (switch to the Cisco IOS crypto engine) or **crypto esa shutdown** *slot* (switch to the ESA crypto engine)
Verify that the current crypto engine is the engine for which you want to delete keys.	**show crypto engine configuration**
Delete the DSS keys for the current crypto engine.	**crypto zeroize** (for the Cisco IOS crypto engine) or **crypto zeroize** *slot* (for the ESA crypto engine)

After you delete DSS keys for a crypto engine, if you ever want to use that engine for encryption, you must regenerate and exchange new DSS keys for that engine. For the ESA crypto engine, you must also enable the ESA.

CUSTOMIZING ENCRYPTION (CONFIGURE OPTIONS)

This section describes options that you can configure to customize encryption on a router:

- Define Time Duration of Encrypted Sessions
- Shorten Session Setup Times by Pregenerating DH Numbers
- Change Encryption Access List Limits

Define Time Duration of Encrypted Sessions

The default time duration of an encrypted session is 30 minutes. After the default time duration expires, an encrypted session must be renegotiated if encrypted communication is to continue. You can change this default to extend or shorten the time of encrypted sessions.

You might want to shorten session times if you believe that there is a risk of compromised session keys.

You might want to extend session times if your system has trouble tolerating the interruptions caused when sessions are renegotiated.

To change the time duration of encrypted sessions, perform at least the first of the following tasks, in global configuration mode:

Task	Command
Define maximum time duration of encrypted sessions.	**crypto key-timeout** *minutes*
View defined time duration of encrypted sessions.	**show crypto key-timeout**

Shorten Session Setup Times by Pregenerating DH Numbers

Diffie-Hellman (DH) numbers are generated in pairs during the setup of each encrypted session. (DH numbers are used during encrypted session setup to compute the DES session key.) Generating these numbers is a CPU-intensive activity, which can make session setup slow—especially for low-end routers. To speed up session setup time, you may choose to pregenerate DH numbers. It is usually necessary to pregenerate only one or two DH numbers.

To pregenerate DH numbers, perform the following task in global configuration mode:

Task	Command
Pregenerate DH numbers.	**crypto pregen-dh-pairs** *count* [*slot*]

Change Encryption Access List Limits

When you configure encryption access lists, you configure source and destination pairs in criteria statements. Any traffic that matches the criteria is then encrypted.

By default, the maximum number of distinct sources (host or subnets) that you can define in an encryption access list is 100. Also, the maximum number of distinct destinations that you can define for any given source address is 10. For example, if you define six different source addresses, you can define up to 10 destination addresses for each of the six sources, for a total of 60 access list criteria statements.

Why Do These Limits Exist?

These limits exist because of the amount of memory that must be reserved for encryption connections. If there are more potential connections, there must be more memory preallocated.

When Should the Limits Be Changed?

For most situations, the defaults of 100 maximum sources and 10 maximum destinations per source are sufficient. Cisco recommends that you do not change the defaults unless you actually exceed the number of sources or destinations per source.

However, in some situations you might want to change one or both of these maximum values. For example, if more than 10 remote sites need to connect to one server behind your router, then you need more than 10 destination addresses (one for each remote site) to pair up with the server's source address in the local router's encryption access list. In this case, you need to change the default of 10 maximum destination addresses per source address.

When changing limits, you should consider the amount of memory that will be allocated. In general, if you increase one value, decrease the other value. This prevents your router from running out of memory because too much memory was preallocated.

How Much Memory Is Preallocated If the Limits Are Changed?

The amount of memory reserved for encrypted connections changes if you change the defaults.

For every additional source, the following additional bytes of memory will be allocated:

$$64 + (68 \times \text{the specified number of maximum destinations})$$

For every additional destination, the following additional bytes of memory will be allocated:

$$68 \times \text{the specified number of maximum sources}$$

For example, if you specify 5 maximum sources, and 250 maximum destinations per source, the memory allocated for encryption connections is calculated as follows:

$$\{5 \times [64 + (68 \times 250)]\} + \{250 \times (68 \times 5)\} = 170320 \text{ bytes}$$

How Are the Limits Changed?

To change the default limits, perform one or both of the following tasks in global configuration mode, then reboot the router for the changes to take effect:

Task	Command
Change the maximum number of distinct sources (hosts or subnets) that you can define in the encryption access list statements.	**crypto sdu entities** *number*
Change the maximum number of destinations (hosts or subnets) per source that you can define in the encryption access list statements.	**crypto sdu connections** *number*

— **NOTES** ——————————————————————————————————

You must reboot the router for these changes to take effect.

For an example of changing these values, see section "Example of Changing Encryption Access List Limits," found later in this chapter.

TURNING OFF ENCRYPTION

You can turn off encryption for certain router interfaces, or you can turn off encryption completely for the entire router.

- To turn off encryption at all the interfaces governed by a single crypto engine, you can delete DSS keys for that engine. Deleting DSS keys is described in this section.

- To turn off encryption at certain random interfaces, you can remove the crypto maps from the interfaces with the **no crypto map** (**interface configuration**) command.

- To turn off encryption completely for a router, you can delete the DSS keys for all the router's crypto engines. Again, deleting DSS keys is described in this section.

Deleting DSS keys deconfigures encryption for the crypto engine and also reduces security risk by ensuring that the keys cannot be misused if you lose physical control over the router or ESA.

After you delete DSS keys for a crypto engine, you will not be able to perform encryption on the interfaces governed by that crypto engine.

— **CAUTION** ——————————————————————————————————

DSS keys cannot be recovered after they have been deleted. Use this function only after careful consideration.

For all platforms other than Cisco 7200 series routers, to delete DSS public/private keys for a crypto engine, perform the following task in global configuration mode:

Task	Command
Delete DSS keys for a crypto engine.	**crypto zeroize** [*slot*][1]

1. Only Cisco 7200 and 7500 series routers require the *slot* argument.

For a Cisco 7200 series router, to delete DSS public/private keys for a crypto engine, refer to section "Delete DSS Keys," found earlier in this chapter.

TESTING AND TROUBLESHOOTING ENCRYPTION

This section discusses how to verify your configuration and the correct operation of encryption. This section also discusses diagnosing encryption problems.

You should complete all the required configuration tasks (as described earlier in this chapter) before trying to test or troubleshoot your encryption configuration.

This section includes the following topics:

- Test the Encryption Configuration
- Diagnose Connection Problems
- Diagnose Other Miscellaneous Problems
- Use Debug Commands

Test the Encryption Configuration

If you want to test the encryption setup between peer routers, you can attempt to manually establish a session using the IP address of a local host and a remote host that have been specified in an encryption access list. (The encryption list must be specified in a crypto map definition, and that crypto map must be applied to an interface before this test will be successful.)

To test the encryption setup, perform the following tasks in privileged EXEC mode:

Task	Command
Set up a test encryption session.	**test crypto initiate-session** *src-ip-addr dst-ip-addr map-name seq-num*
View the connection status.	**show crypto connections**

An example at the end of this chapter explains how to interpret the **show crypto connections** command output.

Diagnose Connection Problems

If you need to verify the state of a connection, you can perform the following tasks in privileged EXEC mode:

Task	Command
Check status of all encryption connections.	**show crypto connections**
Check status of a crypto map.	**show crypto map**
Check that connection is established and that packets are being encrypted.	**show crypto engine connections active**

Diagnose Other Miscellaneous Problems

When using encryption, you might encounter some of the following problems:

- Dropped Packets
- Difficulty Establishing Telnet Sessions
- Invalid DSS Public/Private Keys
- ESA Crypto Engine Not Active
- Password Requested When You Generate DSS Keys
- Router Hanging

Dropped Packets

Packets are normally dropped while an encrypted session is being set up. If this poses a problem for your network, you should extend the length of encryption sessions as described previously in the section "Define Time Duration of Encrypted Sessions." The longer the session time, the fewer the interruptions caused by session renegotiation.

Packets might also be dropped if you switch crypto engines in a Cisco 7200 series router with an ESA. If this is a problem, you should only switch crypto engines when encrypted traffic is light.

IP fragments are always dropped on VIP2 interfaces, because IP fragmentation is not supported with encryption on VIP2 interfaces.

Difficulty Establishing Telnet Sessions

Hosts might experience difficulty in establishing Telnet sessions if the session uses two encrypting peer routers to create the connection. This difficulty is more likely to occur if the peer routers are low-end routers such as Cisco 2500 series routers. Telnet sessions can fail to be established when a Telnet connection attempt times out before the encrypted session setup is complete.

If a Telnet session fails to establish, the host should wait a short time (a few seconds might be sufficient), and then attempt the Telnet connection again. After the short wait, the encrypted session setup should be complete, and the Telnet session can be established. Enabling pregeneration of DH numbers (described later in this chapter) might also help by speeding up encryption session connection setup times.

Invalid DSS Public/Private Keys

If NVRAM fails, or if your ESA is tampered with or replaced, DSS public/private keys will no longer be valid. If this happens, you will need to regenerate and re-exchange DSS keys. Generating and exchanging DSS keys are described earlier in the "Configuring Encryption" section.

ESA Crypto Engine Not Active

If an installed ESA is not active when you boot a router, the router displays a message similar to teh following message, indicating that the router switched over to the Cisco IOS crypto engine:

```
There are no keys on the ESA in slot 2- ESA not enabled

...switching to SW crypto engine
```

You can also determine if the ESA crypto engine is not active by using the **show crypto engine brief** command—look at the "crypto engine state" field in the output. If no crypto engine is active, the state field indicates "pending."

The ESA crypto engine will not be active if you removed and reinstalled the ESA, if the ESA was tampered with, or if encryption is not configured correctly for the ESA.

If the Cisco IOS crypto engine is active, but you want to use the ESA crypto engine instead, make sure that the ESA crypto engine is reset (**crypto clear-latch** command); and for Cisco 7200 series routers, also make sure that the ESA crypto engine is enabled (**crypto esa enable** command). You might also need to complete or verify additional configuration; refer to the instructions for configuring encryption with an ESA, in section "Configuring Encryption with an ESA in a VIP2" or section "Configuring Encryption with an ESA in a Cisco 7200 Series Router," each found earlier in the chapter.

To verify that the ESA has DSS keys, you can use the **show crypto card** command and look at the "DSS Key set" field in the output. If the field contains "Yes," the ESA has DSS keys generated and stored. In this case, you might only need to reset and enable the ESA to make it active.

Password Requested When You Generate DSS Keys

- If you attempt to generate DSS keys for the Cisco IOS crypto engine on a Cisco 7200 series router with an installed ESA without DSS keys, the router might assume that you are trying to generate keys for the ESA and prompt for the ESA password.
  - If you want to generate keys for the ESA, you must supply the ESA password. If you do not know the password, you must reset the ESA as described in section "Configuring Encryption with an ESA in a Cisco 7200 Series Router," found earlier in chapter.
  - If you want to generate keys for the Cisco IOS crypto engine, not the ESA crypto engine, you must select the Cisco IOS crypto engine to make it the active engine.

To select the Cisco IOS crypto engine, perform the following task in global configuration mode:

Task	Command
Shut down the ESA.	**crypto esa shutdown** *slot*

- ○ When the Cisco IOS crypto engine is active, you can generate keys for the router, and you will not be prompted for a password.
- If you want to generate DSS keys for an ESA in a VIP2 (for Cisco RSP7000 and 7500 series routers), you must enter the ESA password. If you do not know the password, you must reset the ESA as described in the section "Configuring Encryption with an ESA in a VIP2," found earlier in this chapter.

Router Hanging

If you remove a configured ESA from a VIP2, you must reboot the router. If you do not, the router might hang when it tries to access the absent ESA.

Use Debug Commands

Debug commands are also available to assist in problem-solving.

ENCRYPTION CONFIGURATION EXAMPLES

The following sections provide examples of configuring and testing your router for network data encryption:

- Example of Generating DSS Public/Private Keys
- Example of Exchanging DSS Public Keys
- Example of Enabling DES Encryption Algorithms
- Examples of Setting Up Encryption Access Lists, Defining Crypto Maps, and Applying Crypto Maps to Interfaces
- Example of Changing Encryption Access List Limits
- Examples of Configuring Encryption with GRE Tunnels
- Examples of ESA-Specific Encryption Configuration Tasks
- Examples of Deleting DSS Keys
- Example of Testing the Encryption Connection

Example of Generating DSS Public/Private Keys

The following example illustrates two encrypting peer routers (named Apricot and Banana) generating their respective DSS public/private keys. Apricot is a Cisco 2500 series router.

Banana is a Cisco 7500 series router with an RSP in chassis slot 4 and an ESA/VIP2 in chassis slot 2.

Apricot

```
Apricot(config)# crypto gen-signature-keys Apricot
Generating DSS keys .... [OK]
Apricot(config)#
```

Banana

```
Banana(config)# crypto gen-signature-keys BananaIOS 4
Generating DSS keys .... [OK]
Banana(config)# crypto gen-signature-keys BananaESA 2
% Initialize the crypto card password. You will need
    this password in order to generate new signature
    keys or clear the crypto card extraction latch.

Password: <passwd>

Re-enter password: <passwd>

Generating DSS keys .... [OK]
Banana(config)#
```

The password entered in this example is a new password that you create when you generate DSS keys for an ESA crypto engine for the first time. If you ever generate DSS keys a second time for the same ESA crypto engine, you must use the same password to complete the key regeneration.

Example of Exchanging DSS Public Keys

The following is an example of a DSS public key exchange between two peer encrypting routers (Apricot and Banana). Apricot is a Cisco 2500 series router, and Banana is a Cisco 7500 series router with an ESA. In this example, Apricot sends its Cisco IOS DSS public key, and Banana sends its ESA DSS public key. DSS keys have already been generated as shown in the previous example.

Before any commands are entered, one administrator must call the other administrator. After the phone call is established, the two administrators decide which router is "PASSIVE" and which is "ACTIVE" (an arbitrary choice). In this example, router Apricot is ACTIVE and router Banana is PASSIVE. To start, PASSIVE enables a connection as follows:

Banana (PASSIVE)

```
Banana(config)# crypto key-exchange passive
Enter escape character to abort if connection does not complete.
Wait for connection from peer[confirm]<Return>
Waiting ....
```

PASSIVE must wait while ACTIVE initiates the connection and sends a DSS public key.

Apricot (ACTIVE)

```
Apricot(config)# crypto key-exchange 192.168.114.68 Apricot
Public key for Apricot:
   Serial Number 01461300
   Fingerprint   0F1D 373F 2FC1 872C D5D7

Wait for peer to send a key[confirm]<Return>
Waiting ....
```

After ACTIVE sends a DSS public key, the key's serial number and Fingerprint display on both terminals, as shown previously and as follows:

Banana (PASSIVE)

```
Public key for Apricot:
   Serial Number 01461300
   Fingerprint   0F1D 373F 2FC1 872C D5D7
Add this public key to the configuration? [yes/no]: y
```

Now the two administrators both must verbally verify that their two screens show the same serial number and Fingerprint. If they do, PASSIVE will accept the DSS key as shown previously by typing **y**, and continue by sending ACTIVE a DSS public key:

```
Send peer a key in return[confirm]<Return>
Which one?

BananaIOS? [yes]: n
BananaESA? [yes]: <Return>
Public key for BananaESA:
   Serial Number 01579312
   Fingerprint   BF1F 9EAC B17E F2A1 BA77

Banana(config)#
```

Both administrators observe Banana's serial number and Fingerprint on their screens. Again, they verbally verify that the two screens show the same numbers.

Apricot (ACTIVE):

```
Public key for BananaESA:
   Serial Number 01579312
   Fingerprint   BF1F 9EAC B17E F2A1 BA77

Add this public key to the configuration? [yes/no]: y
Apricot(config)#
```

ACTIVE accepts Apricot's DSS public key. Both administrators hang up the phone, and the key exchange is complete.

Figure 23–6 shows complete screens of the two routers. The steps are numbered on the figure to show the sequence of the entire exchange.

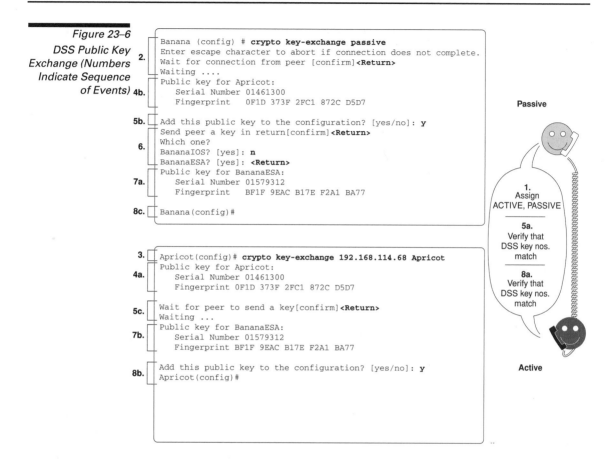

Figure 23–6
DSS Public Key
Exchange (Numbers
Indicate Sequence
of Events)

Example of Enabling DES Encryption Algorithms

In this example, a router (Apricot) globally enables two DES algorithms: the basic DES algorithm with 8-bit Cipher Feedback (CFB), and the 40-bit DES algorithm with 8-bit CFB. Another router (Banana) globally enables three DES algorithms: the basic DES algorithm with 8-bit CFB, the basic DES algorithm with 64-bit CFB, and the 40-bit DES algorithm with 8-bit CFB.

The following commands are entered from the global configuration mode.

Apricot

```
crypto algorithm des cfb-8
crypto algorithm 40-bit-des cfb-8
```

Banana

```
crypto algorithm des cfb-8
crypto algorithm des cfb-64
crypto algorithm 40-bit-des cfb-8
```

Examples of Setting Up Encryption Access Lists, Defining Crypto Maps, and Applying Crypto Maps to Interfaces

The following two examples show how to set up interfaces for encrypted transmission. Participating routers will be configured as encrypting peers for IP packet encryption.

Example 1

In the first example, a team of researchers at a remote site communicate with a research coordinator at headquarters. Company-confidential information is exchanged by IP traffic that consists only of TCP data. Figure 23–7 shows the network topology.

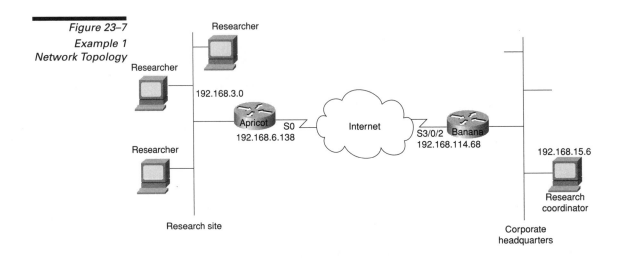

Figure 23–7
Example 1
Network Topology

Apricot is a Cisco 2500 series router, and Banana is a Cisco 7500 series router with an ESA/VIP2 in chassis slot 3.

Apricot

```
Apricot(config)# access-list 101 permit tcp 192.168.3.0 0.0.0.15 host 192.168.15.6
Apricot(config)# crypto map Research 10
Apricot(config-crypto-map)# set peer BananaESA
```

```
Apricot(config-crypto-map)# set algorithm des cfb-8
Apricot(config-crypto-map)# match address 101
Apricot(config-crypto-map)# exit
Apricot(config)# interface s0
Apricot(config-if)# crypto map Research
Apricot(config-if)# exit
Apricot(config)#
```

Banana

```
Banana(config)# access-list 110 permit tcp host 192.168.15.6 192.168.3.0 0.0.0.15
Banana(config)# crypto map Rsrch 10
Banana(config-crypto-map)# set peer Apricot
Banana(config-crypto-map)# set algorithm des cfb-8
Banana(config-crypto-map)# set algorithm des cfb-64
Banana(config-crypto-map)# match address 110
Banana(config-crypto-map)# exit
Banana(config)# interface s3/0/2
Banana(config-if)# crypto map Rsrch
Banana(config-if)# exit
Banana(config)#
```

Because Banana set two DES algorithms for crypto map Rsrch, Banana could use either algorithm with traffic on the S3/0/2 interface. However, because Apricot only set one DES algorithm (CFB-8 DES) for the crypto map Research, that is the only DES algorithm that will be used for all encrypted traffic between Apricot and Banana.

Example 2

In the second example, employees at two branch offices and at headquarters must communicate sensitive information. A mix of TCP and UDP traffic is transmitted by IP packets. Figure 23–8 shows the network topology used in this example.

Apricot is a Cisco 2500 series router and connects to the Internet through interface S1. Both Banana and Cantaloupe are Cisco 7500 series routers with ESA cards. Banana connects to the Internet using the ESA-governed VIP2 interface S2/1/2. Cantaloupe is already using every VIP2 interface (governed by the ESA card) to connect to several offsite financial services, so it must connect to the Internet using a serial interface (S3/1) in slot 3. (Cantaloupe's interface S3/1 is governed by the Cisco IOS crypto engine.)

Apricot will be using one interface to communicate with both Banana and Cantaloupe. Because only one crypto map can be applied to this interface, Apricot creates a crypto map that has two distinct definition sets by using two different *seq-num* values with the same *map-name*.

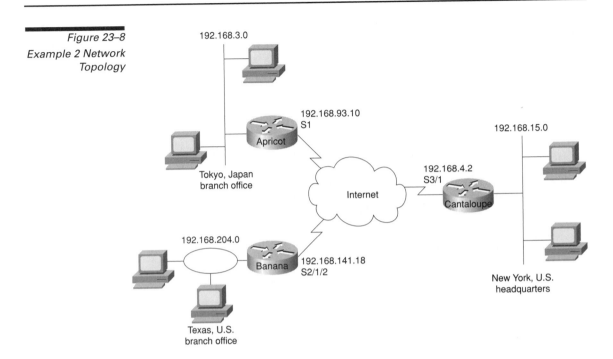

Figure 23–8
Example 2 Network Topology

By using *seq-num* values of 10 and 20, Apricot creates a single crypto map named "TXandNY" that contains a subset of definitions for encrypted sessions with Banana, and a second distinct subset for definitions for encrypted sessions with Cantaloupe.

Banana and Cantaloupe each also use a single interface to communicate with the other two routers, and therefore will use the same strategy as Apricot does for creating crypto maps.

In this example, we assume that Apricot has generated DSS keys with the *key-name* "Apricot.TokyoBranch," Banana has generated DSS keys with the *key-name* "BananaESA.TXbranch," and Cantaloupe has generated DSS keys with the *key-name* "CantaloupeIOS.NY." We also assume that each router has exchanged DSS public keys with the other two routers, and that each router has enabled each DES algorithm that is specified in the crypto maps.

Apricot

```
Apricot(config)# access-list 105 permit tcp 192.168.3.0 0.0.0.15 192.168.204.0 0.0.0.255
Apricot(config)# access-list 105 permit udp 192.168.3.0 0.0.0.15 192.168.204.0 0.0.0.255
Apricot(config)# access-list 106 permit tcp 192.168.3.0 0.0.0.15 192.168.15.0 0.0.0.255
Apricot(config)# access-list 106 permit udp 192.168.3.0 0.0.0.15 192.168.15.0 0.0.0.255
Apricot(config)# crypto map TXandNY 10
Apricot(config-crypto-map)# set peer BananaESA.TXbranch
Apricot(config-crypto-map)# set algorithm 40-bit-des cfb-8
Apricot(config-crypto-map)# match address 105
Apricot(config-crypto-map)# exit
Apricot(config)# crypto map TXandNY 20
```

```
Apricot(config-crypto-map)# set peer CantaloupeIOS.NY
Apricot(config-crypto-map)# set algorithm 40-bit-des cfb-64
Apricot(config-crypto-map)# match address 106
Apricot(config-crypto-map)# exit
Apricot(config)# interface s1
Apricot(config-if)# crypto map TXandNY
Apricot(config-if)# exit
Apricot(config)#
```

Banana

```
Banana(config)# access-list 110 permit tcp 192.168.204.0 0.0.0.255 192.168.3.0 0.0.0.15
Banana(config)# access-list 110 permit udp 192.168.204.0 0.0.0.255 192.168.3.0 0.0.0.15
Banana(config)# access-list 120 permit tcp 192.168.204.0 0.0.0.255 192.168.15.0 0.0.0.255
Banana(config)# access-list 120 permit udp 192.168.204.0 0.0.0.255 192.168.15.0 0.0.0.255
Banana(config)# crypto map USA 10
Banana(config-crypto-map)# set peer Apricot.TokyoBranch
Banana(config-crypto-map)# set algorithm 40-bit-des cfb-8
Banana(config-crypto-map)# match address 110
Banana(config-crypto-map)# exit
Banana(config)# crypto map USA 20
Banana(config-crypto-map)# set peer CantaloupeIOS.NY
Banana(config-crypto-map)# set algorithm des cfb-64
Banana(config-crypto-map)# match address 120
Banana(config-crypto-map)# exit
Banana(config)# interface s2/1/2
Banana(config-if)# crypto map USA
Banana(config-if)# exit
Banana(config)#
```

Cantaloupe

```
Cantaloupe(config)# access-list 101 permit tcp 192.168.15.0 0.0.0.255 192.168.3.0 0.0.0.15
Cantaloupe(config)# access-list 101 permit udp 192.168.15.0 0.0.0.255 192.168.3.0 0.0.0.15
Cantaloupe(config)# access-list 102 permit tcp 192.168.15.0 0.0.0.255 192.168.204.0
0.0.0.255
Cantaloupe(config)# access-list 102 permit udp 192.168.15.0 0.0.0.255 192.168.204.0
0.0.0.255
Cantaloupe(config)# crypto map satellites 10
Cantaloupe(config-crypto-map)# set peer Apricot.TokyoBranch
Cantaloupe(config-crypto-map)# set algorithm 40-bit-des cfb-64
Cantaloupe(config-crypto-map)# match address 101
Cantaloupe(config-crypto-map)# exit
Cantaloupe(config)# crypto map satellites 20
Cantaloupe(config-crypto-map)# set peer BananaESA.TXbranch
Cantaloupe(config-crypto-map)# set algorithm des cfb-64
Cantaloupe(config-crypto-map)# match address 102
Cantaloupe(config-crypto-map)# exit
Cantaloupe(config)# interface s3/1
Cantaloupe(config-if)# crypto map satellites
Cantaloupe(config-if)# exit
Cantaloupe(config)#
```

The previous configurations will result in DES encryption algorithms being applied to encrypted IP traffic as shown in Figure 23–9.

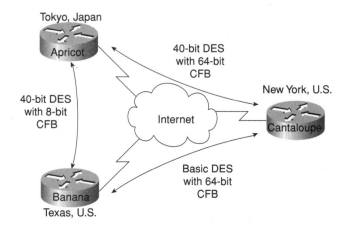

Figure 23–9
Example 2 DES Encryption
Algorithms

Example of Changing Encryption Access List Limits

In this example, there are 50 remote sites connecting to a single server. The connections between the server and each site need to be encrypted. The server is located behind the local router named Apricot. Each of the remote sites connects through its own router.

Because of the large number of destination addresses that must be paired with the same source address in the local encryption access list, the default limits are changed.

```
Apricot(config)# crypto sdu connections 60
%Please reboot for the new connection size to take effect

Apricot(config)# crypto sdu entities 5
%Please reboot for the new table size to take effect
```

Even though there is only one server, and only 50 remote sites, this example defines 5 sources and 60 destinations. This allows room for future growth of the encryption access list. If another source or destination is added later, the limits will not have to be increased and the router rebooted again, which is a disruptive process.

Examples of Configuring Encryption with GRE Tunnels

This section offers two example configurations for encryption with GRE tunnels:

- Example of Encrypting Only GRE Tunnel Traffic
- Example of Encrypting Both GRE Tunnel Traffic and Other Non-GRE Traffic

Example of Encrypting Only GRE Tunnel Traffic

This configuration causes all traffic through the GRE tunnel to be encrypted. No other traffic at the interface will be encrypted. The GRE tunnel is from router Apricot to router Banana. (Only partial configuration files are shown for each router.)

Apricot

```
crypto map BananaMap 10
 set algorithm 40-bit-des
 set peer Banana
 match address 101
!
interface Tunnel0
 no ip address
 ipx network 923FA800
 tunnel source 10.1.1.2
 tunnel destination 10.1.1.1
 crypto map BananaMap
!
interface Serial0
 ip address 10.1.1.2 255.255.255.0
 crypto map BananaMap
!
access-list 101 permit gre host 10.1.1.2 host 10.1.1.1
```

Banana

```
crypto map ApricotMap 10
 set algorithm 40-bit-des
 set peer Apricot
 match address 102
!
interface Tunnel0
 no ip address
 ipx network 923FA800
 tunnel source 10.1.1.1
 tunnel destination 10.1.1.2
 crypto map ApricotMap
!
interface Serial0
 ip address 10.1.1.1 255.255.255.0
 clockrate 2000000
 no cdp enable
 crypto map ApricotMap
!
access-list 102 permit gre host 10.1.1.1 host 10.1.1.2
```

Example of Encrypting Both GRE Tunnel Traffic and Other Non-GRE Traffic

This configuration encrypts all GRE tunnel traffic, and it also encrypts TCP traffic between two hosts with the IP addresses 172.16.25.3 and 192.168.3.5. The GRE tunnel is from router Apricot to router Banana. (Only partial configuration files are shown for each router.)

Apricot

```
crypto map BananaMapTunnel 10
 set algorithm 40-bit-des
 set peer Banana
 match address 101
!
crypto map BananaMapSerial 10
 set algorithm 40-bit-des
 set peer Banana
 match address 101
crypto map BananaMapSerial 20
 set algorithm 40-bit-des
 set peer Banana
 match address 110
!
interface Tunnel0
 no ip address
 ipx network 923FA800
 tunnel source 10.1.1.2
 tunnel destination 10.1.1.1
 crypto map BananaMapTunnel
!
interface Serial0
 ip address 10.1.1.2 255.255.255.0
 crypto map BananaMapSerial
!
access-list 101 permit gre host 10.1.1.2 host 10.1.1.1
access-list 110 permit tcp host 172.16.25.3 host 192.168.3.5
```

Banana

```
crypto map ApricotMapTunnel 10
 set algorithm 40-bit-des
 set peer Apricot
 match address 102
!
crypto map ApricotMapSerial 10
 set algorithm 40-bit-des
 set peer Apricot
 match address 102
crypto map ApricotMapSerial 20
 set algorithm 40-bit-des
 set peer Apricot
 match address 112
```

```
 !
interface Tunnel0
 no ip address
 ipx network 923FA800
 tunnel source 10.1.1.1
 tunnel destination 10.1.1.2
 crypto map ApricotMapTunnel
 !
interface Serial0
 ip address 10.1.1.1 255.255.255.0
 clockrate 2000000
 no cdp enable
 crypto map ApricotMapSerial
 !
access-list 102 permit gre host 10.1.1.1 host 10.1.1.2
access-list 112 permit tcp host 192.168.3.5 host 172.16.25.3
```

Examples of ESA-Specific Encryption Configuration Tasks

This section includes examples of the following:

- Examples of Resetting an ESA
- Example of Enabling an ESA (Cisco 7200 Series Routers Only)
- Example of Selecting a Different Crypto Engine (Cisco 7200 Series Routers Only)

Examples of Resetting an ESA

The following example resets an ESA on a Cisco 7500 series router. The ESA is in a VIP2 that is in slot 4 of the router chassis.

```
Banana(config)# crypto clear-latch 4
% Enter the crypto card password.
Password: <passwd>
Banana(config)#
```

The following example resets an ESA without DSS keys, for a Cisco 7200 series router. The ESA is in the router chassis slot 2.

```
Apricot(config)# crypto clear-latch 2
% Enter the crypto card password.
Password: <passwd>
ESA in slot 2 not enabled.
[OK]
Apricot(config)#
```

The following example resets an ESA with DSS keys, for a Cisco 7200 series router; the ESA was previously in use on the same router, but was removed and reinstalled with OIR. No changes to the encryption configuration are desired by the administrator. The ESA is in the router chassis slot 2.

```
Apricot(config)# crypto clear-latch 2
% Enter the crypto card password.
```

```
Password: <passwd>
Keys were found for this ESA- enable ESA now? [yes/no]: yes
...switching to HW crypto engine
[OK]
Apricot(config)#
```

The following example resets an ESA with DSS keys, for a Cisco 7200 series router; the ESA was previously used in a different router, and requires new DSS keys to be generated and exchanged before the ESA can become operational. The ESA is in the router chassis slot 2.

```
Apricot(config)# crypto clear-latch 2
% Enter the crypto card password.
Password: <passwd>
Keys were found for this ESA- enable ESA now? [yes/no]: no
ESA in slot 2 not enabled.
[OK]
Apricot(config)#
```

Example of Enabling an ESA (Cisco 7200 Series Routers Only)

The following example enables an ESA in the router chassis slot 2:

```
Apricot(config)# crypto esa enable 2
...switching to HW crypto engine
Apricot(config)#
```

Example of Selecting a Different Crypto Engine (Cisco 7200 Series Routers Only)

Select a different crypto engine only if the new engine is fully configured for encryption.

The following example switches from the Cisco IOS crypto engine to the ESA crypto engine. The ESA crypto engine is in the router chassis slot 4.

```
Apricot(config)# crypto esa enable 4
...switching to HW crypto engine
Apricot(config)#
```

The following example switches from the ESA crypto engine to the Cisco IOS crypto engine. The ESA crypto engine is in the router chassis slot 4.

```
Apricot(config)# crypto esa shutdown 4
...switching to SW crypto engine
Apricot(config)#
```

Examples of Deleting DSS Keys

This section includes an example for a Cisco 7500 series router and an example for a Cisco 7200 series router with an installed ESA.

Example for a Cisco 7500 Series Router

The following example deletes all the DSS keys on a Cisco 7500 series router. The RSP is in chassis slot 3, and a VIP2 is in chassis slot 4. Deleting all the DSS keys turns off encryption completely for the router. The Cisco IOS crypto engine keys are deleted first, then the VIP2 crypto engine keys.

```
Apricot(config)# crypto zeroize 3
Warning! Zeroize will remove your DSS signature keys.
Do you want to continue? [yes/no]: y
Keys to be removed are named Apricot.IOS.
Do you really want to remove these keys? [yes/no]: y
[OK]
Apricot(config)# crypto zeroize 4
Warning! Zeroize will remove your DSS signature keys.
Do you want to continue? [yes/no]: y
Keys to be removed are named Apricot.VIP.
Do you really want to remove these keys? [yes/no]: y
[OK]
Apricot(config)#
```

Example for a Cisco 7200 Series Router

The following example deletes DSS keys only for an ESA, in chassis slot 2 of a Cisco 7200 series router. The Cisco IOS crypto engine DSS keys are not deleted in this example.

1. View existing DSS keys:

```
Apricot# show crypto mypubkey
crypto public-key Apricot.IOS 01709642
BDD99A6E EEE53D30 BC0BFAE6 948C40FB 713510CB 32104137 91B06C8D C2D5B422
D9C154CA 00CDE99B 425DB9FD FE3162F1 1E5866AF CF66DD33 677259FF E5C24812
quit
crypto public-key Apricot.ESA 01234567
866AFCF6 E99B425D FDFE3162 BC0BFAE6 13791B06 713510CB 4CA00CDE 0BC0BFAE
3791B06C 154C0CDE F11E5866 AE6948C4 DD336772 3F66DF33 355459FF 2350912D
quit

Apricot#
```

This output shows that DSS keys exist for both the Cisco IOS crypto engine and for the ESA crypto engine.

2. Determine the Active Crypto Engine:

```
Apricot# show crypto engine configuration
engine name:      Apricot.IOS
engine type:      software
serial number:    01709642
platform:         rsp crypto engine

Encryption Process Info:
input queue top:  44
input queue bot:  44
input queue count: 0

Apricot#
```

The output shows that the Cisco IOS crypto engine is the active engine.

3. Because you want to delete DSS keys for the ESA crypto engine, change to the ESA crypto engine:

```
Apricot# config terminal
Enter configuration commands, one per line.  End with CNTL/Z.
Apricot(config)# crypto esa enable 2
...switching to HW crypto engine
Apricot(config)#
```

4. Verify that the ESA crypto engine is the active engine:

```
Apricot(config)# exit
Apricot# show crypto engine configuration
engine name:       Apricot.ESA
engine type:       hardware
serial number:     01234567
platform:          esa crypto engine

Encryption Process Info:
input queue top:   0
input queue bot:   0
input queue count: 0

Apricot#
```

The output shows that the ESA crypto engine is now the active engine.

5. Delete the ESA DSS keys:

```
Apricot# config terminal
Enter configuration commands, one per line.  End with CNTL/Z.
Apricot(config)# crypto zeroize 2
Warning! Zeroize will remove your DSS signature keys.
Do you want to continue? [yes/no]: y
Keys to be removed are named Apricot.ESA.
Do you really want to remove these keys? [yes/no]: y
[OK]

Apricot(config)#
```

6. View existing DSS keys:

```
Apricot(config)# exit
Apricot# show crypto mypubkey
crypto public-key Apricot.IOS 01709642
BDD99A6E EEE53D30 BC0BFAE6 948C40FB 713510CB 32104137 91B06C8D C2D5B422
D9C154CA 00CDE99B 425DB9FD FE3162F1 1E5866AF CF66DD33 677259FF E5C24812
quit

Apricot#
```

The output shows that the ESA crypto engine keys have been deleted.

7. Determine the active crypto engine:

```
Apricot# show crypto engine configuration
engine name:       Apricot.IOS
engine type:       software
```

```
serial number:       01709642
platform:            rsp crypto engine

Encryption Process Info:
input queue top:     0
input queue bot:     0
input queue count:   0

Apricot#
```

The output shows that the system has defaulted back to the Cisco IOS crypto engine as the active engine.

Example of Testing the Encryption Connection

The following example sets up and verifies a test encryption session.

Assume the same network topology and configuration as in the previous example and shown in Figure 23–8.

In this example, router Apricot sets up a test encryption session with router Banana and then views the connection status to verify a successful encrypted session connection.

Step 1 Router Apricot sets up a test encryption connection with router Banana.
```
Apricot# test crypto initiate-session 192.168.3.12 192.168.204.110
    BananaESA.TXbranch 10
Sending CIM to: 192.168.204.110 from: 192.168.3.12.
Connection id: -1
```

Notice the Connection id value is −1. A negative value indicates that the connection is being set up.

Step 2 Router Apricot issues the **show crypto connections** command.
```
Apricot# show crypto connections
Pending Connection Table
PE                UPE              Timestamp              Conn_id
192.168.3.10     192.168.204.100 Mar 01 1993 00:01:09   -1

Connection Table
PE                UPE              Conn_id New_id  Alg     Time
192.168.3.10     192.168.204.100 -1       1       0       Not Set
                 flags:PEND_CONN
```

Look in the Pending Connection Table for an entry with a Conn_id value equal to the previously shown Connection id value—in this case, look for an entry with a Conn_id value of −1. If this is the first time an encrypted connection has been attempted, there will only be one entry (as shown).

Note the PE and UPE addresses for this entry.

Step 3 Now, look in the Connection Table for an entry with the same PE and UPE addresses. In this case, there is only one entry in both tables, so finding the right Connection Table entry is easy.

Step 4   At the Connection Table entry, note the Conn_id and New_id values. In this case, Conn_id equals –1 (as in the Pending Connection Table), and New_id equals 1. The New_id value of 1 will be assigned to the test connection when setup is complete. (Positive numbers are assigned to established, active connections.)

Step 5   Apricot waits a few seconds for the test connection to establish and then reissues the **show crypto connections** command.

```
Apricot# show crypto connections
Connection Table
PE                UPE              Conn_id New_id  Alg    Time
192.168.3.10      192.168.204.100 1       0       0      Mar 01 1993 00:02:00
                  flags:TIME_KEYS
```

Again, look for the Connection Table entry with the same PE and UPE addresses as shown before. In this entry, notice that the Conn_id value has changed to 1. This indicates that our test connection has been successfully established, because the Conn_id value has changed to match the New_id value of Step 4. Also, New_id has been reset to 0 at this point, indicating that there are no new connections currently being set up.

In the command output of Step 5, there is no longer a Pending Connection Table being displayed, which indicates that there are currently no pending connections. This is also a good clue that the test connection was successfully established.

The **show crypto connections** command is explained in greater detail in Chapter 24. There you can find a description of how connection ID's are assigned during and following connection setup.

Network Data Encryption Commands

This chapter describes network data encryption commands. Cisco provides network data encryption as a means to safeguard network data that travels from one Cisco router to another, across unsecured networks.

For configuration information, see Chapter 23, "Configuring Network Data Encryption."

ACCESS-LIST (ENCRYPTION)

To define an encryption access list by number, use the extended IP **access-list** global configuration command. To remove a numbered encryption access list, use the **no** form of this command.

> **access-list** *access-list-number* [**dynamic** *dynamic-name* [**timeout** *minutes*]] {**deny** | **permit**}
> *protocol source source-wildcard destination destination-wildcard* [**precedence**
> *precedence*] [**tos** *tos*] [**log**]
> **no access-list** *access-list-number*

For Internet Control Message Protocol (ICMP), you can also use the following syntax:

> **access-list** *access-list-number* [**dynamic** *dynamic-name* [**timeout** *minutes*]] {**deny** | **permit**}
> **icmp** *source source-wildcard destination destination-wildcard* [*icmp-type* [*icmp-code*] |
> *icmp-message*] [**precedence** *precedence*] [**tos** *tos*] [**log**]

For Internet Group Management Protocol (IGMP), you can also use the following syntax:

> **access-list** *access-list-number* [**dynamic** *dynamic-name* [**timeout** *minutes*]] {**deny** | **permit**}
> **igmp** *source source-wildcard destination destination-wildcard* [**igmp-type**]
> [**precedence** *precedence*] [**tos** *tos*] [**log**]

For TCP, you can also use the following syntax:

> **access-list** *access-list-number* [**dynamic** *dynamic-name* [**timeout** *minutes*]] {**deny** | **permit**}
> **tcp** *source source-wildcard* [*operator port* [*port*]] *destination destination-wildcard*
> [*operator port* [*port*]] [**established**] [**precedence** *precedence*] [**tos** *tos*] [**log**]

For User Datagram Protocol (UDP), you can also use the following syntax:

> **access-list** *access-list-number* [**dynamic** *dynamic-name* [**timeout** *minutes*]] {**deny** | **permit**}
> **udp** *source source-wildcard* [*operator port* [*port*]] *destination destination-wildcard*
> [*operator port* [*port*]] [**precedence** *precedence*] [**tos** *tos*] [**log**]

Syntax Description

access-list-number	Number of an encryption access list. This is a decimal number from 100 to 199.
dynamic *dynamic-name*	(Optional) Identifies this encryption access list as a dynamic encryption access list. Refer to lock-and-key access documented in Chapter 17, "Configuring Lock-and-Key Security (Dynamic Access Lists)."
timeout *minutes*	(Optional) Specifies the absolute length of time (in minutes) that a temporary access list entry can remain in a dynamic access list. The default is an infinite length of time and allows an entry to remain permanently. Refer to lock-and-key access documented in Chapter 17.
deny	Does not encrypt/decrypt IP traffic if the conditions are matched.
permit	Encrypts/decrypts IP traffic if the conditions are matched.
protocol	Name or number of an IP protocol. It can be one of the keywords **eigrp**, **gre**, **icmp**, **igmp**, **igrp**, **ip**, **ipinip**, **nos**, **ospf**, **tcp**, or **udp**, or an integer in the range 0 to 255 representing an IP protocol number. To match any Internet protocol, including ICMP, TCP, and UDP, use the keyword **ip**. Some protocols allow further qualifiers, as described in text that follows.
source	Number of the network or host from which the packet is being sent. There are three other ways to specify the source: • Use a 32-bit quantity in 4-part dotted-decimal format. • Use the keyword any as an abbreviation for a *source* and *source-wildcard* of 0.0.0.0 255.255.255.255. This keyword is normally not recommended (see section "Usage Guidelines"). • Use **host** *source* as an abbreviation for a *source* and *source-wildcard* of source 0.0.0.0.
source-wildcard	Wildcard bits (mask) to be applied to source. There are three other ways to specify the source wildcard: • Use a 32-bit quantity in 4-part dotted-decimal format. Place 1's in the bit positions you want to ignore.

source-wildcard, Continued	• Use the keyword **any** as an abbreviation for a *source* and *source-wildcard* of 0.0.0.0 255.255.255.255. This keyword is normally *not* recommended (see section "Usage Guidelines").
	• Use **host** source as an abbreviation for a *source* and *source-wildcard* of *source* 0.0.0.0.
destination	Number of the network or host to which the packet is being sent. There are three other ways to specify the destination:
	• Use a 32-bit quantity in 4-part dotted-decimal format.
	• Use the keyword **any** as an abbreviation for the *destination* and *destination-wildcard* of 0.0.0.0 255.255.255.255. This keyword is normally *not* recommended (see section "Usage Guidelines").
	• Use **host** *destination* as an abbreviation for a *destination* and *destination-wildcard* of *destination* 0.0.0.0.
destination-wildcard	Wildcard bits to be applied to the destination. There are three other ways to specify the destination wildcard:
	• Use a 32-bit quantity in 4-part dotted-decimal format. Place 1's in the bit positions you want to ignore.
	• Use the keyword **any** as an abbreviation for a *destination* and *destination-wildcard* of 0.0.0.0 255.255.255.255. This keyword is normally *not* recommended (see section "Usage Guidelines").
	• Use **host** *destination* as an abbreviation for a *destination* and *destination-wildcard* of *destination* 0.0.0.0.
precedence *precedence*	(Optional) Packets can be matched for encryption by precedence level, as specified by a number from 0 to 7 or by name as listed in section "Usage Guidelines."
tos *tos*	(Optional) Packets can be matched for encryption by type of service level, as specified by a number from 0 to 15 or by name as listed in section "Usage Guidelines."
icmp-type	(Optional) ICMP packets can be matched for encryption by ICMP message type. The type is a number from 0 to 255.
icmp-code	(Optional) ICMP packets that are matched for encryption by ICMP message type can also be matched by the ICMP message code. The code is a number from 0 to 255.
icmp-message	(Optional) ICMP packets can be matched for encryption by an ICMP message type name or ICMP message type and code name. The possible names are discussed in section "Usage Guidelines."

igmp-type   (Optional) IGMP packets can be matched for encryption by IGMP message type or message name. A message type is a number from 0 to 15. IGMP message names are listed in section "Usage Guidelines."

operator   (Optional) Compares source or destination ports. Possible operands include **lt** (less than), **gt** (greater than), **eq** (equal), **neq** (not equal), and **range** (inclusive range).

                           If the operator is positioned after the *source* and *source-wildcard*, it must match the source port.

                           If the operator is positioned after the *destination* and *destination-wildcard*, it must match the destination port.

                           The **range** operator requires two port numbers. All other operators require one port number.

port   (Optional) The decimal number or name of a TCP or UDP port. A port number is a number from 0 to 65535.

                           TCP port names are listed in section "Usage Guidelines." TCP port names can be used only when filtering TCP.

                           UDP port names are listed in section "Usage Guidelines." UDP port names can be used only when filtering UDP.

established   (Optional) For the TCP protocol only: Indicates an established connection. A match occurs if the TCP datagram has the ACK or RST bits set. The nonmatching case is that of the initial TCP datagram to form a connection.

log   (Optional) Causes an informational logging message about the packet that matches the entry to be sent to the console. (The level of messages logged to the console is controlled by the **logging console** command.)

                           The message includes the access list number, whether the packet was encrypted/decrypted or not; the protocol, whether it was TCP, UDP, ICMP, or a number; and, if appropriate, the source and destination addresses and source and destination port numbers. The message is generated for the first packet that matches, and then at 5-minute intervals, including the number of packets encrypted/decrypted or not in the prior 5-minute interval.

Default

No numbered encryption access lists are defined, and therefore, no traffic will be encrypted/decrypted. After being defined, all encryption access lists contain an implicit "deny" ("do not encrypt/decrypt") statement at the end of the list.

Command Mode

Global configuration

Usage Guidelines

This command first appeared in Cisco IOS Release 11.2.

Use encryption access lists to control which packets on an interface are encrypted/decrypted, and which are transmitted as plain text (unencrypted).

When a packet is examined for an encryption access list match, encryption access list statements are checked in the order that the statements were created. After a packet matches the conditions in a statement, no more statements will be checked. This means that you need to consider carefully the order in which you enter the statements.

To use the encryption access list, you must first specify the access list in a crypto map and then apply the crypto map to an interface, using the **crypto map** (**global configuration**) and **crypto map** (**interface configuration**) commands.

Fragmented IP packets, other than the initial fragment, are immediately accepted by any extended IP access list. Extended access lists used to control virtual terminal line access or restrict contents of routing updates must not match the TCP source port, the type of service value, or the packet's precedence.

NOTES

After an access list is created initially, any subsequent additions (possibly entered from the terminal) are placed at the end of the list. You cannot selectively add or remove access list command lines from a specific access list.

CAUTION

When creating encryption access lists, it is *not* recommended that you use the **any** keyword to specify source or destination addresses. Using the **any** keyword with a **permit** statement could cause extreme problems if a packet enters your router and is destined for a router that is not configured for encryption. This would cause your router to attempt to set up an encryption session with a nonencrypting router.

If you incorrectly use the **any** keyword with a **deny** statement, you might inadvertently prevent all packets from being encrypted, which could present a security risk.

NOTES

If you view your router's access lists by using a command such as **show ip access-lists**, *all* extended IP access lists will be shown in the command output. This includes extended IP access lists that are used for traffic filtering purposes as well as those that are used for encryption. The show command output does not differentiate between the two uses of the extended access lists.

The following is a list of precedence names:

- critical
- flash
- flash-override
- immediate
- internet
- network
- priority
- routine

The following is a list of type of service (TOS) names:

- max-reliability
- max-throughput
- min-delay
- min-monetary-cost
- normal

The following is a list of ICMP message type names and ICMP message type and code names:

- administratively-prohibited
- alternate-address
- conversion-error
- dod-host-prohibited
- dod-net-prohibited
- echo
- echo-reply
- general-parameter-problem
- host-isolated
- host-precedence-unreachable
- host-redirect
- host-tos-redirect
- host-tos-unreachable
- host-unknown
- host-unreachable
- information-reply
- information-request

- mask-reply
- mask-request
- mobile-redirect
- net-redirect
- net-tos-redirect
- net-tos-unreachable
- net-unreachable
- network-unknown
- no-room-for-option
- option-missing
- packet-too-big
- parameter-problem
- port-unreachable
- precedence-unreachable
- protocol-unreachable
- reassembly-timeout
- redirect
- router-advertisement
- router-solicitation
- source-quench
- source-route-failed
- time-exceeded
- timestamp-reply
- timestamp-request
- traceroute
- ttl-exceeded
- unreachable

The following is a list of IGMP message names:

- dvmrp
- host-query
- host-report
- pim
- trace

The following is a list of TCP port names that can be used instead of port numbers. Refer to the current Assigned Numbers RFC to find a reference to these protocols. Port numbers corresponding to these protocols can also be found by typing a ? in the place of a port number.

- bgp
- chargen
- daytime
- discard
- domain
- echo
- finger
- ftp
- ftp-data
- gopher
- hostname
- irc
- klogin
- kshell
- lpd
- nntp
- pop2
- pop3
- smtp
- sunrpc
- syslog
- tacacs-ds
- talk
- telnet
- time
- uucp
- whois
- www

The following is a list of UDP port names that can be used instead of port numbers. Refer to the current Assigned Numbers RFC to find a reference to these protocols. Port numbers corresponding to these protocols can also be found by typing a ? in the place of a port number.

- biff
- bootpc
- bootps
- discard
- dns
- dnsix
- echo
- mobile-ip
- nameserver
- netbios-dgm
- netbios-ns
- ntp
- rip
- snmp
- snmptrap
- sunrpc
- syslog
- tacacs-ds
- talk
- tftp
- time
- who
- xdmcp

Example

The following example creates a numbered encryption access list that specifies a class C subnet for the source and a class C subnet for the destination of IP packets. When the router uses this encryption access list, all TCP traffic that is exchanged between the source and destination subnets will be encrypted.

```
Apricot(config)# access-list 101 permit tcp 172.21.3.0 0.0.0.255 172.22.2.0 0.0.0.255
```

This encryption access list will be applied to an interface as an outbound encryption access list after the router administrator defines a crypto map and applies the crypto map to the interface.

Related Commands

Search online to find documentation for related commands.

access-list (extended) (used for traffic filtering purposes)
crypto map (global configuration)
crypto map (interface configuration)
ip access-list extended (encryption)
show ip access-lists

CLEAR CRYPTO CONNECTION

To terminate an encrypted session in progress, use the **clear crypto connection** global configuration command.

> **clear crypto connection** *connection-id*

Syntax Description

connection-id   Identifies the encrypted session to terminate.

Default

Encrypted sessions will normally terminate when the session times out.

Command Mode

Global configuration

Usage Guidelines

This command first appeared in Cisco IOS Release 11.2.

Use this command to terminate an encrypted session currently in progress. You can first perform the **show crypto connections** command to learn the connection id value.

Example

The following example clears a pending encrypted session. (You could also clear an established encrypted session in the same way.)

```
Apricot# show crypto connections
Pending Connection Table
PE              UPE             Timestamp           Conn_id
192.168.3.10    192.168.204.100 Mar 01 1993 00:01:09 -1

Connection Table
PE              UPE             Conn_id New_id  Alg     Time
```

```
192.168.3.10    192.168.204.100 -1     1        0        Not Set
                flags:PEND_CONN

Apricot# clear crypto connection -1
Apricot# show crypto connections
Connection Table
PE              UPE             Conn_id New_id  Alg     Time
192.168.3.10    192.168.204.100 0       0       0       Mar 01 1993 00:02:00
                flags:BAD_CONN

Apricot#
```

First, a **show crypto connections** command is issued to learn the connection ID for the pending connection (-1). This value is then used to specify which connection to clear.

Notice that after the connection is cleared, the Pending Connection Table containing the connection entry (connection id of -1) has disappeared from the **show crypto connections** output. Also, the Connection Table no longer shows a -1 Conn_id.

Related Commands

Search online to find documentation for related commands.

show crypto connections

CRYPTO ALGORITHM 40-BIT-DES

To globally enable 40-bit Data Encryption Standard (DES) algorithm types, use the **crypto algorithm 40-bit-des** global configuration command. Use the **no** form of this command to globally disable a 40-bit DES algorithm type.

> **crypto algorithm 40-bit-des [cfb-8 | cfb-64]**
> **no crypto algorithm 40-bit-des [cfb-8 | cfb-64]**

Syntax Description

cfb-8
: (Optional) Selects the 8-bit Cipher FeedBack (CFB) mode of the 40-bit DES algorithm. If no CFB mode is specified when you issue the command, 64-bit CFB mode is the default.

cfb-64
: (Optional) Selects the 64-bit CFB mode of the 40-bit DES algorithm. If no CFB mode is specified when you issue the command, 64-bit CFB mode is the default.

Default

One DES algorithm is enabled by default, even if you never issue this command. If you are running a nonexportable image, the basic DES algorithm with 8-bit CFB is enabled by default. (The basic DES algorithm uses a 56-bit DES key.) If you are running an exportable image, the 40-bit DES algorithm with 8-bit CFB is enabled by default.

If you do not know if your image is exportable or nonexportable, you can perform the **show crypto algorithms** command to determine which DES algorithms are currently enabled.

Command Mode

Global configuration

Usage Guidelines

This command first appeared in Cisco IOS Release 11.2.

Use this command to enable a 40-bit DES algorithm type. Enabling a DES algorithm type once allows it to be used by all crypto engines of a router.

You must enable all DES algorithms that will be used to communicate with any other peer encrypting router. If you do not enable a DES algorithm, you will not be able to use that algorithm, even if you try to assign the algorithm to a crypto map at a later time.

If your router tries to set up an encrypted communication session with a peer router, and the two routers do not have the same DES algorithm enabled at both ends, the encrypted session will fail. If at least one common DES algorithm is enabled at both ends, the encrypted session can proceed.

Forty-bit DES uses a 40-bit DES key, which is easier for attackers to "crack" than basic DES, which uses a 56-bit DES key. However, some international applications might require you to use 40-bit DES, because of export laws.

NOTES

If you are running an exportable image, you can only enable and use 40-bit variations of DES. You cannot enable or use the basic DES algorithms, which are not available with exportable images.

Eight-bit CFB is more commonly used than 64-bit CFB, but requires more CPU processing time. If you do not specify 8-bit or 64-bit CFB, 64-bit CFB will be selected by default.

Example

The following example enables 40-bit DES with 8-bit CFB and 40-bit DES with 64-bit CFB:

```
crypto algorithm 40-bit-des cfb-8
crypto algorithm 40-bit-des cfb-64
```

Related Commands

Search online to find documentation for related commands.

crypto algorithm des
show crypto algorithms

CRYPTO ALGORITHM DES

To globally enable Data Encryption Standard (DES) algorithm types that use a 56-bit DES key, use the **crypto algorithm des** global configuration command. Use the **no** form of this command to globally disable a DES algorithm type.

crypto algorithm des [cfb-8 | cfb-64]
no crypto algorithm des [cfb-8 | cfb-64]

Syntax Description

cfb-8   (Optional) Selects the 8-bit Cipher FeedBack (CFB) mode of the basic DES algorithm. If no CFB mode is specified when you issue the command, 64-bit CFB mode is the default.

cfb-64   (Optional) Selects the 64-bit CFB mode of the basic DES algorithm. If no CFB mode is specified when you issue the command, 64-bit CFB mode is the default.

Default

One DES algorithm is enabled by default, even if you never issue this command. If you are running a nonexportable image, the basic DES algorithm with 8-bit CFB is enabled by default. (The basic DES algorithm uses a 56-bit DES key.) If you are running an exportable image, the 40-bit DES algorithm with 8-bit CFB is enabled by default.

If you do not know if your image is exportable or nonexportable, you can perform the **show crypto algorithms** command to determine which DES algorithms are currently enabled.

Command Mode

Global configuration

Usage Guidelines

This command first appeared in Cisco IOS Release 11.2.

Use this command to enable a DES algorithm type that uses a 56-bit DES key. Enabling a DES algorithm type once allows it to be used by all crypto engines of a router.

You must enable all DES algorithms that will be used to communicate with any other peer encrypting router. If you do not enable a DES algorithm, you will not be able to use that algorithm, even if you try to assign the algorithm to a crypto map at a later time.

If your router tries to set up an encrypted communication session with a peer router, and the two routers do not have the same DES algorithm enabled at both ends, the encrypted session will fail. If at least one common DES algorithm is enabled at both ends, the encrypted session can proceed.

NOTES

If you are running an exportable image, you can only enable and use 40-bit variations of DES. You cannot enable or use the basic DES algorithms, which are not available with exportable images.

Eight-bit CFB is more commonly used than 64-bit CFB but requires more CPU processing time. If you do not specify 8-bit or 64-bit CFB, 64-bit CFB will be selected by default.

Example

The following example enables DES with 8-bit CFB and DES with 64-bit CFB:

```
crypto algorithm des cfb-8
crypto algorithm des cfb-64
```

Related Commands

Search online to find documentation for related commands.

crypto algorithm 40-bit-des
show crypto algorithms

CRYPTO CLEAR-LATCH

To reset an Encryption Service Adapter (ESA), use the **crypto clear-latch** global configuration command. This command resets the ESA by clearing a hardware extraction latch that is set when an ESA is removed and reinstalled in the chassis.

   crypto clear-latch *slot*

Syntax Description

slot   Identifies the ESA to reset. On a Cisco 7200 series router, this is the ESA chassis slot number. On a Cisco RSP7000 or 7500 series router, this is the chassis slot number of the ESA's second-generation Versatile Interface Processor (VIP2).

Default

The ESA latch is not cleared.

Command Mode

Global configuration

Usage Guidelines

This command first appeared in Cisco IOS Release 11.2.

If an ESA is installed for the first time, or removed and reinstalled, the ESA will not function unless you reset it by using this command. Before the ESA is reset, the hardware extraction latch is set and the Tampered LED is on.

To complete this command, you must enter the ESA password. If the ESA does not have a password, you must create one at this time. (The ESA might not have a password if it has never been previously used, or if the **crypto zeroize** command was previously issued for the ESA.)

If you have forgotten a previously assigned password, you have to use the **crypto zeroize** command instead of the **crypto clear-latch** command to reset the ESA. After issuing the **crypto zeroize** command, you must regenerate and re-exchange DSS keys. When you regenerate DSS keys, you will be prompted to create a new password.

Example

The following example resets an ESA card. The ESA card is housed in a VIP2 that is in slot 1.

```
Apricot(config)# crypto clear-latch 1
% Enter the crypto card password.
Password: <passwd>
Apricot(config)#
```

Related Commands

Search online to find documentation for related commands.

crypto gen-signature-keys
crypto zeroize

CRYPTO ESA

To enable (select) either the ESA crypto engine or the Cisco IOS crypto engine in Cisco 7200 series routers, use the **crypto esa** global configuration command.

    crypto esa {enable | shutdown} *slot*

Syntax Description

enable	Selects the ESA crypto engine by enabling the ESA.
shutdown	Selects the Cisco IOS crypto engine by shutting down the ESA.
slot	The ESA chassis slot number.

Default

The Cisco IOS crypto engine is the selected (active) crypto engine.

Command Mode

Global configuration

Usage Guidelines

This command first appeared in Cisco IOS Release 11.2P.

This command only applies to Cisco 7200 series routers with an installed ESA.

Until the ESA is enabled, the Cisco IOS crypto engine will function as the crypto engine.

If you want to select the ESA crypto engine with this command, all other encryption configuration must already have been completed for the ESA.

If you select a crypto engine (either the ESA or the Cisco IOS crypto engine) that has not been completely configured for encryption, the router will not be able to encrypt any traffic. Any existing encryption sessions will abruptly terminate. Therefore, you must complete all encryption configuration for before you enable a crypto engine with this command.

NOTES

If any encryption session is in progress when you switch from one crypto engine to the other, the session will be torn down, and a new session will be established using the newly selected crypto engine. This could cause a momentary delay for encrypted traffic.

Examples

The following example enables an ESA in the router chassis slot 2:

```
Apricot(config)# crypto esa enable 2
...switching to HW crypto engine
Apricot(config)#
```

The following example switches from the Cisco IOS crypto engine to the ESA crypto engine. The ESA crypto engine is in the router chassis slot 4.

```
Apricot(config)# crypto esa enable 4
...switching to HW crypto engine
Apricot(config)#
```

The following example switches from the ESA crypto engine to the Cisco IOS crypto engine. The ESA crypto engine is in the router chassis slot 4.

```
Apricot(config)# crypto esa shutdown 4
...switching to SW crypto engine
Apricot(config)
```

CRYPTO GEN-SIGNATURE-KEYS

To generate a Digital Signature Standard (DSS) public/private key pair, use the **crypto gen-signature-keys** global configuration command.

crypto gen-signature-keys *key-name* [*slot*]

Syntax Description

key-name   A name you assign to the crypto engine. This will name either the Cisco IOS software crypto engine, a second-generation Versatile Interface Processor (VIP2) crypto engine, or an Encryption Service Adapter (ESA) crypto engine. Any character string is valid. Using a fully qualified domain name might make it easier to identify public keys.

slot   (Optional) Identifies the crypto engine. This argument is available only on Cisco 7200, RSP7000, and 7500 series routers.

If no slot is specified, the Cisco IOS crypto engine will be selected.

Use the chassis slot number of the crypto engine location. For the Cisco IOS crypto engine, this is the chassis slot number of the Route Switch Processor (RSP). For the VIP2 crypto engine, this is the chassis slot number of the VIP2. For the ESA crypto engine, this is the chassis slot number of the ESA (Cisco 7200) or of the VIP2 (Cisco RSP7000 and 7500).

Default

No DSS public/private keys are defined.

Command Mode

Global configuration

Usage Guidelines

This command first appeared in Cisco IOS Release 11.2.

Use this command to generate a DSS public/private key pair. This is the first configuration task required to set up a router for network data encryption.

If you have a Cisco 7200, RSP7000, or 7500 series router, use the *slot* argument. You must perform this command once for each crypto engine you plan to use.

NOTES

DSS keys of the Cisco IOS crypto engine are saved to a private portion of NVRAM when you perform a **copy running-config startup-config** (previously **write memory**) command. DSS keys are *not* saved with your configuration when you perform a **copy running-config rcp** or **copy running-config tftp** (previously **write network**) command.

If you are using a Cisco 7200, RSP7000, or 7500 series router with an ESA, DSS keys generated for the ESA crypto engine are automatically saved to tamper-resistant memory of the ESA during the DSS key generation process.

If NVRAM fails, or if your ESA is tampered with or replaced, DSS public/private keys will no longer be valid. If this happens, you will need to regenerate and re-exchange DSS keys.

The ESA Password

If you are using a Cisco 7200, RSP7000, or 7500 series router with an ESA, you will be prompted to enter a password when you generate DSS keys for the ESA crypto engine.

If you previously reset the ESA with the **crypto zeroize** command, you must create a new password at this time.

If you previously reset the ESA with the **crypto clear-latch** command, you created a password at that time; use that same password now. If you have forgotten the password, the only workaround is to first use the **crypto zeroize** command and then regenerate DSS keys.

If you ever again need to regenerate DSS keys for the ESA, you will be required to enter the same ESA password to complete the DSS key regeneration.

Examples

The following example generates a DSS public/private key pair for the first time on a Cisco 2500 series router:

```
Apricot(config)# crypto gen-signature-keys Apricot
Generating DSS keys .... [OK]
Apricot(config)#
```

The following example generates DSS public/private key pairs for a Cisco 7500 series router with an RSP in slot 4 and a VIP2 (with an ESA) in slot 3. The ESA was previously reset with the **crypto zeroize** command. Notice that when DSS keys are generated for the ESA, you must type a newly created password:

```
Apricot(config)# crypto gen-signature-keys ApricotRSP 4
Generating DSS keys .... [OK]
Apricot(config)# crypto gen-signature-keys ApricotESA 3
% Initialize the crypto card password. You will need
    this password in order to generate new signature
    keys or clear the crypto card extraction latch.

Password: <passwd>

Re-enter password: <passwd>

Generating DSS keys .... [OK]
Apricot(config)#
```

In the previous example, the ESA crypto engine provides encryption services for the VIP2 interfaces, and the Cisco IOS crypto engine (located in the RSP) provides encryption services for all other designated ports.

The next example shows DSS keys being generated a second time, for the same ESA crypto engine shown in the previous example (DSS keys already exist for this crypto engine). Notice that the password used in the previous example must be entered in this example to complete the DSS key regeneration.

```
Apricot(config)# crypto gen-signature-keys ApricotESA 3
% Generating new DSS keys will require re-exchanging
    public keys with peers who already have the public key
    named ApricotESA!
Generate new DSS keys? [yes/no]: y
% Enter the crypto card password.
Password: <passwd>
Generating DSS keys .... [OK]
```

Related Commands

Search online to find documentation for related commands.

show crypto mypubkey

CRYPTO KEY-EXCHANGE

To exchange Digital Signature Standard (DSS) public keys, the administrator of the peer encrypting router that is designated ACTIVE must use the **crypto key-exchange** global configuration command.

> **crypto key-exchange** *ip-address key-name* [*tcp-port*]

Syntax Description

ip-address   The IP address of the peer router (designated PASSIVE) participating with you in the key exchange.

key-name   Identifies the crypto engine—either the Cisco IOS crypto engine, a second-generation Versatile Interface Processor (VIP2) crypto engine, or an Encryption Service Adapter (ESA) crypto engine. This name must match the *key-name* argument assigned when you generated DSS keys using the **crypto gen-signature-keys** command.

tcp-port   (Optional) Cisco IOS software uses the unassigned[1] TCP port number of 1964 to designate a key exchange. You may use this optional keyword to select a different number to designate a key exchange, if your system already uses the port number 1964 for a different purpose. If this keyword is used, you must use the same value as the PASSIVE router's tcp-port value.

1. 1964 is a TCP port number that has not been preassigned by the Internetworking Engineering Task Force (IETF).

Default

No DSS keys are exchanged.

Command Mode

Global configuration

Usage Guidelines

This command first appeared in Cisco IOS Release 11.2.

Peer encrypting routers must exchange DSS public keys before any encrypted communication can occur.

If you have a Cisco 7200, RSP7000, or 7500 series router, you will need to exchange DSS public keys for each crypto engine you plan to use.

To exchange DSS public keys, the two router administrators must call each other on the phone and verbally assign one router to the PASSIVE role, and the other router to the ACTIVE role.

The PASSIVE administrator uses the **crypto key-exchange passive** command to start the DSS key exchange. Then the ACTIVE administrator uses the **crypto key-exchange** command to send the first DSS public key. During the key exchange sequence, the two administrators must remain on the phone to verify the receipt of DSS keys. To verify the receipt of DSS keys, the administrators should compare screens to match DSS key serial numbers and Fingerprints. Screen prompts will guide both administrators through the exchange.

Example

The following example shows a DSS key exchange sequence from the point of view of a router named Banana. Banana is designated ACTIVE. The other router is named Apricot. Apricot is designated PASSIVE, and has previously generated DSS keys with the *key-name* Apricot. Banana has previously generated DSS keys with the *key-name* BananaESA:

```
Banana(config)# crypto key-exchange 172.21.114.68 BananaESA
Public key for BananaESA:
   Serial Number 01461300
   Fingerprint   0F1D 373F 2FC1 872C D5D7

Wait for peer to send a key[confirm]<Return>
Waiting ....
Public key for Apricot:
   Serial Number 01579312
   Fingerprint   BF1F 9EAC B17E F2A1 BA77

Add this public key to the configuration? [yes/no]: y
Banana(config)#
```

Related Commands

Search online to find documentation for related commands.

crypto key-exchange passive
crypto public-key
show crypto mypubkey

show crypto pubkey
show crypto pubkey name
show crypto pubkey serial

CRYPTO KEY-EXCHANGE PASSIVE

To enable an exchange of Digital Signature Standard (DSS) public keys, the administrator of the peer encrypting router that is designated PASSIVE must use the **crypto key-exchange passive** global configuration command.

> **crypto key-exchange passive** [*tcp-port*]

Syntax Description

tcp-port   (Optional) Cisco IOS software uses the unassigned[1] TCP port number of 1964 to designate a key exchange. You may use this optional keyword to select a different number to designate a key exchange, if your system already uses the port number 1964 for a different purpose. If this keyword is used, you must use the same value as the ACTIVE router's tcp-port value.

1. 1964 is a TCP port number that has not been preassigned by the Internetworking Engineering Task Force (IETF).

Default

No DSS keys are exchanged.

Command Mode

Global configuration

Usage Guidelines

This command first appeared in Cisco IOS Release 11.2.

Peer encrypting routers must exchange DSS public keys before any encrypted communication can occur.

To exchange DSS public keys, the two router administrators must call each other on the phone and verbally assign one router to the PASSIVE role, and the other router to the ACTIVE role.

Then the PASSIVE administrator should use the **crypto key-exchange passive** command to start the DSS key exchange. During the key exchange sequence, the two administrators must remain on the phone to verify the receipt of DSS keys. To verify the receipt of DSS keys, the administrators should compare screens to match DSS key serial numbers and Fingerprints. Screen prompts will guide both administrators through the exchange.

Example

The following example shows a DSS key exchange sequence from the point of view of a router named Apricot. Apricot is designated PASSIVE, and has previously generated DSS keys with the *key-name* Apricot. The other router is named Banana and has previously generated DSS keys with the *key-name* BananaESA:

```
Apricot(config)# crypto key-exchange passive
Enter escape character to abort if connection does not complete.
Wait for connection from peer[confirm]<Return>
Waiting ....
Public key for BananaESA:
   Serial Number 01461300
   Fingerprint   0F1D 373F 2FC1 872C D5D7
Add this public key to the configuration? [yes/no]: y
Send peer a key in return[confirm]<Return>
Which one?

Apricot? [yes]: <Return>
Public key for Apricot:
   Serial Number 01579312
   Fingerprint   BF1F 9EAC B17E F2A1 BA77

Apricot(config)#
```

Related Commands

Search online to find documentation for related commands.

crypto key-exchange
crypto public-key
show crypto mypubkey
show crypto pubkey
show crypto pubkey name
show crypto pubkey serial

CRYPTO KEY-TIMEOUT

To specify the time duration of encrypted sessions, use the **crypto key-timeout** global configuration command. Use the **no** form to restore the time duration of encrypted sessions to the default of 30 minutes.

> **crypto key-timeout** *minutes*
> **no crypto key-timeout** *minutes*

Syntax Description

minutes	Specifies the time duration of encrypted sessions. Can be from 1 to 1440 minutes (24 hours) in 1-minute increments. Specified by an integer from 1 to 1440.
	When the **no** form of the command is used, this argument is optional. Any value supplied for the argument is ignored by the router.

Default

Encrypted sessions time out in 30 minutes.

Command Mode

Global configuration

Usage Guidelines

This command first appeared in Cisco IOS Release 11.2.

After an encrypted communication session is established, it is valid for a specific length of time. After this length of time, the session times out. A new session must be negotiated, and a new Data Encryption Standard (DES) (session) key must be generated for encrypted communication to continue. Use this command to change the time that an encrypted communication session will last before it expires (times out).

Examples

The following example sets encrypted session timeouts to 2 hours:

```
crypto key-timeout 120
```

The following example shows one way to restore the default session time of 30 minutes:

```
no crypto key-timeout
```

The following example shows another way to restore the default session time of 30 minutes:

```
crypto key-timeout 30
```

Related Commands

Search online to find documentation for related commands.

show crypto key-timeout

CRYPTO MAP (GLOBAL CONFIGURATION)

To create or modify a crypto map definition and enter the crypto map configuration mode, use the **crypto map** global configuration command. Use the **no** form of this command to delete a crypto map definition.

> **crypto map** *map-name seq-num*
> **no crypto map** *map-name seq-num*

Syntax Description

map-name   The name you assign to the crypto map.

seq-num   Identifies the sequence number (definition set) of the crypto map. See additional explanation for using this argument in section "Usage Guidelines."

Default

No crypto maps exist.

Command Mode

Global configuration.

Performing this command invokes the crypto map configuration command mode.

Usage Guidelines

This command first appeared in Cisco IOS Release 11.2.

Use this command to create a new crypto map definition, or to modify an existing crypto map definition. Crypto maps link together definitions of encryption access lists, peer routers, and Data Encryption Standard (DES) algorithms. A crypto map must later be applied to an interface for the definitions to take effect; this is done using the **crypto map (interface configuration)** command.

When you issue the **crypto map (global configuration)** command, the router will invoke the crypto map configuration command mode. While in this mode, you will specify the crypto map definitions. Crypto map configuration command mode commands are used to create these definitions.

A crypto map definition must have three parts. First, you specify which remote peer encrypting router (crypto engine) will provide the far-end encryption services (the remote encryption endpoint). This is accomplished using the **set peer** command. Next, you specify which encryption access list(s) will participate in encryption services with the peer router. This is accomplished using the **match address** command. Finally, you specify which DES algorithm(s) to apply to the encrypted packets in the access list. This is accomplished using either the **set algorithm 40-bit-des** command or the **set algorithm des** command.

Because only one crypto map can be applied to a given interface, the *seq-num* argument provides a way to create several distinct definition sets that coexist within a single crypto map. Figure 24–1 illustrates the sequence number concept.

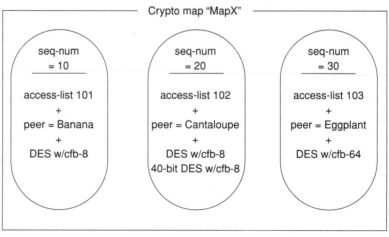

Figure 24–1
Crypto Map with
Subdefinitions

Having multiple distinct definition sets is useful if one router port will provide the encryption interface to more than one peer router.

Example

The following example creates a crypto map and defines the map parameters:

```
Apricot(config)# crypto map Research 10
Apricot(config-crypto-map)# set peer BananaESA.HQ
Apricot(config-crypto-map)# set algorithm des cfb-8
Apricot(config-crypto-map)# match address 101
Apricot(config-crypto-map)# exit
Apricot(config)#
```

Related Commands

Search online to find documentation of related commands.

crypto map (interface configuration)
match address
set algorithm 40-bit-des
set algorithm des
set peer
show crypto map
show crypto map interface
show crypto map tag

CRYPTO MAP (INTERFACE CONFIGURATION)

To apply a previously defined crypto map to an interface, use the **crypto map** interface configuration command. Use the **no** form of the command to eliminate the crypto map from the interface.

crypto map *map-name*
no crypto map *map-name*

Syntax Description

map-name The name that identifies the crypto map. This is the name you assigned when creating the crypto map.

When the **no** form of the command is used, this argument is optional. Any value supplied for the argument is ignored by the router.

Default

No crypto maps are assigned to interfaces.

Command Mode

Interface configuration

Usage Guidelines

This command first appeared in Cisco IOS Release 11.2.

Use this command to assign a crypto map to an interface. You must assign a crypto map to an interface before that interface can provide encryption services. Only one crypto map can be assigned to an interface. If there are multiple subdefinitions to the crypto map (for example, crypto map Research 10 and crypto map Research 20), each subdefinition will be applied when the single crypto map is applied.

Example

The following example assigns crypto map "Research" to the serial interface 0:

```
Apricot(config)# interface serial 0
Apricot(config-if)# crypto map Research
Apricot(config-if)# exit
Apricot(config)#
```

Related Commands

Search online to find documentation for related commands.

crypto map (global configuration)
show crypto map
show crypto map interface
show crypto map tag

CRYPTO PREGEN-DH-PAIRS

To enable pregeneration of Diffie-Hellman (DH) public numbers, use the **crypto pregen-dh-pairs** global configuration command. Use the **no** form to disable pregeneration of DH public numbers for all crypto engines.

> **crypto pregen-dh-pairs** *count* [*slot*]
> **no crypto pregen-dh-pairs**

Syntax Description

count	Specifies how many DH public numbers to pregenerate and hold in reserve. Specified by an integer from 0 to 10.
slot	(Optional) Identifies the crypto engine. This argument is available only on Cisco 7200, RSP7000, and 7500 series routers.
	If no slot is specified, the Cisco IOS crypto engine will be selected.
	Use the chassis slot number of the crypto engine location. For the Cisco IOS crypto engine, this is the chassis slot number of the Route Switch Processor (RSP). For the VIP2 crypto engine, this is the chassis slot number of the VIP2. For the ESA crypto engine, this is the chassis slot number of the ESA (Cisco 7200) or of the VIP2 (Cisco RSP7000 and 7500).

Default

DH number pairs are generated only when needed, during encrypted session setup.

Command Mode

Global configuration

Usage Guidelines

This command first appeared in Cisco IOS Release 11.2.

Each encrypted session uses a unique pair of DH numbers. Every time a new session is set up, new DH number pairs must be generated. When the session completes, these numbers are discarded. Generating new DH number pairs is a CPU-intensive activity, which can make session setup slow—especially for low-end routers.

To speed up session setup, you can choose to have a specified amount of DH number pairs pregenerated and held in reserve. Then, when an encrypted communication session is being set up, a DH number pair will be provided from that reserve. After a DH number pair is used, the reserve is automatically replenished with a new DH number pair, so that there should always be a DH number pair ready for use.

It is usually not necessary to have more than one or two DH number pairs pregenerated, unless your router will be setting up multiple encrypted sessions so frequently that a pregenerated reserve of one or two DH number pairs will be depleted too quickly.

If you have a Cisco 7200, RSP7000, or 7500 series router, you can perform this command for each crypto engine in service.

Setting the number of pregenerated pairs to be zero disables pregeneration but allows you to use the pairs already in reserve. Using the **no** form of the command disables pregeneration for *all* crypto engines of your router and deletes any DH number pairs currently in reserve. If you have a Cisco 7200, RSP7000, or 7500 series router and want to discontinue pregenerating DH numbers for only one crypto engine, set the *count* argument to 0, and specify the crypto engine with the *slot* argument.

Examples

The following example turns on pregeneration of DH public number pairs for a Cisco 2500 series router. Two DH number pairs will be held in constant reserve.

```
crypto pregen-dh-pairs 2
```

The following example turns on pregeneration of DH public numbers for the ESA crypto engine of a VIP2 card in slot 3 of a Cisco 7500 series router. One DH number pair will be held in constant reserve.

```
crypto pregen-dh-pairs 1 3
```

Related Commands

Search online to find documentation for related commands.

show crypto pregen-dh-pairs

CRYPTO PUBLIC-KEY

To manually specify the Digital Signature Standard (DSS) public key of a peer encrypting router, use the **crypto public-key** global configuration command. Use the **no** form of this command to delete the DSS public key of a peer encrypting router.

> **crypto public key** *key-name serial-number*
> > *hex-key-data*
> > *hex-key-data...*
> > quit
> **no crypto public key** *key-name serial-number*

Syntax Description

key-name   Identifies the crypto engine of the peer encrypting router.

serial-number   The serial number of the peer encrypting router's public DSS key.

When the **no** form of the command is used, this argument is optional. Any value supplied for the argument is ignored by the router.

hex-key-data   The DSS public key of the peer encrypting router, in hexadecimal format.

quit   When you are done entering the public key, type **quit** to exit the hex input mode.

Default

No peer encrypting router DSS keys are known.

Command Mode

Global configuration

Performing this command invokes the hex input mode. To complete the command, you must return to the global configuration mode by typing **quit** at the config-pubkey prompt.

Usage Guidelines

This command first appeared in Cisco IOS Release 11.2.

You can choose to use this command to specify DSS public keys of peer encrypting routers, instead of using the **crypto key-exchange passive** and **crypto key-exchange** commands. The administrator of the peer router can provide you with the exact values for the *key-name*, *serial-number*, and *hex-key-data* command arguments. The administrator of the peer router can discover these values by performing the **show crypto mypubkey** command at the peer router.

You should press **Return** after typing the *serial-number* argument. You will then be in the hex input mode. Enter the peer DSS public key in hexadecimal data. Entering the data will take more than one line; press **Return** to continue entering hexadecimal data on a new line. After typing in the hexadecimal data, you should press **Return** to get to a new line of the config-pubkey prompt, then type **quit** to complete the command.

Example

The following example specifies the DSS public key of a peer encrypting router:

```
Apricot(config)# crypto public-key BananaCryptoEngine 01709644
Enter a public key as a hexadecimal number ....

Apricot(config-pubkey)# C31260F4 BD8A5ACE 2C1B1E6C 8B0ABD27 01493A50
Apricot(config-pubkey)# 2E90AF19 8B29122B 2D479B15 437A0F7C BCBE5300
Apricot(config-pubkey)# 29859ED7 EAA2848E A31D7FD6 C8911D9A 9701CA00
Apricot(config-pubkey)# A6A66946
Apricot(config-pubkey)# quit
Apricot(config)# exit
Apricot#
%SYS-5-CONFIG_I: Configured from console by console
Apricot# show crypto pubkey
crypto public-key BananaCryptoEngine 01709644
C31260F4 BD8A5ACE 2C1B1E6C 8B0ABD27 01493A50 2E90AF19 8B29122B 2D479B15
437A0F7C BCBE5300 29859ED7 EAA2848E A31D7FD6 C8911D9A 9701CA00 A6A66946
quit

Apricot#
```

Related Commands

Search online to find documentation for related commands.

crypto key-exchange
crypto key-exchange passive
show crypto mypubkey
show crypto pubkey
show crypto pubkey name
show crypto pubkey serial

CRYPTO SDU CONNECTIONS

To change the maximum number of destinations (hosts or subnets) per source that you can define in encryption access list statements, use the **crypto sdu connections** global configuration command. Use the **no** form of the command to restore the default.

> **crypto sdu connections** *number*
> **no crypto sdu connections** *number*

Syntax Description

number   Specifies the maximum number of destinations per source. Use a value from 3 to 500.

This argument is not required when using the **no** form of the command.

Default

A maximum of 10 destinations can be paired with each source specified in encryption access list criteria statements.

Command Mode

Global configuration

Usage Guidelines

This command first appeared in Cisco IOS Release 11.3.

When you configure encryption access lists, you configure source and destination pairs in criteria statements. Any traffic that matches the criteria is then encrypted.

By default, the maximum number of distinct sources (host or subnets) that you can define in your encryption access lists is 100. Also, the maximum number of distinct destinations that you can define for any given source address is 10. For example, if you define 6 different source addresses, you can define up to 10 destination addresses for each of the 6 sources, for a total of 60 access list criteria statements.

Use this command if you need to specify more than 10 destinations for a particular source (host or subnet) in encryption access list statements.

For most situations, the defaults of 100 maximum sources and 10 maximum destinations per source are sufficient. Cisco recommends that you do not change the defaults unless you actually exceed the number of sources or destinations per source.

NOTES ──

You must reboot the router before this command takes effect.

Memory Impact

The amount of memory reserved for encrypted connections changes if you change the defaults with this command.

When using this command, you should consider the amount of memory that will be allocated. In general, use the **crypto sdu entities** and **crypto sdu connections** commands together: If you increase one value, decrease the other value. This prevents your router from running out of memory because too much memory was preallocated.

For every additional source specified with the **crypto sdu entities** command, the following additional bytes of memory will be allocated:

$$64 + (68 \times \text{the specified number of maximum destinations})$$

For every additional destination specified with the **crypto sdu connections,** the following additional bytes of memory will be allocated:

$$68 \times \text{the specified number of maximum sources}$$

For example, if you specify 5 maximum sources, and 250 maximum destinations per source, the memory allocated for encryption connections is calculated as follows:

$$\{5 \times [64 + (68 \times 250)]\} + \{250 \times (68 \times 5)\} = 170320 \text{ bytes}$$

Example

In this example, there are 50 remote sites connecting to a single server. The connections between the server and each site need to be encrypted. The server is located behind the local router named Apricot. Each of the remote sites connects through its own router.

Because of the large number of destination addresses that must be paired with the same source address in the local encryption access list, the default limits are changed.

```
Apricot(config)# crypto sdu connections 60
%Please reboot for the new connection size to take effect

Apricot(config)# crypto sdu entities 5
%Please reboot for the new table size to take effect
```

Note that the maximum number of sources is reduced to balance the increase in maximum destinations per source. This prevents too much memory from being preallocated to encryption connections.

Also note that even though there is only one server, and only 50 remote sites, this example defines 5 sources and 60 destinations. This allows room for future growth of the encryption access list. If another source or destination is added later, the limits will not have to be increased and the router rebooted again, which is a disruptive process.

Related Commands

Search online to find documentation for related commands.

crypto sdu entities

CRYPTO SDU ENTITIES

To change the maximum number of sources (hosts or subnets) that you can define in encryption access list statements, use the **crypto sdu entities** global configuration command. Use the **no** form of the command to restore the default.

crypto sdu entities *number*
no crypto sdu entities [*number*]

Syntax Description

number	Specifies the maximum number of sources. Use a value from 3 to 500.
	This argument is not required when using the **no** form of the command.

Default

A maximum of 100 sources can be specified in encryption access list criteria statements.

Command Mode

Global configuration

Usage Guidelines

This command first appeared in Cisco IOS Release 11.3.

When you configure encryption access lists, you configure source and destination pairs in criteria statements. Any traffic that matches the criteria is then encrypted.

By default, the maximum number of distinct sources (host or subnets) that you can define in your encryption access lists is 100. Also, the maximum number of distinct destinations that you can define for any given source address is 10. For example, if you define 6 different source addresses, you can define up to 10 destination addresses for each of the 6 sources, for a total of 60 access list criteria statements.

Use this command if you need to specify more than 100 sources (host or subnet) in encryption access list statements.

For most situations, the defaults of 100 maximum sources and 10 maximum destinations per source are sufficient. Cisco recommends that you do not change the defaults unless you actually exceed the number of sources or destinations per source.

NOTES ──

You must reboot the router before this command takes effect.

Memory Impact

The amount of memory reserved for encrypted connections changes if you change the defaults with this command.

When using this command, you should consider the amount of memory that will be allocated. In general, use the **crypto sdu entities** and **crypto sdu connections** commands together: If you increase one value, decrease the other value. This prevents your router from running out of memory because too much memory was preallocated.

For every additional source specified with the **crypto sdu entities** command, the following additional bytes of memory will be allocated:

$$64 + (68 \times \text{the specified number of maximum destinations})$$

For every additional destination specified with the **crypto sdu connections**, the following additional bytes of memory will be allocated:

$$68 \times \text{the specified number of maximum sources}$$

For example, if you specify 5 maximum sources, and 250 maximum destinations per source, the memory allocated for encryption connections is calculated as follows:

$$\{5 \times [64 + (68 \times 250)]\} + \{250 \times (68 \times 5)\} = 170320 \text{ bytes}$$

Example

In this example, there are 50 remote sites connecting to a single server. The connections between the server and each site need to be encrypted. The server is located behind the local router named Apricot. Each of the remote sites connects through its own router.

Because of the large number of destination addresses that must be paired with the same source address in the local encryption access list, the default limits are changed.

```
Apricot(config)# crypto sdu connections 60
%Please reboot for the new connection size to take effect

Apricot(config)# crypto sdu entities 5
%Please reboot for the new table size to take effect
```

Note that the maximum number of sources is reduced to balance the increase in maximum destinations per source. This prevents too much memory from being preallocated to encryption connections.

Also note that even though there is only one server, and only 50 remote sites, this example defines 5 sources and 60 destinations. This allows room for future growth of the encryption access list. If another source or destination is added later, the limits will not have to be increased and the router rebooted again, which is a disruptive process.

Related Commands

Search online to find documentation for related commands.

crypto sdu connections

CRYPTO ZEROIZE

To delete the Digital Signature Standard (DSS) public/private key pair of a crypto engine, use the **crypto zeroize** global configuration command.

crypto zeroize [*slot*]

CAUTION

DSS keys cannot be recovered after they have been removed. Use this command only after careful consideration.

Syntax Description

slot   (Optional) Identifies the crypto engine. This argument is available only on Cisco 7200, RSP7000, and 7500 series routers.

If no slot is specified, the Cisco IOS crypto engine will be selected.

Use the chassis slot number of the crypto engine location. For the Cisco IOS crypto engine, this is the chassis slot number of the Route Switch Processor (RSP). For the VIP2 crypto engine, this is the chassis slot number of the VIP2. For the ESA crypto engine, this is the chassis slot number of the ESA (Cisco 7200) or of the VIP2 (Cisco RSP7000 and 7500).

Default

DSS public/private keys will remain valid indefinitely.

Command Mode

Global configuration

Usage Guidelines

This command first appeared in Cisco IOS Release 11.2.

If you choose to stop using encryption on a router, completely or for a specific crypto engine only, you may delete the public/private DSS key pair(s) for your router's crypto engine(s). However, after you delete DSS key pairs for a specified crypto engine, you will no longer be able to use that crypto engine to have any encrypted sessions with peer routers, unless you regenerate and re-exchange new DSS keys. If only one crypto engine is configured at your router, issuing this command will prevent you from performing any encryption at the router.

CAUTION

If you use this command on a Cisco 7200 series router, the current active crypto engine's DSS keys will be deleted. Be certain that the engine for which you want to delete keys is the engine that is currently selected. You can use the **show crypto engine configuration** command to verify the current crypto engine. If the current crypto engine is not the engine for which you want to delete DSS keys, you must select the correct crypto engine using the **crypto esa** command.

This command can be used if you lose the password required to complete the **crypto clear-latch** or **crypto gen-signature-keys** commands. After using the **crypto zeroize** command, you will need to regenerate and re-exchange new DSS keys. You will be prompted to supply a new password when you regenerate new DSS keys with the **crypto gen-signature-keys** command.

Example

The following example deletes the DSS public/private key of a router named Apricot, which is a Cisco 7500 series router with an RSP in slot 4:

```
Apricot(config)# crypto zeroize 4
Warning! Zeroize will remove your DSS signature keys.
Do you want to continue? [yes/no]: y
Keys to be removed are named ApricotIOS.
Do you really want to remove these keys? [yes/no]: y
[OK]
Apricot(config)#
```

Related Commands

Search online to find documentation for related commands.

crypto gen-signature-keys

DENY

To set conditions for a named encryption access list, use the **deny** access-list configuration command. The **deny** command prevents IP traffic from being encrypted/decrypted if the conditions are matched. To remove a deny condition from an encryption access list, use the **no** form of this command.

> **deny** *source* [*source-wildcard*]
> **no deny** *source* [*source-wildcard*]
>
> **deny** *protocol source source-wildcard destination destination-wildcard* [**precedence** *precedence*] [**tos** *tos*] [**log**]
>
> **no deny** *protocol source source-wildcard destination destination-wildcard* [**precedence** *precedence*] [**tos** *tos*] [**log**]

For ICMP, you can also use the following syntax:

> **deny icmp** *source source-wildcard destination destination-wildcard* [*icmp-type* [*icmp-code*] | *icmp-message*] [**precedence** *precedence*] [**tos** *tos*] [**log**]

For IGMP, you can also use the following syntax:

> **deny igmp** *source source-wildcard destination destination-wildcard* [*igmp-type*] [**precedence** *precedence*] [**tos** *tos*] [**log**]

For TCP, you can also use the following syntax:

deny tcp *source source-wildcard* [*operator port* [*port*]] *destination destination-wildcard*
[*operator port* [*port*]] [**established**] [**precedence** *precedence*] [**tos** *tos*] [**log**]

For UDP, you can also use the following syntax:

deny udp *source source-wildcard* [*operator port* [*port*]] *destination destination-wildcard*
[*operator port* [*port*]] [**precedence** *precedence*] [**tos** *tos*] [**log**]

Syntax Description

source	Number of the network or host from which the packet is being sent. There are two alternative ways to specify the source: • Use a 32-bit quantity in 4-part, dotted-decimal format. • Use the keyword **any** as an abbreviation for a *source* and *source-wildcard* of 0.0.0.0 255.255.255.255. This keyword is normally *not* recommended (see section "Usage Guidelines").
source-wildcard	(Optional) Wildcard bits to be applied to the source. There are two alternative ways to specify the source wildcard: • Use a 32-bit quantity in 4-part, dotted-decimal format. Place ones in the bit positions you want to ignore. • Use the keyword **any** as an abbreviation for a *source* and *source-wildcard* of 0.0.0.0 255.255.255.255. This keyword is normally *not* recommended (see section "Usage Guidelines").
protocol	Name or number of an IP protocol. It can be one of the keywords **eigrp, gre, icmp, igmp, igrp, ip, ipinip, nos, ospf, tcp,** or **udp,** or an integer in the range 0 through 255 representing an IP protocol number. To match any Internet protocol (including ICMP, TCP, and UDP), use the keyword **ip.** Some protocols allow further qualifiers, described later.
source	Number of the network or host from which the packet is being sent. There are three alternative ways to specify the source: • Use a 32-bit quantity in 4-part, dotted-decimal format. • Use the keyword **any** as an abbreviation for a *source* and *source-wildcard* of 0.0.0.0 255.255.255.255. This keyword is normally *not* recommended (see section "Usage Guidelines"). • Use **host** *source* as an abbreviation for a *source* and *source-wildcard* of *source* 0.0.0.0.

source-wildcard

Wildcard bits to be applied to source. There are three alternative ways to specify the source wildcard:
• Use a 32-bit quantity in 4-part, dotted-decimal format. Place ones in the bit positions you want to ignore.
• Use the keyword **any** as an abbreviation for a *source* and *source-wildcard* of 0.0.0.0 255.255.255.255. This keyword is normally *not* recommended (see section "Usage Guidelines").
• Use **host** *source* as an abbreviation for a *source* and *source-wildcard* of *source* 0.0.0.0.

destination

Number of the network or host to which the packet is being sent. There are three alternative ways to specify the destination:
• Use a 32-bit quantity in 4-part, dotted-decimal format.
• Use the keyword **any** as an abbreviation for the *destination* and *destination-wildcard* of 0.0.0.0 255.255.255.255. This keyword is normally *not* recommended (see section "Usage Guidelines").
• Use **host** *destination* as an abbreviation for a *destination* and *destination-wildcard* of *destination* 0.0.0.0.

destination-wildcard

Wildcard bits to be applied to the destination. There are three alternative ways to specify the destination wildcard:
• Use a 32-bit quantity in 4-part, dotted-decimal format. Place ones in the bit positions you want to ignore.
• Use the keyword **any** as an abbreviation for a *destination* and *destination-wildcard* of 0.0.0.0 255.255.255.255. This keyword is normally *not* recommended (see section "Usage Guidelines").
• Use **host** *destination* as an abbreviation for a *destination* and *destination-wildcard* of *destination* 0.0.0.0.

precedence *precedence*

(Optional) Packets can be matched for encryption by precedence level, as specified by a number from 0 to 7 or by name as listed in section "Usage Guidelines" of the **access-list (encryption)** command.

tos *tos*

(Optional) Packets can be matched for encryption by type of service level, as specified by a number from 0 to 15 or by name as listed in section "Usage Guidelines" of the **access-list (encryption)** command.

icmp-type

(Optional) ICMP packets can be matched for encryption by ICMP message type. The type is a number from 0 to 255.

icmp-code   (Optional) ICMP packets that are matched for encryption by ICMP message type can also be matched by the ICMP message code. The code is a number from 0 to 255.

icmp-message   (Optional) ICMP packets can be matched for encryption by an ICMP message type name or ICMP message type and code name. The possible names are found in section "Usage Guidelines" of the **access-list** (**encryption**) command.

igmp-type   (Optional) IGMP packets can be matched for encryption by IGMP message type or message name. A message type is a number from 0 to 15. IGMP message names are listed in section "Usage Guidelines" of the **access-list** (**encryption**) command.

operator   (Optional) Compares source or destination ports. Possible operands include **lt** (less than), **gt** (greater than), **eq** (equal), **neq** (not equal), and **range** (inclusive range).

                   If the operator is positioned after the *source* and *source-wildcard*, it must match the source port.

                   If the operator is positioned after the *destination* and *destination-wildcard*, it must match the destination port.

                   The **range** operator requires two port numbers. All other operators require one port number.

port   (Optional) The decimal number or name of a TCP or UDP port. A port number is a number from 0 to 65,535. TCP and UDP port names are listed in section "Usage Guidelines" of the **access-list** (**encryption**) command. TCP port names can only be used when filtering TCP. UDP port names can only be used when filtering UDP.

established   (Optional) For the TCP protocol only: Indicates an established connection. A match occurs if the TCP datagram has the ACK or RST bits set. The nonmatching case is that of the initial TCP datagram to form a connection.

log   (Optional) Causes an informational logging message about the packet that matches the entry to be sent to the console. (The level of messages logged to the console is controlled by the **logging console** command.)

                   The message includes the access list number, whether the packet was permitted or denied; the protocol, whether it was TCP, UDP, ICMP or a number; and, if appropriate, the source and destination addresses, and source and destination port numbers. The message is generated for the first packet that matches, and then at 5-minute intervals, including the number of packets permitted or denied in the prior 5-minute interval.

Default

There is no specific condition under which a packet is prevented from being encrypted/decrypted. However, if a packet does not match any **deny** or **permit** command statements, the packet will not be encrypted/decrypted. (See section "Usage Guidelines" that follows for more information about matching encryption access list conditions.)

Command Mode

Access-list configuration

Usage Guidelines

This command first appeared in Cisco IOS Release 11.2.

Use this command to specify conditions under which a packet will not be encrypted/decrypted. Use this command after you use the **ip access-list extended (encryption)** command.

After a named encryption access list is fully specified using **permit** and **deny** commands, the encryption access list must be specified in a crypto map, and the crypto map must be applied to an interface. After this is accomplished, packets will be either encrypted/decryped or not encrypted/decrypted at the router depending on the conditions defined within the **permit** and **deny** commands.

If a packet matches the conditions in any **deny** command, the packet will not be encrypted/decrypted. Also, if a packet does not match any conditions in either a **deny** or a **permit** command, the packet will not be encrypted/decrypted. This occurs because all encryption access lists contain an implicit "deny" ("do not encrypt/decrypt") statement at the end of the list.

CAUTION

When creating encryption access lists, it is *not* recommended that you use the **any** keyword to specify source or destination addresses for **permit** or **deny** commands. Using the **any** keyword with a **permit** command could cause extreme problems if a packet enters your router and is destined for a router that is not configured for encryption. This would cause your router to attempt to set up an encryption session with a nonencrypting router.

If you incorrectly use the **any** keyword with a **deny** command, you might inadvertently prevent all packets from being encrypted, which could present a security risk.

Examples

1. Inappropriately Configured Access List: Example 1

   This first example shows a named encryption access list configured in an inappropriate way. After this list is applied to an interface using a crypto map, no UDP traffic will be encrypted. This occurs even though there are **permit** commands.

```
ip access-list extended Apricotcryptomap10
 deny UDP any any
```

```
  permit UDP 192.168.33.145  0.0.0.15  172.31.0.0  0.0.255.255
  permit UDP 192.168.33.145  0.0.0.15  10.0.0.0  0.255.255.255
```

2. Inappropriately Configured Access List: Example 2

   The second example shows another inappropriate configuration for an encryption access list. This example will cause the router to encrypt all UDP traffic leaving the interface, including traffic to routers not configured for encryption. When this happens, the router will attempt to set up an encryption session with a non-encrypting router.

```
ip access-list extended Apricotcryptomap10
  permit UDP 192.168.33.145  0.0.0.15  172.31.0.0  0.0.255.255
  permit UDP 192.168.33.145  0.0.0.15  10.0.0.0  0.255.255.255
  permit UDP any any
```

3. Example of a Correctly Configured Access List

   The third example will encrypt/decrypt only traffic that matches the source and destination addresses defined in the two permit statements. All other traffic will not be encrypted/decrypted.

```
ip access-list extended Apricotcryptomap10
  permit UDP 192.168.33.145  0.0.0.15  172.31.0.0  0.0.255.255
  permit UDP 192.168.33.145  0.0.0.15  10.0.0.0  0.255.255.255
```

Related Commands

Search online to find documentation for related commands.

access-list (encryption)
ip access-list extended (encryption)
permit
show ip access-list

IP ACCESS-LIST EXTENDED (ENCRYPTION)

To define an encryption access list by name, use the **ip access-list extended** global configuration command. To remove a named encryption access list, use the **no** form of this command.

> ip access-list extended *name*
> no ip access-list extended *name*

Syntax Description

name	Name of the encryption access list. Names cannot contain a space or quotation mark, and must begin with an alphabetic character to prevent ambiguity with numbered access lists.

Default

There is no named encryption access list.

Command Mode

Global configuration.

Performing this command invokes the access-list configuration command mode.

Usage Guidelines

This command first appeared in Cisco IOS Release 11.2.

Use this command to configure a named IP access list (as opposed to a numbered IP access list). This command will take you into access-list configuration mode. From this mode you use the **deny** and **permit** commands to define the conditions for which traffic will be encrypted/decrypted or not encrypted/decrypted.

To use the encryption access list, you must first specify the access list in a crypto map definition, and then apply the crypto map to an interface.

Examples

1. Inappropriately Configured Access List: Example 1

    The first example shows a named encryption access list configured in an inappropriate way. After this list is applied to an interface using a crypto map, no UDP traffic will be encrypted. This occurs even though there are **permit** commands.

    ```
    ip access-list extended Apricotcryptomap10
     deny UDP any any
     permit UDP 192.168.33.145  0.0.0.15  172.31.0.0  0.0.255.255
     permit UDP 192.168.33.145  0.0.0.15  10.0.0.0  0.255.255.255
    ```

2. Inappropriately Configured Access List: Example 2

    The second example shows another inappropriate configuration for an encryption access list. This example will cause the router to encrypt all UDP traffic leaving the interface, including traffic to routers not configured for encryption. When this happens, the router will attempt to set up an encryption session with a non-encrypting router.

    ```
    ip access-list extended Apricotcryptomap10
     permit UDP 192.168.33.145  0.0.0.15  172.31.0.0  0.0.255.255
     permit UDP 192.168.33.145  0.0.0.15  10.0.0.0  0.255.255.255
     permit UDP any any
    ```

3. Example of a Correctly Configured Access List

    The third example will encrypt/decrypt only traffic that matches the source and destination addresses defined in the two permit statements. All other traffic will not be encrypted/decrypted.

    ```
    ip access-list extended Apricotcryptomap10
     permit UDP 192.168.33.145  0.0.0.15  172.31.0.0  0.0.255.255
     permit UDP 192.168.33.145  0.0.0.15  10.0.0.0  0.255.255.255
    ```

Part IV

Command Reference

Related Commands

Search online to find documentation for related commands.

access-list (encryption)
crypto map (global configuration)
crypto map (interface configuration)
deny
ip access-list (used for traffic filtering purposes)
permit
show ip access-list

MATCH ADDRESS

To specify an encryption access list within a crypto map definition, use the **match address** crypto map configuration command. Use the **no** form of this command to eliminate an encryption access list from a crypto map definition.

> **match address** [*access-list-number* | *name*]
> **no match address** [*access-list-number* | *name*]

Syntax Description

access-list-number	Identifies the numbered encryption access list. This value should match the access-list-number argument of the numbered encryption access list being matched.
name	Identifies the named encryption access list. This name should match the *name* argument of the named encryption access list being matched.

Default

No access lists are matched to the crypto map.

Command Mode

Crypto map configuration

Usage Guidelines

This command first appeared in Cisco IOS Release 11.2.

Use this command to specify an encryption access list for a given crypto map definition. This access list was previously defined using the **access-list (encryption)** or **ip access-list extended (encryption)** command.

The encryption access list you specify with this command will be applied to an interface as an outbound encryption access list, after you define a crypto map and apply the crypto map to the interface.

Example

The following example creates a crypto map and defines an encryption access list for the map:

```
Apricot(config)# crypto map Research 10
Apricot(config-crypto-map)# match address 101
```

Related Commands

Search online to find documentation for related commands.

access-list (encryption)
crypto map (global configuration)
ip access-list extended (encryption)
show crypto map
show crypto map interface
show crypto map tag

PERMIT

To set conditions for a named encryption access list, use the **permit** access-list configuration command. The **permit** command causes IP traffic to be encrypted/decrypted if the conditions are matched. To remove a permit condition from an encryption access list, use the **no** form of this command.

> **permit** *source* [*source-wildcard*]
> **no permit** *source* [*source-wildcard*]

> **permit** *protocol source source-wildcard destination destination-wildcard* [**precedence** *precedence*] [**tos** *tos*] [**log**]
> **no permit** *protocol source source-wildcard destination destination-wildcard* [**precedence** *precedence*] [**tos** *tos*] [**log**]

For ICMP, you can also use the following syntax:

> **permit icmp** *source source-wildcard destination destination-wildcard* [*icmp-type* [*icmp-code*] | *icmp-message*] [**precedence** *precedence*] [**tos** *tos*] [**log**]

For IGMP, you can also use the following syntax:

> **permit igmp** *source source-wildcard destination destination-wildcard* [*igmp-type*] [**precedence** *precedence*] [**tos** *tos*] [**log**]

For TCP, you can also use the following syntax:

> **permit tcp** *source source-wildcard* [*operator port* [*port*]] *destination destination-wildcard* [*operator port* [*port*]] [**established**] [**precedence** *precedence*] [**tos** *tos*] [**log**]

For UDP, you can also use the following syntax:

> **permit udp** *source source-wildcard* [*operator port* [*port*]] *destination destination-wildcard* [*operator port* [*port*]] [**precedence** *precedence*] [**tos** *tos*] [**log**]

Syntax Description

source	Number of the network or host from which the packet is being sent. There are two alternative ways to specify the source: • Use a 32-bit quantity in 4-part, dotted-decimal format. • Use the keyword **any** as an abbreviation for a *source* and *source-wildcard* of 0.0.0.0 255.255.255.255. This keyword is normally *not* recommended (see section "Usage Guidelines").
source-wildcard	(Optional) Wildcard bits to be applied to the source. There are two alternative ways to specify the source wildcard: • Use a 32-bit quantity in 4-part, dotted-decimal format. Place ones in the bit positions you want to ignore. • Use the keyword **any** as an abbreviation for a *source* and *source-wildcard* of 0.0.0.0 255.255.255.255. This keyword is normally *not* recommended (see section "Usage Guidelines").
protocol	Name or number of an IP protocol. It can be one of the keywords **eigrp, gre, icmp, igmp, igrp, ip, ipinip, nos, ospf, tcp,** or **udp,** or an integer in the range 0 through 255 representing an IP protocol number. To match any Internet protocol (including ICMP, TCP, and UDP), use the keyword **ip**. Some protocols allow further qualifiers described later.
source	Number of the network or host from which the packet is being sent. There are three alternative ways to specify the source: • Use a 32-bit quantity in 4-part, dotted-decimal format. • Use the keyword **any** as an abbreviation for a *source* and *source-wildcard* of 0.0.0.0 255.255.255.255. This keyword is normally *not* recommended (see section "Usage Guidelines"). • Use **host** *source* as an abbreviation for a *source* and *source-wildcard* of source 0.0.0.0.
source-wildcard	Wildcard bits to be applied to source. There are three alternative ways to specify the source wildcard: • Use a 32-bit quantity in 4-part, dotted-decimal format. Place ones in the bit positions you want to ignore. • Use the keyword **any** as an abbreviation for a *source* and *source-wildcard* of 0.0.0.0 255.255.255.255. This keyword is normally *not* recommended (see section "Usage Guidelines"). • Use **host** *source* as an abbreviation for a *source* and *source-wildcard* of source 0.0.0.0.

destination	Number of the network or host to which the packet is being sent. There are three alternative ways to specify the destination: • Use a 32-bit quantity in 4-part, dotted-decimal format. • Use the keyword **any** as an abbreviation for the *destination* and *destination-wildcard* of 0.0.0.0 255.255.255.255. This keyword is normally *not* recommended (see section "Usage Guidelines"). • Use **host** *destination* as an abbreviation for a *destination* and *destination-wildcard* of *destination* 0.0.0.0.
destination-wildcard	Wildcard bits to be applied to the destination. There are three alternative ways to specify the destination wildcard: • Use a 32-bit quantity in 4-part, dotted-decimal format. Place ones in the bit positions you want to ignore. • Use the keyword **any** as an abbreviation for a *destination* and *destination-wildcard* of 0.0.0.0 255.255.255.255. This keyword is normally *not* recommended (see section "Usage Guidelines"). • Use **host** *destination* as an abbreviation for a *destination* and *destination-wildcard* of *destination* 0.0.0.0.
precedence *precedence*	(Optional) Packets can be matched for encryption by precedence level, as specified by a number from 0 to 7 or by name as listed in section "Usage Guidelines" of the **access-list (encryption)** command.
tos *tos*	(Optional) Packets can be matched for encryption by type of service level, as specified by a number from 0 to 15 or by name as listed in section "Usage Guidelines" of the **access-list (encryption)** command.
icmp-type	(Optional) ICMP packets can be matched for encryption by ICMP message type. The type is a number from 0 to 255.
icmp-code	(Optional) ICMP packets that are matched for encryption by ICMP message type can also be matched by the ICMP message code. The code is a number from 0 to 255.
icmp-message	(Optional) ICMP packets can be matched for encryption by an ICMP message type name or ICMP message type and code name. The possible names are found in section "Usage Guidelines" of the **access-list (extended)** command.

igmp-type   (Optional) IGMP packets can be matched for encryption by
                       IGMP message type or message name. A message type is a num-
                       ber from 0 to 15. IGMP message names are listed in section
                       "Usage Guidelines" of the **access-list (extended)** command.

operator   (Optional) Compares source or destination ports. Possible oper-
                       ands include **lt** (less than), **gt** (greater than), **eq** (equal), **neq** (not
                       equal), and **range** (inclusive range).

                       If the operator is positioned after the *source* and *source-wild-
                       card*, it must match the source port.

                       If the operator is positioned after the *destination* and *destina-
                       tion-wildcard*, it must match the destination port.

                       The **range** operator requires two port numbers. All other oper-
                       ators require one port number.

port   (Optional) The decimal number or name of a TCP or UDP port.
                       A port number is a number from 0 to 65535. TCP and UDP port
                       names are listed in section "Usage Guidelines" of the **access-list
                       (extended)** command. TCP port names can only be used when fil-
                       tering TCP. UDP port names can only be used when filtering UDP.

established   (Optional) For the TCP protocol only: Indicates an established
                       connection. A match occurs if the TCP datagram has the ACK
                       or RST bits set. The nonmatching case is that of the initial TCP
                       datagram to form a connection.

log   (Optional) Causes an informational logging message about the
                       packet that matches the entry to be sent to the console. (The
                       level of messages logged to the console is controlled by the **log-
                       ging console** command.)

                       The message includes the access list number, whether the packet
                       was permitted or denied; the protocol, whether it was TCP,
                       UDP, ICMP or a number; and, if appropriate, the source and
                       destination addresses and source and destination port numbers.
                       The message is generated for the first packet that matches, and
                       then at 5-minute intervals, including the number of packets per-
                       mitted or denied in the prior 5-minute interval.

Default

There is no specific condition under which a packet is caused to be encrypted/decrypted. However,
if a packet does not match any **deny** or **permit** command statements, the packet will not be

encrypted/decrypted. (See section "Usage Guidelines" for more information about matching encryption access list conditions.)

Command Mode

Access-list configuration

Usage Guidelines

This command first appeared in Cisco IOS Release 11.2.

Use this command following the **ip access-list extended (encryption)** command to specify conditions under which a packet will be encrypted/decrypted.

After a named encryption access list is fully specified using **permit** and **deny** commands, the encryption access list must be specified in a crypto map, and the crypto map must be applied to an interface. After this is accomplished, packets will be either encrypted/decryped or not encrypted/decrypted at the router depending on the conditions defined within the **permit** and **deny** commands.

If a packet matches the conditions in any **permit** command, the packet will be encrypted/decrypted. If a packet does not match any conditions in either a **deny** or a **permit** command, the packet will not be encrypted/decrypted. This occurs because all encryption access lists contain an implicit "deny" ("do not encrypt/decrypt") statement at the end of the list.

CAUTION

When creating encryption access lists, it is *not* recommended that you use the **any** keyword to specify source or destination addresses for **permit** or **deny** commands. Using the **any** keyword with a **permit** command could cause extreme problems if a packet enters your router and is destined for a router that is not configured for encryption. This would cause your router to attempt to set up an encryption session with a nonencrypting router.

If you incorrectly use the **any** keyword with a **deny** command, you might inadvertently prevent all packets from being encrypted, which could present a security risk.

Examples

1. Inappropriately Configured Access List: Example 1

   The first example shows a named encryption access list configured in an inappropriate way. After this list is applied to an interface using a crypto map, no UDP traffic will be encrypted. This occurs even though there are **permit** commands.

   ```
   ip access-list extended Apricotcryptomap10
    deny UDP any any
    permit UDP 192.168.33.145  0.0.0.15  172.31.0.0  0.0.255.255
    permit UDP 192.168.33.145  0.0.0.15  10.0.0.0  0.255.255.255
   ```

2. Inappropriately Configured Access List: Example 2

   The second example shows another inappropriate configuration for an encryption access list. This example will cause the router to encrypt all UDP traffic leaving the interface, including traffic to routers not configured for encryption. When this happens, the router will attempt to set up an encryption session with a non-encrypting router.

   ```
   ip access-list extended Apricotcryptomap10
    permit UDP 192.168.33.145  0.0.0.15  172.31.0.0  0.0.255.255
    permit UDP 192.168.33.145  0.0.0.15  10.0.0.0  0.255.255.255
    permit UDP any any
   ```

3. Example of a Correctly Configured Access List

   The third example will encrypt/decrypt only traffic that matches the source and destination addresses defined in the two permit statements. All other traffic will not be encrypted/decrypted.

   ```
   ip access-list extended Apricotcryptomap10
    permit UDP 192.168.33.145  0.0.0.15  172.31.0.0  0.0.255.255
    permit UDP 192.168.33.145  0.0.0.15  10.0.0.0  0.255.255.255
   ```

Related Commands

Search online to find documentation for related commands.

access-list (encryption)
deny
ip access-list extended (encryption)
show ip access-list

SET ALGORITHM 40-BIT-DES

To specify a 40-bit Data Encryption Standard (DES) algorithm type within a crypto map definition, use the **set algorithm 40-bit-des** crypto map configuration command. Use the **no** form of this command to disable a 40-bit DES algorithm type within a crypto map definition.

   set algorithm 40-bit-des [cfb-8 | cfb-64]
   no set algorithm 40-bit-des [cfb-8 | cfb-64]

Syntax Description

cfb-8   (Optional) Selects the 8-bit Cipher FeedBack (CFB) mode of the 40-bit DES algorithm. If no CFB mode is specified when the command is issued, 64-bit CFB mode is the default.

cfb-64   Selects the 64-bit CFB mode of the 40-bit DES algorithm. If no CFB mode is specified when the command is issued, 64-bit CFB mode is the default.

Default

If no DES algorithm is specified within a crypto map, all globally enabled DES algorithms will be matched to the map by default. See the **crypto algorithm 40-bit-des** or **crypto algorithm des** command descriptions to learn about globally enabling DES algorithms.

Command Mode

Crypto map configuration

Usage Guidelines

This command first appeared in Cisco IOS Release 11.2.

Use this command to specify 40-bit DES algorithm types for a given crypto map definition. Forty-bit DES algorithm types use a 40-bit DES key. The DES algorithms specified within a crypto map definition will be used to encrypt/decrypt all traffic at an interface when the crypto map is applied to the interface.

NOTES

If you are running an exportable image, you can only use 40-bit variations of DES. You cannot enable or use the basic DES algorithms, which are not available with exportable images.

Example

The following example defines a 40-bit DES algorithm type for a crypto map:

```
Apricot(config)# crypto map Research 10
Apricot(config-crypto-map)# set algorithm 40-bit-des cfb-8
```

Related Commands

Search online to find documentation for related commands.

crypto map (global configuration)
set algorithm des
show crypto map
show crypto map interface
show crypto map tag

SET ALGORITHM DES

To enable basic Data Encryption Standard (DES) algorithm types within a crypto map definition, use the **set algorithm des** crypto map configuration command. Use the **no** form of this command to disable a basic DES algorithm type within a crypto map definition.

set algorithm des [cfb-8 | cfb-64]
no set algorithm des [cfb-8 | cfb-64]

Syntax Description

cfb-8   (Optional) Selects the 8-bit Cipher FeedBack (CFB) mode of the basic DES algorithm. If no CFB mode is specified when the command is issued, 64-bit CFB mode is the default.

cfb-64   (Optional) Selects the 64-bit CFB mode of the basic DES algorithm. If no CFB mode is specified when the command is issued, 64-bit CFB mode is the default.

Default

If no DES algorithm is specified within a crypto map, all globally enabled DES algorithms will be matched to the map by default. See the **crypto algorithm 40-bit-des** or **crypto algorithm des** command descriptions to learn about globally enabling DES algorithms.

Command Mode

Crypto map configuration

Usage Guidelines

This command first appeared in Cisco IOS Release 11.2.

Use this command to specify basic DES algorithm types for a given crypto map definition. Basic DES algorithm types use a 56-bit DES key. The DES algorithms specified within a crypto map definition will be used to encrypt/decrypt all traffic at an interface when the crypto map is applied to the interface.

NOTES

If you are running an exportable image, you can only use 40-bit variations of DES. You cannot enable or use the basic DES algorithms, which are not available with exportable images.

Example

The following example defines a DES algorithm type for a crypto map:

```
Apricot(config)# crypto map Research 10
Apricot(config-crypto-map)# set algorithm des cfb-8
```

Related Commands

Search online to find documentation for related commands.

crypto map (global configuration)
set algorithm 40-bit-des
show crypto map
show crypto map interface
show crypto map tag

SET PEER

To specify a peer encrypting router within a crypto map definition, use the **set peer** crypto map configuration command. Use the **no** form of this command to eliminate a peer encrypting router from a crypto map definition.

> **set peer** *key-name*
> **no set peer** *key-name*

Syntax Description

key-name   Identifies the crypto engine of the peer encrypting router.

Default

No peer is defined by default.

Command Mode

Crypto map configuration

Usage Guidelines

This command first appeared in Cisco IOS Release 11.2.

Use this command to specify a peer encrypting router as the remote encryption route endpoint for a given crypto map definition.

Example

The following example creates a crypto map and defines a peer router for the map:

```
Apricot(config)# crypto map Research 10
Apricot(config-crypto-map)# set peer BananaESA.HQ
```

Related Commands

Search online to find documentation for related commands.

crypto map (global configuration)
show crypto map
show crypto map interface
show crypto map tag

SHOW CRYPTO ALGORITHMS

To view which Data Encryption Standard (DES) algorithm types are globally enabled for your router, use the **show crypto algorithms** privileged EXEC command. This displays all basic DES and 40-bit DES algorithm types globally enabled.

> **show crypto algorithms**

Syntax Description

This command has no arguments or keywords.

Command Mode

Privileged EXEC

Usage Guidelines

This command first appeared in Cisco IOS Release 11.2.

Sample Display

The following is sample output from the **show crypto algorithms** command:

```
Apricot# show crypto algorithms
   des cfb-8
```

Related Commands

Search online to find documentation for related commands.

crypto algorithm 40-bit-des
crypto algorithm des

SHOW CRYPTO CARD

To view the operational status of an Encryption Service Adapter (ESA), use the **show crypto card** privileged EXEC command. This command is available only on Cisco 7200, RSP7000, or 7500 series routers with an installed ESA.

> **show crypto card** [*slot*]

Syntax Description

slot   This argument is used only on Cisco RSP7000 and 7200 series routers.

Identifies the ESA to show. Use the chassis slot number of the VIP2 containing the ESA.

Command Mode

Privileged EXEC

Usage Guidelines

This command first appeared in Cisco IOS Release 11.2.

Sample Display

The following is sample output from the **show crypto card** command:

```
Apricot# show crypto card 1
Crypto card in slot: 1

Tampered:        No
Xtracted:        No
Password set:    Yes
DSS Key set:     Yes
FW version:      5049702
```

Table 24–1 explains each field.

Table 24–1 *Show Crypto Card Field Descriptions*

Field	Description
Tampered	"Yes" indicates that somebody attempted to physically remove the tamper shield cover from the ESA card. Such an action causes the ESA card to clear its memory, similar to if a **crypto zeroize** command had been issued for the ESA.
Xtracted	"Yes" indicates that the ESA card had been extracted (removed) from the router.
Password set	"Yes" indicates that the ESA card password has already been set. This password is set with the **crypto clear-latch** or **crypto gen-signature-keys** command, and is required for subsequent issues of the **crypto clear-latch** and **crypto gen-signature-keys** commands.
DSS Key set	"Yes" indicates that DSS keys are generated and ready for use. DSS keys are generated using the **crypto gen-signature-keys** command.
FW version	Version number of the firmware running on the ESA card.

SHOW CRYPTO CONNECTIONS

To view current and pending encrypted session connections, use the **show crypto connections** privileged EXEC command.

   show crypto connections

Syntax Description

This command has no arguments or keywords.

Command Mode

Privileged EXEC

Usage Guidelines

This command first appeared in Cisco IOS Release 11.2.

Sample Display

The following is sample output from the **show crypto connections** command:

```
Apricot# show crypto connections
Pending Connection Table
PE              UPE            Timestamp             Conn_id
172.21.115.22   172.21.115.18  Mar 01 1993 00:01:09  -1

Connection Table
PE              UPE            Conn_id New_id Alg     Time
172.21.115.22   172.21.115.18  -1       1      0      Not Set
                flags:PEND_CONN
```

Table 24–2 explains each field.

Table 24–2 *Show Crypto Connections Field Descriptions*

Field	Description
PE	"Protected Entity." This shows a representative source IP address as specified in the crypto map's encryption access list. This IP address can be any host that matches a source in the encryption access list that is being used in the connection.
UPE	"Unprotected Entity." This shows a representative destination IP address as specified in the crypto map's encryption access list. This IP address can be any host that matches a destination in the encryption access list that is being used in the connection.
Timestamp	Identifies the time when the connection was initiated.
Conn_id	A number used to identify and track the connection. This can be a positive integer value from 1 to 299, or any negative integer value. Each connection is assigned a negative connection id when the connection is pending (being set up). Once the connection is established, a positive connection id is assigned to the connection.
New_id	Lists the connection id number that will be assigned to a connection, after the connection is set up. The New_id value will be a positive number from 0 to 299.
	If the New_id value is 0, there is no pending connection.
	If the New_id value is a positive integer, a connection is pending.
	As soon as the pending connection has been established, the New_id value will be transferred to the Conn_id for the established connection, and New_id will be reset to 0.

Table 24–2   *Show Crypto Connections Field Descriptions, Continued*

Field	Description
Alg	Identifies the DES encryption algorithm used for the current connection.
	10 = basic DES (56 bit) with 8-bit Cipher FeedBack (CFB)
	11 = basic DES (56 bit) with 64-bit CFB
	1 = 40-bit DES with 8-bit CFB
	2 = 40-bit DES with 64-bit CFB
	0 = no connection
Time	Identifies the time when the connection was initiated.
flags	PEND_CONN = identifies the table entry as a pending connection
	XCHG_KEYS = the connection has timed out; for encrypted communication to occur again, the router must first exchange DH numbers and generate a new session (DES) key
	TIME_KEYS = the encrypted communication session is currently in progress (a session key is currently installed, and the session is counting down to timeout)
	BAD_CONN = no existing or pending connection exists for this table entry
	UNK_STATUS = invalid status (error)

SHOW CRYPTO ENGINE BRIEF

To view all crypto engines within a Cisco 7200, RSP7000, or 7500 series router, use the **show crypto engine brief** privileged EXEC command.

   show crypto engine brief

Syntax Description

This command has no arguments or keywords.

Command Mode

Privileged EXEC

Usage Guidelines

This command first appeared in Cisco IOS Release 11.2.

This command is only available on Cisco 7200, RSP7000, and 7500 series routers.

Sample Display

The following is sample output from the **show crypto engine brief** command. In this example, the router has two crypto engines: a Cisco IOS crypto engine and a Encryption Service Adapter (ESA) crypto engine. Both crypto engines have Digital Signature Standard (DSS) keys generated.

```
Apricot# show crypto engine brief
crypto engine name:    ApricotESA
crypto engine type:    ESA
crypto engine state:   dss key generated
crypto firmware version:  5049702
crypto engine in slot: 1

crypto engine name:    ApricotIOS
crypto engine type:    software
crypto engine state:   dss key generated
crypto lib version:    2.0.0
crypto engine in slot: 4
```

Table 24–3 explains each field.

Table 24–3   *Show Crypto Engine Brief Field Descriptions*

Field	Description
crypto engine name	Name of the crypto engine as assigned with the *key-name* argument in the **crypto gen-signature-keys** command.
crypto engine type	If "software" is listed, the crypto engine resides in either the Route Switch Processor (RSP) (the Cisco IOS crypto engine) or in a second-generation Versatile Interface Processor (VIP2).
	If "crypto card" is listed, the crypto engine is associated with an Encryption Service Adapter (ESA).
crypto engine state	The state "installed" indicates that a crypto engine is located in the given slot, but is not configured for encryption.
	The state "dss key generated" indicates the crypto engine found in that slot has DSS keys already generated.
	In a Cisco 7200 series router, the state "installed (ESA pending)" indicates that the ESA crypto engine will be replaced with the Cisco IOS crypto engine as soon as it becomes available.
crypto firmware version	Version number of the crypto firmware running on the ESA.
crypto lib version	Version number of the crypto library running on the router.

Table 24–3 *Show Crypto Engine Brief Field Descriptions, Continued*

Field	Description
crypto engine in slot	Chassis slot number of the crypto engine. For the Cisco IOS crypto engine, this is the chassis slot number of the Route Switch Processor (RSP). For the VIP2 crypto engine, this is the chassis slot number of the VIP2. For the ESA crypto engine, this is the chassis slot number of the ESA (Cisco 7200) or of the VIP2 (Cisco RSP7000 and 7500).

Related Commands

Search online to find documentation for related commands.

show crypto engine configuration

SHOW CRYPTO ENGINE CONFIGURATION

To view the Cisco IOS crypto engine of your router, use the **show crypto engine configuration** privileged EXEC command.

> **show crypto engine configuration**

Syntax Description

This command has no arguments or keywords.

Command Mode

Privileged EXEC

Usage Guidelines

This command first appeared in Cisco IOS Release 11.2.

Sample Displays

The following is sample output from the **show crypto engine configuration** command for a Cisco 2500 series router:

```
Apricot# show crypto engine configuration
engine name:      Apricot
engine type:      software
serial number:    01709642
platform:         rp crypto engine

Encryption Process Info:
input queue top:    75
```

```
input queue bot:     75
input queue count:   0
```

The following is sample output from the **show crypto engine configuration** command for a Cisco 7500 series router:

```
Banana# show crypto engine configuration
engine name:         BananaIOS
engine type:         software
serial number:       02863239
platform:            rsp crypto engine

Encryption Process Info:
input queue top:     44
input queue bot:     44
input queue count:   0
```

Table 24–4 explains each field.

Table 24–4 *Show Crypto Engine Configuration Field Descriptions*

Field	Description
engine name	Name of the crypto engine as assigned with the *key-name* argument in the **crypto gen-signature-keys** command.
engine type	Should always display "software."
serial number	Serial number of the Route Processor or Route Switch Processor.
platform	If the router is a Cisco RSP7000 or 7500 series router, this field will display "rsp crypto engine."
	If the router is a Cisco 7200 series router, this field will display "rp crypto engine."
input queue top (Encryption Process Info)	The queue location of the (inbound) packet next in line to be processed (decrypted). This packet will come off the top of the circular queue next. (This field is useful for debugging purposes.)
input queue bot (Encryption Process Info)	The queue location of the (inbound) packet last in line to be processed (decrypted). The packet is the most recently received and queued at the bottom of the circular queue. (This field is useful for debugging purposes.)
input queue count (Encryption Process Info)	The total number of packets currently in the circular queue. These are inbound packets waiting for processing. (This field is useful for debugging purposes.)

Related Commands

Search online to find documentation for related commands.

show crypto engine brief

SHOW CRYPTO ENGINE CONNECTIONS ACTIVE

To view the current active encrypted session connections for all crypto engines, use the **show crypto engine connections active** privileged EXEC command.

    show crypto engine connections active [*slot*]

Syntax Description

slot   (Optional) Identifies the crypto engine. This argument is available only on Cisco 7200, RSP7000, and 7500 series routers.

                If no slot is specified, the Cisco IOS crypto engine will be selected.

                Use the chassis slot number of the crypto engine location. For the Cisco IOS crypto engine, this is the chassis slot number of the Route Switch Processor (RSP). For the VIP2 crypto engine, this is the chassis slot number of the VIP2. For the ESA crypto engine, this is the chassis slot number of the ESA (Cisco 7200) or of the VIP2 (Cisco RSP7000 and 7500).

Command Mode

Privileged EXEC

Usage Guidelines

This command first appeared in Cisco IOS Release 11.2.

Sample Display

The following is sample output from the **show crypto engine connections active** command:

```
Apricot# show crypto engine connections active
Connection Interface  IP-Address    State Algorithm    Encrypt Decrypt
2          Ethernet0  172.21.114.9  set   DES_56_CFB64 41      32
3          Ethernet1  172.29.13.2   set   DES_56_CFB64 110     65
4          Serial0    172.17.42.1   set   DES_56_CFB64 36      27
```

Table 24–5 explains each field.

Table 24–5 *Show Crypto Engine Connections Active Field Descriptions*

Field	Description
Connection	Identifies the connection by its number. Each active encrypted session connection is identified by a positive number from 1 to 299. These connection numbers correspond to the table entry numbers.
Interface	Identifies the interface involved in the encrypted session connection. This will display only the actual interface, not a subinterface (even if a subinterface is defined and used for the connection).

Table 24–5 *Show Crypto Engine Connections Active Field Descriptions, Continued*

Field	Description
IP-Address	Identifies the IP address of the interface.
	Note that if a subinterface is used for the connection, this field will display "unassigned."
State	The state "set" indicates an active connection.
Algorithm	Identifies the Data Encryption Standard (DES) algorithm used to encrypt/decrypt packets at the interface.
Encrypt	Shows the total number of encrypted outbound IP packets.
Decrypt	Shows the total number of decrypted inbound IP packets.

Related Commands

Search online to find documentation for related commands.

show crypto engine connections dropped-packets

SHOW CRYPTO ENGINE CONNECTIONS DROPPED-PACKETS

To view information about packets dropped during encrypted sessions for all router crypto engines, use the **show crypto engine connections dropped-packets** privileged EXEC command.

   show crypto engine connections dropped-packets

Syntax Description

This command has no arguments or keywords.

Command Mode

Privileged EXEC

Usage Guidelines

This command first appeared in Cisco IOS Release 11.2.

Sample Display

The following is sample output from the **show crypto engine connections dropped-packets** command:

```
Apricot# show crypto engine connections dropped-packets
Interface    IP-Address      Drop Count
Ethernet0/0  172.21.114.165 4
```

The Drop Count number indicates the total number of dropped packets for the lifetime of the crypto engine.

Related Commands

Search online to find documentation for related commands.

show crypto engine connections active

SHOW CRYPTO KEY-TIMEOUT

To view the current setting for the time duration of encrypted sessions, use the **show crypto key-timeout** privileged EXEC command.

> **show crypto key-timeout**

Syntax Description

This command has no arguments or keywords.

Command Mode

Privileged EXEC

Usage Guidelines

This command first appeared in Cisco IOS Release 11.2.

Sample Display

The following is sample output from the **show crypto key-timeout** command:

```
Apricot# show crypto key-timeout
Session keys will be re-negotiated every 120 minutes.
```

Related Commands

Search online to find documentation for related commands.

crypto key-timeout

SHOW CRYPTO MAP

To view all created crypto maps of your router, use the **show crypto map** privileged EXEC command.

> **show crypto map**

Syntax Description

This command has no arguments or keywords.

Command Mode

Privileged EXEC

Usage Guidelines

This command first appeared in Cisco IOS Release 11.2.

Sample Displays

The following is sample output from the **show crypto map** command performed at a Cisco 2500 series router.

```
Apricot# show crypto map

Crypto Map "Canada" 10
        Connection Id = UNSET    (2 established,    0 failed)
        Crypto Engine = ApricotIOS (2)
        Algorithm = 40-bit-des cfb-64
        Peer = Banana
        PE = 172.21.114.9
        UPE = 192.168.23.116
        Extended IP access list 101
                access-list 101 permit ip host 10.0.0.1 host 192.168.15.0
                access-list 101 permit ip host 172.21.114.9 host 192.168.23.116
```

The following is sample output from the **show crypto map** command performed at a Cisco 7500 series router. Two crypto maps are shown: a crypto map named ResearchSite with sub-definitions 10 and 20, and another crypto map named HQ.

```
Banana# show crypto map

Crypto Map "ResearchSite" 10
        Connection Id = 6        (6 established,    0 failed)
        Crypto Engine = BananaIOS (4)
        Algorithm = 40-bit-des cfb-64
        Peer = Apricot
        PE = 192.168.15.0
        UPE = 10.0.0.1
        Extended IP access list 102
                access-list 102 permit ip host 192.168.15.0 host 10.0.0.1
Crypto Map "ResearchSite" 20
        Connection Id = UNSET    (0 established,    0 failed)
        Crypto Engine = BananaIOS (4)
        Algorithm = 56-bit-des cfb-64
        Peer = Cantaloupe
        PE = 192.168.129.33
        UPE = 172.21.114.165
        Extended IP access list 103
                access-list 103 permit ip host 192.168.129.33 host 172.21.114.165
Crypto Map "HQ" 10
        Connection Id = UNSET    (3 established,    0 failed)
        Crypto Engine = BananaESA (2)
```

```
Algorithm = 56-bit-des cfb-64
Peer = Eggplant
PE = 192.168.129.10
UPE = 10.1.2.3
Extended IP access list 104
        access-list 104 permit ip host 192.168.129.10 host 10.1.2.3
```

The command output separately lists each crypto map subdefinition.

If more than one subdefinition exists for a crypto map, each subdefinition will be listed separately by sequence number (per the *seq-num* argument of the **crypto map (global configuration)** command). The sequence number is shown following the crypto map name.

Table 24–6 explains each field.

Table 24–6 *Show Crypto Map Field Descriptions*

Field	Description
Connection Id	Identifies the connection by its number. Each active encrypted session connection is identified by a positive number from 1 to 299. A value of UNSET indicates that no connection currently exists and is using the crypto map.
established	Indicates the total number of encrypted connections that have been successfully established using the crypto map.
failed	Indicates the total number of attempted encrypted connections that failed to be established while using the crypto map.
Crypto Engine	Lists the name of the governing crypto engine, followed by the crypto engine slot number in parentheses.
	The slot number could be the Route Switch Processor (RSP) slot number, indicating a Cisco IOS crypto engine, or a second-generation Versatile Interface Processor (VIP2) slot number, indicating a VIP2 or an ESA crypto engine, or (Cisco 7200 only) an ESA slot number, indicating an ESA crypto engine.
	(Not displayed on routers other than Cisco 7200, RSP7000, or 7500 series routers.)
Algorithm	Indicates the type of DES encryption algorithm used by the crypto map.
Peer	Indicates the name of the crypto map of the remote peer encrypting router.
PE	"Protected Entity." This shows a representative source IP address as specified in the crypto map's encryption access list. This IP address can be any host that matches a source in the encryption access list that is being used in the connection.

Table 24–6 *Show Crypto Map Field Descriptions, Continued*

Field	Description
UPE	"Unprotected Entity." This shows a representative destination IP address as specified in the crypto map's encryption access list. This IP address can be any host that matches a destination in the encryption access list that is being used in the connection.
Extended IP access list	Lists the access list associated with the crypto map. If no access list is associated, the message "No matching address list set" is displayed.

Related Commands

Search online to find documentation for related commands.

crypto map (global configuration)
crypto map (interface configuration)
show crypto map interface
show crypto map tag

SHOW CRYPTO MAP INTERFACE

To view the crypto map applied to a specific interface, use the **show crypto map interface** privileged EXEC command.

> **show crypto map interface** *interface*

Syntax Description

interface   Designates the router interface.

Command Mode

Privileged EXEC

Usage Guidelines

This command first appeared in Cisco IOS Release 11.2.

Sample Display

The following is sample output from the **show crypto map interface** command:

```
Apricot# show crypto map interface ethernet0

Crypto Map "ResearchSite" 10
        Connection Id = 6        (6 established,     0 failed)
        Crypto Engine = BananaIOS (4)
        Algorithm = 40-bit-des cfb-64
        Peer = Apricot
```

```
                PE = 192.168.15.0
                UPE = 10.0.0.1
                Extended IP access list 102
                        access-list 102 permit ip host 192.168.15.0 host 10.0.0.1
      Crypto Map "ResearchSite" 20
                Connection Id = UNSET     (0 established,     0 failed)
                Crypto Engine = BananaIOS (4)
                Algorithm = 56-bit-des cfb-64
                Peer = Cantaloupe
                PE = 192.168.129.33
                UPE = 172.21.114.165
                Extended IP access list 103
                        access-list 103 permit ip host 192.168.129.33 host 172.21.114.165
```

Table 24–7 explains each field.

Table 24–7 *Show Crypto Map Interface Field Descriptions*

Field	Description
Connection Id	Identifies the connection by its number. Each active encrypted session connection is identified by a positive number from 1 to 299. A value of UNSET indicates that no connection currently exists and is using the crypto map.
established	Indicates the total number of encrypted connections that have been successfully established using the crypto map.
failed	Indicates the total number of attempted encrypted connections that failed to be established while using the crypto map.
Crypto Engine	Lists the name of the governing crypto engine, followed by the crypto engine slot number in parentheses.
	The slot number could be the Route Switch Processor (RSP) slot number, indicating a Cisco IOS crypto engine, or a second-generation Versatile Interface Processor (VIP2) slot number, indicating a VIP2 or an ESA crypto engine, or (Cisco 7200 only) an ESA slot number, indicating an ESA crypto engine.
	(Not displayed on routers other than Cisco 7200, RSP7000, or 7500 series routers.)
Algorithm	Indicates the type of DES encryption algorithm used by the crypto map.
Peer	Indicates the name of the crypto map of the remote peer encrypting router.
PE	"Protected Entity." This shows a representative source IP address as specified in the crypto map's encryption access list. This IP address can be any host that matches a source in the encryption access list that is being used in the connection.

Table 24–7 *Show Crypto Map Interface Field Descriptions, Continued*

Field	Description
UPE	"Unprotected Entity." This shows a representative destination IP address as specified in the crypto map's encryption access list. This IP address can be any host that matches a destination in the encryption access list that is being used in the connection.
Extended IP access list	Lists the access list associated with the crypto map. If no access list is associated, the message "No matching address list set" is displayed.

Related Commands

Search online to find documentation for related commands.

crypto map (global configuration)
crypto map (interface configuration)
show crypto map
show crypto map tag

SHOW CRYPTO MAP TAG

To view a specific crypto map, use the **show crypto map tag** privileged EXEC command.

> **show crypto map tag** *map-name*

Syntax Description

map-name   Identifies the crypto map by its name. This should match the map-name argument assigned during crypto map creation.

Command Mode

Privileged EXEC

Usage Guidelines

This command first appeared in Cisco IOS Release 11.2.

Sample Display

The following is sample output from the **show crypto map tag** command:

```
Apricot# show crypto map tag HQ

Crypto Map "HQ" 10
        Connection Id = UNSET    (3 established,    0 failed)
        Crypto Engine = BananaESA (2)
        Algorithm = 56-bit-des cfb-64
        Peer = Eggplant
```

```
PE = 192.168.129.10
UPE = 10.1.2.3
Extended IP access list 104
        access-list 104 permit ip host 192.168.129.10 host 10.1.2.3
```

Table 24–8 explains each field.

Table 24–8 *Show Crypto Map Tag Field Descriptions*

Field	Description
Connection Id	Identifies the connection by its number. Each active encrypted session connection is identified by a positive number from 1 to 299. A value of UNSET indicates that no connection currently exists and is using the crypto map.
established	Indicates the total number of encrypted connections that have been successfully established using the crypto map.
failed	Indicates the total number of attempted encrypted connections that failed to be established while using the crypto map.
Crypto Engine	Lists the name of the governing crypto engine, followed by the crypto engine slot number in parentheses.
	The slot number could be the Route Switch Processor (RSP) slot number, indicating a Cisco IOS crypto engine, or a second-generation Versatile Interface Processor (VIP2) slot number, indicating a VIP2 or an ESA crypto engine, or (Cisco 7200 only) an ESA slot number, indicating an ESA crypto engine.
	(Not displayed on routers other than Cisco 7200, RSP7000, or 7500 series routers.)
Algorithm	Indicates the type of DES encryption algorithm used by the crypto map.
Peer	Indicates the name of the crypto map of the remote peer encrypting router.
PE	"Protected Entity." This shows a representative source IP address as specified in the crypto map's encryption access list. This IP address can be any host that matches a source in the encryption access list that is being used in the connection.
UPE	"Unprotected Entity." This shows a representative destination IP address as specified in the crypto map's encryption access list. This IP address can be any host that matches a destination in the encryption access list that is being used in the connection.
Extended IP access list	Lists the access list associated with the crypto map. If no access list is associated, the message "No matching address list set" is displayed.

Related Commands

Search online to find documentation for related commands.

crypto map (global configuration)
crypto map (interface configuration)
show crypto map
show crypto map interface

SHOW CRYPTO MYPUBKEY

To view Digital Signature Standard (DSS) public keys (for all your router crypto engines) in hexadecimal form, use the **show crypto mypubkey** EXEC command.

> **show crypto mypubkey [rsp]**

Syntax Description

rsp   (Optional) This argument is available only on Cisco 7200, RSP7000, and 7500 series routers.

If this argument is used, only the DSS public keys for the Route Switch Processor (RSP) (Cisco IOS crypto engine) will be displayed.

If this argument is not used, DSS public keys for all crypto engines will be displayed.

Command Mode

EXEC

Usage Guidelines

This command first appeared in Cisco IOS Release 11.2.

Sample Display

The following is sample output from the **show crypto mypubkey** command for a Cisco 2500 series router with a crypto engine called "Apricot.branch":

```
Apricot# show crypto mypubkey

crypto public-key Apricot.branch 01709642
BDD99A6E EEE53D30 BC0BFAE6 948C40FB 713510CB 32104137 91B06C8D C2D5B422
D9C154CA 00CDE99B 425DB9FD FE3162F1 1E5866AF CF66DD33 677259FF E5C24812
quit
```

Related Commands

Search online to find documentation for related commands.

show crypto pubkey
show crypto pubkey name
show crypto pubkey serial

SHOW CRYPTO PREGEN-DH-PAIRS

To view the number of Diffie-Hellman (DH) number pairs currently generated, use the **show crypto pregen-dh-pairs** privileged EXEC command.

> **show crypto pregen-dh-pairs** [*slot*]

Syntax Description

slot   (Optional) Identifies the crypto engine. This argument is available only on Cisco 7200, RSP7000, and 7500 series routers.

If no slot is specified, the Cisco IOS crypto engine will be selected.

Use the chassis slot number of the crypto engine location. For the Cisco IOS crypto engine, this is the chassis slot number of the Route Switch Processor (RSP). For the VIP2 crypto engine, this is the chassis slot number of the VIP2. For the ESA crypto engine, this is the chassis slot number of the ESA (Cisco 7200) or of the VIP2 (Cisco RSP7000 and 7500).

Command Mode

Privileged EXEC

Usage Guidelines

This command first appeared in Cisco IOS Release 11.2.

Sample Display

The following is sample output from the **show crypto pregen-dh-pairs** command:

```
Apricot# show crypto pregen-dh-pairs

Number of pregenerated DH pairs: 1
```

The number 1 shown in the output indicates that there is one DH number pair ready and available for the next encrypted connection.

Related Commands

Search online to find documentation for related commands.

crypto pregen-dh-pairs

SHOW CRYPTO PUBKEY

To view all peer router Digital Signature Standard (DSS) public keys known to your router, use the **show crypto pubkey** EXEC command.

> **show crypto pubkey**

Syntax Description

This command has no arguments or keywords.

Command Mode

EXEC

Usage Guidelines

This command first appeared in Cisco IOS Release 11.2.

Sample Display

The following is sample output from the **show crypto pubkey** command. In this example, router Apricot has exchanged DSS public keys with two other routers, named Banana and Cantaloupe. Banana has a crypto engine named BananaESA, and Cantaloupe has a crypto engine named CantaloupeIOS:

```
Apricot# show crypto pubkey

crypto public-key BananaESA 01580120
8A1D0765 DE172C96 3DE9575D D1EEC69B A40107CA D0E2C55D CC17D6E9 3D45D042
DD4959AA BFC556EC AF5B2931 90FC883B 48F7A61A 9C9E5C25 06775ECB E1EDC966
quit
crypto public-key CantaloupeIOS 00198A0F
BBCD227D B8630AAA F888B6DC A9D64781 108FF9A1 157645C9 52F96EC0 6FB9E5F3
51BA8A76 2DFA532B 48856D46 B91B74C3 C2FEB617 85916A3F 27C8A9C2 311CF872
quit
```

Related Commands

Search online to find documentation for related commands.

crypto gen-signature-keys
crypto key-exchange
show crypto pubkey
show crypto pubkey name
show crypto pubkey serial

SHOW CRYPTO PUBKEY NAME

To view a specific peer router Digital Signature Standard (DSS) public key known by its name, use the **show crypto pubkey name** EXEC command.

> **show crypto pubkey name** *key-name*

Syntax Description

key-name   Identifies the crypto engine of the peer router.

Command Mode

EXEC

Usage Guidelines

This command first appeared in Cisco IOS Release 11.2.

Sample Display

The following is sample output from the **show crypto pubkey name** command. In this example, router Apricot has exchanged DSS public keys with a router named Banana. Banana has a crypto engine named BananaESA:

```
Apricot# show crypto pubkey name BananaESA

crypto public-key BananaESA 01580120
8A1D0765 DE172C96 3DE9575D D1EEC69B A40107CA D0E2C55D CC17D6E9 3D45D042
DD4959AA BFC556EC AF5B2931 90FC883B 48F7A61A 9C9E5C25 06775ECB E1EDC966
quit
```

Related Commands

Search online to find documentation for related commands.

show crypto mypubkey
show crypto pubkey
show crypto pubkey serial

SHOW CRYPTO PUBKEY SERIAL

To view a specific peer router Digital Signature Standard (DSS) public key known by its serial number, use the **show crypto pubkey serial** EXEC command.

   show crypto pubkey serial *serial-number*

Syntax Description

serial-number   Identifies the serial number of the crypto engine.

Command Mode

EXEC

Usage Guidelines

This command first appeared in Cisco IOS Release 11.2.

Part IV

Command Reference

Sample Display

The following is sample output from the **show crypto pubkey serial** command. In this example, router Apricot has exchanged DSS public keys with a router named Cantaloupe. Cantaloupe has a crypto engine with the serial number 00198A0F:

```
Apricot# show crypto pubkey serial 00198A0F

crypto public-key cantaloupeIOS 00198A0F
BBCD227D B8630AAA F888B6DC A9D64781 108FF9A1 157645C9 52F96EC0 6FB9E5F3
51BA8A76 2DFA532B 48856D46 B91B74C3 C2FEB617 85916A3F 27C8A9C2 311CF872
quit
```

Related Commands

Search online to find documentation for related commands.

show crypto mypubkey
show crypto pubkey
show crypto pubkey name

TEST CRYPTO INITIATE-SESSION

To set up a test encryption session, use the **test crypto initiate-session** privileged EXEC command.

    test crypto initiate-session *src-ip-addr dst-ip-addr map-name seq-num*

Syntax Description

src-ip-addr	IP address of source host. Should be included in an encryption access list definition as a valid IP address source address.
dst-ip-addr	IP address of destination host. Should be included in an encryption access list definition as a valid IP address destination address.
map-name	Names the crypto map to be used.
seq-num	Names the crypto map sequence number.

Command Mode

Privileged EXEC

Usage Guidelines

This command first appeared in Cisco IOS Release 11.2.

Use this command to set up a test encryption session. This command can be used after you have completed all the essential encryption configuration tasks for your router. After issuing this command, use the **show crypto connections** command to verify the status of the connection just created.

Example

The following example sets up and verifies a test encryption session.

Router Apricot sets up a test encryption session with router Banana and then views the connection status to verify a successful encrypted session connection.

Step 1   Router Apricot sets up a test encryption connection with router Banana.

```
Apricot# test crypto initiate-session 192.168.3.12 192.168.204.110
BananaESA.TXbranch 10
Sending CIM to: 192.168.204.110 from: 192.168.3.12.
Connection id: -1
```

Notice the Connection id value is -1. A negative value indicates that the connection is being set up. (CIM stands for Connection Initiation Message.)

Step 2   Router Apricot issues the **show crypto connections** command.

```
Apricot# show crypto connections
Pending Connection Table
PE                UPE               Timestamp             Conn_id
192.168.3.10      192.168.204.100 Mar 01 1993 00:01:09  -1


Connection Table
PE                UPE               Conn_id New_id  Alg    Time
192.168.3.10      192.168.204.100 -1       1       0      Not Set
                  flags:PEND_CONN
```

Look in the Pending Connection Table for an entry with a Conn_id value equal to the previously shown Connection id value—in this case, look for an entry with a Conn_id value of -1. If this is the first time an encrypted connection has been attempted, there will only be one entry (as shown).

Note the PE and UPE addresses for this entry.

Step 3   Now, look in the Connection Table for an entry with the same PE and UPE addresses. In this case, there is only one entry in both tables, so finding the right Connection Table entry is easy.

Step 4   At the Connection Table entry, note the Conn_id and New_id values. In this case, Conn_id equals -1, and New_id equals 1. The New_id value of 1 will be assigned to the test connection when setup is complete. (Positive numbers are assigned to established, active connections.)

Step 5   Apricot waits a moment for the test connection to set up, and then reissues the **show crypto connections** command.

```
Apricot# show crypto connections
Connection Table
```

```
PE               UPE              Conn_id New_id  Alg    Time
192.168.3.10     192.168.204.100 1       0       10     Mar 01 1993 00:02:00
                 flags:TIME_KEYS
```

Again, look for the Connection Table entry with the same PE and UPE addresses as shown before. In this entry, notice that the Conn_id value has changed to 1. This indicates that our test connection has been successfully established, because the Conn_id value has changed to match the New_id value of Step 4. Also, New_id has been reset to 0 at this point., indicating that there are no new connections currently being set up.

In the command output of Step 5, there is no longer a Pending Connection Table being displayed, which indicates that there are currently no pending connections. This is also a good clue that the test connection was successfully established.

The **show crypto connections** command is explained in greater detail previously in this chapter, including a description of how connection ids are assigned during and following connection setup.

Related Commands

Search online to find documentation for related commands.

show crypto connections

PART V

Other Security Features

## CHAPTER 25

Configuring Passwords and Privileges

Using passwords and assigning privilege levels is a simple way of providing terminal access control in your network.

This chapter describes the following topics and tasks:

- Protecting Access to Privilege EXEC Commands
- Encrypting Passwords
- Configuring Multiple Privilege Levels
- Recovering a Lost Enable Password
- Recovering a Lost Line Password
- Configuring Identification Support

For a complete description of the commands used in this chapter, see Chapter 26, "Passwords and Privileges Commands." For configuration examples using the commands in this chapter, refer to section "Passwords and Privileges Configuration Examples," located at the end of the this chapter.

PROTECTING ACCESS TO PRIVILEGE EXEC COMMANDS

The following tasks provide a way to control access to the system configuration file and privilege EXEC (enable) commands:

- Set or Change a Static Enable Password
- Protect Passwords with Enable Password and Enable Secret
- Set or Change a Line Password
- Set TACACS Password Protection for Privilege EXEC Mode

Set or Change a Static Enable Password

To set or change a static password that controls access to privileged EXEC (enable) mode, perform the following task in global configuration mode:

Task	Command
Establish a new password or change an existing password for the privileged command level.	**enable password** *password*

For examples of how to define enable passwords for different privilege levels, see section "Multiple Levels of Privileges Examples" at the end of this chapter.

Protect Passwords with Enable Password and Enable Secret

To provide an additional layer of security, particularly for passwords that cross the network or are stored on a TFTP server, you can use either the **enable password** or **enable secret** commands. Both commands accomplish the same thing; that is, they allow you to establish an encrypted password that users must enter to access enable mode (the default), or any privilege level you specify.

We recommend that you use the **enable secret** command, because it uses an improved encryption algorithm. Use the **enable password** command only if you boot an older image of the Cisco IOS software, or if you boot older boot ROMs that do not recognize the **enable secret** command.

If you configure the **enable secret** command, it takes precedence over the **enable password** command; the two commands cannot be in effect simultaneously.

To configure the router to require an enable password, perform one of the following tasks in global configuration mode:

Task	Command
Establish a password for a privilege command mode.	**enable password** [**level** *level*] {*password* | *encryption-type encrypted-password*}
Specify a secret password, saved using a non-reversible encryption method. (When enable password and enable secret are both set, users must enter the enable secret password.)	**enable secret** [**level** *level*] {*password* | *encryption-type encrypted-password*}

Use either of these commands with the **level** option to define a password for a specific privilege level. After you specify the level and set a password, give the password only to users who need to have access at this level. Use the **privilege level** configuration command to specify commands accessible at various levels.

If you have the **service password-encryption** command enabled, the password you enter is encrypted. When you display it with the **show running-config** command, it is displayed in encrypted form.

If you specify an encryption type, you must provide an encrypted password—an encrypted password you copy from another router configuration.

NOTES

You cannot recover a lost encrypted password. You must clear NVRAM and set a new password. See section "Recovering a Lost Enable Password" or section "Recovering a Lost Line Password" in this chapter if you have lost or forgotten your password.

Set or Change a Line Password

To set or change a password on a line, perform the following task in global configuration mode:

Task	Command
Establish a new password or change an existing password for the privileged command level.	**password** *password*

Set TACACS Password Protection for Privilege EXEC Mode

You can set the TACACS protocol to determine whether a user can access privileged EXEC (enable) mode. To do so, perform the following task in global configuration mode:

Task	Command
Set the TACACS-style user ID and password-checking mechanism at the privileged EXEC level.	**enable use-tacacs**

When you set TACACS password protection at the privileged EXEC mode, the **enable** EXEC command prompts for both a new username and a password. This information is then passed to the TACACS server for authentication. If you are using the extended TACACS, it also passes any existing UNIX user identification code to the TACACS server.

CAUTION

If you use the **enable use-tacacs** command, you must also specify **tacacs-server authenticate enable**, or you will be locked out of the privilege EXEC (enable) mode.

When used without extended TACACS, the **enable use-tacacs** command allows anyone with a valid username and password to access the privileged EXEC mode, creating a potential security problem. This occurs because the TACACS query resulting from entering the **enable** command is indistinguishable from an attempt to log in without extended TACACS.

ENCRYPTING PASSWORDS

Because protocol analyzers can examine packets (and read passwords), you can increase access security by configuring the Cisco IOS software to encrypt passwords. Encryption prevents the password from being readable in the configuration file.

Configure the Cisco IOS software to encrypt passwords by performing the following task in global configuration mode:

Task	Command
Encrypt a password.	service password-encryption

The actual encryption process occurs when the current configuration is written or when a password is configured. Password encryption is applied to all passwords, including authentication key passwords, the privileged command password, console and virtual terminal line access passwords, and BGP neighbor passwords. The **service password-encryption** command is primarily useful for keeping unauthorized individuals from viewing your password in your configuration file.

CAUTION

The **service password-encryption** command does not provide a high level of network security. If you use this command, you should also take additional network security measures.

Although you cannot recover a lost encrypted password (that is, you cannot get the original password back), you can recover from a lost encrypted password. See section "Recovering a Lost Enable Password" or section "Recovering a Lost Line Password" in this chapter if you have lost or forgotten your password.

CONFIGURING MULTIPLE PRIVILEGE LEVELS

By default, the Cisco IOS software has two modes of password security: user mode (EXEC) and privilege mode (enable). You can configure up to 16 hierarchical levels of commands for each mode. By configuring multiple passwords, you can allow different sets of users to have access to specified commands.

For example, if you want the **configure** command to be available to a more restricted set of users than the **clear line** command, you can assign level 2 security to the **clear line** command and distribute the level 2 password fairly widely, and assign level 3 security to the **configure** command and distribute the password to level 3 commands to fewer users.

The following tasks describe how to configure additional levels of security:

- Set the Privilege Level for a Command
- Change the Default Privilege Level for Lines
- Display Current Privilege Levels
- Log In to a Privilege Level

Set the Privilege Level for a Command

To set the privilege level for a command, perform the following tasks in global configuration mode:

Task	Command
Set the privilege level for a command.	**privilege** *mode* **level** *level command*
Specify the enable password for a privilege level.	**enable password level** *level* [*encryption-type*] *password*

Change the Default Privilege Level for Lines

To change the default privilege level for a given line or a group of lines, perform the following task in line configuration mode:

Task	Command
Specify a default privilege level for a line.	**privilege level** *level*

Display Current Privilege Levels

To display the current privilege level you can access based on the password you used, perform the following task in EXEC mode:

Task	Command
Display your current privilege level.	**show privilege**

Log In to a Privilege Level

To log in to a router at a specified privilege level, perform the following task in EXEC mode:

Task	Command
Log in to a specified privilege level.	**enable** *level*

To exit to a specified privilege level, perform the following task in EXEC mode:

Task	Command
Exit to a specified privilege level.	**disable** *level*

RECOVERING A LOST ENABLE PASSWORD

You can restore access to enable mode on a router when the password is lost using one of the three procedures described in this section. The procedure you use depends on your router platform. Table 25–1 shows which password recovery procedure to use with each router platform.

You can perform password recovery on most of the platforms without changing hardware jumpers, but all platforms require the configuration to be reloaded. Password recovery can be done only from the console port on the router.

Table 25–1   *Platform-Specific Password Recovery Procedures*

Password Recovery Procedure	Router Platform
Password Recovery Procedure 1	Cisco 2000 series
	Cisco 2500 series
	Cisco 3000 series
	Cisco 4000 series with 680x0 Motorola CPU
	Cisco 7000 series running Cisco IOS Release 10.0 or later in ROMs installed on the RP card
	IGS series running Cisco Release IOS 9.1 or later in ROMs
Password Recovery Procedure 2	Cisco 1003
	Cisco 1600 series
	Cisco 3600 series
	Cisco 4500 series
	Cisco 7200 series
	Cisco 7500 series
	IDT Orion-based routers
	AS5200 and AS5300 platforms

Password Recovery Process

Both password recovery procedures involve the following basic steps:

Step 1   Configure the router to boot up without reading the configuration memory (NVRAM). This is sometimes called the test system mode.

Step 2   Reboot the system.

Step 3   Access enable mode (which can be done without a password if you are in test system mode).

Step 4   View or change the password, or erase the configuration.

Step 5   Reconfigure the router to boot up and read the NVRAM as it normally does.

Step 6   Reboot the system.

NOTES

Some password recovery requires that a terminal issue a Break signal; you must be familiar with how your terminal or PC terminal emulator issues this signal. For example, in ProComm, the keys Alt-B by default generates the Break signal, and in a Windows terminal you press Break or CTRL-Break. A Windows terminal also allows you to define a function key as a BREAK signal. To do so, select function keys from the Terminal window and define one as Break by entering the characters ^$B (**Shift 6**, **Shift 4**, and uppercase **B**).

Password Recovery Procedure 1

Use this procedure to recover lost passwords on the following Cisco routers:

- Cisco 2000 series
- Cisco 2500 series
- Cisco 3000 series
- Cisco 4000 series with 680x0 Motorola CPU
- Cisco 7000 series running Cisco IOS Release 10.0 or later in ROMs installed on the RP card.
  The router can be booting Cisco IOS Release 10.0 software in Flash memory, but it needs the actual ROMs on the processor card too.
- IGS Series running Cisco IOS Release 9.1 or later in ROMs

To recover a password using Procedure 1, perform the following steps:

Step 1   Attach a terminal or PC with terminal emulation software to the console port of the router.

Step 2   Enter the **show version** command and record the setting of the configuration register. It is usually 0x2102 or 0x102.

The configuration register value is on the last line of the display. Note whether the configuration register is set to enable Break or disable Break.

The factory-default configuration register value is 0x2102. Notice that the third digit from the left in this value is 1, which disables Break. If the third digit is *not* 1, Break is enabled.

Step 3   Turn off the router, then turn it on.

Step 4   Press the **Break** key on the terminal within 60 seconds of turning on the router.

The rommon> prompt with no router name appears. If it does not appear, the terminal is not sending the correct Break signal. In that case, check the terminal or terminal emulation setup.

Step 5   Enter **o/r0x42** at the rommon> prompt to boot from Flash memory or **o/r0x41** to boot from the boot ROMs.

Note that the first character is the letter o, not the numeral zero. If you have Flash memory and it is intact, 0x42 is the best setting. Use 0x41 only if the Flash memory is erased or not installed. If you use 0x41, you can only view or erase the configuration. You cannot change the password.

Step 6   At the rommon> prompt, enter the initialize command to initialize the router.

This causes the router to reboot but ignore its saved configuration and use the image in Flash memory instead.

The system configuration display appears.

Step 7   Enter **no** in response to the System Configuration Dialog prompts until the following message appears:
```
Press RETURN to get started!
```

Step 8   Press **Return**.

The Router> prompt appears.

Step 9   Enter the **enable** command.

The Router# prompt appears.

Step 10   Choose one of the following options:

- To view the password, if it is not encrypted, enter the **show startup-config** command.

- To change the password (if it is encrypted, for example), enter the **configure terminal** command to make the changes to the configuration, or the **write memory** command to save the changes to NVRAM. For example:
```
Router # configure terminal
Router(config)# enable password 1234abcd
Router(config)# ctrl-z
Router # write memory
```

- To erase the configuration, enter the **write erase** command.

Step 11   Enter the **configure terminal** command at the EXEC prompt to enter configuration mode.

Step 12   Enter the **config-register** command and whatever value you recorded in Step 2.

Step 13   Press **Ctrl-Z** to quit from the configuration editor.

Step 14   Enter the **reload** command at the privileged EXEC prompt and issue the **write memory** command to save the configuration.

Password Recovery Procedure 2

Use this procedure to recover lost passwords on the following Cisco routers:

- Cisco 1003
- Cisco 1600 series
- Cisco 3600 series
- Cisco 4500 series
- Cisco 7200 series
- Cisco 7500 series
- IDT Orion-Based Routers
- AS5200 and AS5300 platforms

To recover a password using Procedure 2, perform the following steps:

Step 1   Attach a terminal or PC with terminal emulation software to the console port of the router.

Step 2   Enter the **show version** command and record the setting of the configuration register. It is usually 0x2102 or 0x102.

The configuration register value is on the last line of the display. Note whether the configuration register is set to enable Break or disable Break.

The factory-default configuration register value is 0x2102. Notice that the third digit from the left in this value is 1, which disables Break. If the third digit is *not* 1, Break is enabled.

Step 3   Turn off the router, then turn it on.

Step 4   Press the **Break** key on the terminal within 60 seconds of turning on the router.

The rommon> prompt appears. If it doesn't appear, the terminal is not sending the correct Break signal. In that case, check the terminal or terminal emulation setup.

Step 5   Enter the **config-register** command at the rommon> prompt.

The following prompt appears:

```
Do you wish to change configuration[y/n]?
```

Step 6   Enter **yes** and press **Return.**

Step 7   Enter **no** to subsequent questions until the following prompt appears:

```
ignore system config info[y/n]?
```

Step 8   Enter **yes.**

Step 9   Enter **no** to subsequent questions until the following prompt appears:

```
change boot characteristics[y/n]?
```

Step 10   Enter **yes.**

The following prompt appears:

```
enter to boot:
```

Step 11   At this prompt, either enter **2** and press Return if Flash memory or, if Flash memory is erased, enter **1**. If Flash memory is erased, the Cisco 4500 must be returned to Cisco for service. If you enter **1**, you can only view or erase the configuration. You cannot change the password.

A configuration summary is displayed and the following prompt appears:

```
Do you wish to change configuration[y/n]?
```

Step 12   Answer **no** and press **Return.**

The following prompt appears:

```
rommon>
```

Step 13   Enter the **reload** command at the privileged EXEC prompt or, for Cisco 4500 series and Cisco 7500 series routers, power cycle the router.

Step 14   As the router boots, enter **no** to all the setup questions until the following prompt appears:

```
Router>
```

Step 15   Enter the **enable** command to enter enable mode.

The Router# prompt appears.

Step 16   Choose one of the following options:

- To view the password, enter the **show configuration** command.
- To change the password (if it is encrypted, for example), enter the **configure terminal** command to make the changes to the configuration, and enter the **write memory** command to save the changes. For example:

```
Router # configure terminal
Router (config)# enable password 1234abcd
Router (config)# ctrl-z
Router # write memory
```

- To Erase the configuration, enter the **write erase** command.

Step 17   Enter the **configure terminal** command at the prompt.

Step 18   Enter the **config-register** command and whatever value you recorded in Step 2.

Step 19   Press **Ctrl-Z** to quit from the configuration editor.

Step 20   Enter the **reload** command at the prompt and issue the **write memory** command to save the configuration.

RECOVERING A LOST LINE PASSWORD

If your router has the nonvolatile memory option, you can accidentally lock yourself out of enable mode if you enable password checking on the console terminal line and then forget the line password. To recover a lost line password, perform the following steps:

Step 1   Force the router into factory diagnostic mode.

            See the hardware installation and maintenance publication for your product for specific information about setting the processor configuration register to factory diagnostic mode. Table 25–2 summarizes the hardware or software settings required by various products to set factory diagnostic mode.

Step 2   Enter **Yes** when asked if you want to set the manufacturers' addresses.

            The following prompt appears:

```
TEST-SYSTEM >
```

Step 3   Issue the **enable** command to enter enable mode:

```
TEST-SYSTEM > enable
```

Step 4   Enter the **show startup-config** command to review the system configuration and find the password. Do not change anything in the factory diagnostic mode.

```
TEST-SYSTEM # show startup-config
```

Step 5   To resume normal operation, restart the router or reset the configuration register.

Step 6   Log in to the router with the password that was shown in the configuration file.

NOTES

All debugging capabilities are turned on during diagnostic mode.

See the hardware installation and maintenance publication for your product for specific information about configuring the processor configuration register for factory diagnostic mode. Table 25–2 summarizes the hardware or software settings required by the various products to set factory diagnostic mode.

Table 25–2 *Factory Diagnostic Mode Settings for the Configuration Register*

Platform	Setting
Modular products	Set jumper in bit 15 of the processor configuration register, then restart; remove the jumper when finished.
Cisco AS5100 Cisco AS5200 Cisco AS5300 Cisco 1600 series Cisco 2500 series Cisco 3000 series Cisco 3600 series Cisco 4000 series Cisco 4500 series Cisco 7000 series Cisco 7200 series Cisco 7500 series	Use the **config-register** command to set the processor configuration register to 0x8000, then **initialize** and **boot** the system. Use the **reload** command to restart and set the processor configuration register to 0x2102 when finished.

CONFIGURING IDENTIFICATION SUPPORT

Identification support allows you to query a Transmission Control Protocol (TCP) port for identification. This feature enables an unsecure protocol, described in RFC 1413, to report the identity of a client initiating a TCP connection and a host responding to the connection. With identification support, you can connect a TCP port on a host, issue a simple text string to request information, and receive a simple text-string reply.

To configure identification support, perform the following task in global configuration mode:

Task	Command
Enable identification support.	ip identd

PASSWORDS AND PRIVILEGES CONFIGURATION EXAMPLES

This section describes multiple privilege level and username authentication examples and contains the following sections:

- Multiple Levels of Privileges Examples
- Username Examples

Multiple Levels of Privileges Examples

This section provides examples of using multiple privilege levels to specify who can access different sets of commands.

Allow Users to Clear Lines Examples

If you want to allow users to clear lines, you can do either of the following:

- Change the privilege level for the **clear** and **clear line** commands to 1 or "ordinary user level," as follows. This allows any user to clear lines.

  ```
  privilege exec level 1 clear line
  ```

- Change the privilege level for the **clear** and **clear line** commands to level 2. To do so, use the **privilege level** global configuration command to specify privilege level 2. Then define an enable password for privilege level 2 and tell only those users who need to know what the password is.

  ```
  enable password level 2 pswd2
  privilege exec level 2 clear line
  ```

Define an Enable Password for System Operators Examples

In the following example, you define an enable password for privilege level 10 for system operators and make **clear** and **debug** commands available to anyone with that privilege level enabled.

```
enable password level 10 pswd10
privilege exec level 10 clear line
privilege exec level 10 debug ppp chap
privilege exec level 10 debug ppp error
privilege exec level 10 debug ppp negotiation
```

The following example lowers the privilege level of the **show running-config** command and most configuration commands to operator level so that the configuration can be viewed by an operator. It leaves the privilege level of the **configure** command at 15. Individual configuration commands are displayed in the **show running-config** output only if the privilege level for a command has been lowered to 10. Users are allowed to see only those commands that have a privilege level less than or equal to their current privilege level.

```
enable password level 15 pswd15
privilege exec level 15 configure
enable password level 10 pswd10
privilege exec level 10 show running-config
```

Disable a Privilege Level Example

In the following example, the **show ip route** command is set to privilege level 15. To keep all **show ip** and **show** commands from also being set to privilege level 15, these commands are specified to be privilege level 1.

```
privilege exec level 15 show ip route
privilege exec level 1 show ip
privilege exec level 1 show
```

Username Examples

The following sample configuration sets up secret passwords on Routers A, B, and C to enable the three routers to connect to each other.

To authenticate connections between Routers A and B, enter the following commands:

On Router A:

```
username B password a-b_secret
```

On Router B:

```
username A password a-b_secret
```

To authenticate connections between Routers A and C, enter the following commands:

On Router A:

```
username C password a-c_secret
```

On Router C:

```
username A password a-c_secret
```

To authenticate connections between Routers B and C, enter the following commands:

On Router B:

```
username C password b-c_secret
```

On Router C:

```
username B password b-c_secret
```

For example, suppose you enter the following command:

```
username bill password westward
```

The system displays this command as follows:

```
username bill password 7 21398211
```

The encrypted version of the password is 21398211. The password was encrypted by the Cisco-defined encryption algorithm, as indicated by the "7."

However, if you enter the following command, the system determines that the password is already encrypted and performs no encryption. Instead, it displays the command exactly as you entered it:

```
username bill password 7 21398211
username bill password 7 21398211
```

CHAPTER 26

Passwords and Privileges Commands

This chapter describes the commands used to establish password protection and configure privilege levels. Password protection lets you restrict access to a network or a network device. Privilege levels let you define what commands users can issue after they have logged in to a network device.

For information on how to establish password protection or configure privilege levels, see Chapter 25, "Configuring Passwords and Privileges." For configuration examples using the commands in this chapter, see section "Passwords and Privilege Levels Configuration Examples," located at the end of Chapter 25.

ENABLE

To log on to the router at a specified level, use the **enable** EXEC command.

```
enable [level]
```

Syntax Description

level   (Optional) Defines the privilege level that a user logs in to on the router.

Default

Level 15

Command Mode

EXEC

Usage Guidelines

This command first appeared in Cisco IOS Release 10.0.

NOTES

The enable command is associated with privilege level 0. If you configure AAA authorization for a privilege level greater than 0, this command will not be included in the privilege level command set.

Example

In the following example, the user is logging on to privilege level 5 on a router:
```
enable 5
```

Related Commands

Search online to find documentation for related commands.

disable
privilege level (global)
privilege level (line)

ENABLE PASSWORD

To set a local password to control access to various privilege levels, use the **enable password** global configuration command. Use the **no** form of this command to remove the password requirement.

> **enable password** [**level** *level*] {*password* | *encryption-type encrypted-password*}
> **no enable password** [**level** *level*]

Syntax Description

level *level*	(Optional) Level for which the password applies. You can specify up to 16 privilege levels, using numbers 0 through 15. Level 1 is normal EXEC-mode user privileges. If this argument is not specified in the command or the **no** form of the command, the privilege level defaults to 15 (traditional enable privileges).
password	Password users type to enter enable mode.
encryption-type	(Optional) Cisco-proprietary algorithm used to encrypt the password. Currently the only encryption type available is 7. If you specify *encryption-type*, the next argument you supply must be an encrypted password (a password already encrypted by a Cisco router).
encrypted-password	Encrypted password you enter, copied from another router configuration.

Default

No password is defined. The default is level 15.

Command Mode

Global configuration

Usage Guidelines

This command first appeared in Cisco IOS Release 10.0.

Use this command with the **level** option to define a password for a specific privilege level. After you specify the level and the password, give the password to the users who need to access this level. Use the **privilege level (global)** configuration command to specify commands accessible at various levels.

You will not ordinarily enter an encryption type. Typically, you enter an encryption type only if you copy and paste into this command a password that has already been encrypted by a Cisco router.

CAUTION

If you specify an encryption type and then enter a cleartext password, you will not be able to re-enter enable mode. You cannot recover a lost password that has been encrypted by any method.

If the **service password-encryption** command is set, the encrypted form of the password you create with the **enable password** command is displayed when a **show startup-config** command is entered.

You can enable or disable password encryption with the **service password-encryption** command.

An enable password is defined as follows:

- Must contain from 1 to 25 uppercase and lowercase alphanumeric characters.
- Must not have a number as the first character.
- Can have leading spaces, but they are ignored. However, intermediate and trailing spaces are recognized.
- Can contain the question mark (?) character if you precede the question mark with the key combination Crtl-V when you create the password; for example, to create the password *abc?123*, do the following:
  - Enter **abc**
  - Type **Crtl-V**
  - Enter **?123**

  When the system prompts you to enter the enable password, you need not precede the question mark with the **Ctrl-V**; you can simply enter **abc?123** at the password prompt.

Examples

In the following example, the password *pswd2* is enabled for privilege level 2:

```
enable password level 2 pswd2
```

In the following example the encrypted password 1i5Rkls3LoyxzS8t9, which has been copied from a router configuration file, is set for privilege level 2 using encryption type 7:

```
enable password level 2 7 $1$i5Rkls3LoyxzS8t9
```

Related Commands

Search online to find documentation for related commands.

disable
enable
enable secret
privilege level (global)
service password-encryption
show privilege
show startup-config

ENABLE SECRET

To specify an additional layer of security over the **enable password** command, use the **enable secret** global configuration command. Use the **no** form of this command to turn off the enable secret function.

> **enable secret** [level *level*] {*password* | *encryption-type encrypted-password*}
> **no enable secret** [level *level*]

Syntax Description

level *level*   (Optional) Level for which the password applies. You can specify up to 16 privilege levels, using numbers 0 through 15. Level 1 is normal EXEC-mode user privileges. If this argument is not specified in the command or in the **no** form of the command, the privilege level defaults to 15 (traditional enable privileges). The same holds true for the **no** form of the command.

password   Password for users to enter enable mode. This password should be different from the password created with the **enable password** command.

encryption-type   (Optional) Cisco-proprietary algorithm used to encrypt the password. Currently, the only encryption type available for this command is 5. If you specify *encryption-type*, the next argument you supply must be an encrypted password (a password encrypted by a Cisco router).

encrypted-password   Encrypted password you enter, copied from another router configuration.

Default

No password is defined. The default level is 15.

Command Mode

Global configuration

Usage Guidelines

This command first appeared in Cisco IOS Release 11.0.

Use this command in conjunction with the **enable password** command to provide an additional layer of security over the enable password. The **enable secret** command provides better security by storing the enable secret password using a non-reversible cryptographic function. The added layer of security encryption provides is useful in environments where the password crosses the network or is stored on a TFTP server.

You will not ordinarily enter an encryption type. Typically, you enter an encryption type only if you paste into this command an encrypted password that you copied from a router configuration file.

CAUTION

If you specify an encryption type and then enter a cleartext password, you will not be able to re-enter enable mode. You cannot recover a lost password that has been encrypted by any method.

If you use the same password for the **enable password** and **enable secret** commands, you receive an error message warning that this practice is not recommended, but the password will be accepted. By using the same password, however, you undermine the additional security the **enable secret** command provides.

NOTES

After you set a password using **enable secret** command, a password set using the **enable password** command works only if the **enable secret** is disabled or an older version of Cisco IOS software is being used, such as when running an older rxboot image. Additionally, you cannot recover a lost password that has been encrypted by any method.

If **service password-encryption** is set, the encrypted form of the password you create here is displayed when a **show startup-config** command is entered.

You can enable or disable password encryption with the **service password-encryption** command.

An enable password is defined as follows:

- Must contain from 1 to 25 uppercase and lowercase alphanumeric characters
- Must not have a number as the first character

- Can have leading spaces, but they are ignored. However, intermediate and trailing spaces are recognized.
- Can contain the question mark (?) character if you precede the question mark with the key combination **Crtl-V** when you create the password; for example, to create the password *abc?123*, do the following:
  - ○ Enter **abc**
  - ○ Type **Crtl-V**
  - ○ Enter **?123**

  When the system prompts you to enter the enable password, you need not precede the question mark with the **Ctrl-V**; you can simply enter **abc?123** at the password prompt.

Examples

The following example specifies the enable secret password of gobbledegook:

```
enable secret gobbledegook
```

After specifying an enable secret password, users must enter this password to gain access. Any passwords set through enable password will no longer work.

```
Password: gobbledegook
```

In the following example the encrypted password 1FaD0$Xyti5Rkls3LoyxzS8, which has been copied from a router configuration file, is enabled for privilege level 2 using encryption type 5:

```
enable password level 2 5 $1$FaD0$Xyti5Rkls3LoyxzS8
```

Related Commands

Search online to find documentation for related commands.

enable
enable password

IP IDENTD

To enable identification support, use the **ip identd** global configuration command. Use the **no** form of this command to disable this feature.

ip identd
no ip identd

Syntax Description

This command has no arguments or keywords.

Default

Identification support is not enabled.

Command Mode

Global configuration

Usage Guidelines

This command first appeared in Cisco IOS Release 11.1.

The **ip identd** command returns accurate information about the host TCP port; however, no attempt is made to protect against unauthorized queries.

Example

In the following example, identification support is enabled:

```
ip identd
```

PASSWORD

To specify a password on a line, use the **password** line configuration command. Use the **no** form of this command to remove the password.

password *password*
no password

Syntax Description

password   Character string that specifies the line password. The first character cannot be a number. The string can contain any alphanumeric characters, including spaces, up to 80 characters. You cannot specify the password in the format *number-space-anything*. The space after the number causes problems. For example, *hello 21* is a legal password, but *21 hello* is not. The password checking is case sensitive. For example, the password *Secret* is different than the password *secret*.

Default

No password is specified.

Command Mode

Line configuration

Usage Guidelines

This command first appeared in Cisco IOS Release 10.0.

When an EXEC process is started on a line with password protection, the EXEC prompts for the password. If the user enters the correct password, the EXEC prints its normal privileged prompt. The user can try three times to enter a password before the EXEC exits and returns the terminal to the idle state.

Part
V

Command Reference

Example

The following example removes the password from virtual terminal lines 1 to 4:
```
line vty 1 4
  no password
```

Related Commands

Search online to find documentation for related commands.

enable password

PRIVILEGE LEVEL (GLOBAL)

To set the privilege level for a command, use the **privilege level** global configuration command. Use the **no** form of this command to revert to default privileges for a given command.

> **privilege** *mode* **level** *level command*
> **no privilege** *mode* **level** *level command*

Syntax Description

mode	Configuration mode. See Table 26–1 for a list of options for this argument.
level	Privilege level associated with the specified command. You can specify up to 16 privilege levels, using numbers 0 through 15.
command	Command to which privilege level is associated.

Table 26–1 shows the acceptable options for the mode argument in the **privilege level** command.

Table 26–1 *Mode Argument Options*

Argument Options	Mode
configuration	Global configuration
controller	Controller configuration
exec	EXEC
hub	Hub configuration
interface	Interface configuration
ipx-router	IPX router configuration
line	Line configuration
map-class	Map class configuration

Table 26-1 *Mode Argument Options, Continued*

Argument Options	Mode
map-list	Map list configuration
route-map	Route map configuration
router	Router configuration

Defaults

Level 15 is the level of access permitted by the **enable** password.

Level 1 is normal EXEC-mode user privileges.

Command Mode

Global configuration

Usage Guidelines

This command first appeared in Cisco IOS Release 10.3.

The password for a privilege level defined using the **privilege level** global configuration command is configured using the **enable password** command.

Level 0 can be used to specify a more limited subset of commands for specific users or lines. For example, you can allow user "guest" to use only the **show users** and **exit** commands.

> **NOTES**
>
> There are five commands associated with privilege level 0: **disable**, **enable**, **exit**, **help**, and **logout**. If you configure AAA authorization for a privilege level greater than 0, these five commands will not be included.

When you set a command to a privilege level, all commands whose syntax is a subset of that command are also set to that level. For example, if you set the **show ip route** command to level 15, the **show** commands and **show ip** commands are automatically set to privilege level 15—unless you set them individually to different levels.

Example

The commands in the following example set the **configure** command to privilege level 14 and establish SecretPswd14 as the password users must enter to use level 14 commands.

```
privilege exec level 14 configure
enable secret level 14 SecretPswd14
```

Related Commands

Search online to find documentation for related commands.

enable password
enable secret
privilege level (line)

PRIVILEGE LEVEL (LINE)

To set the default privilege level for a line, use the **privilege level** line configuration command. Use the **no** form of this command to restore the default user privilege level to the line.

> **privilege level** *level*
> **no privilege level**

Syntax Description

level   Privilege level associated with the specified line.

Defaults

Level 15 is the level of access permitted by the enable password.

Level 1 is normal EXEC-mode user privileges.

Command Mode

Line configuration

Usage Guidelines

This command first appeared in Cisco IOS Release 10.3.

Users can override the privilege level you set using this command by logging in to the line and enabling a different privilege level. They can lower the privilege level by using the **disable** command. If users know the password to a higher privilege level, they can use that password to enable the higher privilege level.

You can use level 0 to specify a subset of commands for specific users or lines. For example, you can allow user "guest" to use only the **show users** and **exit** commands.

You might specify a high level of privilege for your console line to restrict who uses the line.

Examples

The commands in the following example configure the auxiliary line for privilege level 5. Anyone using the auxiliary line has privilege level 5 by default.

```
line aux 0
 privilege level 5
```

The command in the following example sets all **show ip** commands, which includes all **show** commands, to privilege level 7:

```
privilege exec level 7 show ip route
```

This is equivalent to the following command:

```
privilege exec level 7 show
```

The commands in the following example set **show ip route** to level 7 and the **show** and **show ip** commands to level 1:

```
privilege exec level 7 show ip route
privilege exec level 1 show ip
```

Related Commands

Search online to find documentation for related commands.

enable password
privilege level (line)

SERVICE PASSWORD-ENCRYPTION

To encrypt passwords, use the **service password-encryption** global configuration command. Use the **no** form of this command to disable this service.

service password-encryption
no service password-encryption

Syntax Description

This command has no arguments or keywords.

Default

No encryption

Command Mode

Global configuration

Usage Guidelines

This command first appeared in Cisco IOS Release 10.0.

The actual encryption process occurs when the current configuration is written or when a password is configured. Password encryption is applied to all passwords, including username passwords, authentication key passwords, the privileged command password, console and virtual terminal line access passwords, and BGP neighbor passwords. This command is primarily useful for keeping unauthorized individuals from viewing your password in your configuration file.

Part
V

Command Reference

When password encryption is enabled, the encrypted form of the passwords is displayed when a **show running-config** command is entered.

CAUTION

This command does not provide a high level of network security. If you use this command, you should also take additional network security measures.

NOTES

You cannot recover a lost encrypted password. You must clear NVRAM and set a new password.

Example
The following example causes password encryption to take place:
```
service password-encryption
```

Related Commands
Search online to find documentation for related commands.

enable password
key-string
neighbor password

SHOW PRIVILEGE

To display your current level of privilege, use the **show privilege** EXEC command.
```
show privilege
```

Syntax Description
This command has no arguments or keywords.

Command Mode
EXEC

Usage Guidelines
This command first appeared in Cisco IOS Release 10.3.

Sample Display
The following is sample output from the **show privilege** command. The current privilege level is 15.
```
Router# show privilege
Current privilege level is 15
```

Related Commands

Search online to find documentation for related commands.

enable password
enable secret

USERNAME

To establish a username-based authentication system, enter the **username** global configuration command.

> **username** *name* {**nopassword** | **password** *password* [*encryption-type encrypted-password*]}
> **username** *name* **password** *secret*
> **username** *name* [**access-class** *number*]
> **username** *name* [**autocommand** *command*]
> **username** *name* [**callback-dialstring** *telephone-number*]
> **username** *name* [**callback-rotary** *rotary-group-number*]
> **username** *name* [**callback-line** [**tty**] *line-number* [*ending-line-number*]]
> **username** *name* [**nocallback-verify**]
> **username** *name* [**noescape**] [**nohangup**]
> **username** *name* [**privilege** *level*]

Syntax Description

name	Host name, server name, user ID, or command name. The *name* argument can be only one word. White spaces and quotation marks are not allowed.
nopassword	No password is required for this user to log in. This is usually most useful in combination with the **autocommand** keyword.
password	Specifies a possibly encrypted password for this username.
password	Password a user enters.
encryption-type	(Optional) Single-digit number that defines whether the text immediately following is encrypted, and, if so, what type of encryption is used. Currently defined encryption types are 0, which means that the text immediately following is not encrypted, and 7, which means that the text is encrypted using a Cisco-defined encryption algorithm.
encrypted-password	Encrypted password a user enters.
password	(Optional) Password to access the name argument. A password must be from 1 to 25 characters, can contain embedded spaces, and must be the last option specified in the **username** command.

secret	For CHAP authentication: specifies the secret for the local router or the remote device. The secret is encrypted when it is stored on the local router. The secret can consist of any string of up to 11 ASCII characters. There is no limit to the number of username and password combinations that can be specified, allowing any number of remote devices to be authenticated.
access-class	(Optional) Specifies an outgoing access list that overrides the access list specified in the **access-class** line configuration command. It is used for the duration of the user's session.
number	Access list number.
autocommand	(Optional) Causes the specified command to be issued automatically after the user logs in. When the command is complete, the session is terminated. Because the command can be any length and contain embedded spaces, commands using the **autocommand** keyword must be the last option on the line.
command	The command string. Because the command can be any length and contain embedded spaces, commands using the **autocommand** keyword must be the last option on the line.
callback-dialstring	(Optional) For asynchronous callback only: permits you to specify a telephone number to pass to the DCE device.
telephone-number	For asynchronous callback only: telephone number to pass to the DCE device.
callback-rotary	(Optional) For asynchronous callback only: permits you to specify a rotary group number. The next available line in the rotary group is selected.
rotary-group-number	For asynchronous callback only: integer between 1 and 100 that identifies the group of lines on which you want to enable a specific username for callback.
callback-line	(Optional) For asynchronous callback only: specific line on which you enable a specific username for callback.
tty	(Optional) For asynchronous callback only: standard asynchronous line.
line-number	For asynchronous callback only: relative number of the terminal line (or the first line in a contiguous group) on which you want to enable a specific username for callback. Numbering begins with zero.
ending-line-number	(Optional) Relative number of the last line in a contiguous group on which you want to enable a specific username for callback. If you omit the keyword (such as **tty**), then *line-number* and *ending-line-number* are absolute rather than relative line numbers.

nocallback-verify	(Optional) Authentication not required for EXEC callback on the specified line.
noescape	(Optional) Prevents a user from using an escape character on the host to which that user is connected.
nohangup	(Optional) Prevents the security server from disconnecting the user after an automatic command (set up with the **autocommand** keyword) has completed. Instead, the user gets another login prompt.
privilege	(Optional) Sets the privilege level for the user.
level	(Optional) Number between 0 and 15 that specifies the privilege level for the user.

Default

No username-based authentication system is established.

Command Mode

Global configuration

Usage Guidelines

The following commands first appeared in Cisco IOS Release 10.0:
username *name* {**nopassword** | **password** *password* [*encryption-type encrypted-password*]}
username *name* **password** *secret*
username *name* [**access-class** *number*]
username *name* [**autocommand** *command*]
username *name* [**noescape**] [**nohangup**]
username *name* [**privilege** *level*]

The following commands first appeared in Cisco IOS Release 11.1:
username *name* [**callback-dialstring** *telephone-number*]
username *name* [**callback-rotary** *rotary-group-number*]
username *name* [**callback-line** [**tty**] *line-number* [*ending-line-number*]]
username *name* [**nocallback-verify**]

The **username** command provides username and/or password authentication for login purposes only. (Note that it does not provide username and/or password authentication for enable mode when the **enable use-tacacs** command is also configured.)

Multiple **username** commands can be used to specify options for a single user.

Add a **username** entry for each remote system that the local router communicates with and requires authentication from. The remote device must have a **username** entry for the local router. This entry must have the same password as the local router's entry for that remote device.

Part
V

Command Reference

This command can be useful for defining usernames that get special treatment. For example, you can use this command to define an "info" username that does not require a password, but connects the user to a general-purpose information service.

The **username** command is required as part of the configuration for the Challenge Handshake Authentication Protocol (CHAP). Add a **username** entry or each remote system from which the local router requires authentication.

NOTES

To enable the local router to respond to remote CHAP challenges, one **username** *name* entry must be the same as the **hostname** *name* entry that has already been assigned to your router.

If there is no *secret* specified and the **debug serial-interface** command is enabled, an error is displayed when a link is established and the CHAP challenge is not implemented. CHAP debugging information is available using the **debug serial-interface** and **debug serial-packet** commands.

Examples

To implement a service similar to the UNIX **who** command, which can be entered at the login prompt and lists the current users of the router, the **username** command takes the following form:

```
username who nopassword nohangup autocommand show users
```

To implement an information service that does not require a password to be used, the command takes the following form:

```
username info nopassword noescape autocommand telnet nic.ddn.mil
```

To implement an ID that works even if the TACACS servers all break, the command takes the following form:

```
username superuser password superpassword
```

The following example configuration enables CHAP on interface serial 0. It also defines a password for the local server, Adam, and a remote server, Eve.

```
hostname Adam
interface serial 0
 encapsulation ppp
 ppp authentication chap
 username Adam password oursystem
 username Eve password theirsystem
```

When you look at your configuration file, the passwords will be encrypted and the display will look similar to the following:

```
hostname Adam
interface serial 0
 encapsulation ppp
 ppp authentication chap
 username Adam password 7 1514040356
 username Eve password 7 121F0A18
```

Related Commands

Search online to find documentation for related commands.

arap callback
callback-forced-wait
debug callback
ppp callback

## CHAPTER 27

Neighbor Router Authentication: Overview and Guidelines

You can prevent your router from receiving fraudulent route updates by configuring neighbor router authentication.

This chapter describes neighbor router authentication as part of a total security plan. This chapter describes what neighbor router authentication is, how it works, and why you should use it to increase your overall network security.

This chapter refers to neighbor router authentication as *neighbor authentication*. Neighbor router authentication is also sometimes called *route authentication*.

IN THIS CHAPTER

This chapter describes the following topics:

- Benefits of Neighbor Authentication
- Protocols That Use Neighbor Authentication
- When to Configure Neighbor Authentication
- How Neighbor Authentication Works
- Key Management (Key Chains)

BENEFITS OF NEIGHBOR AUTHENTICATION

When configured, neighbor authentication occurs whenever routing updates are exchanged between neighbor routers. This authentication ensures that a router receives reliable routing information from a trusted source.

Without neighbor authentication, unauthorized or deliberately malicious routing updates could compromise the security of your network traffic. A security compromise could occur if an unfriendly party diverts or analyzes your network traffic. For example, an unauthorized router could send a fictitious routing update to convince your router to send traffic to an incorrect destination. This diverted traffic could be analyzed to learn confidential information of your organization, or merely used to disrupt your organization's ability to effectively communicate using the network.

Neighbor Authentication prevents any such fraudulent route updates from being received by your router.

PROTOCOLS THAT USE NEIGHBOR AUTHENTICATION

Neighbor authentication can be configured for the following routing protocols:

- Border Gateway Protocol (BGP)
- DRP Server Agent
- Intermediate System-to-Intermediate System (IS-IS)
- IP Enhanced Interior Gateway Routing Protocol (IGRP)
- Open Shortest Path First (OSPF)
- Routing Information Protocol (RIP) version 2

WHEN TO CONFIGURE NEIGHBOR AUTHENTICATION

You should configure any router for neighbor authentication if that router meets all of these conditions:

- The router uses any of the routing protocols previously mentioned.
- It is conceivable that the router might receive a false route update.
- If the router were to receive a false route update, your network might be compromised.
- If you configure a router for neighbor authentication, you also need to configure the neighbor router for neighbor authentication.

HOW NEIGHBOR AUTHENTICATION WORKS

When neighbor authentication has been configured on a router, the router authenticates the source of each routing update packet that it receives. This is accomplished by the exchange of an authenticating key (sometimes referred to as a password) that is known to both the sending and the receiving router.

There are two types of neighbor authentication used: *plain text authentication* and *Message Digest Algorithm Version 5 (MD5) authentication*. Both forms work in the same way, with the exception that MD5 sends a "message digest" instead of the authenticating key itself. The message digest is created using the key and a message, but the key itself is not sent, preventing it from being read while it is being transmitted. Plain text authentication sends the authenticating key itself over the wire.

NOTES

Note that plain text authentication is not recommended for use as part of your security strategy. Its primary use is to avoid accidental changes to the routing infrastructure. Using MD5 authentication, however, is a recommended security practice.

CAUTION

As with all keys, passwords, and other security secrets, it is imperative that you closely guard authenticating keys used in neighbor authentication. The security benefits of this feature rely upon your keeping all authenticating keys confidential. Also, when performing router management tasks via Simple Network Management Protocol (SNMP), do not ignore the risk associated with sending keys using non-encrypted SNMP.

Plain Text Authentication

Each participating neighbor router must share an authenticating key. This key is specified at each router during configuration. Multiple keys can be specified with some protocols; each key must then be identified by a key number.

In general, when a routing update is sent, the following authentication sequence occurs:

Step 1 A router sends a routing update with a key and the corresponding key number to the neighbor router. In protocols that can have only one key, the key number is always zero.

Step 2 The receiving (neighbor) router checks the received key against the same key stored in its own memory.

Step 3 If the two keys match, the receiving router accepts the routing update packet. If the two keys did not match, the routing update packet is rejected.

These protocols use plain text authentication:

- DRP Server Agent
- IS-IS
- OSPF
- RIP version 2

MD5 Authentication

MD5 authentication works similarly to plain text authentication, except that the key is never sent over the wire. Instead, the router uses the MD5 algorithm to produce a *message digest* of the key (also called a *hash*). The message digest is then sent instead of the key itself. This ensures that nobody can eavesdrop on the line and learn keys during transmission.

These protocols use MD5 authentication:

- OSPF
- RIP version 2
- BGP
- IP Enhanced IGRP

KEY MANAGEMENT (KEY CHAINS)

You can configure key chains for these routing protocols:

- RIP version 2
- IP Enhanced IGRP
- DRP Server Agent

These routing protocols both offer the additional function of managing keys by using key chains. When you configure a key chain, you specify a series of keys with lifetimes, and the Cisco IOS software rotates through each of these keys. This decreases the likelihood that keys will be compromised.

Each key definition within the key chain must specify a time interval for which that key will be activated (its "lifetime"). Then, during a given key's lifetime, routing update packets are sent with this activated key. Keys cannot be used during time periods for which they are not activated. Therefore, it is recommended that for a given key chain, key activation times overlap to avoid any period of time for which no key is activated. If a time period occurs during which no key is activated, neighbor authentication cannot occur, and therefore routing updates will fail.

Multiple key chains can be specified. Note that the router needs to know the time to be able to rotate through keys in synchronization with the other participating routers, so that all routers are using the same key at the same moment.

CHAPTER █ 28

Configuring
IP Security Options

Cisco provides IP Security Option (IPSO) support as described in RFC 1108. Cisco's implementation is only minimally compliant with RFC 1108 because the Cisco IOS software only accepts and generates a 4-byte IPSO.

IPSO is generally used to comply with the U.S. Government's Department of Defense security policy.

For a complete description of IPSO commands, see Chapter 29, "IP Security Options Commands."

IN THIS CHAPTER

This chapter describes how to configure IPSO for both the basic and extended security options described in RFC 1108. This chapter also describes how to configure auditing for IPSO. This chapter includes the following sections:

- Configuring Basic IP Security Options
- Configuring Extended IP Security Options
- Configuring the DNSIX Audit Trail Facility
- IPSO Configuration Examples

CONFIGURING BASIC IP SECURITY OPTIONS

Cisco's basic IPSO support provides the following features:

- Defines security level on a per-interface basis
- Defines single-level or multilevel interfaces
- Provides a label for incoming packets
- Strips labels on a per-interface basis
- Reorders options to put any basic security options first

To configure basic IPSO, complete the tasks in the following sections:

- Enable IPSO and Set the Security Classifications
- Specify How IP Security Options Are Processed

Enable IPSO and Set the Security Classifications

To enable IPSO and set security classifications on an interface, perform either of the following tasks in interface configuration mode:

Task	Command
Set an interface to the requested IPSO classification and authorities.	ip security dedicated *level authority* [*authority...*]
Set an interface to the requested IPSO range of classifications and authorities.	ip security multilevel *level1* [*authority1...*] to *level2 authority2* [*authority2...*]

Use the **no ip security** command to reset an interface to its default state.

Specify How IP Security Options Are Processed

To specify how IP security options are processed, perform any of the following optional tasks in interface configuration mode:

Task	Command
Enable an interface to ignore the authorities field of all incoming packets.	ip security ignore-authorities
Classify packets that have no IPSO with an implicit security label.	ip security implicit-labelling [*level authority* [*authority...*]]
Accept packets on an interface that has an extended security option present.	ip security extended-allowed
Ensure that all packets leaving the router on an interface contain a basic security option.	ip security add
Remove any basic security option that might be present on a packet leaving the router through an interface.	ip security strip
Prioritize security options on a packet.	ip security first
Treat as valid any packets that have Reserved1 through Reserved4 security levels.	ip security reserved-allowed

Default Values for Command Keywords

In order to fully comply with IPSO, the default values for the minor keywords have become complex. Default value usages include the following:

- The default for all of the minor keywords is *off*, with the exception of **implicit-labelling** and **add.**
- The default value of **implicit-labelling** is *on* if the interface is unclassified Genser; otherwise, it is *off.*
- The default value for **add** is *on* if the interface is not "unclassified Genser"; otherwise, it is *off.*

Table 28–1 provides a list of all default values.

Table 28–1   *Default Security Keyword Values*

Interface Type	Level	Authority	Implicit Labeling	Add IPSO
None	None	None	On	Off
Dedicated	Unclassified	Genser	On	Off
Dedicated	Any	Any	Off	On
Multilevel	Any	Any	Off	On

The default value for any interface is "dedicated, unclassified Genser." Note that this implies implicit labeling. This might seem unusual, but it makes the system entirely transparent to packets without options. This is the setting generated when you specify the **no ip security** interface configuration command.

CONFIGURING EXTENDED IP SECURITY OPTIONS

Our extended IPSO support is compliant with the Department of Defense Intelligence Information System Network Security for Information Exchange (DNSIX) specification documents. Extended IPSO functionality can unconditionally accept or reject Internet traffic that contains extended security options by comparing those options to configured allowable values. This support allows DNSIX networks to use additional security information to achieve a higher level of security than that achievable with basic IPSO.

We also support a subset of the security features defined in the DNSIX Version 2.1 specification. Specifically, we support DNSIX definitions of the following:

- How extended IPSO is processed
- Audit trail facility

There are two kinds of extended IPSO fields defined by the DNSIX 2.1 specification and supported by our implementation of extended IPSO—Network Level Extended Security Option (NLESO) and Auxiliary Extended Security Option (AESO) fields.

NLESO processing requires that security options be checked against configured allowable information, source, and compartment bit values, and requires that the router be capable of inserting extended security options in the IP header.

AESO is similar to NLESO, except that its contents are not checked and are assumed to be valid if its source is listed in the AESO table.

To configure extended IPSO, complete the tasks in the following sections:

- Configure Global Default Settings
- Attach ESOs to an Interface
- Attach AESOs to an Interface

DNSIX Version 2.1 causes slow-switching code.

See section "IPSO Configuration Examples," located at the end of this chapter.

Configure Global Default Settings

To configure global default setting for extended IPSO, including AESOs, perform the following task in global configuration mode:

Task	Command
Configure system-wide default settings.	**ip security eso-info** *source compartment-size default-bit*

Attach ESOs to an Interface

To specify the minimum and maximum sensitivity levels for an interface, perform the following tasks in interface configuration mode:

Task	Command
Set the minimum sensitivity level for an interface.	**ip security eso-min** *source compartment-bits*
Set the maximum sensitivity level for an interface.	**ip security eso-max** *source compartment-bits*

Attach AESOs to an Interface

To specify the extended IPSO sources that are to be treated as AESO sources, perform the following task in interface configuration mode:

Task	Command
Specify AESO sources.	ip security aeso *source compartment-bits*

CONFIGURING THE DNSIX AUDIT TRAIL FACILITY

The audit trail facility is a UDP-based protocol that generates an audit trail of IPSO security violations. This facility allows the system to report security failures on incoming and outgoing packets. The Audit Trail Facility sends DNSIX audit trail messages when a datagram is rejected because of IPSO security violations. This feature allows you to configure organization-specific security information.

The DNSIX audit trail facility consists of two protocols:

- DNSIX Message Deliver Protocol (DMDP) provides a basic message-delivery mechanism for all DNSIX elements.
- Network Audit Trail Protocol (NAT) provides a buffered logging facility for applications to use to generate auditing information. This information is then passed on to DMDP.

To configure the DNSIX auditing facility, complete the tasks in the following sections:

- Enable the DNSIX Audit Trail Facility
- Specify Hosts to Receive Audit Trail Messages
- Specify Transmission Parameters

Enable the DNSIX Audit Trail Facility

To enable the DNSIX audit trail facility, perform the following task in global configuration mode:

Task	Command
Start the audit writing module.	dnsix-nat source *ip-address*

Specify Hosts to Receive Audit Trail Messages

To define and change primary and secondary addresses of the host to receive audit messages, perform the following tasks in global configuration mode:

Task	Command
Specify the primary address for the audit trail	dnsix-nat primary *ip-address*
Specify the secondary address for the audit trail.	dnsix-nat secondary *ip-address*
Specify the address of a collection center that is authorized to change primary and secondary addresses. Specified hosts are authorized to change the destination of audit messages.	dnsix-nat authorized-redirection *ip-address*

Specify Transmission Parameters

To specify transmission parameters, perform the following tasks in global configuration mode:

Task	Command
Specify the number of records in a packet before it is sent to a collection center.	**dnsix-nat transmit-count** *count*
Specify the number of transmit retries for DMDP.	**dnsix-dmdp retries** *count*

IPSO CONFIGURATION EXAMPLES

There are two examples in this section:

Example 1

In this example, three Ethernet interfaces are presented. These interfaces are running at security levels of Confidential Genser, Secret Genser, and Confidential to Secret Genser, as shown in Figure 28–1.

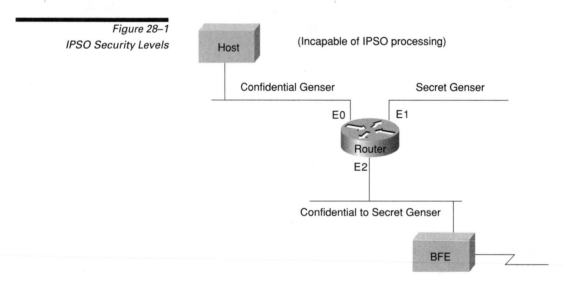

Figure 28–1
IPSO Security Levels

The following commands set up interfaces for the configuration in the preceding figure.

```
interface ethernet 0
 ip security dedicated confidential genser
interface ethernet 1
 ip security dedicated secret genser
interface ethernet 2
 ip security multilevel confidential genser to secret genser
```

It is possible for the setup to be much more complex.

Example 2

In the following example, there are devices on Ethernet 0 that cannot generate a security option, and so they must accept packets without a security option. These hosts do not understand security options; therefore, never place one on such interfaces. Furthermore, there are hosts on the other two networks that are using the extended security option to communicate information, so you must allow these to pass through the system. Finally, there also is a host (a Blacker Front End) on Ethernet 2 that requires the security option to be the first option present, and this condition also must be specified. The new configuration follows:

```
interface ethernet 0
 ip security dedicated confidential genser
 ip security implicit-labelling
 ip security strip
interface ethernet 1
 ip security dedicated secret genser
 ip security extended-allowed
!
interface ethernet 2
 ip security multilevel confidential genser to secret genser
 ip security extended-allowed
 ip security first
```

## CHAPTER 29

IP Security Options Commands

This chapter describes IP Security Options (IPSO) commands. IPSO is generally used to comply with the U.S. Government's Department of Defense security policy.

For IPSO configuration information, see Chapter 28, "Configuring IP Security Options."

DNSIX-DMDP RETRIES

To set the retransmit count used by the Department of Defense Intelligence Information System Network Security for Information Exchange (DNSIX) Message Delivery Protocol (DMDP), use the **dnsix-dmdp retries** global configuration command. To restore the default number of retries, use the **no** form of this command.

> **dnsix-dmdp retries** *count*
> **no dnsix-dmdp retries** *count*

Syntax Description

count	Number of times DMDP will retransmit a message. It can be an integer from 0 to 200. The default is 4 retries, or until acknowledged.

Default

Retransmits messages up to 4 times, or until acknowledged.

Command Mode

Global configuration

Usage Guidelines

This command first appeared in Cisco IOS Release 10.0.

Example

The following example sets the number of times DMDP will attempt to retransmit a message to 150:

```
dnsix-dmdp retries 150
```

Related Commands

Search online to find documentation for related commands.

dnsix-nat authorized-redirection
dnsix-nat primary
dnsix-nat secondary
dnsix-nat source
dnsix-nat transmit-count

DNSIX-NAT AUTHORIZED-REDIRECTION

To specify the address of a collection center that is authorized to change the primary and secondary addresses of the host to receive audit messages, use the **dnsix-nat authorized-redirection** global configuration command. To delete an address, use the **no** form of this command.

> **dnsix-nat authorized-redirection** *ip-address*
> **no dnsix-nat authorized-redirection** *ip-address*

Syntax Description

ip-address   IP address of the host from which redirection requests are permitted.

Default

An empty list of addresses

Command Mode

Global configuration

Usage Guidelines

This command first appeared in Cisco IOS Release 10.0.

Use multiple **dnsix-nat authorized-redirection** commands to specify a set of hosts that are authorized to change the destination for audit messages. Redirection requests are checked against the configured list, and if the address is not authorized, the request is rejected and an audit message is generated. If no address is specified, no redirection messages are accepted.

Example

The following example specifies that the address of the collection center that is authorized to change the primary and secondary addresses is 193.1.1.1.

```
dnsix-nat authorization-redirection 193.1.1.1.
```

DNSIX-NAT PRIMARY

To specify the IP address of the host to which DNSIX audit messages are sent, use the **dnsix-nat primary** global configuration command. To delete an entry, use the **no** form of this command.

> **dnsix-nat primary** *ip-address*
> **no dnsix-nat primary** *ip-address*

Syntax Description

ip-address   IP address for the primary collection center.

Default

Messages are not sent.

Command Mode

Global configuration

Usage Guidelines

This command first appeared in Cisco IOS Release 10.0.

An IP address must be configured before audit messages can be sent.

Example

The following example configures an IP address as the address of the host to which DNSIX audit messages are sent:

```
dnsix-nat primary 194.1.1.1
```

DNSIX-NAT SECONDARY

To specify an alternate IP address for the host to which DNSIX audit messages are sent, use the **dnsix-nat secondary** global configuration command. To delete an entry, use the **no** form of this command.

> **dnsix-nat secondary** *ip-address*
> **no dnsix-nat secondary** *ip-address*

Syntax Description

ip-address   IP address for the secondary collection center.

Default

No alternate IP address is known.

Command Mode

Global configuration

Usage Guidelines

This command first appeared in Cisco IOS Release 10.0.

When the primary collection center is unreachable, audit messages are sent to the secondary collection center instead.

Example

The following example configures an IP address as the address of an alternate host to which DNSIX audit messages are sent:

```
dnsix-nat secondary 193.1.1.1
```

DNSIX-NAT SOURCE

To start the audit writing module and to define audit trail source address, use the **dnsix-nat source** global configuration command. To disable the DNSIX audit trail writing module, use the **no** form of this command.

> **dnsix-nat source** *ip-address*
> **no dnsix-nat source** *ip-address*

Syntax Description

ip-address   Source IP address for DNSIX audit messages.

Default

Disabled

Command Mode

Global configuration

Usage Guidelines

This command first appeared in Cisco IOS Release 10.0.

You must issue the **dnsix-nat source** command before any of the other **dnsix-nat** commands. The configured IP address is used as the source IP address for DMDP protocol packets sent to any of the collection centers.

Example

The following example enables the audit trail writing module, and specifies that the source IP address for any generated audit messages should be the same as the primary IP address of Ethernet interface 0.

```
dnsix-nat source 128.105.2.5
interface ethernet 0
 ip address 128.105.2.5 255.255.255.0
```

DNSIX-NAT TRANSMIT-COUNT

To have the audit writing module collect multiple audit messages in the buffer before sending the messages to a collection center, use the **dnsix-nat transmit-count** global configuration command. To revert to the default audit message count, use the **no** form of this command.

> **dnsix-nat transmit-count** *count*
> **no dnsix-nat transmit-count** *count*

Syntax Description

count   Number of audit messages to buffer before transmitting to the server. It can be an integer from 1 to 200.

Default

One message is sent at a time.

Command Mode

Global configuration

Usage Guidelines

This command first appeared in Cisco IOS Release 10.0.

An audit message is sent as soon as the message is generated by the IP packet-processing code. The audit writing module can, instead, buffer up to several audit messages before transmitting to a collection center.

Example

The following example configures the system to buffer five audit messages before transmitting them to a collection center:

```
dnsix-nat transmit-count 5
```

IP SECURITY ADD

To add a basic security option to all outgoing packets, use the **ip security add** interface configuration command. To disable the adding of a basic security option to all outgoing packets, use the **no** form of this command.

> **ip security add**
> **no ip security add**

Syntax Description

This command has no arguments or keywords.

Default

Disabled, when the security level of the interface is "Unclassified Genser" (or unconfigured). Otherwise, the default is enabled.

Command Mode

Interface configuration

Usage Guidelines

This command first appeared in Cisco IOS Release 10.0.

If an outgoing packet does not have a security option present, this interface configuration command will add one as the first IP option. The security label added to the option field is the label that was computed for this packet when it first entered the router. Because this action is performed after all the security tests have been passed, this label will either be the same as or will fall within the range of the interface.

Example

The following example adds a basic security option to each packet leaving Ethernet interface 0:

```
interface ethernet 0
  ip security add
```

Related Commands

Search online to find documentation for related commands.

ip security dedicated
ip security extended-allowed
ip security first
ip security ignore-authorities
ip security implicit-labelling
ip security multilevel
ip security reserved-allowed
ip security strip

IP SECURITY AESO

To attach Auxiliary Extended Security Options (AESOs) to an interface, use the **ip security aeso** interface configuration command. To disable AESO on an interface, use the **no** form of this command.

       ip security aeso *source compartment-bits*
       no ip security aeso *source compartment-bits*

Syntax Description

source	Extended Security Option (ESO) source. This can be an integer from 0 to 255.
compartment-bits	Compartment bits in hexadecimal.

Default

Disabled

Command Mode

Interface configuration

Usage Guidelines

This command first appeared in Cisco IOS Release 10.0.

Compartment bits are specified only if this AESO is to be inserted in a packet. On every incoming packet at this level on this interface, these AESOs should be present.

Beyond being recognized, no further processing of AESO information is performed. AESO contents are not checked and are assumed to be valid if the source is listed in the configurable AESO table.

Configuring any per-interface extended IP security option (IPSO) information automatically enables **ip security extended-allowed** (disabled by default).

Example

In the following example, the extended security option source is defined as 5, and the compartments bits are set to 5:

```
interface ethernet 0
  ip security aeso 5 5
```

Related Commands

Search online to find documentation for related commands.

ip security eso-info
ip security eso-max
ip security eso-min
ip security extended-allowed

Part
V

Command Reference

IP SECURITY DEDICATED

To set the level of classification and authority on the interface, use the **ip security dedicated** interface configuration command. To reset the interface to the default classification and authorities, use the **no** form of this command.

> **ip security dedicated** *level authority [authority...]*
> **no ip security dedicated** *level authority [authority...]*

Syntax Description

level   Degree of sensitivity of information. The level keywords are listed in Table 29–1.

authority   Organization that defines the set of security levels that will be used in a network. The authority keywords are listed in Table 29–2.

Default

Disabled

Command Mode

Interface configuration

Usage Guidelines

This command first appeared in Cisco IOS Release 10.0.

All traffic entering the system on this interface must have a security option that exactly matches this label. Any traffic leaving via this interface will have this label attached to it.

The following definitions apply to the descriptions of the IP security options (IPSO) in this section:

- **level**—The degree of sensitivity of information. For example, data marked TOPSECRET is more sensitive than data marked SECRET. The level keywords and their corresponding bit patterns are shown in Table 29–1.

Table 29–1 *IPSO Level Keywords and Bit Patterns*

Level Keyword	Bit Pattern
Reserved4	0000 0001
TopSecret	0011 1101
Secret	0101 1010
Confidential	1001 0110
Reserved3	0110 0110

Table 29-1 *IPSO Level Keywords and Bit Patterns, Continued*

Level Keyword	Bit Pattern
Reserved2	1100 1100
Unclassified	1010 1011
Reserved1	1111 0001

- **authority**—An organization that defines the set of security levels that will be used in a network. For example, the Genser authority consists of level names defined by the U.S. Defense Communications Agency (DCA). The authority keywords and their corresponding bit patterns are shown in Table 29–2.

Table 29-2 *IPSO Authority Keywords and Bit Patterns*

Authority Keyword	Bit Pattern
Genser	1000 0000
Siop-Esi	0100 0000
DIA	0010 0000
NSA	0001 0000
DOE	0000 1000

- **label**—A combination of a security level and an authority or authorities.

Example

The following example sets a confidential level with Genser authority:

```
ip security dedicated confidential Genser
```

Related Commands

Search online to find documentation for related commands.

ip security add
ip security extended-allowed
ip security first
ip security ignore-authorities
ip security implicit-labelling
ip security multilevel
ip security reserved-allowed
ip security strip

IP SECURITY ESO-INFO

To configure system-wide defaults for extended IP Security Option (IPSO) information, use the **ip security eso-info** global configuration command. To return to the default settings, use the **no** form of this command.

> **ip security eso-info** *source compartment-size default-bit*
> **no ip security eso-info** *source compartment-size default-bit*

Syntax Description

source   Hexadecimal or decimal value representing the extended IPSO source. This is an integer from 0 to 255.

compartment-size   Maximum number of bytes of compartment information allowed for a particular extended IPSO source. This is an integer from 1 to 16.

default-bit   Default bit value for any unsent compartment bits.

Default

Disabled

Command mode

Global configuration

Usage Guidelines

This command first appeared in Cisco IOS Release 10.0.

This command configures Extended Security Option (ESO) information, including Auxiliary Extended Security Option (AESO). Transmitted compartment info is padded to the size specified by the *compartment-size* argument.

Example

In the following example, system-wide defaults for source, compartment size, and the default bit value are set:

```
ip security eso-info 100 5 1
```

Related Commands

Search online to find documentation for related commands.

ip security eso-max
ip security eso-min

IP SECURITY ESO-MAX

To specify the maximum sensitivity level for an interface, use the **ip security eso-max** interface configuration command. To return to the default, use the **no** form of this command.

> **ip security eso-max** *source compartment-bits*
> **no ip security eso-max** *source compartment-bits*

Syntax Description

source	Extended Security Option (ESO) source. This is an integer from 1 to 255.
compartment-bits	Compartment bits in hexadecimal.

Default

Disabled

Command Mode

Interface configuration

Usage Guidelines

This command first appeared in Cisco IOS Release 10.0.

The command is used to specify the minimum sensitivity level for a particular interface. Before the per-interface compartment information for a particular Network Level Extended Security Option (NLESO) source can be configured, the **ip security eso-info** global configuration command must be used to specify the default information.

On every incoming packet on the interface, these extended security options should be resent at the minimum level and should match the configured compartment bits. Every outgoing packet must have these ESOs.

On every packet transmitted or received on this interface, any NLESO sources present in the IP header should be bounded by the minimum sensitivity level and bounded by the maximum sensitivity level configured for the interface.

When transmitting locally generated traffic out this interface or adding security information (with the **ip security add** command), the maximum compartment bit information can be used to construct the NLESO sources placed in the IP header.

A maximum of 16 NLESO sources can be configured per interface. Due to IP header length restrictions, a maximum of nine of these NLESO sources appear in the IP header of a packet.

Part
V

Command Reference

Example

In the following example, the specified ESO source is 240 and the compartment bits are specified as 500:

```
interface ethernet 0
  ip security eso-max 240 500
```

Related Commands

Search online to find documentation for related commands.

ip security eso-info
ip security eso-min

IP SECURITY ESO-MIN

To configure the minimum sensitivity for an interface, use the **ip security eso-min** interface configuration command. To return to the default, use the **no** form of this command.

> **ip security eso-min** *source compartment-bits*
> **no ip security eso-min** *source compartment-bits*

Syntax Description

source	Extended Security Option (ESO) source. This is an integer from 1 to 255.
compartment-bits	Compartment bits in hexadecimal.

Default

Disabled

Command Mode

Interface configuration

Usage Guidelines

This command first appeared in Cisco IOS Release 10.0.

The command is used to specify the minimum sensitivity level for a particular interface. Before the per-interface compartment information for a particular Network Level Extended Security Option (NLESO) source can be configured, the **ip security eso-info** global configuration command must be used to specify the default information.

On every incoming packet on this interface, these extended security options should be resent at the minimum level and should match the configured compartment bits. Every outgoing packet must have these ESOs.

On every packet transmitted or received on this interface, any NLESO sources present in the IP header should be bounded by the minimum sensitivity level and bounded by the maximum sensitivity level configured for the interface.

When transmitting locally generated traffic out this interface or adding security information (with the **ip security add** command), the maximum compartment bit information can be used to construct the NLESO sources placed in the IP header.

A maximum of 16 NLESO sources can be configured per interface. Due to IP header length restrictions, a maximum of nine of these NLESO sources appear in the IP header of a packet.

Example

In the following example, the specified ESO source is 5 and the compartment bits are specified as 5:

```
interface ethernet 0
 ip security eso-min 5 5
```

Related Commands

Search online to find documentation for related commands.

ip security eso-info
ip security eso-max

IP SECURITY EXTENDED-ALLOWED

To accept packets on an interface that has an extended security option present, use the **ip security extended-allowed** interface configuration command. To restore the default, use the **no** form of this command.

ip security extended-allowed
no ip security extended-allowed

Syntax Description

This command has no arguments or keywords.

Default

Disabled

Command Mode

Interface configuration

Usage Guidelines

This command first appeared in Cisco IOS Release 10.0.

Packets containing extended security options are rejected.

Example

The following example allows interface Ethernet 0 to accept packets that have an extended security option present:

```
interface ethernet 0
 ip security extended-allowed
```

Related Commands

Search online to find documentation for related commands.

ip security add
ip security dedicated
ip security first
ip security ignore-authorities
ip security implicit-labelling
ip security multilevel
ip security reserved-allowed
ip security strip

IP SECURITY FIRST

To prioritize the presence of security options on a packet, use the **ip security first** interface configuration command. To disable this function, use the **no** form of this command.

ip security first
no ip security first

Syntax Description

This command has no arguments or keywords.

Default

Disabled

Command Mode

Interface configuration

Usage Guidelines

This command first appeared in Cisco IOS Release 10.0.

If a basic security option is present on an outgoing packet, but it is not the first IP option, then the packet is moved to the front of the options field when this interface configuration command is used.

Example

The following example ensures that if a basic security option is present in the options field of a packet exiting interface Ethernet 0, the packet is moved to the front of the options field:

```
interface ethernet 0
  ip security first
```

Related Commands

Search online to find documentation for related commands.

ip security add
ip security dedicated
ip security extended-allowed
ip security ignore-authorities
ip security implicit-labelling
ip security multilevel
ip security reserved-allowed
ip security strip

IP SECURITY IGNORE-AUTHORITIES

To have the Cisco IOS software ignore the authorities field of all incoming packets, use the **ip security ignore-authorities** interface configuration command. To disable this function, use the **no** form of this command.

ip security ignore-authorities
no ip security ignore-authorities

Syntax Description

This command has no arguments or keywords.

Default

Disabled

Command Mode

Interface configuration

Usage Guidelines

This command first appeared in Cisco IOS Release 10.0.

When the packet's authority field is ignored, the value used in place of this field is the authority value declared for the specified interface. The **ip security ignore-authorities** can only be configured on interfaces with dedicated security levels.

Example

The following example causes interface Ethernet 0 to ignore the authorities field on all incoming packets:

```
interface ethernet 0
  ip security ignore-authorities
```

Related Commands

Search online to find documentation for related commands.

ip security add
ip security dedicated
ip security extended-allowed
ip security first
ip security implicit-labelling
ip security multilevel
ip security reserved-allowed
ip security strip

IP SECURITY IMPLICIT-LABELLING

To force the Cisco IOS software to accept packets on the interface, even if they do not include a security option, use the **ip security implicit-labelling** interface configuration command. To disable this function, use the **no** form of this command.

> **ip security implicit-labelling** [*level authority* [*authority...*]]
> **no ip security implicit-labelling** [*level authority* [*authority...*]]

Syntax Description

level	(Optional) Degree of sensitivity of information. If your interface has multilevel security set, you must specify this argument. (See the *level* keywords listed in Table 29–1 in the **ip security dedicated** command section.)
authority	(Optional) Organization that defines the set of security levels that will be used in a network. If your interface has multilevel security set, you must specify this argument. You can specify more than one. (See the *authority* keywords listed in Table 29–2 in the **ip security dedicated** command section.)

Default

Enabled, when the security level of the interface is "Unclassified Genser" (or unconfigured). Otherwise, the default is disabled.

Command Mode

Interface configuration

Usage Guidelines

This command first appeared in Cisco IOS Release 10.0.

If your interface has multilevel security set, you must use the expanded form of the command (with the optional arguments as noted in brackets), because the arguments are used to specify the precise level and authority to use when labeling the packet. If your interface has dedicated security set, the additional arguments are ignored.

Example

In the following example, an interface is set for security and will accept unlabeled packets:

```
ip security dedicated confidential genser
ip security implicit-labelling
```

Related Commands

Search online to find documentation for related commands.

ip security add
ip security dedicated
ip security extended-allowed
ip security first
ip security ignore-authorities
ip security multilevel
ip security reserved-allowed
ip security strip

IP SECURITY MULTILEVEL

To set the range of classifications and authorities on an interface, use the **ip security multilevel** interface configuration command. To disable this function, use the **no** form of this command.

> **ip security multilevel** *level1* [*authority1*...] **to** *level2 authority2* [*authority2*...]
> **no ip security multilevel**

Syntax Description

level1   Degree of sensitivity of information. The classification level of incoming
                          packets must be equal to or greater than this value for processing to occur.
                          (See the *level* keywords found in Table 29–1 in the **ip security dedicated**
                          command section.)

authority1	(Optional) Organization that defines the set of security levels that will be used in a network. The authority bits must be a superset of this value. (See the *authority* keywords listed in Table 29–2 in the **ip security dedicated** command section.)
to	Separates the range of classifications and authorities.
level2	Degree of sensitivity of information. The classification level of incoming packets must be equal to or less than this value for processing to occur. (See the *level* keywords found in Table 29–1 in the **ip security dedicated** command section.)
authority2	Organization that defines the set of security levels that will be used in a network. The authority bits must be a proper subset of this value. (See the *authority* keywords listed in Table 29–2 in the **ip security dedicated** command section.)

Default
Disabled

Command Mode
Interface configuration

Usage Guidelines
This command first appeared in Cisco IOS Release 10.0.

All traffic entering or leaving the system must have a security option that falls within this range. Being within range requires that the following two conditions be met:

- The classification level must be greater than or equal to *level1* and less than or equal to *level2*.
- The authority bits must be a superset of *authority1* and a proper subset of *authority2*. That is, *authority1* specifies those authority bits that are required on a packet, while *authority2* specifies the required bits plus any optional authorities that also can be included. If the *authority1* field is the empty set, then a packet is required to specify any one or more of the authority bits in *authority2*.

Example
The following example specifies levels Unclassified to Secret and NSA authority:

```
ip security multilevel unclassified to secret nsa
```

Related Commands

Search online to find documentation for related commands.

ip security add
ip security dedicated
ip security extended-allowed
ip security first
ip security ignore-authorities
ip security implicit-labelling
ip security reserved-allowed
ip security strip

IP SECURITY RESERVED-ALLOWED

To treat as valid any packets that have Reserved1 through Reserved4 security levels, use the **ip security reserved-allowed** interface configuration command. To disable this feature, use the **no** form of this command.

> **ip security reserved-allowed**
> **no ip security reserved-allowed**

Syntax Description

This command has no arguments or keywords.

Default

Disabled

Command Mode

Interface configuration

Usage Guidelines

This command first appeared in Cisco IOS Release 10.3.

When you set multilevel security on an interface, and indicate, for example, that the highest range allowed is Confidential, and the lowest is Unclassified, the Cisco IOS software neither allows nor operates on packets that have security levels of Reserved3 and Reserved2 because they are undefined.

If you use the IP Security Option (IPSO) to block transmission out of unclassified interfaces, and you use one of the Reserved security levels, you *must* enable this feature to preserve network security.

Example

The following example allows a security level of Reserved through Ethernet interface 0:

```
interface ethernet 0
  ip security reserved-allowed
```

Related Commands

Search online to find documentation for related commands.

ip security add
ip security dedicated
ip security extended-allowed
ip security first
ip security ignore-authorities
ip security implicit-labelling
ip security multilevel
ip security strip

IP SECURITY STRIP

To remove any basic security option on outgoing packets on an interface, use the **ip security strip** interface configuration command. To disable this function, use the **no** form of this command.

> **ip security strip**
> **no ip security strip**

Syntax Description

This command has no arguments or keywords.

Default

Disabled

Command Mode

Interface configuration

Usage Guidelines

This command first appeared in Cisco IOS Release 10.0.

The removal procedure is performed after all security tests in the router have been passed. This command is not allowed for multilevel interfaces.

Example

The following example removes any basic security options on outgoing packets on Ethernet interface 0:

```
interface ethernet 0
  ip security strip
```

Related Commands

Search online to find documentation for related commands.

ip security add
ip security dedicated
ip security extended-allowed
ip security first
ip security ignore-authorities
ip security implicit-labelling
ip security multilevel
ip security reserved-allowed

SHOW DNSIX

To display state information and the current configuration of the DNSIX audit writing module, use the **show dnsix** privileged EXEC command.

> show dnsix

Syntax Description

This command has no arguments or keywords.

Command Mode

Privileged EXEC

Usage Guidelines

This command first appeared in Cisco IOS Release 10.0.

Sample Display

The following is sample output from the **show dnsix** command:

```
Router# show dnsix

Audit Trail Enabled with Source 128.105.2.5
        State: PRIMARY
        Connected to 128.105.2.4
        Primary 128.105.2.4
        Transmit Count 1
        DMDP retries 4
        Authorization Redirection List:
                128.105.2.4
        Record count: 0
        Packet Count: 0
        Redirect Rcv: 0
```

Appendixes

RADIUS Attributes

Remote Authentication Dial-In User Server (RADIUS) attributes are used to define specific authentication, authorization, and accounting (AAA) elements in a user profile, which is stored on the RADIUS daemon. This appendix lists the RADIUS attributes currently supported.

RADIUS IETF ATTRIBUTES

Table A–1 lists the supported RADIUS (IETF) attributes. In cases where the attribute has a security server-specific format, the format is specified.

Table A–1 *Supported RADIUS (IETF) Attributes*

Number	Attribute	Description	Cisco IOS Release 11.1	Cisco IOS Release 11.2	Cisco IOS Release 11.3
1	User-Name	Indicates the name of the user being authenticated.	yes	yes	yes
2	User-Password	Indicates the user's password or the user's input following an Access-Challenge. Passwords longer than 16 characters are encrypted using the IETF Draft #2 (or later) specifications.	yes	yes	yes

Table A–1 *Supported RADIUS (IETF) Attributes, Continued*

Number	Attribute	Description	Cisco IOS Release 11.1	Cisco IOS Release 11.2	Cisco IOS Release 11.3
3	CHAP-Password	Indicates the response value provided by a PPP Challenge-Handshake Authentication Protocol (CHAP) user in response to an Access-Challenge.	yes	yes	yes
4	NAS-IP Address	Specifies the IP address of the network access server that is requesting authentication.	yes	yes	yes
5	NAS-Port	Indicates the physical port number of the network access server that is authenticating the user. The NAS-Port value (32 bits) consists of one or two 16-bit values (depending on the setting of the **radius-server extended-portnames** command). Each 16-bit number should be viewed as a 5-digit decimal integer for interpretation as follows: For asynchronous terminal lines, async network interfaces, and virtual async interfaces, the value is **00ttt**, where **ttt** is the line number or async interface unit number. For ordinary synchronous network interface, the value is **10xxx**. For channels on a primary rate ISDN interface, the value is **2ppcc**. For channels on a basic rate ISDN interface, the value is **3bb0c**. For other types of interfaces, the value is **6nnss**.	yes	yes	yes

Table A–1 *Supported RADIUS (IETF) Attributes, Continued*

Number	Attribute	Description	Cisco IOS Release 11.1	Cisco IOS Release 11.2	Cisco IOS Release 11.3
6	Service-Type	Indicates the type of service requested or the type of service to be provided. • In a request: Framed for known PPP or SLIP connection. Administrative-user for **enable** command. • In response: Login—Make a connection. Framed—Start SLIP or PPP. Administrative User—Start an EXEC or **enable ok.** Exec User—Start an EXEC session.	yes	yes	yes
7	Framed-Protocol	Indicates the framing to be used for framed access.	yes	yes	yes
8	Framed-IP-Address	Indicates the address to be configured for the user.	yes	yes	yes
9	Framed-IP-Netmask	Indicates the IP netmask to be configured for the user when the user is a router to a network. This attribute value results in a static route being added for Framed-IP-Address with the mask specified.	yes	yes	yes
10	Framed-Routing	Indicates the routing method for the user when the user is a router to a network. Only "None" and "Send and Listen" values are supported for this attribute.	yes	yes	yes

Table A–1   *Supported RADIUS (IETF) Attributes, Continued*

Number	Attribute	Description	Cisco IOS Release 11.1	Cisco IOS Release 11.2	Cisco IOS Release 11.3
11	Filter-Id	Indicates the name of the filter list for the user and is formatted as follows: %d, %d.in, or %d.out. This attribute is associated with the most recent service-type command. For login and EXEC, use %d or %d.out as the line access list value from 0 to 199. For Framed service, use %d or %d.out as interface output access list, and %d.in for input access list. The numbers are self-encoding to the protocol to which they refer.	yes	yes	yes
13	Framed-Compression	Indicates a compression protocol used for the link. This attribute results in a "/compress" being added to the PPP or SLIP autocommand generated during EXEC authorization. Not currently implemented for non-EXEC authorization.	yes	yes	yes
14	Login-IP-Host	Indicates the host to which the user will connect when the Login-Service attribute is included.	yes	yes	yes
15	Login-Service	Indicates the service that should be used to connect the user to the login host.	yes	yes	yes
16	Login-Port	Defines the TCP port with which the user is to be connected when the Login-Service attribute is also present.	yes	yes	yes
18	Reply-Message	Indicates text that might be displayed to the user.	yes	yes	yes

Table A–1 *Supported RADIUS (IETF) Attributes, Continued*

Number	Attribute	Description	Cisco IOS Release 11.1	Cisco IOS Release 11.2	Cisco IOS Release 11.3
22	Framed-Route	Provides routing information to be configured for the user on this network access server. The RADIUS RFC format (net/bits [router [metric]]) and the old style dotted mask (net mask [router [metric]]) are supported. If the router field is omitted or 0, the peer IP address is used. Metrics are currently ignored.	yes	yes	yes
24	State	Allows state information to be maintained between the network access server and the RADIUS server. This attribute is applicable only to CHAP challenges.	yes	yes	yes
26	Vendor-Specific	Allows vendors to support their own extended attributes not suitable for general use. The Cisco RADIUS implementation supports one vendor-specific option using the format recommended in the specification. Cisco's vendor-ID is 9, and the supported option has vendor-type 1, which is named "cisco-avpair." The value is a string of the format: `protocol : attribute sep value`			

Table A–1 *Supported RADIUS (IETF) Attributes, Continued*

Number	Attribute	Description	Cisco IOS Release 11.1	Cisco IOS Release 11.2	Cisco IOS Release 11.3

26	Vendor-Specific, Continued	"Protocol" is a value of the Cisco "protocol" attribute for a particular type of authorization. "Attribute" and "value" are an appropriate AV pair defined in the Cisco TACACS+ specification, and "sep" is "=" for mandatory attributes and "*" for optional attributes. This allows the full set of features available for TACACS+ authorization to also be used for RADIUS. For example:
		
		`cisco-avpair=`
		`"ip:addr-pool=first"`
		`cisco-avpair= "shell:priv-lvl=15"`
		
		The first example causes Cisco's "multiple named ip address pools" feature to be activated during IP authorization (during PPP's IPCP address assignment). The second example causes a "NAS Prompt" user to have immediate access to EXEC commands.
			yes	yes	yes

27	Session-Timeout	Sets the maximum number of seconds of service to be provided to the user before the session terminates. This attribute value becomes the per-user "absolute timeout." This attribute is not valid for PPP sessions.	yes	yes	yes
28	Idle-Timeout	Sets the maximum number of consecutive seconds of idle connection allowed to the user before the session terminates. This attribute value becomes the per-user "session-timeout." This attribute is not valid for PPP sessions.	yes	yes	yes

Table A–1 *Supported RADIUS (IETF) Attributes, Continued*

Number	Attribute	Description	Cisco IOS Release 11.1	Cisco IOS Release 11.2	Cisco IOS Release 11.3
34	Login-LAT-Service	Indicates the system with which the user is to be connected by LAT. This attribute is only available in the EXEC mode.	yes	yes	yes
35	Login-LAT-Node	Indicates the node with which the user is to be automatically connected by LAT.	no	no	no
36	Login-LAT-Group	Identifies the LAT group codes that this user is authorized to use.	no	no	no
49	Terminate-Cause	Reports details on why the connection was terminated.	no	no	no

For more information about RADIUS configuration tasks, see Chapter 9, "Configuring RADIUS."

RADIUS ACCOUNTING ATTRIBUTES

Table A–2 lists the supported RADIUS (IETF) accounting attributes. In cases where the attribute has a security server-specific format, the format is specified.

Table A–2 *Supported RADIUS (IETF) Accounting Attributes*

Number	Attribute	Description	Cisco IOS Release1 1.1	Cisco IOS Release1 1.2	Cisco IOS Release1 1.3
25	Class	Arbitrary value that the network access server includes in all accounting packets for this user if supplied by the RADIUS server.	yes	yes	yes
30	Called-Station-Id	Allows the network access server to send the telephone number the user called as part of the Access-Request packet (using Dialed Number Identification [DNIS] or similar technology). This attribute is only supported on ISDN, and modem calls on the Cisco AS5200 if used with PRI.	yes	yes	yes

Table A–2 *Supported RADIUS (IETF) Accounting Attributes, Continued*

Number	Attribute	Description	Cisco IOS Release1 1.1	Cisco IOS Release1 1.2	Cisco IOS Release1 1.3
31	Calling-Station-Id	Allows the network access server to send the telephone number the call came from as part of the Access-Request packet (using Automatic Number Identification or similar technology). This attribute has the same value as "remote-addr" from TACACS+. This attribute is only supported on ISDN, and modem calls on the Cisco AS5200 if used with PRI.	yes	yes	yes
40	Acct-Status-Type	Indicates whether this Accounting-Request marks the beginning of the user service (start) or the end (stop).	yes	yes	yes
41	Acct-Delay-Time	Indicates how many seconds the client has been trying to send a particular record.	yes	yes	yes
42	Acct-Input-Octets	Indicates how many octets have been received from the port over the course of this service being provided.	yes	yes	yes
43	Acct-Output-Octets	Indicates how many octets have been sent to the port in the course of delivering this service.	yes	yes	yes
44	Acct-Session-Id	A unique accounting identifier that makes it easy to match start and stop records in a log file. Acct-Session ID numbers restart at 1 each time the router is power cycled or the software is reloaded.	yes	yes	yes

Table A–2 *Supported RADIUS (IETF) Accounting Attributes, Continued*

Number	Attribute	Description	Cisco IOS Release1 1.1	Cisco IOS Release1 1.2	Cisco IOS Release1 1.3
45	Acct-Authentic	Indicates how the user was authenticated, whether by RADIUS, the network access server itself, or another remote authentication protocol. This attribute is set to "radius" for users authenticated by RADIUS; "remote" for TACACS+ and Kerberos; or "local" for local, enable, line, and if-needed methods. For all other methods, the attribute is omitted.	yes	yes	yes
46	Acct-Session-Time	Indicates how long (in seconds) the user has received service.	yes	yes	yes
47	Acct-Input-Packets	Indicates how many packets have been received from the port over the course of this service being provided to a framed user.	yes	yes	yes
48	Acct-Output-Packets	Indicates how many packets have been sent to the port in the course of delivering this service to a framed user.	yes	yes	yes
61	NAS-Port-Type	Indicates the type of physical port the network access server is using to authenticate the user.	yes	yes	yes

For more information about configuring RADIUS accounting, see Chapter 9.

RADIUS VENDOR-PROPRIETARY ATTRIBUTES

Although an Internet Engineering Task Force (IETF) draft standard for RADIUS specifies a method for communicating vendor-proprietary information between the network access server and the

RADIUS server, some vendors have extended the RADIUS attribute set in a unique way. Table A–3 lists the supported vendor-proprietary RADIUS attributes:

Table A–3   *Supported Vendor-Proprietary RADIUS Attributes*

Number	Vendor-Proprietary Attribute	Description
17	Change-Password	Specifies a request to change a user's password.
21	Password-Expiration	Specifies an expiration date for a user's password in the user's file entry.
194	Maximum-Time	Specifies the maximum length of time (in seconds) allowed for any session. After the session reaches the time limit, its connection is dropped.
195	Terminate-Cause	Reports details on why the connection was terminated.
208	PW-Lifetime	Enables you to specify on a per-user basis the number of days that a password is valid.
209	IP-Direct	Specifies in a user's file entry the IP address to which the Cisco router redirects packets from the user. When you include this attribute in a user's file entry, the Cisco router bypasses all internal routing and bridging tables and sends all packets received on this connection's WAN interface to the specified IP address.
210	PPP-VJ-Slot-Comp	Instructs the Cisco router not to use slot compression when sending VJ-compressed packets over a PPP link.
212	PPP-Async-Map	Gives the Cisco router the asynchronous control character map for the PPP session. The specified control characters are passed through the PPP link as data and used by applications running over the link.
217	IP-Pool-Definition	Defines a pool of addresses using the following format: X a.b.c Z; where X is the pool index number, a.b.c is the pool's starting IP address, and Z is the number of IP addresses in the pool. For example, 3 10.0.0.1 5 allocates 10.0.0.1 through 10.0.0.5 for dynamic assignment.
218	Assign-IP-Pool	Tells the router to assign the user and IP address from the IP pool.
228	Route-IP	Indicates whether IP routing is allowed for the user's file entry.

Table A–3   *Supported Vendor-Proprietary RADIUS Attributes, Continued*

Number	Vendor-Proprietary Attribute	Description
233	Link-Compression	Defines whether to turn on or turn off "stac" compression over a PPP link.
234	Target-Util	Specifies the load-threshold percentage value for bringing up an additional channel when PPP multilink is defined.
235	Maximum-Channels	Specifies allowed/allocatable maximum number of channels.
242	Data-Filter	Defines per-user IP data filters. These filters are retrieved only when a call is placed using a RADIUS outgoing profile or answered using a RADIUS incoming profile. Filter entries are applied on a first-match basis; therefore, the order in which filter entries are entered is important.
243	Call-Filter	Defines per-user IP data filters. On a Cisco router, this attribute is identical to the Data-Filter attribute.
244	Idle-Limit	Specifies the maximum time (in seconds) that any session can be idle. When the session reaches the idle time limit, its connection is dropped.

For more information about configuring RADIUS to recognize vendor-proprietary attributes, see Chapter 9.

APPENDIX B

TACACS+
Attribute-Value Pairs

Terminal Access Controller Access Control System Plus (TACACS+) attribute-value (AV) pairs are used to define specific authentication, authorization, and accounting elements in a user profile, which is stored on the TACACS+ daemon. This appendix lists the TACACS+ AV pairs currently supported.

TACACS+ AV PAIRS

Table B–1 lists the supported TACACS+ AV pairs.

Table B–1 *Supported TACACS+ AV Pairs*

Attribute	Description	Cisco IOS Release 11.0	Cisco IOS Release1 1.1	Cisco IOS Release1 1.2	Cisco IOS Release1 1.3
service=x	The primary service. Specifying a service attribute indicates that this is a request for authorization or accounting of that service. Current values are **slip, ppp, arap, shell, tty-daemon, connection,** and **system**. This attribute must always be included.	yes	yes	yes	yes

Table B–1   *Supported TACACS+ AV Pairs, Continued*

Attribute	Description	Cisco IOS Release 11.0	Cisco IOS Release1 1.1	Cisco IOS Release1 1.2	Cisco IOS Release1 1.3
protocol=x	A protocol that is a subset of a service. An example would be any PPP NCP. Currently known values are **lcp, ip, ipx, atalk, vines, lat, xremote, tn3270, telnet, rlogin, pad, vpdn, osicp, deccp, ccp, cdp, bridging, xns, nbf, bap,** and **unknown.**	yes	yes	yes	yes
cmd=x	A shell (EXEC) command. This indicates the command name for a shell command that is to be run. This attribute must be specified if service equals "shell." A NULL value indicates that the shell itself is being referred to.	yes	yes	yes	yes
cmd-arg=x	An argument to a shell (EXEC) command. This indicates an argument for the shell command that is to be run. Multiple cmd-arg attributes may be specified, and they are order dependent.	yes	yes	yes	yes
acl=x	ASCII number representing a connection access list. Used only when service=shell.	yes	yes	yes	yes
inacl=x	ASCII identifier for an interface input access list. Used with service=ppp and protocol=ip. Per-user access lists do not currently work with ISDN interfaces.	yes	yes	yes	yes

Table B–1 *Supported TACACS+ AV Pairs, Continued*

Attribute	Description	Cisco IOS Release 11.0	Cisco IOS Release1 1.1	Cisco IOS Release1 1.2	Cisco IOS Release1 1.3
inacl#<n>	ASCII access list identifier for an input access list to be installed and applied to an interface for the duration of the current connection. Used with service=ppp and protocol=ip, and service service=ppp and protocol =ipx. Per-user access lists do not currently work with ISDN interfaces.	no	no	no	yes
outacl=x	ASCII identifier for an interface output access list. Used with service=ppp and protocol=ip, and service service=ppp and protocol=ipx. Contains an IP output access list for SLIP or PPP/IP (for example, outacl=4). The access list itself must be preconfigured on the router. Per-user access lists do not currently work with ISDN interfaces.	yes (PPP/IP only)	yes	yes	yes
outacl#<n>	ACSII access list identifier for an interface output access list to be installed and applied to an interface for the duration of the current condition. Used with service=ppp and protocol=ip, and service service=ppp and protocol=ipx. Per-user access lists do not currently work with ISDN interfaces.	no	no	no	yes

Table B–1   *Supported TACACS+ AV Pairs, Continued*

Attribute	Description	Cisco IOS Release 11.0	Cisco IOS Release1 1.1	Cisco IOS Release1 1.2	Cisco IOS Release1 1.3
zonelist=x	A numeric zonelist value. Used with service=arap. Specifies an AppleTalk zonelist for ARA (for example, zonelist=5).	yes	yes	yes	yes
addr=x	A network address. Used with service=slip, service=ppp, and protocol=ip. Contains the IP address that the remote host should use when connecting via SLIP or PPP/IP. For example, addr=10.2.3.4.	yes	yes	yes	yes

addr-pool=x	Specifies the name of a local pool from which to get the address of the remote host. Used with service=ppp and protocol=ip.
	
	Note that **addr-pool** works in conjunction with local pooling. It specifies the name of a local pool (which must be preconfigured on the network access server). Use the **ip-local pool** command to declare local pools. For example:
	
	`ip address-pool local`
	`ip local pool boo 10.0.0.1`
	`    10.0.0.10`
	`ip local pool moo 10.0.0.1`
	`    10.0.0.20`
	
	You can then use TACACS+ to return addr-pool=boo or addr-pool=moo to indicate the address pool from which you want to get this remote node's address.
		yes	yes	yes	yes

Table B-1 *Supported TACACS+ AV Pairs, Continued*

Attribute	Description	Cisco IOS Release 11.0	Cisco IOS Release1 1.1	Cisco IOS Release1 1.2	Cisco IOS Release1 1.3
routing=x	Specifies whether routing information is to be propagated to and accepted from this interface. Used with service=slip, service=ppp, and protocol=ip. Equivalent in function to the /routing flag in SLIP and PPP commands. Can either be true or false (for example, routing=true).	yes	yes	yes	yes
route	Specifies a route to be applied to an interface. Used with service=slip, service=ppp, and protocol=ip. During network authorization, the route attribute can be used to specify a per-user static route, to be installed by TACACS+ as follows: `route="dst_address mask [gateway]"` This indicates a temporary static route that is to be applied. The *dst_address*, *mask*, and *gateway* are expected to be in the usual dotted-decimal notation, with the same meanings as in the familiar **ip route** configuration command on a network access server. If *gateway* is omitted, the peer's address is the gateway. The route is expunged when the connection terminates.	no	yes	yes	yes

Table B–1   *Supported TACACS+ AV Pairs, Continued*

Attribute	Description	Cisco IOS Release 11.0	Cisco IOS Release1 1.1	Cisco IOS Release1 1.2	Cisco IOS Release1 1.3
route#<n>	As with the route AV pair, this specifies a route to be applied to an interface, but these routes are numbered, allowing multiple routes to be applied. Used with service=ppp and protocol=ip, and service=ppp and protocol=ipx.	no	no	no	yes
timeout=x	The number of minutes before an EXEC or ARA session disconnects (for example, timeout=60). A value of zero indicates no timeout. Used with service=arap.	yes	yes	yes	yes
idletime=x	Sets a value, in minutes, after which an idle session is terminated. Does not work for PPP. A value of zero indicates no timeout.	no	yes	yes	yes
autocmd=x	Specifies an autocommand to be executed at EXEC startup (for example, autocmd=telnet muruga.com). Used only with service=shell.	yes	yes	yes	yes
noescape=x	Prevents user from using an escape character. Used with service=shell. Can be either true or false (for example, noescape=true).	yes	yes	yes	yes

Table B–1 *Supported TACACS+ AV Pairs, Continued*

Attribute	Description	Cisco IOS Release 11.0	Cisco IOS Release1 1.1	Cisco IOS Release1 1.2	Cisco IOS Release1 1.3
nohangup=x	Used with service=shell. Specifies the nohangup option, which means that after an EXEC shell is terminated, the user is presented with another login (username) prompt. Can be either true or false (for example, nohangup=false).	yes	yes	yes	yes
priv-lvl=x	Privilege level to be assigned for the EXEC. Used with service=shell. Privilege levels range from 0 to 15, with 15 being the highest.	yes	yes	yes	yes
callback-dialstring	Sets the telephone number for a callback (for example: callback-dialstring=408-555-121 2). Value is NULL, or a dial string. A NULL value indicates that the service may choose to get the dial string through other means. Used with service=arap, service=slip, service=ppp, service=shell. Not valid for ISDN.	no	yes	yes	yes
callback-line	The number of a TTY line to use for callback (for example: callback-line=4). Used with service=arap, service=slip, service=ppp, service=shell. Not valid for ISDN.	no	yes	yes	yes

Table B–1   *Supported TACACS+ AV Pairs, Continued*

Attribute	Description	Cisco IOS Release 11.0	Cisco IOS Release1 1.1	Cisco IOS Release1 1.2	Cisco IOS Release1 1.3
callback-rotary	The number of a rotary group (between 0 and 100 inclusive) to use for callback (for example: callback-rotary=34). Used with service=arap, service=slip, service=ppp, service=shell. Not valid for ISDN.	no	yes	yes	yes
nocallback-verify	Indicates that no callback verification is required. The only valid value for this parameter is 1 (for example, nocallback-verify=1). Used with service=arap, service=slip, service=ppp, service=shell. There is no authentication on callback. Not valid for ISDN.	no	yes	yes	yes
tunnel-id	Specifies the username that will be used to authenticate the tunnel over which the individual user MID will be projected. This is analogous to the *remote name* in the **vpdn outgoing** command. Used with service=ppp and protocol=vpdn.	no	no	yes	yes
ip-addresses	Space-separated list of possible IP addresses that can be used for the endpoint of a tunnel. Used with service=ppp and protocol=vpdn.	no	no	yes	yes
nas-password	Specifies the password for the network access server during the L2F tunnel authentication. Used with service=ppp and protocol=vpdn.	no	no	yes	yes

Table B–1 *Supported TACACS+ AV Pairs, Continued*

Attribute	Description	Cisco IOS Release 11.0	Cisco IOS Release1 1.1	Cisco IOS Release1 1.2	Cisco IOS Release1 1.3
gw-password	Specifies the password for the home gateway during the L2F tunnel authentication. Used with service=ppp and protocol=vpdn.	no	no	yes	yes
rte-ftr-in#<n>	Specifies an input access list definition to be installed and applied to routing updates on the current interface for the duration of the current connection. Used with service=ppp and protocol=ip, and with service=ppp and protocol=ipx.	no	no	no	yes
rte-ftr-out#<n>	Specifies an output access list definition to be installed and applied to routing updates on the current interface for the duration of the current connection. Used with service=ppp and protocol=ip, and with service=ppp and protocol=ipx.	no	no	no	yes
sap#<n>	Specifies static Service Advertising Protocol (SAP) entries to be installed for the duration of a connection. Used with service=ppp and protocol=ipx.	no	no	no	yes
sap-fltr-in#<n>	Specifies an input SAP filter access list definition to be installed and applied on the current interface for the duration of the current connection. Used with service=ppp and protocol=ipx.	no	no	no	yes

Table B–1 *Supported TACACS+ AV Pairs, Continued*

Attribute	Description	Cisco IOS Release 11.0	Cisco IOS Release1 1.1	Cisco IOS Release1 1.2	Cisco IOS Release1 1.3
sap-fltr-out#<n>	Specifies an output SAP filter access list definition to be installed and applied on the current interface for the duration of the current connection. Used with service=ppp and protocol=ipx.	no	no	no	yes
pool-def#<n>	Used to define IP address pools on the network access server. Used with service=ppp and protocol=ip.	no	no	no	yes
source-ip=x	Used as the source IP address of all VPDN packets generated as part of a VPDN tunnel. This is equivalent to the Cisco **vpdn outgoing** global configuration command.	no	no	yes	yes

For more information about configuring TACACS+, see Chapter 11, "Configuring TACACS+." For more information about configuring TACACS+ authentication, see Chapter 5, "Configuring Authorization."

TACACS+ Accounting AV Pairs

Table B–2 lists the supported TACACS+ accounting AV pairs.

Table B–2 *Supported TACACS+ Accounting AV Pairs*

Attribute	Description	Cisco IOS Release1 1.0	Cisco IOS Release 11.1	Cisco IOS Release 11.2	Cisco IOS Release1 1.3
service	The service the user used.	yes	yes	yes	yes
port	The port the user was logged in to.	yes	yes	yes	yes

Table B–2 *Supported TACACS+ Accounting AV Pairs, Continued*

Attribute	Description	Cisco IOS Release1 1.0	Cisco IOS Release 11.1	Cisco IOS Release 11.2	Cisco IOS Release1 1.3
task_id	Start and stop records for the same event must have matching (unique) task_id numbers.	yes	yes	yes	yes
start_time	The time the action started (in seconds since the epoch, 12:00 a.m. Jan 1 1970). The clock must be configured to receive this information.	yes	yes	yes	yes
stop_time	The time the action stopped (in seconds since the epoch.) The clock must be configured to receive this information.	yes	yes	yes	yes
elapsed_time	The elapsed time in seconds for the action. Useful when the device does not keep real-time.	yes	yes	yes	yes
timezone	The time zone abbreviation for all timestamps included in this packet.	yes	yes	yes	yes
priv_level	The privilege level associated with the action.	yes	yes	yes	yes
cmd	The command the user executed.	yes	yes	yes	yes
protocol	The protocol associated with the action.	yes	yes	yes	yes
bytes_in	The number of input bytes transferred during this connection.	yes	yes	yes	yes
bytes_out	The number of output bytes transferred during this connection.	yes	yes	yes	yes
paks_in	The number of input packets transferred during this connection.	yes	yes	yes	yes

Table B–2 *Supported TACACS+ Accounting AV Pairs, Continued*

Attribute	Description	Cisco IOS Release1 1.0	Cisco IOS Release 11.1	Cisco IOS Release 11.2	Cisco IOS Release1 1.3
paks_out	The number of output packets transferred during this connection.	yes	yes	yes	yes
event	Information included in the accounting packet that describes a state change in the router. Events described are accounting starting and accounting stopping.	yes	yes	yes	yes
reason	Information included in the accounting packet that describes the event that caused a system change. Events described are system reload, system shutdown, or when accounting is reconfigured (turned on or off).	yes	yes	yes	yes

For more information about configuring TACACS+, see Chapter 11. For more information about configuring TACACS+ accounting, see Chapter 7, "Configuring Accounting."

Index

527